S0-CPE-067

GETTING HELP

ALSO BY CHRISTINE AMMER
The New A to Z of Women's Health

GETTING HELP

A CONSUMER'S GUIDE
═══ TO THERAPY ═══

CHRISTINE AMMER

with Nathan T. Sidley, MD

PARAGON HOUSE
New York

The ideas, procedures, and suggestions contained in this book are not intended to replace the services of a trained health professional. All matters regarding your physical or mental health require supervision.

The cases and examples cited in this book are based on actual situations and people. Names and identifying details have been changed to protect privacy.

First Paragon House edition, 1991

Published in the United States by

Paragon House
90 Fifth Avenue
New York, NY 10011

Copyright 1982, 1991 by Christine Ammer

All rights reserved. No part of this book may be
reproduced, in any form, without written permission
from the publisher, unless by a reviewer who wishes
to quote brief passages.
10   9   8   7   6   5   4   3   2   1

Library of Congress Cataloging-in-Publication Data
Ammer, Christine.
[Common sense guide to mental health care]
Getting help : the consumer's guide to therapy / Christine Ammer
with Nathan T. Sidley. — 1st Paragon House ed.
p.   cm.
Reprint. Originally published: The common sense guide to mental
health care. 1st ed. Lexington, Mass. : Lewis Pub. Co., ©1982.
Includes index.
ISBN 1-55778-369-1 : $22.95
1. Psychotherapy—Popular works.   2. Mental illness—Popular
works.   3. Consumer education.   I. Sidley, Nathan T., 1929–
II. Title.
[RC480.515.A45   1991]
362.2—dc20   90-39110
                              CIP

Manufactured in the United States of America

The paper used in this publication meets the minimum requirements of
American National Standard for Information Sciences—Permanence of Paper
for Printed Library Materials, ANSI Z39.48-1984.

To the National Alliance for the Mentally Ill
for their fine work in informing the public, in advocacy,
and most of all in lending support to the mentally ill
and their families

CONTENTS

Contents

the Elderly • Elderly Home Care • Preventive Care
for Former Patients • Home Mental Health-Care
Services • Outpatient Commitment • Returning to
Work • For Those in Trouble with the Law • Coping
with Life Crises • Crisis Intervention • Employee
Assistance Programs (EAPs) • Reducing Stress •
Divorce Mediation • Social and Environmental
Stress • Community Mental Health Care • The Men-
tal Health Association • Regular Checkups?

ACKNOWLEDGMENTS

PROFOUND GRATITUDE is due to the many experts and friends who gave unstintingly of their time to answer questions and make invaluable suggestions, criticisms, and corrections. Among those who merit special thanks for their help with the first edition are Karen Ann Ammer, Research Assistant, Mental Health Policy Research Program, Woodrow Wilson School of Public and International Affairs, Princeton University; Cynthia P. Anderson, ACSW, psychiatric social worker; Theodore Anderson, M.D., former Medical Director, Stoney Brook Counseling Center, and Assistant Clinical Professor of Psychiatry, Boston University Medical School; Maureen Burke-Green, R.N., Director, Arlington Branch, Mystic Valley Partial Hospitalization Program; the late Mary Fischelis, R.N., Psychiatric Nursing Coordinator, Emerson Hospital; Anne O. Freed, MSW, Director, Counseling Services, Family Service Association of Greater Boston, and Adjunct Professor of Social Work, Boston University School of Social Work; Marvin Goldfarb, Director, Home Care Services, Minuteman Home Care Corporation; Jon E. Gudeman, M.D., Center Director, Massachusetts Mental Health Center, and Associate Professor of Psychiatry, Harvard University Medical School; John G. Gunderson, M.D., Director of Psychotherapy, McLean Hospital, and Associate Professor of

Psychiatry, Harvard University Medical School; James Harburger, M.D., Chief of Psychiatry, Cambridge Branch, Harvard Community Health Plan; Bernie Jenkins, Director, Mental Health Association of Central Middlesex; Norine Johnson, Ph.D., Director, Psychology Department, Kennedy Memorial Hospital for Children; Rosemary Johnson, MSW, Director, CONTACT-Boston; Peter J. Lang, Ph.D., Research Professor of Clinical Psychology, University of Florida; Nancy Langman-Dorwart, R.N., Director of Consultation and Education, Mystic Valley Comprehensive Community Mental Health Center; Robert E. Larson, Jr., Executive Director, CONTACT Teleministries, USA; the Reverend Polly Laughland-Guild, Follen Community Church; John F. Morrall, M.D., Chief, Psychiatric Services, V.A. Outpatient Clinic, Boston; Anne Newton, National Council on Crime and Delinquency; Penelope Penland, Ph.D., clinical psychologist; Michael Singer, Ph.D., clinical psychologist, Eliot Community Mental Health Center; Fay Snider, MSW, Codirector, Institute of Family Life and Learning; John J. Spillane, M.D., Assistant Director, Admissions and Evaluation Services, McLean Hospital; Joan Stewart, Center for Mental Health and Psychiatric Services, American Hospital Association; Harold N. Weiner, Family Service Association of America; Jerome Weinstein, Director, Divorce Resource and Mediation Center.

For the second edition, special thanks to (again) Cynthia P. Anderson and Theodore Anderson, and also to Kathryn Apgar, LICSW, Center for Counseling, Family Service of Greater Boston; William Chrisemer, Acting Executive Director, Community Human Services, Lexington, MA; Paul J. Cote, Jr., Executive Director, Center for Mental Health and Mental Retardation, Watertown, MA; Louise Davy, Executive Director, Mental Health Association of Central Middlesex; Robert A. Fein, Assistant Commissioner, Forensic Mental Health, Massachusetts; Erna Greene, President, Alliance for the Mentally Ill of Central Middlesex; Lyneath Floyd, R.N., Manager, Psychiatry and Addiction Unit, Emerson Hospital; Robert Patterson, M.D., Director, Mental Health Connections; Divvie Powell, R.N., Manager, Mental Health, WalthamWeston Hospital; Lois Pulliam, Alliance for the Mentally Ill of Central Middlesex; Anne M. Snodgrass, R.N., Waltham-Weston Hospital; Robert Stern, M.D., Executive Director, Eliot Community Mental Health Center; Mary Ellen Turner, LICSW, Family Service of Greater Boston.

This book has been vastly improved through their assistance; its errors and shortcomings are wholly the authors' responsibility.

PREFACE

In recent years more and more people have become involved with mental health services of one kind or another, ranging from special education in the school classroom to support groups of various kinds offered by clinics, churches, or other organizations, from counseling for short-term temporary problems to hospitalization for more serious illness. They may find themselves involved both directly, when they or their relatives or friends seek treatment, and indirectly, as a matter of public interest. Mental health care is one of the largest health expenditures in both federal and state budgets. In addition to personal and humanitarian concerns, it therefore has become an important issue politically, economically, judicially, and financially.

As consumers and citizens we can only behave intelligently and safely when we understand the issues and the alternatives. Even in a time of personal crisis there often are choices we can and should make in our own best interest. Yet where mental health services are concerned, a number of factors conspire against us as consumers. First, there is lingering public prejudice against mental health problems, leading to fear and shame that we will be considered "crazy" or "unstable" or even worse, which may keep us from asking necessary and perfectly legitimate questions. Second, traditional methods of psychiatry call for giving very little information to patients lest it interfere with the healing process, and to some extent the reluctance to disclose basic facts and opinions persists among many practitioners. Third, knowledge about the human mind is not yet (and perhaps never will be) a precise science, and therefore practitioners frequently disagree concerning just what is wrong with an individual and what treatment is appropriate. This does not mean such a person cannot be helped—far from it, and many can be and are—but it can make the process of finding treatment bewildering and cumbersome. And finally, mental health practitioners, like other professionals, are apt to favor the methods and disciplines they know best, and to overlook or disdain others that may be equally effective.

For all these reasons we saw the need for an accurate, up-to-date, straightforward guide to mental health care. Our emphasis throughout is on the consumer's viewpoint. You can only make good decisions if you know what to ask and how to evaluate the information you are given. We hope our guidelines make it easier to find your way.

Chapter

1

BUYING THERAPY AND OTHER MENTAL HEALTH SERVICES

HEALTH CARE is a commodity. We buy medical care in order to treat an illness or injury, to prevent an illness from becoming worse, or to maintain good health by making sure no undetected condition will undermine it. All but the last are true for mental health services, too. Most of us do not have regular mental health checkups comparable to regular physicals, but we probably should, and perhaps one day it will be common practice.

In the meantime, all of us are indirect buyers of mental health services. Billions of tax dollars are spent on them each year. In addition, millions of Americans are direct consumers of mental health services, mostly in some form of psychotherapy. And 2 million to 2.5 million Americans suffer from a mental illness serious enough to prevent them from functioning.

A recent study indicates that even these statistics represent but the tip of the iceberg. Almost one-third of all Americans suffer from acute mental illness sometime during their lives, and major mental disorders afflict almost 15 percent of the population. The frequency of mental illness has long been underestimated, it is believed, because the majority of sufferers *never seek* treatment at all.

In view of the fact that billions of dollars are spent on mental health services there should be lots of services provided, and in fact there are. Why, then, does so much mental illness go untreated? One problem is that mental health services are hard to find and even harder to evaluate. Furthermore, just when we need mental health services the most—when we are in emotional distress, sometimes in desperate straits—we are likely to be too distraught to make sensible decisions and choices.

Mental health care often has been described as a maze; even professionals frequently lose their way in it. There are no hard-and-fast rules for what service is most suitable for a particular client, or what treatment is most effective for a particular disorder. The standards for providers are murky, too. Literally anyone can hang out a shingle saying "Counselor" or "Therapist" and undertake treatment, regardless of training or experience or competence. Indeed, it is estimated that there are currently as many as one million unregulated lay therapists. We would not think of entrusting the care of our bodies to just anyone, and we certainly should not do so with our minds.

The indications for buying mental health services are not very clearcut. It is a lot easier to distinguish between a small cut and a large, festering wound than to tell if an emotional problem is mild and self-limited or potentially serious and in need of professional treatment.

Then, even if we decide we need treatment and can locate a licensed professional to provide it, how do we know it is the best or even the right treatment? Psychiatry is the only branch of medicine in which there are *no* generally accepted treatment guidelines. Recently the American Psychiatric Association tried to solve this dilemma by issuing a treatment manual, *Treatments of Psychiatric Disorders* (1989), the product of six years' work that amounts to three thousand pages in four volumes. The very idea of such a project gave rise to controversy before it was even begun. Its critics claim that knowledge concerning human mental processes is still far too sketchy to develop guidelines for treating any malfunctions of them.

In order to find appropriate treatment for our problems and to get our money's worth from the treatment, we need to know more. We need to know when to seek help, what kinds of service are available, how to find one appropriate for the particular problem at hand, how much the service will cost, how to evaluate whether or not a treatment is satisfactory. And, given the particular nature of mental illness, we need to know our legal rights, too.

Mental illness is a frightening concept for most of us. That is all the more reason to find some rational ways of deciding what might be wrong and figuring out what to do about it. In spite of the inadequacy of present-day knowledge and the lack of hard-and-fast rules for appropriate treatment, help is available and it often does work very well.

Chapter

2

WHAT IS MENTAL ILLNESS?

WHAT ACTUALLY is mental illness? It is a term for a group of disorders that cause severe disturbances in thinking, feeling, and relating, and result in a greatly diminished capacity for coping with the ordinary demands of life. More specifically, it is *any one or more* of the following conditions persisting over a long period of time and to a marked degree, so that it adversely affects one's life:

1. An inability to learn or work that cannot be explained by intellectual, sensory, or health factors.
2. An inability to build or maintain satisfactory personal relationships with family members, friends, and teachers or employers.
3. Inappropriate kinds of behavior or feelings under normal circumstances.
4. A general pervasive mood of unhappiness.
5. A tendency to develop physical symptoms or fears associated with personal or school or work problems.

Note, however, that all of us experience some of these conditions now and then. When we do, we are apt to say we are having a "problem." A so-called problem is regarded as a mental illness when it lasts long enough and is severe enough to interfere significantly with one's life.

WHO IS MENTALLY ILL?

It can be anyone—your neighbor, your friend, your relative, yourself. A mentally ill person doesn't necessarily look or act ill, at least not all the time. There are no barriers whatever. Age, education, income— none is a factor. Mental illness can affect two-year-olds and octogenarians, adults who are grade-school dropouts and those with advanced degrees, poor and rich, women and men.

At any one time, it is estimated that 15 percent of the nation's population are afflicted by a major mental disorder and that at least that many more suffer from milder disturbances.

NINE CASES

Betty A., 47, has a medicine cabinet full of pills. At least once a month she calls her family doctor, complaining of stomach upsets, sleeplessness, backache, and a host of other ailments. Her doctor rarely can find a physical cause for her symptoms but each time suggests that she try some new medication. It usually doesn't help for long.

John B., 25, lost his job last week after getting in a fist fight with a fellow worker. It is the fourth time in less than a year that his violent behavior has gotten him in trouble. This time the other man, whose jaw he broke, is planning to sue him.

Jane C., 68, has been grief-stricken since her husband died eighteen months ago. She weeps constantly, and lately she has been having more and more trouble remembering things. Last week she couldn't find her car after parking it at the shopping center; yesterday she went visiting and left her dinner on the stove, causing a small fire in her kitchen.

William D., 36, has quit his job and moved out of his family's suburban home, leaving his wife and children. He has rented an elegant high-rise apartment in the city and is about to buy an expensive cabin cruiser. However, he hasn't enough in the bank to meet the payments on the family car, let alone buy any luxury items.

Kathy E., 17, refuses to eat, claiming she is far too fat. She has lost twenty-five pounds in the past two months and was, if anything, quite slender to begin with.

Wanda F., 28, a housewife with three young children, is afraid to leave her house. One evening four months ago she went shopping for groceries while her husband took care of the children, and she found herself standing paralyzed in an aisle of the store, panic-stricken and unable to move. A neighbor who saw her helped her get home. Since then she has been seized with fear every time she plans to go out, and now she cannot even take her children for a walk.

Donald G., 19, who was an A student in high school, dropped out of college during his freshman year and now spends all his time in his room at home, refusing to leave except for meals. He scarcely speaks to his family and has seen none of his former friends. His mother sometimes hears him talking behind his closed door, even though she knows he is alone and there is no telephone in the room.

Harry and Mary H., a couple in their late thirties, quarrel constantly. They have two children, and Harry has two other children from two previous marriages. He has walked out on Mary several times, vowing he would not return. He is drinking heavily, their sex life has dwindled to zero, and their older child, Mark, has begun to have terrible temper tantrums and nightmares.

Stephen I., 10, is not doing well in his third-grade class, even though he is repeating the grade. He has been allowed out for recess only once all year, his teacher making him stay in because of his disruptive and destructive behavior. He is sent to the principal's office several times a week. The school now wants to suspend him.

These situations have a number of features in common:

• They are not unusual. Chances are you know one or more individuals who resemble one or more of these persons.
• A person is behaving markedly differently from those around him, or quite differently from his or her previous pattern. Donald was an excellent student in high school and functioned well enough to be admitted to college; Harry and Mary loved each other enough to marry and have two children; Jane had never "lost" her car before or started a fire.

- The person in question is suffering. Betty is in physical discomfort or pain much of the time; John suffers the humiliations of being fired and facing a lawsuit; Kathy hates her appearance; Stephen is miserable about constantly being punished.
- Those close to the person also are suffering. William's family may lose their car if he cannot meet payments; Stephen's and Kathy's parents are frantic with worry; Donald's mother doesn't know what to do about him.
- Financial cost is incurred, both directly and in lost productive capacity: The unemployment of John and William (and the consequent loss of purchasing power), the cost of a teacher's time in dealing with Stephen's problems, the postponement and likely loss of income that Donald will earn after he completes his education, medical bills incurred by Betty and by Kathy's parents—all drain financial resources.
- Each of these situations represents a common mental illness.

Common as such problems are, there still is substantial fear and prejudice against mental illness, which can be a major factor in stopping a person from getting help. Afraid to admit to a handicap, one does nothing about it, although many would greatly benefit from treatment.

THE STIGMA OF MENTAL ILLNESS

Few of us mind saying we don't feel well if something is physically wrong, but mental illness is not something we readily admit to. Indeed, we avoid the very term. At best we regard mental illness as embarrassing; at worst it is shameful.

Like most prejudices, the stigma of mental illness arises from misconception and myth. Some common ones are:

- **Mental patients (or former patients) may become violent.**
  THE TRUTH is that some severely ill individuals do behave violently and aggressively, but their proportion among mental patients is quite small. Most mentally ill persons are quiet and withdrawn.

- **Mental illness is hereditary, and marrying into a family with mental illness makes it likely that your children will go crazy.**
  THE TRUTH is that certain forms of mental illness do seem to have a genetic component, but we know very little about the mechanism of inherited mental disorders. When a parent has a mental illness, the children may or may not develop a mental illness; usually they do not.
- **Mentally ill persons act crazy.**
  THE TRUTH is that some do and many others don't. Many are able to function well enough so that their illness is not noticeable except to family members and close friends, and sometimes not even to them.
- **Mental illness is incurable, and a person who has been treated for an emotional disturbance can never again be wholly trusted.**
  THE TRUTH is that many mental illnesses can be cured, in the sense that the person never again has a serious mental disorder. Mental illness does not necessarily recur. In fact, about half of those ill enough to require hospitalization recover sufficiently so that they never again require any treatment (in or out of a hospital).
- **Maladjustment in mothers and other family members can cause such serious mental illnesses as autism and schizophrenia.**
  THE TRUTH is that this older theory about what causes these disorders is no longer considered valid. Rather, they are believed to involve a disturbance in the function of the brain's neurotransmitters, which is only partially understood but often does respond to drug treatment. (See Chapter 27 for further explanation.)

Prejudice makes us reluctant to describe ourselves or a friend or relative as "mentally ill." Instead we use such euphemisms as "troubled," "emotionally disturbed," "distressed," "having personal problems," or "needing help." These expressions, along with cruder terms such as "lunatic," "insane," "crazy," "mad," "nuts," and "nervous breakdown," all mean much the same thing: that a person has some kind of mental disorder, which may be mild or severe, short-lived or long-term.

MENTAL ILLNESS IS HARD TO LIVE WITH

When a person is physically ill we are inclined to make allowances, even when the illness causes us annoyance or difficulty of some kind, or when the patient acts grouchy or unpleasant. It is harder to remember that the mentally ill person, too, is suffering, and is just as much in need of understanding and support.

Mental illness often manifests itself in unpleasant ways. Among them are extreme lassitude and weariness ("I just can't seem to do it/ make up my mind/get going; I just don't care"); belligerence and quarrelsomeness, with the ill person seeming always ready to pick a fight; exaggerated worry and anxiety over trifles; suspiciousness and mistrust ("Everyone is picking on me; they're out to get me"); extreme selfishness and self-absorption ("What's in it for me?"); and poor emotional control, with violent outbursts out of proportion to the cause and often at inappropriate times. Such behavior inevitably irritates others.

Well-meaning relatives and friends may be tempted to scold or badger the ill person to change his or her behavior. But telling a mentally ill person to "snap out of it" or "shape up" is rarely helpful and may, by putting additional pressure on him or her, make matters worse. The behavior is part of the illness. Though a troubled person can often act normally for brief periods, over the long term he or she can no more change behavior at will than a man with pneumonia can clear his lungs on command. A depressed woman might smile when told to but she cannot change her underlying mood, no matter how hard she tries.

Chapter

3

CAUSES OF MENTAL ILLNESS

ANCIENT AND primitive peoples attributed disturbances in thinking and feeling to evil spirits and other kinds of magic. Today most—but not all—authorities believe that the most serious and disabling mental disorders involve a malfunction of the brain's neurotransmitters (discussed in more detail in Chapter 27). What causes such malfunctioning in the first place is not known, nor do we know if it is involved in the milder mental disorders as well. Among the contributing factors often cited are *heredity,* which may predispose one to become ill, and *stress,* which may trigger the onset of illness. In some organic disorders with mental symptoms, removal of the underlying cause— correction of a hormone deficiency or removal of a tumor—eliminates the symptoms completely. For others no cure has yet been found.

PHYSICAL CAUSES

Some mental impairments actually are known to be physical illnesses that result from a demonstrable organic cause. This cause may lie in the brain itself or in some other part of the body. Brain tumors, endocrine disorders, cerebral vascular accident (stroke), multiple sclerosis, Huntington's chorea, vitamin deficiency, and head injury are but some of the physical problems that can give rise to mental illness with symptoms identical to those of so-called *functional* mental illness (for which no physical cause has been identified).

Certain organic brain disorders are known to be genetic (inherited) in origin, others are traceable to the environment, and still others involve both genetic and environmental factors. Some inherited defects affect the brain only under particular environmental conditions. For example, phenylketonuria, an inherited deficiency of the enzyme phenylalanine, requires certain external conditions—specifically, the consumption of food containing an essential amino acid that the body cannot break down without this enzyme—to bring on brain damage. Other genetic defects affect the brain immediately, such as Down's syndrome, usually caused by the presence of an extra chromosome. Still others appear only late in life, among them Huntington's chorea.

Environmental causes of brain damage take many forms. Mental retardation and cerebral palsy often result from abnormalities present in the fetal environment (as a baby develops in the womb) or that occur during birth. A mother's exposure during pregnancy to drugs, alcohol, nicotine, or other toxins, or to certain infections, such as rubella (German measles), may cause abnormal brain development in her baby. After birth, bacterial and viral infections, toxic chemicals both within and outside the body, and injury or disease that compromise the brain's blood supply can lead to mental disorders.

DRUGS THAT CAN CAUSE MENTAL SYMPTOMS

Many drugs, both prescription medications and illegal substances, can induce symptoms that mimic various mental illnesses. Some drugs can produce delirium while being taken, whereas others do so when the drug is discontinued; alcohol, barbiturates, and other hypnotic drugs are among the latter.

Anticholinergic drugs, which include medications used to treat parkinsonism and stomach ulcers, as well as certain sedatives, can cause restlessness, irritability, disorientation, hallucinations, and even delirium. Occasionally, widely used ulcer medications such as cimetidine (Tagamet) and ranitidine (Zantac) cause depression.

Antihypertensive drugs, used to control high blood pressure, also may cause depression in some patients. Generally such an effect occurs only with an overdose, but it may occur with normal doses in susceptible individuals. Heart drugs such as digitalis also can cause depression and hallucinations.

Anticonvulsant medications, used to control epileptic seizures, can produce nervousness, mental confusion, and occasionally, hallucinations. Certain ones can cause agitation, anxiety, restlessness, and inability to concentrate; others produce drowsiness or dizziness. Overdoses of insulin, used to control diabetes, can produce anxiety and agitation.

VITAMIN DEFICIENCY

Symptoms resembling mental illness can result from vitamin deficiency. Recent studies have shown that niacin deficiency, which causes pellagra, can in its later stages be accompanied by delusions of persecution and hallucinations, as well as suicidal tendencies. Folic acid deficiency, which can lead to severe anemia, may also be associated with depression, insomnia, and irritability.

SUBSTANCE ABUSE

Both legal substances, such as nicotine and caffeine, and illegal drugs, such as marijuana, cocaine, amphetamines (speed), opiates (morphine, heroin), and hallucinogens (mescaline, PCP, etc.), can give rise to severe mental symptoms. Caffeine in large quantities can cause symptoms identical to an anxiety or panic attack, and the street drugs can give rise to psychotic symptoms.

The fact that the intake of chemical substances such as these can give rise to mental symptoms is yet another indication that such symptoms are probably caused by a biochemical derangement of one sort of another. Certainly this is true of the serious mental illnesses— schizophrenia, manic-depressive disease, and major depression. Further, these major disorders all tend to run in families, pointing to the possibility of inherited susceptibility, and they are likely to respond to drug treatment. Some experts believe that eventually all mental disorders will be found to have organic causes, or at least that certain individuals will be found to have a specific inborn predisposition to develop a mental illness.

THE LANGUAGE OF MENTAL ILLNESS

More important to the lay person is the fact that, whatever their causes, mental illnesses express themselves in behavior, in how people think, act, and feel. Mental health professionals often say that when people behave appropriately they *adapt* well to circumstances; when they do not, their behavior is *maladaptive*. For example, feeling terror in the face of danger or grieving over the death of a loved one is a normal response. Feeling fear when there is no real danger or continuing to grieve unabatedly for many months after a loss is maladaptive.

Imperfect as our knowledge is, mental health professionals have developed a terminology used to distinguish among different kinds of mental illness. The terms and the system of classification they represent are constantly changing as more is learned, but some continue to be in common use. The most severe disorders are referred to as *psychoses* and their acute manifestations as *psychotic episodes*. They involve severe disturbances of thought, communication, memory, and emotion, in which a person may have trouble distinguishing fantasy from reality. These disorders include schizophrenia, manic-depressive disease, and major depression. Less crippling but often even more distressing are *neuroses* or *neurotic disorders,** characterized by unrealistic and inappropriate thoughts, feelings, or actions. Whereas a person undergoing a psychotic episode may not even realize that something is seriously wrong, the neurotic usually is troubled but unable to do anything about it. Some researchers distinguish between neurotics, whom they call "the worried well," and seriously impaired mentally ill persons.

Other common classes of disorder are *substance addiction*, which includes drug addiction and alcoholism; *psychosomatic* or *somatoform disorders*, in which mental problems take the form of physical symptoms; and *personality* or *character disorders*, which include immature and irresponsible behavior that can lead to crimes of var-

---

* DSM-III-R, the most recently revised (1987) *Diagnostic and Statistical Manual of the American Psychiatric Association*, no longer uses *neurosis*, but describes these disorders by their symptoms. However, the word *neurotic* is still in common use. The World Health Organization issues another manual, *International Classification of Disease, 9th Revision (ICD-9)*, which is used in much of the world but not in the United States. It includes neurasthenia (nervous debility and exhaustion), which is not in DSM-III-R.

ious kinds. (Specific disorders and their symptoms are discussed more fully in Chapter 6.)

Although much remains to be learned about the causes of their illness, many mentally ill persons can be successfully treated. First, however, one must be aware of the need for treatment. Before we go on to discuss how you can tell if something is wrong (Chapter 5), we must deal with those occasions when you know something serious is wrong and immediate help is needed: the psychiatric crisis or emergency.

Chapter

4

HELP!
PSYCHIATRIC EMERGENCIES

MOST MENTAL illnesses, like physical illnesses, are not very dramatic. Just as there is a far greater incidence of common colds and stomach upsets than there is of pneumonia and stomach cancers, so there are far more garden-variety emotional problems than psychiatric emergencies.

Sometimes, however, it is obvious that something must be done, and done fast. This situation is called an *emergency* or *crisis*.

Any acute psychiatric disorder can *become* an emergency, but the most serious are those that involve violence or the threat of violence. Violent behavior, or the threat of it, should *never* be overlooked.

WHO IS IN CRISIS?

The following are instances where immediate professional attention and counseling are required:

1. A person threatening himself or herself with death or injury.
2. A person threatening someone else with death or injury.

= 15 =

3. A person making a violent outburst against another person or against someone's property.
4. A victim of physical violence, whether inflicted by a family member or an outsider.
5. A victim of sexual assault.
6. A person behaving in a bizarre, incoherent, or disorganized manner, possibly under the influence of drugs or alcohol.
7. A person undergoing an acute anxiety attack (see Chapter 6).

What should you do? If an individual is in immediate danger of personal harm, or is threatening to commit suicide or to hurt himself or someone else, you must intervene at once and call for help.

WHOM DO YOU CALL?

If a person is threatening to injure someone else or someone's property, or is a victim of violent or sexual assault, call the *police*. The police usually cannot offer treatment of any kind, but they can temporarily restrain a violent person and they can supply transport to a hospital emergency room. For victims of violence, such as rape or child abuse, some police departments offer special services, including counseling. Calling the police may also provide the fastest help for a person clearly unable to take responsibility for her own safety: an individual running wildly into the street, ignoring oncoming traffic, going outside half-naked in below-zero weather, or engaging in similar bizarre and potentially harmful behavior.

Suppose, however, that the person who needs help is neither in immediate physical danger nor an immediate threat to others. Then whom do you call?

If there is time to seek advice concerning local resources, call your *family doctor*, or a private *mental health practitioner* you know (psychologist, psychiatrist, social worker), or the *clergy* (preferably your own pastor or rabbi). Any of these individuals is apt to have experience with similar problems and be familiar with local hospitals, clinics, and other services. If none is available or able to make a recommendation, call any of the following:

1. The emergency ward of your local psychiatric hospital. They are well equipped to advise you.

2. The emergency service of your community mental health center. (If you don't know the name, look in the phone book white pages or yellow pages under Mental Health Center.) Many such centers have a 24-hour telephone emergency line and can either offer help themselves or advise you where to call or go.
3. The emergency room of a nearby general hospital. (If you don't know the name, look in the phone book under Hospital.) If the hospital does not offer psychiatric emergency service itself, it can refer you to the nearest hospital that does. However, before you take yourself or someone else there, be sure to phone first so that the person is expected. Also, it is wise to ask how long a wait might be expected; if it's several hours, you may want to try to find another facility. Although procedures vary from hospital to hospital, a patient in psychiatric crisis is usually seen and evaluated by a psychiatrist, who is either part of the emergency room staff or, more often, simply on call. Since many emergency rooms do not have a psychiatrist or other mental health professional on duty around the clock, a wait of some time (minutes to hours) is to be expected.
4. A telephone hot line. Many areas have such services to provide advice if you are in crisis or you are helping someone else. Hotlines, staffed twenty-four hours a day by volunteers, are likely to be listed in the phone book white pages under such listings as Contact, Crisis, Emergency, Help, Hotline, Suicide. If the problem is specifically drug- or alcohol-related, look in the phone book under Drug(s) or Alcohol(ics). If the crisis is related to Pregnancy or Rape, you may find help under either of these headings. If a young child has been injured by an adult, look under Child Abuse.

A hot line may refer you to a crisis center, usually one of the facilities listed above (hospital-connected). Such a center may offer overnight or brief hospitalization, usually in the emergency ward, with little or no red tape involved in being admitted or released.

If the person you are trying to help resists your assistance or refuses to go for help, you must use your own best judgment. If they are, in your opinion, a danger to self or others, you may have to call the police. If you believe there is a possible threat of such danger, you may want to point it out to a close relative of the person. If you yourself are a close relative, you may wish to consult other family members.

None of these decisions is easy, and there can be no iron-clad rules.

If you are not sure what to do, or what your obligation is, you may want to seek advice from one of the professional sources listed above.

UNTIL HELP ARRIVES

What should you do in the meantime? Whatever the underlying cause of an outbreak of violent behavior, the person is usually prompted to act out of either rage or fear, which in turn comes from a sense of either extreme frustration or extreme helplessness. It is unwise for you to aggravate these feelings by showing anger or contempt. Rather, remain as calm as possible and indicate your desire to help. If the person is endangering his own life, try to engage him in conversation, in talking rather than acting, until help can be summoned. If you yourself are being threatened or are in danger, leave the person as best you can, using your own judgment as to the safest way.

AND AFTERWARD

How does an emergency come about? An individual either has less and less ability to cope with life's ordinary stresses or is faced with an unusual stress so severe that she cannot handle it. Sometimes a relatively well-adjusted person is faced with an overwhelming disaster— the sudden accidental death of a loved one, for example—and requires temporary help in order to adjust to the tragedy. In other cases a crisis has no obvious cause; this situation usually means that a person has been ill for some time and the illness has progressed to the point where it must be treated. In effect the crisis is a call for help.

What happens afterward? That depends on the nature of the emergency, which often can be understood better by identifying the precipitating stress. If it was a catastrophe, such as one's house burning down with several family members killed or injured, counseling and other treatment may be needed until the person has adjusted well enough to function. If the crisis was brought on by an underlying mental illness that has become more severe, longer-term treatment may be required. Often, however, *crisis intervention* or *short-term treatment* (see Chapter 20), taking a week or less, may be all that is needed.

5

DO YOU NEED HELP?
HOW CAN YOU TELL?

How CAN you tell when you or someone you know needs help? How can you tell when symptoms are short-term and self-limiting—when, in effect, you have the psychiatric equivalent of a common cold that requires no special treatment other than rest and plenty of fluids and patience—or when you are on the verge of pneumonia and should be getting treatment?

You know it is not an emergency, yet you believe something may be wrong. You are not really sure if you are right or what you should do.

Recently, a famous psychiatric hospital ran an ad in a local paper. It was seeking volunteers to test the treatment of depression with a new drug. The ad called for individuals who felt depressed (or sad) and who had experienced at least five of the following eight symptoms:

- Sleeping too little or too much
- Eating too little or too much
- Agitation or being slowed down

- Loss of interest or pleasure
- Self-reproach or guilt
- Difficulty thinking, concentrating, or making decisions
- Fatigue or loss of energy
- Feeling that life is not worth living

It is probably safe to say that nine out of every ten persons over the age of fifteen have on occasion felt sad and experienced some—if not all—of these symptoms. Does that mean they are mentally ill? Does it mean they need treatment of some kind?

Not necessarily. One problem with many psychiatric symptoms is their subjective nature. How much sleep is too much? Or too little? In extreme instances, sleep can be monitored. But what about "loss of interest" or "pleasure?" Just what constitutes difficulty in making decisions?

Consider these two cases:

Dean R., 55, has changed his career five times in the past twenty years. His attic and garage are littered with the remains of discarded hobbies—elaborate photographic equipment, wood-working tools, ham radio equipment. Each year or so he takes up another hobby, or a new job, but he soon becomes bored.

Is Dean's loss of interest or pleasure pathologic? Does it represent "fatigue" or "loss of energy?" or "difficulty in making decisions?" Is he in fact suffering from depression?

Arthur S., 37, is now studying for a doctorate in computer science. He already has a master's degree in history and physics, and a doctorate in electrical engineering. Funded by scholarships and student aid, he has never held a job, not even a part-time position in any of his fields of study. Every time he completes his studies in one field he switches to another.

Is Arthur's status as a perpetual student symptomatic of mental illness? Or is he simply the eternal scholar in search of truth and knowledge?

IF YOU THINK YOU HAVE A PROBLEM, YOU MAY BE RIGHT

Suppose both Dean and Arthur decide to answer the hospital's advertisement. Is that significant? Yes, it may well be. When a person thinks something is seriously wrong, that feeling cannot be discounted. Most people do in fact know themselves fairly well, and they can discern changes in their mental functioning. A person looking for help usually does feel she is not functioning as well as before, or as well as possible, and the situation has persisted long enough that it probably will not get better by itself.

Remember, also, that in general the sooner you seek treatment, the better the prospects for improvement. Just as a small infection is easier to cure than a massive one, so a minor mental disorder is more likely to respond to treatment than a major psychotic episode. If you feel persistently anxious without cause, or if you are too frightened to go out, it is time to get help now, not when you are so upset that hiding in a closet is the only comfortable alternative. Similarly, if you are grief-stricken or sad to the point of not caring what happens, get help now; don't wait until you are driven to try suicide.

EARLY WARNING SIGNS

Any of the following feelings or behavior that persists over a period of weeks or months and begins to interfere with other aspects of day-to-day living should be a signal that something is wrong:

- Sadness, either over a specific event (a death, job loss, marriage breakup) or for no reason
- Hopelessness, demoralization, the sense that your life is out of control
- Violent and erratic shifts of mood
- Inability to concentrate or make decisions
- Fear and anger because everything and everyone is against you
- Trouble getting along with other people, in and out of the family; severe marital problems
- Severe sleep disturbances (insomnia, nightmares)
- Sexual problems
- Extreme fear of certain things or situations (dogs, airplanes, heights, crowds)
- Compulsive self-destructive behavior (overeating, drinking, gambling, drug abuse)
- Frequent physical complaints for which no medical cause can be found

If you experience these symptoms or notice them in a relative or friend, it's worth getting (or suggesting that your friend seek) a professional opinion.

Bear in mind, however, that a perfectly competent mental health professional may not be able to tell for sure what is wrong. To a large extent, the diagnosis and prognosis of a mental illness—deciding what is wrong with someone and how (or if) the disorder will respond to treatment—are very much a matter of guesswork. Furthermore, some mental illnesses (sometimes even very severe ones, like acute depression) appear to cure themselves, running their course much as a common cold does.

Unlike a mild upper respiratory infection, however, a mental illness can cause considerable damage, and even death, before it subsides, and it is very difficult to predict which depressed person will get better and which will end up committing suicide. Chances are that any mental illness severe enough to be noticed by family members or friends, or severe enough to make your life unsatisfying for a prolonged period, should at least be evaluated by an experienced professional.

GET A MEDICAL CHECKUP

Before you conclude that your problems are signs of mental illness, get a thorough medical checkup. It doesn't happen all that often, but every health practitioner knows at least one horror story about a patient who was treated for months for anxiety, stress, or hysteria or some other mental condition and then was found to have an organic disease that was responsible for the bizarre symptoms. Most responsible practitioners are alert to this possibility and will recommend a medical workup for any patient whose symptoms are suspicious. But even the most conscientious can sometimes overlook this possibility, so be on the safe side and make an appointment for a thorough checkup with your family doctor or, if you have none, with a hospital outpatient clinic or similar facility. Be sure to report your "mental" symptoms to whoever performs the examination, so that the physician will not fail to order any special procedures, such as an electroencephalogram to measure brain-wave activity, that may be needed to rule out organic disease. Other special tests that may be required include a spinal tap, skull x-ray, blood tests, brain scan, and CAT scan (computerized axial tomography).

A WORD OF CAUTION

Suppose, now, that you or your relative or friend has been told that the physician can find no physical causes for concern or a need for treatment. Does this mean it is time to seek psychiatric help? Maybe.

Before we continue with a description of symptoms of the more common mental illnesses, a word of warning is in order. As every medical and nursing student soon discovers, when you are confronted with a list of symptoms it is very easy to imagine yourself suffering from any number of them. Consider these, for example: weakness, fatigue, increased pigmentation, weight loss. Many if not most medical students, given their rigorous schedule of classes and clinical studies, feel very tired, occasionally weak, and lose weight as a result of lack of sleep and irregular meals. If they also notice that they are getting more freckles (increased pigmentation), should they conclude that they have the beginnings of Addison's disease, a very serious endocrine disorder whose early symptoms were just described?

The same is even more true for readers of mental symptoms, which most often are subjective feelings rather than measurable, observable phenomena. Do not, therefore, be too quick to conclude that your teenager is clinically depressed or that you are "losing your mind." Diagnosis is not easy for expert practitioners. You yourself cannot become a diagnostic expert just by reading this or any other book.

Chapter

6

WHAT COULD BE WRONG? SYMPTOMS OF MENTAL ILLNESSES

UNLIKE PHYSICAL illness, which your doctor has now ruled out for you or your relative, mental disorders are rarely characterized by signs, but, rather, by symptoms. A *sign*, medically speaking, is objective evidence of disease that can be verified, such as a skin rash, rapid pulse, or high blood pressure. A *symptom* is subjective evidence that cannot necessarily be verified, such as a headache, insomnia, or nausea.

Symptoms and signs are what a physician uses to make a diagnosis. Though it is much harder to make a diagnosis when all the evidence (or much of it) is subjective, it can be done, but with necessarily less certainty. Groups of symptoms occurring together, called *syndromes*, usually are considered evidence of particular disorders.

This chapter describes the most common mental illnesses and their symptoms: anxiety and phobias; obsessive-compulsive disorder; depression; suicide; manic-depressive psychosis (bipolar disorder); schizophrenia; somatoform (psychosomatic) disorders; eating disorders; alcoholism and drug abuse; personality disorders. Disorders of old age are described in Chapter 7, and mental disorders of children are discussed in Chapter 8.

ANXIETY

One of the most common psychiatric problems is anxiety, a feeling that all of us experience now and then. Apprehension and tenseness can be normal responses to anticipating a frightening situation, such as making an important speech or taking a crucial examination, just as fear is a normal response to the threat of danger. Whether or not anxiety is justified depends on when it occurs, how long it lasts, and how disabling it is.

To be acutely frightened when one's house catches on fire or the car brakes fail to respond is perfectly reasonable. To continue to fear fire, to be frightened by the sound of sirens, to imagine one is smelling smoke—all these reactions may take place after undergoing such a terrifying experience. But to fear fire obsessively when one has never had a bad experience with it, or to react with increasing panic for many months after a bad experience is not an appropriate emotional reaction. An estimated 15 percent of all adults suffer from *panic disorder.*

We usually use the word *fear* to describe a response to a realistic danger and *anxiety* or *panic* describes the same response when it has no apparent objective cause. The feeling is the same, however—a sense of profound apprehension and dread:

Wanda F. . . . found herself standing paralyzed in an aisle of the store, panic-stricken and unable to move. A neighbor who saw her helped her get home.

An episode of such intense panic is called an *anxiety attack.* Such attacks are often accompanied by physical symptoms, among them:

- Trembling or shaking
- Faintness
- Sweating
- Hot flashes or cold chills
- Numbness or tingling in the hands and/or feet
- Dizziness

- Palpitations (rapid heartbeat)
- Chest pain or constriction
- Difficult or labored breathing, shortness of breath
- Choking or smothering sensation
- Nausea or abdominal distress
- Fear of dying
- Fear of going berserk (out of control)

   In addition, one may experience a sense of unreality, or the fear of impending calamity or death.

   A person who experiences *at least four* of these symptoms *and* a sense of overwhelming panic is said to be having a full-fledged anxiety attack. (Actually, picking four symptoms as a requirement for such an episode is somewhat arbitrary. A person with three symptoms of disabling severity might be more disturbed than one with five in a milder form. Nevertheless, requiring four represents an attempt to establish some common ground for diagnosis, and it is useful provided one does not regard it as a hard-and-fast rule.)

RECURRENT ANXIETY AND PHOBIAS

An anxiety attack ordinarily lasts from a few minutes to an hour or so, usually depending on how quickly the feared object or situation can be avoided. Occasionally such attacks represent an isolated instance. More often, however, they recur, sometimes with increasing frequency. An anxiety attack is so frightening and unpleasant that it often provokes the fear of another such attack; in effect one becomes anxious about being anxious. This situation leads a person to fear and avoid the triggering circumstance: going into a crowded place or small enclosure or high place, or whatever the locale of the previous attack. This kind of fear—the fear of something that actually is neither dangerous nor frightening to most people—is called a *phobia*.

   Wanda's form of anxiety is called *agoraphobia*, literally meaning "fear of the market place." *Phobia* comes from the Greek word *Phobos*, the name of the god who inspired terror and panic. Agoraphobia need not literally involve a market, as Wanda's case does; it can be any open or crowded public place, such as an airline terminal, classroom, theater, or church, and in some cases, any place outside one's own home.

   Agoraphobia is the most common of such phobias. It affects women twice as often as it affects men. Other common phobias connected with anxiety attacks are *claustrophobia*, fear of being enclosed in a small space such as an elevator or airplane; *acrophobia*, fear of heights (balconies, tall bridges, mountain roads); *animal phobias*, especially fear of wasps, spiders, snakes, rats, mice, cats, dogs, or birds; and *social phobias*, fear of appearing ridiculous in public, especially while eating or drinking (in a restaurant), or writing (lest one's hand shake), or walking past a line of people (as in a restaurant, bus, or subway). Some phobic reactions are set off by a frightening experience, such as an attacking dog or an emergency airplane landing. Agoraphobia, however, most often starts with a nonspecific panic attack.

CHRONIC ANXIETY

Another form of anxiety is more chronic in nature, not so much marked by attacks of panic but persisting over a longer time. It is sometimes called *free-floating anxiety* or *generalized anxiety*. It, too, is characterized by a sense of dread and anticipation of some terrible misfortune, and it also tends to be accompanied by other symptoms, some of them physical:

- Difficulty concentrating
- Irritability, feeling "on edge"
- Impatience
- Trouble sleeping
- Motor tension (shakiness, jitteriness, trembling, eye twitch or other twitches, fidgeting)
- Sweating
- Heart pounding
- Dry mouth
- Clammy hands
- Tingling in the hands and/or feet
- Flushing or pallor
- Dizziness, light-headedness
- Diarrhea, nausea, or other gastrointestinal distress
- Lump in throat
- Frequent urination
- Rapid pulse

- Rapid breathing
- Shortness of breath or a sense of smothering

If a generalized feeling of dread persists for six months, during which you feel anxious more often than not, and *at least six* of these symptoms are often present when you are feeling anxious (not during a panic attack), you may be suffering from generalized anxiety and might do well to seek help in coping with it.

RULE OUT PHYSICAL CAUSES

With either specific phobias or generalized free-floating anxiety, the sooner a person seeks help for the symptoms, the better the outlook for relief. In all such cases, however, it is especially important to rule out certain physical disorders before beginning any treatment, since some forms of organic brain disease, hyperthyroidism (overactivity of the thyroid gland), hypoglycemia (low blood sugar), overdoses of or intolerance to stimulants such as caffeine and amphetamine, or withdrawal from certain drugs such as barbiturates all can give rise to anxiety reactions that appear identical to those caused by psychological factors alone.

TREATING ANXIETY

Anxiety disorders of all kinds have been successfully treated in a number of ways. Some of the physical symptoms, such as stomach upset, will respond to appropriate medication, and psychoactive drugs—both tranquilizers and antidepressants—may relieve the feelings of intense terror.

Many practitioners also recommend some form of behavior therapy, especially for helping persons with specific phobias (fear of dogs, heights, flying, etc.). Such a person is gradually desensitized through safe exposures to the object of fear, be it a dog, snake, or airplane. In the case of agoraphobics, they are encouraged gradually to reenter the environment they fear, perhaps accompanied by a supportive person who helps them wait out any panic reaction that occurs.

It is estimated that about one-third of sufferers can be treated with such therapy alone. Another one-third respond to antidepressant drugs alone, and the rest appear to require both medication and behavior therapy. Cognitive therapy also may be very effective. (See Chapter 16 for a fuller account of behavior and cognitive therapy.)

OBSESSIVE-COMPULSIVE DISORDER (OCD)

Closely related to the anxiety disorders but perhaps more obvious to relatives, friends, and even casual observers are the obsessive-compulsive disorders. An *obsession* is a nagging fear, doubt, impulse, or idea that a person cannot put out of his mind, no matter how much he wants to, even though he realizes that the fear is senseless.

Marjorie A., 57, a housewife with a high-school education, is tormented with the idea that her floors are poisonous. A dozen years ago she found ants on her kitchen floor and used a strong insecticide to get rid of them. Since then she has become convinced that the kitchen floor—and in time all the floors in her house—became poisonous and will kill her if she comes in direct contact with it. She never goes barefoot, and in fact is afraid to touch the soles of her feet lest they somehow have become contaminated too.

A *compulsion* is a repetitive, stereotyped form of behavior that a person feels compelled to perform. Washing one's hands many times a day, even when they are obviously not dirty, is one common form of compulsive behavior. Another is lining objects up in a particular order—for example, rearranging the things on top of one's desk in a certain ritual way—and checking frequently to make sure that the order has not been disturbed. Refraining from this behavior results in unbearable anxiety, and sometimes a person arranges her entire life around the compulsive behavior.

Actually, many otherwise normal individuals appear to think obsessively or behave compulsively in one or another area of their lives and do no harm, either to themselves or to others. The "workaholic" is a compulsive achiever who can do very well in life. But when an obsession or compulsion becomes a source of profound stress to the individual, when it is time-consuming (takes up more than one hour a day) or when it interferes with normal functioning (when a person cannot be away from soap and water for more than half an hour at a time because of "needed" hand-washing) treatment is indicated.

Obsessive-compulsive disorder was once viewed as a result of psychologically damaging experiences and unresolved early childhood conflicts. In recent years, however, there has been increasing evidence that the cause may lie in abnormalities of brain function. Studies also indicate that the disorder is far more common than was formerly believed, probably because affected individuals tend to conceal their peculiar behavior and perform it in secret. A combination of drug treatment, usually with certain antidepressants, and behavior therapy helps a large majority of sufferers. (See also the section on obsessive-compulsive disorder in youngsters in Chapter 8.)

DEPRESSION

Often less obvious to the casual acquaintance or friend than either anxiety or phobia but one of the most common of all mental disorders is depression. Formerly called *melancholia,* depression has perhaps the widest range of any mental illness. It may be so mild and chronic that it can scarcely be identified at all, or so profound that a person is barely able to function. It also is potentially fatal. Many individuals who commit suicide suffered from depression. Between these extremes, every imaginable gradation exists.

Depression is called a *mood disorder* or *affective disorder* (*affect* means "mood" or "spirits"), the predominant mood experienced being one of extreme sadness. The overall impression of depression given to others is one of slowed-down functions and diminished reactions (psychiatrists call it *flattened affect*). We all have "highs" and "lows" in our lives; the depressed person seems to have a perpetual "low." When that "low" interferes significantly with day-to-day living, it constitutes a *clinical depression,* one that requires treatment.

Some depressions are *endogenous,* that is, they appear to have no particular triggering cause but seemingly arise "from within." Others are said to be *reactive,* that is, they have a definite beginning, often a loss over which the person grieves, or some other profound emotional stress or trauma.

Jane C. has been grief-stricken since her husband died eighteen months ago . . . weeps constantly, and lately has been having more and more trouble remembering things.

The death of one's spouse or child tops the list of devastating events that can trigger depression. Others are divorce or separation, a serious physical illness such as cancer, a disabling accident, job loss and unemployment, and bankruptcy or other disastrous financial problems. It is natural to grieve over a serious loss, but when the sense of emptiness continues over a period of time and becomes complicated with feelings of worthlessness and despair, so that normal functioning does not resume, a clinical depression has developed. Chronic physical illness and substance abuse, especially of alcohol and cocaine, seem to predispose one to serious depression.

MAJOR DEPRESSION

How can you tell when you or someone you know is suffering from a *major depression?* The dominant mood is prolonged loss of interest in or pleasure from practically all of one's usual activities, accompanied by feelings of sadness, hopelessness, being "down in the dumps," and irritability, all of which persist for a considerable time. Further, the following symptoms are likely to occur:

- Feelings of deep sadness most of the time
- Marked change in appetite, leading to either significant weight loss or weight gain
- Sleeping disturbances: either sleeping too much (hypersomnia) or too little (insomnia); early-morning wakening (two hours before the normal time) is especially common
- Physical agitation and restlessness or an overall physical slowdown
- Greatly decreased interest or pleasure in most activities, including sex; in men, inability to sustain an erection often occurs
- Loss of energy, constant fatigue
- Diminished ability to concentrate and difficulty in making simple decisions
- Feelings of worthlessness, self-reproach, and/or excessive guilt
- Recurrent thoughts of death or wishing to be dead

Anyone who experiences profound sadness along with *any five* of these other symptoms *almost daily for at least two weeks,* and without a logical triggering cause such as the recent death of a loved one, is probably undergoing a major depressive episode.

A major depression may occur once and never recur, or it may, in about half of all cases, occur again. It sometimes recurs *cyclically,* for example, several months of depression followed by a period of relative normalcy, followed again by some months of depression, and so on. In other cases there are clusters of depressive episodes interspersed with normal periods; in some the depressive episodes become more and more frequent. The American Psychiatric Association's diagnostic manual also distinguishes between a melancholic type and a chronic type of major depression. Both are equally severe, but the former responds better to antidepressant drugs or electric shock therapy (ECT), whereas the latter is longer-lasting (two years or more) without a two-month period of relief and seems to be less responsive to medication.

CHRONIC DEPRESSION

A less severe depression, sometimes called *dysthymia* or *depressive neurosis*, differs from a major depression largely in degree. Generally the symptoms are troublesome for a long period of time—off and on for over two years (one year in the case of children and adolescents)—but not quite disabling enough to be called a major depressive episode. They may be more or less constant, or they may be separated by periods of normal mood lasting a few days to a few weeks (but never more than two months at a time). The depressive periods themselves may be characterized by the following symptoms:

- Loss of interest in pleasurable activities and inability to respond positively to pleasurable events
- Tearfulness and weeping
- Feelings of worthlessness
- Brooding about the past, feeling pessimistic about the present and future
- Chronic fatigue, little energy
- Sleep disturbances, either sleeping too much or too little
- Poor appetite or overeating
- Inability to concentrate and difficulty in making decisions

The presence of at least *two* of these symptoms and prolonged sadness (for two years; one year for children and adolescents), never abating for a two-month period, indicate the possibility of a milder but still clinical depression that calls for treatment.

WHO BECOMES DEPRESSED?

How common is clinical depression? Estimates indicate that between 5 and 30 percent of the total population experience this disorder. One recent study suggests that major depression affects 10 million Americans each year.

Almost anyone, from a small child to a very old person, can be affected. In fact, there is a high incidence of depression among teenagers and young adults. High-school counselors and college infirmaries frequently see students with problems that turn out to be depression, at least to some degree. Part of the reason is, no doubt, that adolescence and early adulthood are times of considerable stress and change, as young people strive to find their identity and separate from their parents.

Depression occurs in women two to five times more often than in men, but it is not certain whether this finding is due to the fact that our culture permits women to express feelings, especially negative feelings, more openly and to ask for help more readily, or whether there really is a sex-linked difference. In any event, two to three times as many women seek professional help for depression.

There seems to be a familial component as well, that is, depression runs in families. If one identical twin has an affective disorder (either depression or manic-depressive psychosis, described below), there is a 70 percent chance that the other twin also will be affected. Among nonidentical twins, siblings, parents, and children of depressed individuals, the risk drops to 15 percent. Whether or not there is an inherited biochemical factor in all kinds of depression is not known, but it is strongly suspected, at least in some kinds of depression. Depression also can be a side effect of certain medications, such as the ulcer drugs Tagamet (cimetidine) and Zantac (ranitidine), the antihypertensive Inderal (propranolol) used to control high blood pressure, diuretics, and numerous others. It also is often associated with alcoholism.

SUICIDE

The principal danger of untreated depression is suicide. It is believed that a high proportion—some say as many as 15 percent—of depressed persons eventually succeed in ending their lives. (This figure applies to manic-depressive psychosis and depression combined; manic-depressive psychosis is discussed later in this chapter.) Oddly enough, a depressed person sometimes tends to commit suicide during a period of seeming improvement. The reason, it is believed, is that when a major depression is at its worst, inertia prevents a person from acting; with some improvement one is still overcome by feelings of despair and worthlessness but now has enough energy to plan for death.

The possibility of suicide increases with advancing years. However, in recent years there has been an alarming increase in suicide among younger persons. Suicide is the third leading cause of death (after accidents and homicides) among adolescents and young adults in the United States (ages fifteen through twenty-four). The risk of a depressed person committing suicide is thought to be at least fifty times that of someone who is not depressed. Moreover, statistics for suicide are believed to be underestimates of the real figures because many cases go unreported.

SIX WARNING SIGNALS OF SUICIDE

1. Suicide threats; none should be ignored.
2. Statements revealing a desire to die (such as "They'd be better off without me").
3. One or more previous suicide attempts.
4. Sudden change in behavior (withdrawal, moodiness, apathy).
5. Depression, especially feelings of utter hopelessness.
6. Suddenly making final arrangements, such as giving away personal possessions and/or indicating who is to inherit what.

None of these warning signs should be ignored. Suicide or the threat of it is a genuine emergency. Take some action, even if you find yourself in the position of "betraying a confidence," by getting direct help for someone who is suicidal but refuses to seek counseling. Many people who are considering suicide have given up hope and do not believe anyone can help them. This is not true; in most cases they can be helped.

TREATMENT OF DEPRESSION

Depression responds far better to various kinds of treatment than some other severe mental disorders. Further, both a severe reactive depression and the milder clinical depressions sometimes are self-limiting and cure themselves spontaneously. When this happens, the depression simply runs its course, usually within four to twelve months. Severe endogenous depressions, on the other hand, rarely go away by themselves, but they often respond to antidepressant drugs and/or to electroconvulsive therapy (ECT). Antidepressants, which have been in use since the 1950s, are among the most effective drugs in the psychiatrist's black bag, but they often take a number of weeks to work, during which some patients become so discouraged that they stop taking them and get worse (or become desperate and commit suicide). In some cases, moreover, they do not work. (See Chapters 18 and 19 for more information about antidepressants and ECT.)

Unfortunately, depression sometimes is disguised. Even though a person's mood and behavior may have changed markedly, it is one or another physical symptom—palpitations, chest pain, back pain, trouble swallowing, trouble breathing, stomach upset, fatigue, dizziness, headache, insomnia—that drives a person to the doctor. Troubled by such symptoms, patients often do not bother to mention the mood changes that might warn the practitioner. Unless the primary-care physician is exceptionally alert (and two-thirds of those who do seek treatment see their family doctor first), treatment for depression may be long delayed while the other complaints are treated with sleeping pills, antacids, painkillers, and similar remedies that are useless against depression.

A clinical depression in children or adults may be secondary to a physical illness. Viral infections such as influenza (flu or grippe) and mononucleosis, ulcers, rheumatoid arthritis, and alcoholism are closely associated with depression. Disorders of the thyroid and adrenal glands, diabetes, multiple sclerosis, pancreatic cancer, congestive heart failure, and temporal lobe epilepsy also are often associated with depression. Depression can be a side effect of medication taken for other conditions, such as some antibiotics and blood pressure medications; cortisone and related anti-inflammatory agents used for arthritis; digitalis, used in heart disease; estrogens and progesterones, hormones used in oral contraceptives (birth control pills); and tranquilizers, sometimes given when depression is mistaken for anxiety or some other mental disorder. Therefore, it is vital to tell physicians about any past illnesses and all medications being taken.

MANIC-DEPRESSIVE PSYCHOSIS (BIPOLAR DISORDER)

An estimated one-fourth to one-third of all persons suffering from major depression are believed to have manic-depressive psychosis or bipolar disorder (the rest have *unipolar depression*), which tends to develop in early adulthood or later. Perhaps 1 percent of all Americans suffer from it. This form of depression often occurs in several family members, so a genetic predisposition to develop the condition is almost certainly present. Some researchers believe that the disease can be inherited.

Manic-depressive psychosis is a mood disorder characterized by very extreme "ups" and "downs," the former called *mania*, or *manic episodes*, and the latter called *depression*, or *depressive episodes*. Out of control, the manic patient may decide to run for president of the United States, go on an extravagant shopping spree, make an impulsive (and usually foolish) business investment, or otherwise behave with extreme recklessness.

William D. quit his job and moved out of his family's suburban home, leaving his wife and children. He has rented an elegant high-rise apartment in the city, and is about to buy an expensive cabin cruiser. However, he hasn't enough in the bank to meet the payments on the family car, let alone buy any luxury items.

William's behavior is manic. It will probably be followed by a profound depression in which he feels he is no good to himself or anyone else and becomes too despondent to act at all. Like any profound depression, it can end in suicide (and about 10 percent of cases do).

The manic phase of this disorder is usually considered a psychosis, involving a severe distortion of the patient's perceptions. Behavior may become so bizarre that it resembles an acute schizophrenic episode (see below). However, while schizophrenia tends primarily to disrupt thought processes, manic-depressive disease is primarily a disorder of mood (although its alternating ups and downs may secondarily affect a person's thinking). Schizophrenia often begins in late adolescence, whereas manic-depressive disease usually begins in early adulthood or later.

Manic-depressives often behave quite normally between episodes, and are able to hold jobs and function in a family setting. The more difficult phase of the illness is the manic, but in about 75 percent of cases it can be quite well controlled by means of lithium carbonate, a powerful drug that also appears to lessen the subsequent depression. During the two to three weeks it takes for lithium to become effective, other antipsychotic drugs may be prescribed. The depressive phase of the illness sometimes responds well to antidepressants and occasionally to ECT. Although unipolar depression (without mania) is very common, mania rarely occurs without a preceding or subsequent depression. However, there is no set pattern of these extreme swings. Some individuals have a series of manic episodes, others a series of depressive episodes, and still others have both in various sequences. Months or years may separate such episodes, and in between the person may be quite normal.

WHEN IS IT A MANIC EPISODE?

How can you tell if you or someone you know is undergoing a manic episode?

The predominant symptom is an extended period during which the person's mood is markedly elevated and expansive, with sudden shifts to irritability and anger. Further, the following symptoms are likely to be present:

- Increased activity (of any kind) and/or physical restlessness
- Decreased need for rest and sleep
- Flight of ideas, that is, jumping rapidly from one thought or topic of conversation to another
- Talking a great deal and talking very fast
- An inflated ego, the idea (usually false) that one can accomplish anything and everything
- Increased distractibility, attention easily drawn to unimportant details
- Involvement in potentially self-destructive or risky behavior: spending sprees, sexual indiscretions, wild business investments, reckless driving, and so on

A predominantly elated mood accompanied by *three or more* of the above-named symptoms, severe enough to cause impaired functioning in one's normal activities and lasting more than one week or requiring hospitalization, points to the strong possibility of manic-depressive psychosis. The depressive phase, when it occurs, must last at least two weeks.

The American Psychiatric Association also describes *cyclothymia,* a chronic mood disturbance of at least two years' duration involving manic and depressive episodes but of less severity and duration than manic-depressive psychosis.

SCHIZOPHRENIA

Among the most severe mental illnesses is schizophrenia, a disorder that affects one's thought processes, feelings, and ability to relate to other people. The schizophrenic literally cannot think straight; he has distorted perceptions and often confuses fantasy and reality. Moreover, his feelings are completely dulled, so there is either little reaction, or inappropriate reaction, to painful or pleasurable experiences, for example, laughing as a response to hearing that someone has died, weeping at good news, and so on. Finally, social relations are at a minimum, since the schizophrenic tends to withdraw from most contact with others. Typically he feels lonely and misunderstood and has very little self-esteem. Faced with these disordered thoughts and feelings, the schizophrenic withdraws into a private world where the distinction between real and imagined disappears. One characteristic symptom of schizophrenia is auditory hallucinations, that is, hearing sounds and voices that actually do not exist.

Donald, 19 . . . spends all his time in his room . . . scarcely speaks to his family and has seen none of his former friends. His mother sometimes hears him talking behind his closed door, even though she knows he is alone and there is no telephone in the room.

Typically schizophrenia begins in late adolescence or young adulthood, between the ages of sixteen and twenty-five. A first episode after age thirty-five is uncommon and after age forty is rare. It affects men and women with equal frequency, although it affects more men than women in the sixteen to twenty-five age group, and more women in the twenty-five to thirty group. Until the discovery of antipsychotic drugs, schizophrenia was regarded as both incurable and untreatable; in many cases episodes became more frequent and severe, until the patient, by then often in the back ward of a mental hospital, stopped functioning altogether. Such patients would spend their days sitting in a corner and rocking, unable to speak or wash or use the toilet. Today the outlook for most schizophrenics is more hopeful.

How can you tell if someone has schizophrenia? During a schizophrenic episode the person is usually markedly peculiar; schizophrenia gives rise to behavior that is closest to what most people call "crazy." It often is marked by delusions and hallucinations. A *delusion* is a false belief held in the face of either no evidence or strong evidence to the contrary, for example, that you really are Jesus Christ or that the television newscaster is sending you secret messages in code every evening. A *hallucination* is a false sensory stimulus, for example, hearing nonexistent voices or feeling nonexistent insects crawling up your legs.

The following symptoms may occur in schizophrenia:

- *Strange delusions* without any basis in reality, such as that one's actions and/or thoughts are controlled by a computer hooked up to the brain
- *Auditory hallucinations* in which "voices" are either arguing with each other or a voice is commenting on one's actions or telling one what to do
- *Delusions of grandeur*, such as the idea that one is not really oneself but someone "great" such as Napoleon or Jesus Christ
- *Persecution delusions*, such as believing that everyone on the bus is staring at you because they are planning to kill you
- *Incoherent speech*, or speech that does not make sense
- *Inappropriate expression of feelings* (laughing at bad news, crying at good), or no overt reaction to deeply moving events
- *Catatonic behavior* (holding one body position for hours at a time)

If *any one* of these symptoms persists for a period of at least six months, and the person is functioning markedly worse than usual at work, at school, in personal grooming, or in social relations, she could be suffering from some form of schizophrenia.

Schizophrenics in remission have described how it feels to have this disease. The feelings are miserable and terrifying. One has a sense of being unreal, a sense of separation from one's body and behavior (of being an outsider watching oneself), as well as a sense of alienation from others. This feeling is sometimes called *depersonalization*.

Formerly called *dementia praecox* ("precocious madness"), schizophrenia is not a single disorder but a complex of diseases. Often one or another of the symptoms—paranoia (delusions of persecution), incoherent speech and inappropriate affect (feelings), or catatonic behavior—is the principal symptom seen. Also, the course of the illness is variable. In some cases it becomes chronic, and in others, usually only those undergoing effective treatment, it goes into remission, although there often is some residual disability. Generally speaking, the later in life the onset of the disease, the better the outlook for improvement.

Some authorities now differentiate between *process* or *chronic schizophrenia*, with a gradual onset, and *reactive* or *acute schizophrenia*, which develops suddenly in response to some great stress. The latter usually responds better to treatment.

A newer method of subdividing schizophrenia—which like cancer is thought to be not one but an entire group of diseases—differentiates between those who have mostly active (or *positive*) symptoms (delusions, hallucinations, disordered thought or disconnected thinking) and those who have mostly *negative* symptoms (social withdrawal, apathy, lack of drive). Medication tends to help the former more than the latter.

CAUSES OF SCHIZOPHRENIA

Schizophrenia affects approximately 1 percent of the world's population, and 2 to 3 million persons in the United States alone. Studies of identical twins and of children of schizophrenic parents who were raised in foster homes indicate that there probably is a genetic factor in the disease, although its precise role is still unclear.

What appears to be virtually certain is that schizophrenia is a *brain disease*, just as multiple sclerosis and parkinsonism are. It probably is caused by some damage or defect in the limbic system, the brain's gateway through which external stimuli pass, and this damage is thought to occur very early in life. It seems to involve an excess of the neurotransmitter dopamine (see Chapter 27 for more about the brain and neurotransmitters). Other causes that have been suggested, and that may trigger the onset of symptoms, are nutritional deficiency, viral infection, immune-system abnormality, or stress. Schizophrenia is *not* caused by family interactions and is *not* a sane response to a crazy world.

WARNING SIGNS OF SCHIZOPHRENIA

Sometimes the active psychotic phase of the disease is preceded by a set of somewhat less extreme symptoms. These may include:

• Social isolation or withdrawal, usually followed by personality changes, such as frequently becoming angry, suspicious, and/or evasive
• Deteriorating performance at work or at school

- Deteriorating personal hygiene and grooming, such as neglecting to bathe, change one's clothes, comb one's hair, and so on
- Overactive, frenzied behavior and inability to concentrate
- Marked change in sleep patterns, such as reversing night and day behavior (lying in bed all day and being active all night)
- Depression, sometimes difficult to distinguish from a severe clinical depression or manic-depressive psychosis (see above)
- Blunt or flattened affect (little emotional reaction to events that normally arouse emotion), or an inappropriate emotional reaction
- Peculiar speech, digressive or vague, or speaking very little
- A constantly hollow, unhappy tone
- Peculiar behavior, such as hoarding garbage, stealing food, or talking to oneself out loud in public
- Auditory hallucinations (hearing voices that aren't there)
- Lack of energy or initiative
- Odd beliefs or magical thinking
- Unusual perceptions or illusions

These may be early signs of schizophrenia, or they may occur when an acute episode is subsiding.

TREATMENT OF SCHIZOPHRENIA

Acute schizophrenia patients usually need to be hospitalized, particularly during a first episode, so that complete tests and evaluation can be performed and an appropriate schedule of medication can be established. Despite the severity of the disorder, it should be remembered that highly creative and intelligent individuals have suffered from it—the writer Virginia Woolf and the painter Vincent Van Gogh are believed to have been schizophrenics—and that with new medication and research the outlook is improving quickly. Approximately 90 percent of patients recover enough after three to twelve weeks of hospitalization to be discharged. Continuing medication can shorten subsequent episodes, make them milder, and may even abort an attack. (See Chapter 18 for medications used for schizophrenia.)

Approximately one-fourth of cases suffer one schizophrenic episode only and never experience another. Usually such a full recovery occurs within the first two years of illness. (In non-Western society the course and outcome tend to be better, perhaps because the disorder is generally viewed as a temporary condition.) Of the remainder,

25 to 35 percent may be much improved and relatively independent with treatment, and another 15 to 25 percent may improve but require considerable support. The rest either remain hospitalized and unimproved, or are dead, often by suicide. Indeed, suicide among schizophrenics has increased since the large-scale programs of deinstitutionalization were begun in the 1970s and probably results from depression as well as the delusional behavior characteristic of uncontrolled schizophrenia.

Four disorders have names similar to schizophrenia but are believed to be distinctly different from it: (1) *schizophreniform disorder*, which is very similar to schizophrenia in every way except that it lasts a much shorter time (anywhere from one week to six months); (2) *schizoid personality disorder*, in which a person is emotionally cold and aloof, has no warm or tender feelings for anyone at all, is indifferent to praise, criticism, or the feelings of others, but otherwise has no eccentricities of speech, behavior, or thought; (3) *schizotypal personality disorder* (also called *borderline schizophrenia*), in which a person never actually becomes psychotic but shows many of the peculiarities of the schizophrenic (odd speech, magical thinking, self-referential thinking, suspiciousness, social isolation, poor rapport with others, undue sensitivity to real or imagined criticism, and depersonalization); and (4) *schizoaffective disorder*, a disturbance of psychotic severity that combines elements of disordered thought processes and mood disturbance—in effect a combination of schizophrenia and manic-depressive psychosis.

PHYSICAL SYMPTOMS FROM MENTAL CAUSES

The relationship of body and mind is exceedingly complex and still is not understood. We know which nerves transmit the painful impulses of a burned finger to the brain, but we do not understand how anxiety can cause a headache or diarrhea, or how depression can cause constipation.

Certain serious chronic physical illnesses—diabetes, rheumatoid arthritis, and high blood pressure are among them—are affected by how a person feels. At times of stress such an illness worsens, and at calm, relaxed times it improves. Such illnesses are sometimes called *psychosomatic* or *psychophysiological*, but in 1980 the American

Psychiatric Association changed its nomenclature to "psychological factors affecting physical condition" in recognition of the fact that we still don't know how they operate.

Moreover, a person can be feeling extreme pain—crippling lower back pain, for example—without any detectable organic cause whatever. One of Sigmund Freud's most famous cases showed that one can actually imagine oneself to be partially paralyzed, a condition called *conversion hysteria* or *conversion disorder* because here mental symptoms have in effect been converted into physical ones. An entire category of mental illnesses—the so-called *somatoform disorders*—involve physical pain of one kind or another that has no discernible organic cause.

Betty A., 47, has a medicine cabinet full of pills. At least once a month she calls her family doctor, complaining of stomach upsets, sleeplessness, backache, and a host of other ailments. Her doctor rarely can find a physical cause for her symptoms. . . .

Betty suffers from so-called *somatization disorder,* one of the two principal forms of somatoform disorder. It tends to affect principally women (it is rarely diagnosed in men), it usually begins in the teens, and it drives the woman to seek frequent medical attention. In some cases a woman goes from doctor to doctor hoping to find relief; she may even undergo surgery for a nonexistent ulcer or tumor, or some other major medical procedure.

Typically such a person appears, to the physician who treats her, as a demanding and complaining pest, with a long history of physical symptoms, unsuccessful treatment, and unhappy relations with physicians. Indeed, such patients may so anger practitioners that they prefer to avoid them altogether, and therefore they tend to ignore their very real distress. At the worst extreme, such a patient is in danger of having the early signs of a serious physical illness, such as cancer, overlooked until it is too advanced to treat successfully, simply because she has cried "Wolf" for so long that no one pays attention any more.

The second form of common somatoform disorder affects men and women equally but tends to begin somewhat later, between the ages of twenty and thirty. Here the principal symptom is the mistaken belief that one is suffering from a serious disease, although a thorough physical examination does not reveal any evidence of it. No matter how much the doctor—or doctors—reassures the individual that his heart, for example, is in perfectly good working order, he continues to experience various disturbances of heartbeat (too rapid or irregular) or chest pain and lives in mortal fear of an impending fatal heart attack. This form of the disorder is called *hypochondriasis* or *hypochondriacal neurosis*.

How can you tell if someone is really ill or is suffering from psychogenic symptoms? You can suspect the latter if she continues to insist either that she has a serious disease, with fear of it persisting for at least six months (hypochondriasis), even after being carefully checked by a reputable physician who can find nothing wrong, or if there are complaints of at least *thirteen* of the following symptoms,* in addition to maintaining that she is (and has always been) in very poor health (somatization disorder):

- *Trouble swallowing*, hearing, seeing (double or blurred vision), speaking (voice loss), remembering (*amnesia*), or walking; trouble urinating; fainting or passing out; seizures or convulsions; muscle weakness, numbness, or paralysis
- Stomach upsets (stomachache, nausea, vomiting, bloating, intolerance to various foods, diarrhea)
- Menstrual problems (*pain*, irregularity, excessive bleeding)
- Difficult pregnancy (severe *vomiting* throughout or sufficiently severe to require hospitalization)
- Sexual problems (lack of interest in sex, lack of pleasure, pain during intercourse, *burning sensation in sexual organs or rectum*)
- Chest symptoms (pain, *shortness of breath*, palpitations, dizziness)
- Pain (in the back, joints, *extremities*, on urinating, elsewhere)

The hypochondriac has been a figure of fun and a source of annoyance for centuries. The seventeenth-century playwright Molière poked expert fun at him in his *The Imaginary Invalid*. Because hypochondriacs are so persistent about their complaints, one tends to lose patience with them fairly quickly. It is hard to remember that their suffering is nonetheless genuine.

---

* *DSM-III-R*, the American Psychiatric Association's latest *Diagnostic and Statistical Manual* (1987), says two or more of the symptoms in italics suggest high likelihood of somatoform disorder.

EATING DISORDERS

A truly dangerous physical condition believed to be almost wholly mental in origin is *anorexia nervosa.*

Kathy J., refuses to eat, claiming she is far too fat. She has lost twenty-five pounds in the past two months and was, if anything, quite slender to start with.

Kathy may well be among the 5 to 18 percent of young women with this condition who actually starve to death. Like other anorexics, she believes she must lose more weight even when she has already lost as much as 15 percent of her total body weight.

Anorexia afflicts mainly young women in their late teens to early twenties (95 percent of anorexics are female). They not only restrict their eating drastically but may encourage further weight loss by taking strong laxatives and enemas and inducing vomiting after they eat. A related syndrome, called *bulimia* or *bulimia nervosa,* consists of alternate eating binges followed by self-inflicted purging and drastic dieting. Girls with either of these disorders tend to be secretive about their diets, binges, and purges. Depending on how extreme the weight loss, they may stop menstruating, and purging in particular can seriously damage the digestive system.

How can you tell if your friend or your daughter is endangering her health in this way? In this age group, anyone who shows massive weight loss and a marked change in eating habits may be suspected and should be checked by the family physician or pediatrician without much delay. The sooner the condition is discovered, the better the outlook, both physically and mentally. Sometimes, however, the patient may be very resistant to advice, psychotherapy, medication, and other means used to reverse the symptoms, and may require hospitalization for a time.

Difficult to treat, anorexia is, at least one study shows, a culture-specific illness of the West, where a slim figure is considered highly desirable. It is spreading to countries like Japan, which are adopting Western values and ideals.

OBESITY

One of the most common of all eating disorders in America today is obesity, which is defined as weighing 25 percent more than one should (according to fairly standard guidelines put out by insurance companies and medical societies). Obesity is caused by overeating. In some instances it begins in early childhood; in most it begins in adulthood. It is not really known what leads a person to eat far more than the body needs, so that the excess is stored as fat, but it is a dangerous condition, putting one at risk for a variety of serious and potentially life-threatening disorders such as diabetes, hypertension (high blood pressure), cerebral vascular accident (stroke), heart disease, gall bladder disease, osteoarthritis and other orthopedic problems, and some kinds of cancer. Although the American Psychiatric Association does not include obesity in its list of mental disorders, overeating can be influenced by psychological factors, such as emotional stress.

There is little doubt that most obese persons would much prefer a normal weight and the great majority are unable to achieve this desire. Insight therapy occasionally helps them discover why they overeat and how to adjust their habits, but it usually takes a very long time. Various kinds of behavior therapy and supportive self-help groups also have been used to treat obesity, employing a variety of techniques to alter the client's eating habits. Unfortunately many individuals may lose a great deal of weight for a time but then revert to overeating and gain it back. Self-help and support groups aim not only at weight loss but at improving one's self-image and maintaining the weight loss.

ALCOHOL AND DRUG ABUSE

Alcohol abuse and substance dependency also represent physical and behavior problems that are caused, at least in part, by psychologic factors. Here the basic unhappiness or insecurity that leads individuals to begin drinking or taking drugs in order to change how they feel is responsible, but only in part. Some individuals, it is now believed, have an inborn biochemical makeup that makes them become readily addicted to substances that, while not totally harmless for others, do not necessarily lead to addiction. We all know persons who can drink a bottle of wine a day, or consume six ounces of whiskey a day, yet can easily control their alcohol intake at will. They can literally take it or leave it. The alcohol is not really good for them—at best it is a form of junk food, or "empty calories"—but under most normal circumstances it does them no significant harm. For those predisposed to alcoholism, however, one drink almost invariably leads to another, and for some a relatively small amount causes intoxication. Such individuals seem to develop a need for alcohol, and it becomes extremely difficult to control.

Alcohol abuse is a widespread problem. An estimated 13 percent of all American adults have experienced alcohol abuse or dependence sometime in their lives, and about 1.5 million Americans each year seek treatment for it. The toll is enormous. Not only can abusers die of liver disease and other ailments resulting from their high intake but they are implicated in perhaps half of all automobile deaths as well as many other fatal accidents.

Like individuals with eating disorders, alcoholics often conceal their drinking habits. They also try to convince themselves that they are not "problem drinkers." How can you tell if you drink too much? Ask yourself the following questions*:

- Has someone close to you sometimes expressed concern about your drinking?
- When faced with a problem, do you often (or always) turn to alcohol for relief?
- Are you sometimes unable to meet home or work responsibilities because of drinking?
- Have you ever required medical attention of any kind as a result of drinking?
- Have you ever experienced a blackout—a total loss of memory while still awake—when drinking?
- Have you ever come in conflict with the law in connection with your drinking?
- Have you often failed to keep the promises you made to yourself about controlling or cutting out your drinking?

If you have answered yes to even one of these questions, your drinking is probably affecting your life in some major ways and you should do something about it now, before it gets worse.

How can you tell if a relative or friend is becoming (or has already become) dependent on alcohol?

* Developed by the National Institute on Alcohol Abuse and Alcoholism.

- Is he immediately ready to pour a drink when faced with a problem?
- Does she regularly get drunk?
- Is there a record of work missed because of drinking, or regular attendance at work but with an ill-disguised odor of liquor on the breath?
- Has the person's license been suspended for driving while drunk?
- Has the person gotten in trouble with the authorities for no "logical" reason?
- Has the person been involved in several unexplainable accidents?
- Has the person's home life become difficult because of excessive drinking or arguments resulting from drinking?

When one or more of these signs is present, it shows that a person's drinking pattern may be either out of control or heading in that direction. Alcoholics do not necessarily drink regularly. Researchers have found three different patterns of alcohol abuse or dependence: (1) regular intake of large amounts of alcohol; (2) regular heavy weekend drinking; (3) binges of heavy drinking for weeks or months, interspersed with long periods of abstinence.

Many primary-care physicians (family doctors, general practitioners, internists) seem to have a blind spot regarding alcoholism in their patients. The results of one survey of Alcoholics Anonymous members indicated that half had tried to discuss their drinking problem with someone who told them they couldn't possibly be alcoholics, and in one-fourth of these cases the "someone" was a physician. Even psychiatrists sometimes overlook the possibility that a patient's problems are secondary to alcohol abuse.

Alcoholism can be treated. A variety of facilities exist (see alcohol and drug treatment centers in Chapter 20). The programs differ in environment, method, and level of services. Some believe in separating patients from their normal environment (family, friends, school, work). Others believe families must be involved for treatment to succeed and to eliminate codependence.

To find the right program for you or your relative, contact one of the following agencies, most of which can be found through the telephone book: National Council on Alcoholism affiliate in your area; Alcoholics Anonymous; Al-Anon; your community alcoholism or mental health clinic; the social services or human resources department of your city or county; your county medical society; the health office or "troubled employee" program in your company. (See also the resources for alcoholism listed in Appendix A.)

DUAL DIAGNOSIS

Alcohol abuse can induce certain organic mental disorders, specifically dementia (inability to handle complex thoughts, impaired judgment, poor memory), as well as personality changes. Intoxication may involve loss of memory (blackouts), outbursts of rage and violent behavior, and the like. Alcohol abuse therefore can be confused with symptoms of serious mental illness, for example, schizophrenia, manic-depressive psychosis, major depression. But it also can appear in conjunction with these and other mental illnesses, that is, one may be schizophrenic and alcoholic at the same time. Because alcohol abuse can be responsible for such similar symptoms, most clinicians believe it must be treated first, before any mental disorder that might also be present can be properly diagnosed and treated.

Similarly, many of the drugs abused for their psychoactive effects also can produce psychotic symptoms like those of schizophrenia or mania. Some users of marijuana experience strange feelings of "depersonalization" (unreality concerning oneself), loss of "body boundaries," and paranoid delusions. Drugs such as amphetamines, LSD, and PCP (angel dust) produce hallucinations, delusions, and disordered thought processes. As with alcohol, chronic heavy use of drugs can affect the brain, impairing intellectual function and memory. Unless such damage has already occurred, stopping the drug will eliminate these symptoms, enabling more accurate diagnosis of any coexisting mental illness as well as appropriate treatment.

DRUG ABUSE AND ADDICTION

Many substances are called *psychoactive*, that is, they affect the central nervous system and thereby modify mood and behavior. In addition to alcohol, which in our society is legal and considered acceptable provided it is not overused, and caffeine in the form of coffee or tea, widely used as a stimulant, numerous mood-altering substances that are either illegal or available legally only as prescription medications have come into wider use. Among them are amphetamine (speed) or similar stimulants of the nervous system, cannabis (marijuana), cocaine (including the form called "crack"), hallucinogens such as LSD and mescaline, inhalants such as glue and paint thinner, opioids such as heroin and morphine, phencyclidine or PCP (angel dust), sedatives and hypnotics (sleeping pills), and nicotine. *Abuse* of these substances consists of their continued use despite the knowledge that they cause some persistent social, occupational, or physical problem (e.g., driving while "high" is dangerous, cigarette smoking can cause cancer and heart disease, etc.). *Dependence* means that there is significant psychological and/or physical suffering in giving them up.

Substance dependence or addiction can happen to just about anyone. Some individuals begin to use drugs for pure enjoyment, whereas others use them to suppress unpleasant feelings. Still others suffer from physical or mental ailments and become addicted to the medication prescribed for their illness. Although much about addiction is not well understood, it seems clear that some individuals have a combination of biochemical, personal, and social characteristics that together predispose them to become drug-dependent.

Treatment for drug dependence tends to be similar to that for alcoholism, and in fact a worldwide association modeled on Alcoholics Anonymous, Narcotics Anonymous, currently includes approximately fourteen thousand self-help groups, two thousand of them in drug treatment centers (see Chapter 20). How can you tell if you or your relative or friend is addicted? The accompanying list contains a series of twenty-nine questions developed by recovering addicts for Narcotics Anonymous that is intended to uncover drug dependence.

AM I AN ADDICT?

	Yes	No
1. Do you ever use alone?	_____	_____
2. Have you ever substituted one drug for another, thinking that one particular drug was the problem?	_____	_____
3. Have you ever manipulated or lied to a doctor to obtain prescription drugs?	_____	_____
4. Have you ever stolen drugs or stolen to obtain drugs?	_____	_____
5. Do you regularly use a drug when you wake up or when you go to bed?	_____	_____

6. Have you ever taken one drug to overcome the effects of another? _____ _____
7. Do you avoid people or places that do not approve of you using drugs? _____ _____
8. Have you ever used a drug without knowing what it was or what it would do to you? _____ _____
9. Has your job or school performance ever suffered from the effects of your drug use? _____ _____
10. Have you ever been arrested as a result of using drugs? _____ _____
11. Have you ever lied about what or how much you use? _____ _____
12. Do you put the purchase of drugs ahead of your financial responsibilities? _____ _____
13. Have you ever tried to stop or control your using? _____ _____
14. Have you ever been in a jail, hospital, or drug rehabilitation center because of your using? _____ _____
15. Does using interfere with your sleeping or eating? _____ _____
16. Does the thought of running out of drugs terrify you? _____ _____
17. Do you feel it is impossible for you to live without drugs? _____ _____
18. Do you ever question your own sanity? _____ _____
19. Is your drug use making life at home unhappy? _____ _____
20. Have you ever thought you couldn't fit in or have a good time without drugs? _____ _____
21. Have you ever felt defensive, guilty, or ashamed about your using? _____ _____
22. Do you think a lot about drugs? _____ _____
23. Have you had irrational or indefinable fears? _____ _____
24. Has using affected your sexual relationships? _____ _____
25. Have you ever taken drugs you didn't prefer? _____ _____
26. Have you ever used drugs because of emotional pain or stress? _____ _____
27. Have you ever overdosed on any drugs? _____ _____

28. Do you continue to use despite negative con-
    sequences?   _____   _____
29. Do you think you might have a drug prob-
    lem?   _____   _____

NICOTINE DEPENDENCE

Despite overwhelming evidence of the devastating effects of cigarette smoking on health, currently 54 million Americans continue to smoke. Supposedly the large majority of them would like to quit, but for one reason or another they do not. Many individuals do try to stop, but then they resume smoking. Withdrawal symptoms, which include anxiety and irritability, headache, muscle aches, an unpleasant taste in the mouth, and strong cravings for cigarettes, last from a few days to many weeks. The relapse rate is approximately 50 percent within the first six months and 70 percent or more within the first year. Those who are able to quit for one year rarely resume smoking.

Nicotine is genuinely addictive. It is a psychoactive substance that works at specific sites in the brain to cause relaxation yet works in the rest of the body as a stimulant, increasing the heart rate, raising blood pressure, and giving the smoker the feeling of a "lift." Also, smokers develop tolerance for these effects, so that more nicotine is needed to satisfy their craving.

As with alcohol and other drug dependence, some individuals are more addicted than others. Approximately 3 to 5 percent of smokers who want to quit do so simply by stopping, and another 5 percent do so simply because their physicians tell them to. The most effective means is currently thought to be the use of nicotine polyacrilex chewing gum (Nicorette), which provides blood levels of nicotine comparable to that of smoking and therefore mitigates withdrawal symptoms, combined with behavioral therapy or some other kind of counseling in order to overcome the psychological dependence. Even then the relapse rate is close to 50 percent after one year. Other means used are self-help programs and brochures, clinics using a form of group therapy, aversive conditioning (see under behavior therapies in Chapter 16), hypnosis, and acupuncture.

PERSONALITY DISORDERS

Personality disorders (also called *character disorders*) differ from other forms of mental illness in that their predominant feature is an inflexible and maladaptive mode of behavior toward oneself or others. Two types were mentioned earlier: schizoid personality disorder and schizotypal personality disorder (see above, at the end of the section on schizophrenia).

Another kind takes the form of extreme suspiciousness and mistrust.

Mildred J., 28, suspects that others are out to get her, and will do her a bad turn. She is convinced they want to make her look ridiculous, so she is quick to feel slighted and take offense at what, to anyone else, would be a harmless remark or gesture.

Mildred's disorder is called *paranoid personality disorder*, or *paranoia*, which means the feeling of being persecuted ("persecution complex" was an older term for it). It is not as severe as the paranoia sometimes present in schizophrenia, in that Mildred is not psychotic and is able to distinguish reality from fantasy. But it is self-destructive, in that she is always expecting the worst from others and hence goes through life with "a chip on the shoulder." As a result, she has trouble getting along with her co-workers and her boss.

In another form one may find it virtually impossible to state one's opinions, wishes, or demands directly, and instead treats the world with passive resistance.

James K., 22, is seemingly amiable and easygoing. If his family decides on a family outing after supper, he agrees to go but eats his meal very slowly, forcing everyone to wait for him and so delay the activity. Or he may agree to do an errand on his way home from work but repeatedly "forgets" to do it. If he dislikes a fellow worker, he never says so directly but obstructs that person's efforts by failing to do his share of the job, and may even stay home from work.

James can express his negative feelings only indirectly, by refusing to act at all. His illness is called *passive-aggressive personality disorder* and markedly impairs his relations with family, friends, and colleagues. In fact, he has no real friends.

Perhaps the most obviously destructive form of personality disorder is the kind called *antisocial personality disorder*.

John B., 25, lost his job last week after getting in a fist fight with a fellow worker. It is the fourth time in less than a year that his violent behavior has gotten him in trouble. This time the other man, whose jaw he broke, is planning to sue him.

The antisocial person is constantly violating the rights of others and frequently ends up in trouble with the law. Often such a person first has trouble in childhood or early adolescence with school truancy, lying, theft, running away, and/or impulsive behavior. In adult life he generally has a poor work history, with frequent job changes, and an unhappy marriage. Punishment—even jail—does not change the behavior; learning from bitter experience simply does not occur. Occasionally such antisocial behavior ends of its own accord, usually in the late thirties. More often it does not. It is much more common in boys and men than in girls and women. Further, there may be a familial factor as well, since it occurs much more often in near relatives of those with the problem than in the general population. Conventional therapies do not seem to help much, but in recent years some practitioners have reported success with behavior therapy or behavior modification methods (see Chapter 16).

We tend to focus on the harm such individuals do to others, yet in the long run their behavior is harmful to themselves, too. It is their families that usually suffer most. The individuals themselves often seem to have blunted feelings and do not react emotionally as most of us would in deeply moving situations.

HEAD INJURY

A woman suffers severe head injuries from a vicious mugging. A carful of teenagers smashes into a retaining wall, and the driver, who wore no seatbelt, is thrown out of the vehicle. In both cases the victims lie in a coma for several weeks, regain consciousness, and then face a long struggle to regain their physical and mental functions.

Many individuals whose brains are injured in falls, automobile crashes, or other accidents make an excellent *physical* recovery, but for reasons still not understood the recovery of their full mental faculties is much less likely. Only a small percentage are able to return to work or retain the same level of intellectual functioning they had before. A recent study of severely brain-injured individuals over a five-year period showed that upon discharge from the hospital only 7 percent were sufficiently recovered to live independently. Another 29 percent were severely disabled, 19 percent were moderately disabled, and 15 percent were in a state in which they appeared to be conscious but could not communicate or act purposefully.

In addition to experiencing such problems as performing tasks much more slowly than before, having difficulty in making plans, or having a sufficient attention span to complete a task, severely brain-injured persons often have residual psychological problems. Some tend to be very irritable and impetuous. Others develop severe depression. Still others suffer panic attacks. These conditions may require the same kinds of treatment as mental illnesses whose cause is not specifically known, that is, psychotherapy of various kinds, appropriate medication, and extensive rehabilitation.

Chapter

7

MENTAL PROBLEMS OF OLD AGE

JANE, THE sixty-eight-year-old widow described earlier, most certainly exemplifies a case of grieving that has turned into depression. But is it only depression that makes her forget to turn off the stove or "lose" her car? Could her mental condition be the result of aging?

Earlier studies of the elderly suggested that mental illness is especially common, in part due to stresses associated with increased physical illness, loss of significant social supports, isolation, and inadequate income. Depression was thought to be particularly common. More recent research, however, suggests that mental disorders in old age are no more common than in younger people, *except* for those of organic origin.

DEMENTIA AND ALZHEIMER'S

Elderly persons who suffer from lapses of memory, especially forgetting recent events, who become disoriented as to time and place, and who lose their ability to do simple arithmetic may be suffering from an organic mental illness called Alzheimer's disease. Approximately 7 percent of the elderly in the United States—about 2.5 million persons—are so affected, and another 1.5 to 2 million suffer dementia from other causes. Indeed, recent studies show that mild cases of dementia may be even more widespread, as may the incidence of Alzheimer's (one study says 10 percent may be affected).

Alzheimer's, for which no cure has yet been found, is characterized by tangles of nerve material resembling spaghetti strands in brain cells, and by deposits of a protein, beta amyloid, that forms plaques in the brain's blood vessels and tissues. These interfere with an essential neurotransmitter, acetylcholine. Alzheimer's usually begins at age sixty or earlier and involves progressive deterioration. In most cases the patient dies within ten years of its onset.

Another physical cause of senile dementia is a series of small cerebral vascular accidents (CVAs, or strokes), in which infarcts (areas of dead tissue) form in the small arteries of the brain, thereby reducing its supply of blood and oxygen. Unlike a more massive CVA, these "mini-strokes" do not incapacitate the victim all at once but gradually reduce brain function. Approximately one-fourth of all cases of senile dementia are believed to result from such strokes. Unlike Alzheimer's, for which no specific tests are available and diagnosis can only be confirmed by autopsy, a CAT (computerized axial tomography) scan or MRI (magnetic resonance imaging; see Chapter 27 for further description) will reveal the infarcts. Even though neither of these physical causes of mental impairment is at present curable, self-help and family support programs can do a great deal for their victims, often preventing or postponing institutionalization. (See Appendix A for resources.)

The diagnosis of senile dementia is not always clear-cut. The symptoms include:

• Disorientation as to time, especially concerning when events in one's own life occurred
• Disorientation as to place, mistaking one place for some other familiar place
• Disorientation as to identity of others, such as mistaking a doctor for one's own daughter
• Impaired memory, especially relating to recent events (remote memory may remain good)
• Hallucinations, usually visual

- Delusions concerning ordinary, everyday people and events
- Confusion, usually alternating with lucid periods, and with the confusion worse at night

The elderly especially can react to medication in peculiar ways, and some symptoms of senile dementia can be caused by a toxic reaction to drugs they commonly use, such as sleep medications, diuretics for high blood pressure and heart disease, and ulcer drugs such as Tagamet and Zantac. Sometimes psychoactive drugs are used to treat behavioral changes associated with dementia. Some of them may make the symptoms worse. The so-called minor tranquilizers (Valium, Librium, etc.; see the chart in Chapter 18) are especially apt to do so, but antipsychotics and antidepressants also may have such results.

Some of the physical disorders to which the elderly are especially prone can also cause mental symptoms—conditions such as diseases of the heart, lungs, kidneys, or liver, nutritional deficiency, sight or hearing loss, and hypothermia (below-normal body temperature, a common problem in the very old). Other disorders that can cause dementia are a brain lesion (benign tumor, abscess, or cyst), hypothyroidism (underactive thyroid gland), pernicious anemia, chronic poisoning (from the workplace or some other source), and tertiary syphilis. Drug use, including alcoholism, can give rise to such symptoms, as can adverse drug reactions and interactions. In most cases treatment of the primary physical condition can relieve the mental symptoms, even in those where it coexists with Alzheimer's.

DEPRESSION: THE VICIOUS CIRCLE

The signs of dementia in its early stages—bad mood, withdrawal, apathy, indecisiveness—also can be mistaken for depression, and what is really a depression can in turn be mistaken for Alzheimer's. Further, the two may both be present.

Losing one's memory is good cause for sadness. But which comes first? Profound depression can give rise to memory loss, which may be partly or wholly reversed by means of antidepressants and other treatment. In Jane's case, we do not know if her depression affected her memory or if her natural grief turned into depression because of organic brain changes. Even more complicated are cases where a patient has received electroconvulsive treatment (ECT) for depression (see Chapter 19), since a common side effect of such treatment is impaired memory of recent events. Loss of memory can in turn cause depression—in effect, a vicious circle.

Depression also can accompany many of the illnesses that afflict older persons, especially parkinsonism, cancer, and arthritis. Treating depression in these cases can reduce unnecessary suffering and help patients cope better with their medical problems.

CAREFUL DIAGNOSIS

In its early stages senile dementia is especially difficult to diagnose. Careful observation by a knowledgeable person, in addition to sophisticated medical evaluation, may be required. A physician attempting to differentiate between senility and depression may call on family members or long-term friends for information about the patient's history, since the onset of depression is usually more sudden than the slow, gradual process of senility. Also, the individual with organic problems typically minimizes loss of mental function such as memory, whereas the depressed individual tends to exaggerate the loss.

If dementia is suspected, a careful medical workup is indicated, including:

1. A detailed medical and personal history, taken either from the patient or from a knowledgeable family member or friend; it should include an inventory of all medications currently being taken.
2. A comprehensive physical examination, with blood tests (including measuring levels of thyroid hormone and vitamin B_{12}), urine, thyroid, and neurological tests, and vision and hearing evaluation; an electrocardiogram (EKG), chest x-ray, and electroencephalogram (EEG); a brain scan—CAT scan or MRI.
3. Psychologic and intellectual tests especially designed to detect organic brain disease.

As the disease progresses, errors of judgment and memory lapses become more obvious, and the patient is painfully aware of them. However, as memory declines still more, insight is lost, and the emotional burden of the disease falls largely on family members and friends. Eventually not only memory but control of bodily functions is lost, and full-time care is required.

Not only is there no cure for Alzheimer's but the causes are not understood. Some researchers have focused on the unusually high concentration of aluminum found in the nerve cells of people who died from Alzheimer's, but it is not known whether this substance results from the disease or is a factor in its development. A "slow" virus—an infection that takes many years to affect the nerve cells—is suspected by others. There may also be a genetic component— susceptibility to Alzheimer's may be inherited—but no clear pattern of heredity has been established.

If you suspect that your elderly relative is suffering from senile dementia, try to get her evaluated by a physician who specializes in the care of the elderly—a gerontologist or geriatric psychiatrist. If your own doctor cannot direct you, you may be able to locate such a person through your local or state council on elderly affairs, a reputable nursing home, or your local home-care corporation. There is also a national organization for exchanging information and advice among families of Alzheimer's victims, the Alzheimer's and Related Disorders Association (see Appendix A for address). Living with Alzheimer's is discussed in Chapter 23.

For information about geriatric family therapy, see Chapter 17; for psychoactive drugs and their effect on the elderly, Chapter 18; finding a nursing home and evaluating such facilities, Chapters 20 and 22; and preventive care for the elderly, Chapter 25.

Chapter

8

MENTAL ILLNESS IN CHILDREN

AN ESTIMATED 12 to 20 percent of Americans under the age of eighteen experience mental health problems serious enough to impair their lives in some way. Of these perhaps one-third suffer severe mental disability and related handicaps. For many years mental illness in children went unrecognized unless the symptoms were extremely severe. For example, the recognition of a mental disorder, rather than willful disobedience, in instances of children who could not sit still or pay attention is relatively recent and by no means universal.

Stephen I., 10, is not doing well in his third-grade class. . . . He has been allowed out for recess only once all year, his teacher making him stay in because of his disruptive and destructive behavior.

Punishment or suspension from school is not likely to help this ten-year-old, yet it can be hard to differentiate between a child who needs stricter discipline and one who needs treatment. Moreover, parents are often reluctant to acknowledge that their child may have an emotional problem or a mental illness. The stigma is strong, and they may feel it casts blame on them.

Even if parents do admit—or are forced to admit—that something is wrong with their child, it may be difficult to determine just what is the matter. Young children do not readily express their thoughts and feelings in words. They are more likely to show such symptoms as aggressive behavior toward other children, sleep disturbances, eating disturbances, and the like.

When older children are taken to see a mental health professional (and only an estimated one-third of those who need it actually receive a mental health evaluation), their perceptions of their problem tend to be quite different from those of their parents. While parents tend to complain about their conduct and behavior, the children themselves are more likely to report emotional problems, such as anxiety and depression.

ANXIETY AND PHOBIAS

Anxiety disorders in children often take the form of such habits as nail-biting, thumb-sucking, head-banging, rocking, or hair-pulling. Anxiety may also express itself in physical disorders, especially stomach upsets and respiratory difficulties, as well as sleep disturbances. Overanxious children tend to be fearful of new people and new situations, and are excessively wary of body injury. Sometimes their anxiety can create learning problems resembling those of children with attention deficit hyperactivity disorder (see below).

A common form of anxiety disorder in children is *separation anxiety*, that is, excessive clinging to and reluctance to leave the parents or others to whom the child is closely attached. In school-age children this condition may take the form of *school phobia*, that is, persistent fearfulness about leaving home to go to school. On school days such a child often complains of (and experiences) physical symptoms—stomachache, headache, nausea. Although it is natural for children to feel apprehensive when they first start nursery school, kindergarten, and first grade, and in some cases their early school experiences may need to be postponed on this account, generally such fearfulness subsides after a relatively short time. In some youngsters, however, it may persist to the point where school attendance can no longer be avoided and something must be done. Similarly, a child with separation anxiety may become unduly anxious about possible harm befalling his parents, or about being abandoned by the parents, or some similar calamity for which there is no basis in reality.

In other youngsters, acute anxiety may express itself in night terrors, repeated episodes of abrupt waking and panic, or eating disorders such as pica (habitually eating paper, clay, or other nonfoods), refusal to eat, or overeating. Adolescents may develop bulimia or anorexia nervosa (see under eating disorders in Chapter 6), or become dependent on alcohol or drugs.

One recent study* found that phobias are the most common problem in children ages seven to eleven. Although fear of dogs, insects, the dark, and so forth are common in children at various stages, those diagnosed with phobia were afraid enough to have it interfere significantly with their lives. Another common finding was overanxiety, a general state of worry about getting hurt, failing exams, or being disliked by other children, severe enough to interfere with normal living patterns. Anxiety and phobias also were common among teenagers ages fourteen to sixteen, affecting 17 percent of those studied in one report.†

Some of these youngsters can be helped with psychoactive drug treatment. An antidepressant such as imipramine may be effective, although blood levels must be carefully monitored to avoid toxicity. Others may respond to treatment with benzodiazepines, although the duration of treatment must be limited to avoid addiction and the drug must be discontinued very gradually to avoid withdrawal problems. Nonaddicting drugs such as antihistamines also may be useful. (See the chart in Chapter 18 for more about these drugs.)

OBSESSIVE-COMPULSIVE DISORDER

Obsessive-compulsive disorder (see the description of various symptoms in Chapter 6) apparently afflicts far more youngsters than was previously thought. Many adult patients are admitting that their problems began in childhood. One recently published study describes a

---

* Of 789 youngsters ages 7 to 11 treated at a Pittsburgh health maintenance organization, headed by Dr. Elizabeth J. Costello, Duke University Medical Center; reported in *Archives of General Psychiatry*, December 1988.

† By Dr. Patricia Cohen, New York State Psychiatric Institute.

three-year-old who would walk in circles around manhole covers whenever he crossed the street. Later, in kindergarten, he would sit for hours drawing circles on pieces of paper. At age eight he would stand up and sit down seventeen times before finally sitting in a chair, and he would go back and forth through a door seventeen times before finally leaving a room.

A recent study of high school students revealed that obsessive-compulsive disorder occurred in about 1 percent of them. Also, recent research reveals that obsessive-compulsive disorder, whose symptoms are shown in the accompanying table, very likely results from some aberration in the brain's circuitry. The condition often responds to behavior therapy, which entails repeated exposure of the youngster to the stimulus that sets off the repetitive actions. For example, if a youngster feels compelled to wash her hands thirty times a day, her hands might be deliberately soiled and she might then be prevented from washing them. Such therapy seems to work better for treating compulsions than obsessions, which have fewer outward signs. Newer drug treatments, on the other hand, seem to work for both compulsions and obsessions. Three antidepressant drugs in particular have been shown to be quite effective: clomipramine, fluvoxamine, and fluoxetine. Only the last has been approved in the United States at this writing, but the other two, widely tested in Europe, are expected to become available by 1991.

DEPRESSION

Normal behavior varies so much from one childhood stage to another that it sometimes is difficult to know whether a child is suffering from depression or is just going through the terrible twos, sulky sevens, or trying teens. Also, temporary periods of depression, when things go wrong, are just as common among children as adults.

A depressive order in children may take the same form as in adults—a persistent feeling of sadness and low self-esteem with feelings of being worthless and rejected ("I'm no good," "I can't do anything right," "No one likes me"). If such a mood disturbance persists and the child begins to withdraw from siblings and friends, and there has been no external event (illness, hospitalization, loss) that can account for it, the child may need treatment for depression. Like

COMMON SYMPTOMS OF OBSESSIVE-COMPULSIVE DISORDER IN CHILDREN AND ADOLESCENTS*

Obsessions	Reported Symptom at Initial Interview[†]
Concern with dirt, germs, or environmental toxins	28 (40%)
Something terrible happening (fire, death or illness of self or loved one)	17 (24%)
Symmetry, order or exactness	12 (17%)
Scrupulosity (religious obsession)	9 (13%)
Concern or disgust with bodily wastes or secretions (urine, stool, saliva)	6 (8%)
Lucky or unlucky numbers	6 (8%)
Forbidden, aggressive or perverse sexual thoughts, images, or impulses	3 (4%)
Fear might harm others or self	3 (4%)
Concern with household items	2 (3%)
Intrusive nonsense sounds, words, or music	1 (1%)

Compulsions	
Excessive or ritualized handwashing, bathing, showering, toothbrushing, or grooming	60 (85%)
Repeating rituals (going in/out of door, up/down from a chair)	36 (51%)
Checking (doors, locks, stove, appliances, emergency brake, paper route, homework)	32 (46%)
Rituals to remove contact with contaminants	16 (23%)
Touching	14 (20%)
Counting	13 (18%)
Ordering or arranging	12 (17%)
Measures to prevent harm to self or others	11 (16%)
Hoarding or collecting rituals	8 (11%)
Rituals of cleaning household or inanimate objects	4 (6%)
Miscellaneous rituals (e.g., writing, moving, speaking)	18 (26%)

* National Institute of Mental Health Study directed by Judith L. Rapoport, M.D., of 70 children and adolescents, also appearing in *Scientific American,* March 1989. Used by permission. Rapoport is author of *The Boy Who Couldn't Stop Washing* (E. P. Dutton, 1989).
† Totals exceed 70 and percentages total more than 100 because many patients presented more than one symptom.

adults, depressed children often complain of physical ailments, especially stomachache, headache, sleep problems, and fatigue. In a young child depression is sometimes expressed in temper tantrums, aggressive behavior, or nightmares.

Depression is common in adolescents, and major depression (described in Chapter 6) appears to be as common in young adolescents as in adults. Most teenagers seem to experience frequent "highs" and "lows," but a persistent low that remains unaltered by pleasurable events may indicate a need for help. As was pointed out in Chapter 6, suicide is the third leading cause of death among adolescents and young adults, so no teenager's persistent sadness or comments such as "I wish I were dead" should be overlooked. Older children also occasionally express their underlying sadness in a violent way, by truancy, vandalism, or running away from home.

Manic-depressive psychosis in adolescents is often manifested by episodes of impulsivity, irritability, and loss of control alternating with periods of withdrawal. This treatable illness typically goes unrecognized when it is assumed that such storminess is natural to adolescence.

Since adolescents are noted for their quickly changing moods and behavior, it may take careful watching to discern the difference between a mood disorder and normal behavior. The key to recognizing depression is that the change in behavior lasts for weeks or longer. Any youngster who has four or more symptoms of depression for more than a few weeks, or is doing poorly in school, seems socially withdrawn, uncaring, overimpulsive, and no longer interested in activities formerly enjoyed, should be checked for a possible depressive illness. Depression in children and adolescents can and should be treated, lest it lead to subsequent problems in later life. Psychotherapy and/or antidepressant medication, or, in the case of mania, lithium, may be effective; with either medication blood levels should be carefully monitored for toxicity.

WARNING SIGNS OF MENTAL ILLNESS*

Younger Children

Marked change in school performance
Poor grades in school even though trying hard
Considerable worry or anxiety, shown in refusing to go to school, go to sleep, or take part in normal activities
Constant fidgeting, constant movement beyond regular play
Persistent nightmares
Persistent disobedience or aggression (longer than six months) and opposition to authority figures
Frequent, unexplainable temper tantrums

Preadolescents and Adolescents

Marked change in school performance
Abuse of alcohol and/or drugs
Inability to cope with problems and daily activities
Marked changes in sleeping and/or eating habits
Many complaints of physical ailments
Consistent violation of rights of others; opposition to authority, truancy, thefts, vandalism
Intense fear of becoming obese with no relationship to actual body weight
Depression shown in sustained, prolonged negative mood and attitude, often accompanied by poor appetite, difficulty sleeping, or thoughts of death
Frequent outbursts of anger

* Indicating that a psychiatric evaluation may be useful, according to the American Academy of Child and Adolescent Psychiatry.

ANTISOCIAL BEHAVIOR

Lying, stealing, setting fires or other acts of vandalism, getting in trouble with the police—these problems are more likely to attract prompt attention than depression. To some extent, some of these forms of behavior are normal among very young children, who "lie" because they are not able to distinguish between truth and falsehood or "steal" because they fail to understand the concept of property rights. Further, most young children occasionally have trouble controlling their aggressive impulses. But when aggressive behavior physically harms other children, or when there are frequent complaints from other parents, teachers, and neighbors, something is amiss, and professional advice may be needed. (See also the section on juvenile delinquency in Chapter 25.)

CHILDHOOD PSYCHOSIS

There is some disagreement as to whether or not children actually develop schizophrenia. Some authorities maintain that childhood psychosis or schizophrenia—and they tend to use the terms interchangeably—is an appropriate label for any very severe emotional disturbance found in babies as early as three to four months of age and as late as adolescence. Others say that schizophrenia in children is an early form of the adult disorder (described in Chapter 6) but hardly ever begins before age five and increases only slightly between ages five and ten. It affects boys four times more often than girls.

Childhood psychosis is in any event quite rare—less than one child in one thousand is so diagnosed—and in most cases the child's behavior is so different from that of other children that the parents nearly always sense that something serious is wrong. A characteristic symptom is persistent social isolation, that is, lack of friends, no interest in making friends, no pleasure from peer interaction, and general avoidance of contact with other children in play, sports, or other activities. In children other evidence of brain damage is much more prominent than in adult schizophrenics, for example, seizures, dyslexia, hyperactivity, retardation. Since it is difficult to determine which is the primary disorder, the American Psychiatric Association calls this psychosis *childhood-onset pervasive development disorder.*

AUTISM

One of the most tragic and, fortunately, very rare disorders of young children is autism. It afflicts approximately one child in twenty-five hundred, and affects boys four times more often than girls. Its cause is not known. Once thought to be parent-induced, autism today is widely considered an organic brain disorder and most probably is a group of diseases rather than a single one. Recent studies indicate that families with one autistic member are more likely to bear another child with the disorder.

Autism usually begins before the age of two and one-half, and its foremost symptom is an inability to relate to people and to social situations in a normal way. The autistic child acts aloof and inaccessible; he does not smile at his mother or raise his arms to be picked up. He usually does not develop normal speech, although he will cry—sometimes almost constantly—and make noises. If picked up and held, the autistic child often holds his body rigid, seemingly resisting affectionate human contact.

In addition to this aloof behavior, autistic children may show one or more of the following symptoms:

- Severe speech and language disturbance, ranging from not talking at all to bizarre speech patterns (such as echoing aloud everything he hears)
- Preoccupation with particular objects, such as playing with a single toy all day long, day after day
- Resistance to environmental change of any kind—different food, rearranged furniture, changes in schedule, and so on
- Unusual repetitive body movements, such as head-banging, rocking, hand-flapping, and the like
- Failure to react appropriately or consistently to external stimuli, for example, jumping at a soft sound and not responding at all to a loud noise, or not reacting to being burned by a match
- Acute and excessive anxiety without apparent cause
- Lack of a sense of identity, shown in self-injurious behavior (pulling out own hair, biting self, etc.), or reversing personal pronouns ("You want milk" instead of "I want milk")

Autism may be primary (occurs in the absence of other disorders), but, as pointed out above, often appears with other neurologic disorders, including epilepsy, deafness, and blindness. About half of all autistic children have some degree of mental retardation. Superficially the autistic child may resemble a severely retarded child, but in fact physical development is usually normal, and in some areas there is marked intelligence. Some autistic children who scarcely speak can read very well and can repeat complex sentences that have been read to them. On the other hand, they tend to have limited understanding of what they repeat or attach unusual meanings to the words.

The outlook for autistic children is not very hopeful. Even with devoted care, approximately 85 percent eventually end up in institutions, where they remain for life. Those who can develop speech and social relations to levels sufficient to function independently still seem very eccentric to strangers and/or very immature for their years.

Over the past few decades there has been great progress in developing a range of teaching techniques that can and do help severely disturbed children develop appropriate behavior, gain mastery over their abilities, and lead more productive lives. Also, medication sometimes can help to control some of the maladaptive behavior. Information about the facilities in your area is available from the Autism Society of America (see Appendix A).

OTHER DEVELOPMENTAL PROBLEMS

One symptom that often prompts parents to seek professional advice is a child's failure to begin speaking. This symptom, of course, can point not only to autism but to deafness, mental retardation, or some other organic problem, or it may mean nothing at all—some children simply develop certain skills far more slowly than others. Other symptoms that parents may find alarming are failure to crawl, stand, or walk, and eating and sleep disturbances.

When, then, should a parent seek advice about a child's slow development? Here are some cautionary signs:

DURING INFANCY

- Slow motor development; not crawling by seven months, not walking by sixteen months
- Failure to form social attachments—not smiling at three to four months, not acknowledging the parents as special by six months
- Slowness to understand language and to talk—not speaking a single word at twelve months, not responding to own name or to voices, not using many words by eighteen months
- Unusual sensitivities and irritability
- Problems in eating and sleeping
- Failure to show normal physical growth
- Failure to show normal feelings of pleasure and pain

DURING TODDLER YEARS

- Hyperactivity
- Unusual aggressiveness
- Failure to advance language skills

DURING PRESCHOOL AND EARLY SCHOOL YEARS

- Trouble learning, especially reading
- Unusual fears and preoccupations
- Trouble paying attention

What should parents do? The first person to turn to is the family doctor or the child's pediatrician. If the doctor seems uninterested in the problem, or if both physician and parents feel the need for further advice, a child psychiatrist or a psychologist who specializes in child development should be consulted, in order to perform a professional evaluation.

Diagnosing autism or other severely disturbed behavior or mental retardation in a young child is often complicated by the presence of specific sensory or motor defects (for example, impaired hearing may delay learning to speak), of a condition such as cerebral palsy that delays motor development, or of mental retardation, alone or in conjunction with emotional disturbance. Often the symptoms overlap and several problems exist at the same time. Brain-injured and epileptic children have psychiatric disturbances far more frequently than physically normal children, and also far more frequently than children with physical disorders not involving the central nervous system. Psychiatric disorders are especially common among youngsters with temporal lobe epilepsy. Sorting out these difficulties, both physical and psychological, requires expert help.

TOURETTE'S DISORDER

Tourette's disorder, also called *Tourette's syndrome*, named for Gilles de la Tourette, the French physician who first identified it in 1885, is a neurological disease that begins in childhood. The child develops one or more motor tics—spasmodic, uncontrollable muscular contractions—involving the head and other parts of the body, including the torso, arms, and legs. In about half of all cases vocal tics, including various sounds such as clicks, grunts, yelps, or barks, also occur. Often these vocal tics consist of uncontrollable utterances of swear words or obscenities, which have nothing to do with the current situation or the patient's feelings.

In most youngsters Tourette's begins between the ages of four and eight; it nearly always develops before the age of fourteen. Some patients also have obsessional thoughts and engage in compulsive actions. The disorder is at least three times more common in boys than in girls, and since it is more common among close relatives of persons with Tourette's, a genetic component is strongly suspected. Also, many youngsters have Tourette's along with attention-deficit hyperactivity disorder (see below) and many also have obsessive-compulsive disorder, suggesting that all three may be genetically linked.

Tourette's disorder is thought to be the result of a neurotransmitter abnormality, probably involving dopamine or norepinephrine or both. The most effective current treatment is the antipsychotic drug haloperidol (Haldol) in a low dose. Side effects seldom occur when the drug is started with a tiny dose and increased very gradually until symptoms are controlled. For youngsters who do not respond to it, another antipsychotic drug, pimozide (Orap), has been approved specifically for treating Tourette's; however, it may give rise to brain wave abnormalities, so periodic electroencephalograms (EEGs) are advised if it is used. Clonidine, which reduces norepinephrine in some parts of the brain, also may be useful in patients who cannot tolerate or do not respond to haloperidol. The most recent studies suggest that two calcium-channel blocking drugs, verapamil and nifedipine, may be effective. These drugs only control the symptoms. The disorder is lifelong, and symptoms recur when the drugs are stopped.

ATTENTION DEFICIT HYPERACTIVITY DISORDER (ADHD)

As with autism, there is an overlap of symptoms with hyperactivity, learning disabilities, and mental retardation. Frequently it is very hard to tell if a child has organic brain damage of some kind that impairs learning, or if emotional problems are responsible, or if an organic handicap has given rise to (secondary) emotional problems. Stephen, the third-grader whose behavior disrupts the class, is a typical example. Is he hyperactive? Is he retarded? Does he have emotional problems? If more than one is true, which came first?

An estimated 15 percent of all schoolchildren have learning problems caused by mental retardation, emotional problems, or brain dysfunction. Hyperactivity, the condition in which a child can't pay attention long enough to learn anything, is believed to affect as many as one out of ten youngsters. In the 1950s this condition was called "minimal brain damage" because its symptoms are so similar to those of known brain damage, even though no evidence of organic damage can be found in these children. Later came "minimum brain dysfunction" (MBD), another label now in disfavor. The current name, *attention deficit hyperactivity disorder*, refers to the disorder's basic features: inappropriate (for one's age) inattention, impulsiveness, and hyperactivity. About four out of five hyperactive youngsters are boys, and a high proportion are first-born children; the reasons for these findings are not known. Hyperactivity usually appears before the age of seven (in half of cases before age four), but may not be recognized until the child begins school.

WHO IS HYPERACTIVE?

How can you tell the difference between a normal but very lively child and a hyperactive one? In addition to their seemingly constant jumpiness, such children usually show *all* of the following symptoms:

- *Constant fidgeting*—fiddling with hands and feet, squirming in seat, unable to remain seated
- *Impatience*—can't wait turn in games, blurt out answers before question is finished, often interrupt
- *Impulsive behavior*—quick to react and act on impulse, without thought of the consequences
- *Distractibility*—short attention span, easily diverted from the task at hand, shifting from one activity to another
- *Excitability*—easily aroused

If all these symptoms are present, appeared before the age of seven, have persisted for at least six months, and appear in more than one setting (both home *and* school, or school *and* neighborhood), there is cause to suspect hyperactivity.

A variety of other symptoms—mental, physical, and emotional— also may be present. A physical examination usually shows no gross abnormalities, but an EEG may show something amiss.

To evaluate such children thoroughly, a team approach is needed, involving the family physician or pediatrician, a child psychologist, psychiatrist, social worker, speech pathologist, and others trained in special education. The symptoms must be differentiated from mental retardation (impaired intellect) by means of intelligence tests; from organic disorders such as a degenerative disease of the central nervous system; and from psychiatric disorders such as autism, obsessive-compulsive disorder, or depression. The special education

specialists then are enlisted to pinpoint the precise nature of any
existing learning disability, for example, *dyslexia* (perception problems that hamper reading and writing).

The causes of hyperactivity and learning disability are not really
known, but most authorities feel they have multiple causes that vary
from individual to individual. Among them are brain damage (occurring before, during, or after birth), a lag in the development or matura-
tion of some part of the central nervous system (since these
disabilities sometimes are outgrown), a genetic factor (in about half of
all cases other members of the family are affected by a similar problem), a biochemical cause related to the neurotransmitters or another
area of brain chemistry, some other dysfunction in the brain, nutritional deficiencies, and allergies. The symptoms tend to lessen with
age, but attention span and ability to concentrate often remain a
problem throughout life. Also, academic failures frequently produce
low self-esteem and feelings of depression, which sometimes (some
authorities say in as many as one-fourth of cases) find expression in
antisocial behavior.

Treatment for hyperactivity includes psychotherapy, special diets
that restrict artificial flavorings and preservatives, and medication. For
some reason amphetamines (Dexedrine, for one) and methylphenidate
(Ritalin), which usually act as stimulants, dampen the impulsive
behavior of hyperactive youngsters. However, they have undesirable
side effects and can cause addiction. Pemoline (Cylert) appears to be
less addictive, and some antidepressant drugs also may be effective.
Restricting sugar intake, for some time a popular treatment, has to date
not been proved effective in double-blind controlled experiments
although research in this field is continuing.

Every Child Is Different

A special word of caution is in order. To parents their own child is
always different from other children—better in some respects, worse
in others. Parents who want the best for their children—that is, practically all parents—may be inclined to worry too much over individual differences. The range of normal behavior is very wide, and so is
the range of normal development. Differences in intellect, motor coordination, temperament, sociability, and ways of learning are to be
expected. What, then, are the warning signs of a real problem?

1. The child's behavior is very different from that of his peers.
2. Compared to children of the same age, the child has trouble controlling impulsive behavior.
3. The child has trouble getting along with other children of the same age.
4. The child has trouble learning things that others of the same age can learn readily.
5. The child has recurring physical symptoms for which no organic cause can be found (headache, stomachache, etc.).
6. The child is either very withdrawn, retreating from social contact, or is very aggressive toward others.
7. The child's behavior difficulties occur not only at home or at school or in the neighborhood but in at least *two* of these places.
8. The problem behavior has lasted for some months.
9. Efforts by family members and teachers have not helped the child.

The more symptoms that apply, and the longer-lasting the problem has been, without improvement despite efforts to help, the more important it is to seek professional advice soon. For those found to have learning disabilities, the Association for Children and Adults with Learning Disabilities (see Appendix A) can, through its local chapters, provide information about various available services.

MENTAL RETARDATION

In recent years special programs and special education have advanced considerably to help those youngsters who are mentally retarded. Retardation is defined as significantly below-average intellectual functioning along with deficits in adaptive behavior, that is, low intelligence combined with impaired ability to attain the personal independence and social responsibility expected for one's age. In young children it takes the form of lags in sensory-motor development, communication skills (speech and language), self-help skills, and socialization (interaction with others).

It is important to understand that there are *degrees* of mental retardation, and that by far the majority of retarded individuals—an estimated 89 percent of retarded youngsters and adults—fall into the category called "mildly retarded." Of the rest, approximately 6 percent are moderately retarded, 3.5 percent are severely retarded, and 1.5 percent are profoundly retarded. Most mildly retarded children are able to remain at home with their families during the school years and eventually live independently as self-supporting adults. The very fact of retardation, however, subjects both these youngsters and their families to considerable emotional stress, and consequently they are advised to seek as much support as possible from special organizations and community agencies that can serve them. The Association for Retarded Citizens has numerous local offices that provide information on services and programs for mentally retarded children. Local agencies can also be located through your mental health association and through the Council for Exceptional Children (see Appendix A for addresses and phone numbers).

For more about psychotherapy for children, see the section on it in Chapter 16; for residential facilities for children, Chapter 20; for evaluation of children's programs, Chapter 22; and for the family's role, Chapter 23.

Chapter

9

WHAT'S WRONG:
A PROFESSIONAL OPINION

ONCE IT is decided that you, your relative, or your friend will seek treatment for a problem, the next step is to find out whether or not a mental health professional agrees that treatment is indeed indicated. As pointed out before, some practitioners believe that if you *think* you need therapy you undoubtedly do, but not everyone subscribes to this school of thought. Further, what you or your friend may regard as a serious, long-term problem may, in the opinion of a professional, be insufficiently serious to require any treatment or mild enough that a short-term approach seems to be the best course.

A REAL-LIFE CASE

Arlene H., 54, a legal secretary, was brought to the hospital by ambulance at 2 P.M. on a hot August day. While sitting on the steps of her office building during lunch hour, she had suddenly complained of

= 77 =

dizziness and collapsed. *She was conscious by the time she was admitted, but seemed disoriented. A careful physical examination showed nothing out of the ordinary. Asked if she was taking any medication, she said she took only strong headache remedies because she had been getting headaches for the past year. Six months earlier she had seen a neurosurgeon, who had performed nerve conduction tests and found no cause for the headaches.*

At the hospital, Arlene seemed strangely unconcerned, even though she had no recollection of how she got there. The attending physician could find no underlying illness but suspected she was suffering from depression and called in a psychiatrist for consultation.

The weekend intervened, and the psychiatrist who saw her two days later recorded the following statements she made (among others) during the interview:

1. I don't remember how I got here. I think it was yesterday. Today is August 12 (it was actually August 24). I do remember getting dizzy and falling on my way to the bathroom this morning, but that's happened before. Also, the coffee tastes different from how I make it.
2. I'm not a nervous person, but sometimes I'm a little "slow-motion." I've always been good at my work though, but not so much during the past two months.
3. My mother died four months ago. I took care of her for the past four years while she was in and out of the nursing home. I haven't been able to cry for her. But I couldn't cry when my father died, either.
4. My appetite isn't good, and I don't feel well in general, but that began before my mother died.

The psychiatrist also interviewed Arlene's husband, Herb, who said:

1. My wife's changed. She's lost her vitality and pep. She never smiles anymore, and I think she doesn't give a damn about anything.
2. She's changed at work, too, I think. She's not as friendly as she used to be, she doesn't get along so well with people, and she isn't doing her work as well.
3. She gets angry when I ask her about it. I think she's really depressed about her mother's death.

The psychiatrist agreed with the attending physician that this case was puzzling and suggested starting Arlene on an antidepressant drug and performing more tests. A spinal tap and EEG (electroencephalogram to measure brain-wave activity) showed no abnormalities. The psychiatrist returned and spoke briefly with Arlene again, and then told her physician he did not think depression was a significant problem for Arlene. He did not find her condition typical of any functional disorder he had seen. Rather, he thought there might be an organic problem and suggested a CAT (computerized axial tomography) scan.

Arlene's CAT scan was performed a couple of days later. It revealed a brain tumor, which was successfully removed that same week. Two months later she was back at work, functioning normally.

Arlene was among the fortunate. Two alert practitioners realized that there might be something seriously wrong and pursued it until they found out what it was. And she was doubly fortunate that her tumor could be removed without further damaging her brain, and that her functioning was fully restored.

Asked why he suspected organic disease, the psychiatrist later summed up his findings. There were five signs: progressive headache, falling spells, disorientation, decreased intellectual function (both reported at work and evident during the interview), and a kind of apathy or indifference that seemed to him markedly different from "sadness" or "grieving."

A MEDICAL WORKUP

Arlene's experience underlines the importance of a medical checkup to ensure that mental symptoms that cannot be logically explained are not in fact being caused by organic disease. Among other organic disorders that give rise to psychiatric symptoms are *viral encephalitis*, caused by herpes simplex, Epstein-Barr, measles, cytomegalovirus, or some other virus; temporal lobe *epilepsy*; cerebral *syphilis*; *multiple sclerosis*, which in its early stages can give rise to symptoms of depression and in later stages those of paranoid schizophrenia; *Huntington's disease*; *cerebral vascular accident* (stroke); and pernicious *anemia*. Although a medical workup is performed in practically every hospital, it may not be sufficiently thorough.

Most workups for a psychiatric admission (or for a patient suspected of psychiatric problems) begin with a history and mental status examination. Visual hallucinations, headache, and recent head injury should be specifically asked about. Another important question relates to what drugs—street drugs as well as over-the-counter and prescription drugs—are being used. Blood and urine tests should also be performed. A simple blood count can uncover anemia or lead poisoning, and blood chemical screens, which can perform several dozen tests on a single blood sample, can detect endocrine or metabolic imbalances. A thyroid function test, syphilis test, and urinalysis (to detect street drugs) also should be performed.

Electroencephalography (EEG) is usually ordered if there is a history of meningitis, encephalitis, or severe head injury, and it may detect temporal lobe epilepsy. A spinal tap (lumbar puncture), whereby cerebrospinal fluid is withdrawn by a needle from a sac in the lower back, could reveal multiple sclerosis and other neurological disorders.

Computerized axial tomography (CAT or CT) scanning, which uncovered Arlene's tumor, can also reveal Huntington's disease, subdural hematomas (blood clots pressing on the brain), viral encephalitis, and other organic disorders. Newer brain scans—PET scans (positron emission tomography), MRI (magnetic resonance imaging), and others—also are becoming more widely available, yielding more sophisticated diagnoses.

THE EVALUATION PROCESS

After a medical checkup has ruled out various physical problems, you still need a professional opinion concerning your mental problems. Formulating this opinion is called *evaluation* or *assessment*. Most mental health professionals have a set procedure for evaluating clients, which varies somewhat according to the therapist's personal beliefs and training.

Some rely on standardized tests, usually administered by psychologists who specialize in diagnostic testing. Others may rely on one or more interviews with the client, calling in other mental health professionals only if special circumstances seem to warrant it.

Anywhere from *one to three interviews* are on the average needed for an evaluation. At the end of that time the therapist should be able to explain the nature of the problem and what treatment, if any, is recommended.

Among the simplest tests employed are those to determine whether or not an individual's basic cognitive functions are within a normal range. These tests include questions concerning orientation as to place, time, and person (Where are we now? What is today's date and day of the week? What is your name? What is my name?), counting backward from 100 by 7s (100, 93, 86, etc.) or making change correctly, the interpretation of simple proverbs (What does "A stitch in time saves nine" mean?), and questions to test recent and remote memory (What did you eat today? Where were you born?). These questions usually are presented at an initial interview with a person who seems disoriented or otherwise out of touch with reality. More extensive tests are used to check for neurological impairment or other defects due to organic brain disease or injury, personality characteristics, and intelligence. The accompanying chart describes some of the most widely used tests in psychological evaluation.

Sometimes evaluation must be performed in a hospital, where a person can be observed over a period of time by a variety of experts— neurologist, psychiatrist, psychologist, nurses, social workers, speech and other special therapists—who can then combine their findings. Inpatient evaluation is used most often for those who are judged to be a danger to themselves or others (they may be committed for a given period, for observation), for individuals in whom organic brain disease is suspected and who require medical tests, and for children who need medical treatment in addition to psychotherapy or who suffer from physical handicaps such as epilepsy or cerebral palsy. Evaluation for educational aptitude and achievement potential (sometimes called a *core* or *team evaluation* because it involves parents and numerous professionals, such as social worker, teacher, educational psychologist, neurologist) is usually done on an outpatient basis. Typically such an evaluation takes a week, but depending on individual factors it may require more or less time.

A thorough evaluation takes into account not only psychological factors and somatic factors (physical disease) but also environmental factors. A young boy growing up in dire poverty may be slow to acquire speech simply because his parents do not have time or sufficient language skills to talk to him; similarly an undernourished child may do very poorly in school. A family situation where one of the

COMMONLY USED PSYCHOLOGIC TESTS

	For Ages	Assesses	Method
Intelligence Tests			
Bayley Scales of Infant Development	2 to 30 months	Cognitive function and motor development	Doing developmental tasks
Cattell Infant Intelligence Scale	3 to 30 months	Cognitive function and motor development; helps early diagnosis of brain damage; mental retardation	Doing developmental tasks
Stanford-Binet Intelligence Scale Form L-M	2 to adult (best, 3 to 8 years)	Intellectual functioning	Problem-solving
Wechsler Preschool and Primary Scale of Intelligence (WPPSI)	4½ to 6	Intellectual functioning	Problem-solving
Wechsler Intelligence Scale for Children—Revised (WISC-R)	6 to 16	Intellectual functioning	Problem-solving
Wechsler Adult Intelligence Scale—Revised (WAIS-R)	16+	Intellectual functioning	Problem-solving
Personality Tests, Projective*			
Children's Apperception Test (CAT)	3 to 10	Personality conflicts	Make up story based on pictures
Thematic Apperception Test (TAT)	14 to 40	Personality conflicts	Make up story based on pictures
Personality Tests, Nonprojective			
Rorschach Psychodiagnostic Test (Ink-blot)	3 to adult	Personality conflicts, thought processes	Interpret what one sees in a series of ink blots

Test	Age	Measures	Description
Minnesota Multiphasic Personality Inventory—Revised (MMPI-R)	16 to adult	Personality; yields scores on scales representing diagnostic categories (schizophrenia, depression, hysteria, etc.)	Decide if each of 704 statements (for adults), 654 statements (for adolescents) applies to you or not
Millon Clinical Multiaxial Inventory (MCMI)	18 and older	Emotionally disturbed persons for personality disorders and other syndromes that may need treatment	175-item true-false test
Sixteen Personality Factor Questionnaire (16 PF)	16 and older	Normal persons for job placement, vocational guidance, etc.; assesses 16 traits such as anxiety, self-sufficiency, etc.	Multiple-item pencil-paper test
Vineland Social Maturity Test	All ages	Independent social functioning	Interview with individual or guardian

Tests for Learning Disabilities and Organic Brain Damage

Test	Age	Measures	Description
Illinois Test of Psycholinguistic Ability (ITPA)	2 to 10	Auditory and visual perception	Language functioning
Frostig Development Test of Visual Perception	4 to 8	Visual perception	Paper and pencil test
Bender Visual Motor Gestalt Test	3 to adult	Perceptual and motor skills/deficits	Copying geometric figures
Benton Revised Visual Retention Test	8 to adult	Visual memory	Reproduce geometric figures from memory

* Intentionally ambiguous tasks designed to draw different responses from individuals, revealing personal thoughts and feelings.

members is seriously ill or disturbed can cause intolerable stress for some of the other members, giving rise to emotional symptoms. A careful assessment should uncover and take into account the client's life situation.

After the evaluation is completed, you can consider the recommendations made and decide whether or not to act on them. Remember that in most cases this decision is up to the client. The only exceptions are those cases where a person is committed (see Chapter 26 for more about these legal procedures) or is so ill, with thought processes and judgment so severely impaired, that a relative must make the decision.

Further, if you're not satisfied with either the evaluation or the recommendations, get a *second opinion*. It is far better to be sure of your course of action now, before you have invested time and money in a treatment that may not be the best, or even an appropriate one. As pointed out before, the symptoms of mental illness overlap, and diagnosis is more an art than a science. If you are uneasy about the results of one evaluation, consult another qualified professional.

Chapter

10

GETTING HELP—
HOW DO YOU FIND IT?

IT HAS now been decided, and you agree, that mental health care of one kind or another is needed. How can you find a competent practitioner? Even though your problems may not qualify as an emergency, you might first try the same sources that were suggested for one: your family doctor, a private mental health practitioner (psychiatrist, psychologist, social worker) of your acquaintance, or the clergy (preferably your own pastor or rabbi).

YOUR DOCTOR

The old-time family physician who treated every ailment, made house calls at all hours, and knew each family member intimately is a thing of the past, but today's general practitioners, family practitioners, pediatricians, and internists all are frequently called on to provide initial care and referral for persons in emotional distress. Some undertake long-term care as well. Nearly two-thirds of all referrals to private psychiatrists are made by family doctors. Often a mental illness first appears in the form of physical symptoms (lack of sleep, stomach upset, headache, etc.) driving an individual to seek medical advice. Or, even if the distress is obviously mental in origin, one's doctor is still looked on as a trusted adviser. Further, in routine physical examinations the doctor is often in a position to recognize early evidence of mental disorders, especially in children, but also in adults.

In an emergency, as we have said, a physician is likely to know the nearest place for you or your relative to go, and may even be able to give some immediate treatment personally (administer a sedative, for example). As for referring you to a specific therapist, the physician may or may not be a good source.

Some doctors look down on psychotherapy, either because they believe mental problems are better handled medically, or because they feel mental illness is somehow "unreal" (at least, compared to physical illness) and can be "outgrown" or "gotten over" without treatment. When they do make referrals, they often have a strong preference for psychiatrists, who have medical backgrounds like their own, even when a psychologist, social worker, or other therapist might be just as useful and more readily available (and usually less expensive, too).

Does your doctor share these prejudices? It may be hard to find out. If your doctor does seem sympathetic and knowledgeable, and you ask about a therapist, you might inquire what the results have been for patients previously referred to this person—in other words, have other patients been sent to this therapist? If so, how well have they done? Whom would the doctor use for a family member of her own? Some referrals from physicians work out very well, and the conscientious family doctor generally provides some follow-up, even if only in the form of asking "How are things going now?" during the next office visit.

ASKING OTHER PROFESSIONALS

If you happen to know someone in the mental health field, you may ask him for advice. Remember, however, that he may be just as likely as a physician to recommend someone in his own specialty (psychologists tend to refer you to a psychologist, social workers to a social worker, etc.). It is not necessarily bad but it does limit your choices. Also, the professionals you consult may not always know very much about the therapists and facilities they are recommending.

Another source of information is the clergy. A growing number are trained in pastoral counseling (see Chapter 11) and have established contacts with mental health professionals and various facilities. They tend to keep in touch with parishioners after they have been referred elsewhere, so they know something of the results of treatment they have recommended.

Industrial physicians, personnel officers, and employee assistance plan (EAP) representatives of large companies often are experienced with mental health problems and can refer employees to a therapist or clinic. For a child, contact the school counselor or student assistance plan. They, too, are likely to have feedback concerning the outcome of treatment.

COSTS OF HELP

Even at this early stage you must consider the costs of different kinds of help. Finances are a grim reality and few of us budget for a mental breakdown. What good does it do to find a marvelous alcoholism treatment center for Aunt Bertha if it costs $600 a day and she and Uncle Jack are barely making ends meet on his unemployment compensation? Some professionals go so far as to say that the first step in seeking help should be to list one's financial assets. That is something of an exaggeration, but money can't be overlooked entirely. All the money in the world won't help your autistic son if you can't find a therapist or facility agreeing to take him on as a patient. Chapter 24 further discusses payment options for and costs of treatment.

REFERRAL SERVICES

In some places, mainly in larger cities, one may find a therapist through a referral service. Usually such agencies are listed in the yellow pages under Mental Health Services.

REPRESENTATIVE COSTS OF PSYCHOTHERAPY*

Kind of Therapy	Range of Cost per Session	Average Frequency and Duration	Average Total Cost
Psychoanalysis	$60 to $150 (less with trainees)	4 times a week for 4 years	$76,800
Insight or analytic therapy	$75 to $125	1.5 times a week for 2 to 4 years	$21,600
Jungian therapy	$60 to $120 (less at training institutes)	once a week for 3 to 4 years	$15,120
Short-term problem-oriented therapy	$80 (individual)	8 to 30 sessions	$ 1,520
	$90 (couple)		($ 1,710)
Pastoral counseling	$25 to $75	Once a week for 1½ to 2 years	$ 4,200
Client-centered (Rogerian) therapy	$60 to $125	Once a week for 2 years†	$ 8,832
Gestalt therapy	$75 to $125 (less with trainee or in workshops)	Once a week for 3 to 4 years	$16,800
Bioenergetics	$60 to $100	Weekly or biweekly for 2 to 4 years	$ 9,360
Psychodrama	$50 per person	Once a week for 14 weeks	$ 700
Traditional group therapy	$35 to $50 per person (less in clinics)	Once a week for 1 year	$ 2,040
Family therapy	$60 to $100 per family (less in clinics)	Once a week for 6 to 12 months	$ 2,880
Transactional analysis (TA)	$45 per person in group ($70 for individual)	Once a week for 2 years	$ 4,320
			($ 6,720)
Cognitive therapy	$35 per person in group ($50 to $100 for individual)	Once or twice a week for 12 to 25 weeks	$ 945
			($ 2,025)
Behavior therapy	$55 to $75 (in group, $25 to $35 per person)	1.5 times a week for 4 months	$ 1,275
Biofeedback and Hypnotherapy	$150 to $200 for two initial sessions; $75 to $100 thereafter	Once a week for 12 weeks	$ 1,225

* Fees represent overall range and may be much higher or lower in different areas.
† Most often individually negotiated, based on client needs, and therefore extremely variable.

One such agency is Mental Health Connections, a computerized referral service founded by Dr. Robert Patterson, a Massachusetts psychiatrist, that tries to match clients with therapists. Clients call to describe their problem and what type of therapist (according to age, sex, kind of therapy practiced, fees, etc.) they seek. They then are matched, via the service's computer, with one of the 115 or so therapists in the area who are listed with the service. An answering service takes the initial (intake) call, which is returned by the person who handles the data base. The resulting match (of client and therapist) is then sent by modem to the answering service, which contacts the therapist.

The therapist, who may be a psychiatrist, psychologist, social worker, or psychiatric nurse (see Chapter 11 for descriptions of their qualifications), then telephones the client for an appointment and also mails a written self-description. Therapists pay a fee ($125 in 1989) to be listed for a month. If they receive no referrals during the first month, the fee is rolled over to the second month or until they are matched with a client.

The data base provides considerable information about the therapist, including the age groups treated (children, adolescents, adults, elderly) and/or specialized in, the therapy methods used, the types of problem treated, other services provided (psychological testing, consultation to schools, etc.), a description of the office (available by public transport, wheelchair accessibility, evening and weekend office hours, etc.), degrees earned and when and where, number of years of clinical experience, state license number, foreign languages spoken, availability (do they have time for a new client), insurance and health plan participation, charges for initial visit and subsequent visits, and financial adjustments they would make for those who cannot afford their fees. Clients unable to afford any of the therapists with whom they are matched are referred to a mental health clinic.

While the referral service is necessarily limited to those therapists who are willing to pay to be listed, it has the advantage of constant feedback from both therapists and clients. Most people come to it via the yellow pages or friends and acquaintances. Some are repeat customers. The problems presented are mostly of a less serious nature than schizophrenia or a full-blown psychotic episode, but include a wide range. Finally, the client may not like the therapist but then is under no obligation. (See also Chapter 12, discussing how to choose a therapist and on what you should base your choice.)

AGENCIES TO CONSULT

If you or whoever must pay the bills has limited financial means, one of the first things to investigate is the possibility of state or federal programs that can aid the individual in need of help. The best way to get this information is through a community mental health center, local mental health association, or a social agency such as a family service agency. These sources all have knowledgeable staff members.

The community mental health center may or may not be a direct-help agency for all mental health problems. When the center can't handle a problem, it can refer you to other professionals. A phone call should get you an appointment. Some community mental health centers have walk-in clinics where you can make an appointment. (See also below.)

If there is no community mental health center near you, the nearest state mental hospital may be able to tell you about various state-supported mental health programs for which you might be eligible. If you think you are entitled to federal help, the nearest Veterans Administration hospital can give you information on federal programs.

The state mental health association or a county mental health association are local divisions of the National Mental Health Association, an organization whose main jobs are information, referral, and advocacy. The branch nearest you is likely to know of clinics and services available in your area. Most cities and counties have MHA branches, listed in the phone book under Mental Health Association or under the name of your city or county, or in the yellow pages under Mental Health. Some branches publish directories of local resources; if they do not, they will know if any other social agency in your area, such as the United Way, does. They may or may not recommend individual practitioners; more often they will give you the names of several with offices near you.

When you consult an agency, such as a family service agency or MHA branch, you may need both patience and persistence. It is better to describe your problem instead of simply asking about a specific kind of help or facility. Be prepared to explain your problem fully, and let the agency decide what service(s) or facility might be appropriate. For example, if you are trying to find a place to treat alcoholic Aunt Bertha, explain that your aunt is an alcoholic of so many years' standing who has become both drunk and disoriented and who needs medical help to dry out. The agency may then suggest the available facilities. If you ask only for an alcohol detoxification center and there is none nearby, you may be told just that and will have reached a dead end.

Don't give up if the first or second (or third or fourth) agency doesn't have the information you need, or cannot offer help. Ask them whom you should call next, or, if they say they don't know, ask who they think might know.

If you live far from a big city with numerous agencies, a good start for you might be the counseling service or psychology department of a nearby college or university. They sometimes refer students who need help, and are apt to know of local resources. Other sources of referral are the psychiatric service of a local hospital, local schools of psychotherapy or social work, and friends or family members who have had good experience with one or another therapist. These are mainly sources for names of practitioners in your area, but may not tell you much else about them. Chapter 11 discusses their training requirements and qualifications.

Chapter

11

PROVIDERS OF TREATMENT: INDIVIDUAL THERAPISTS

SUPPOSE YOUR problem has been narrowed down to finding a suitable therapist. Or, if you or your child or your Uncle Jack needs to be hospitalized for a time, you will be dealing with one or more individual therapists on a one-to-one basis. Who are these people?

The principal mental health providers in a hospital or other inpatient setting are psychiatrists, neurologists, clinical psychologists, psychiatric social workers, psychiatric nurses, aides (mental health workers), case managers and outreach workers, and occupational therapists. These individuals also may (and often do) work outside a hospital setting. Outside the hospital, psychotherapy also is performed by psychoanalysts, lay analysts, and counselors of various kinds: marriage counselors, family counselors, sex therapists, divorce counselors, rehabilitation counselors, school counselors, vocational guidance counselors, pastoral counselors.

How do these professionals differ from one another? What are their qualifications? Their backgrounds and credentials may not make them the best (or even the right) therapist for you, but at least they tell you something about them.

PSYCHIATRISTS

The psychiatrist has completed four years of medical school and one year of postgraduate training (often called *internship*), and has passed a state licensing examination. Legally this is all that is needed to practice psychiatry—that is, any licensed physician may practice it. However, most psychiatrists also have spent at least three years (usually four) as a resident physician in an institution where mental illness is treated (state hospital, psychiatric service of a general hospital, private mental hospital, or mental health center). This period of residency includes work with physical therapies (see Chapters 18 and 19) and with both individual and group psychotherapy, but it does not include psychoanalysis (see below). The quality of residency programs varies; the best are those affiliated with a medical school (the remaining one-third are less rigorous). Those who want additional special training in psychotherapy usually attend a postgraduate program at a psychotherapy institute (which may or may not be a psychoanalytic institute).

After two years of additional experience following their residency, psychiatrists may take the examinations of the Board of Psychiatry and Neurology of the American Medical Association, which leads to board certification. In the United States not quite half of the more than forty-five thousand psychiatrists currently practicing are board-certified. Approximately half of those who take the board examinations fail them, but they still may (and do) practice psychiatry.

Psychiatrists can become associate members of the American Psychiatric Association (APA) after one year of practice, and full members after three years. More than thirty-six thousand American psychiatrists are members, and more than 75 percent of them are men. Membership indicates professional responsibility but does not signify competence in psychotherapy.

Because psychiatrists are also physicians, they may prescribe drugs and administer physical treatment such as electroconvulsive therapy (ECT). Such treatment by them is covered by any health insurance plan that includes mental health coverage. Of the other mental health professionals, only psychoanalysts who also are physicians may prescribe drugs. There are no other federal standards regarding who may treat what disorder or how.

The *child psychiatrist* specializes in diagnosis and treatment of children. In order to be board-certified in child psychiatry a five-year residency must be completed, including at least two years of supervised clinical experience with adults and two with children, and a special examination in this area is required.

Psychiatrists practice various kinds of psychotherapy—individual, family, group—according to their interests. Some specialize in treating children, others treat only adults, and still others treat patients of any age. Some psychiatrists take on patients with any kind of mental disorder, including psychoses, whereas others concentrate on treating less severe disorders. In a hospital (either general or mental), it is a psychiatrist who is usually in charge of directing the care of all psychiatric inpatients.

Until 1988 only psychiatrists could obtain training at the major psychoanalytic training institutes. Since then, as the result of a lawsuit brought by four psychologists, psychoanalytic training has been open to all mental health professionals.

Both the American Psychiatric Association and the American Medical Association, as well as the licensing boards of some states, require that psychiatrists keep up with new developments in their field by periodically taking courses, attending professional meetings where research results are shared, and the like. Of the mental health professionals in private practice, psychiatrists' fees tend to be higher than those of psychologists and social workers. Also, because three out of four American psychiatrists are male, if you want a woman therapist you are less likely to find one who is a psychiatrist.

NEUROLOGISTS

A neurologist is a physician who specializes in organic disorders of the brain and nervous system. Requirements are a degree in medicine, postgraduate training and experience in this field, certification as a specialist, and a state license to practice. Neurologists usually have received some training in psychiatry. Those who specialize in surgery are called *neurosurgeons* or *neural surgeons*. Consultation with and testing by a neurologist may be required for patients whose mental symptoms are suspected of being caused by an organic disease.

SUMMARY OF STANDARDS FOR
MENTAL HEALTH PROFESSIONALS
(LISTED IN DESCENDING ORDER OF IMPORTANCE)

Psychiatrist
Completed psychiatric residency, preferably in affiliation with a medical school
Member of the American Psychiatric Association
Board-certified by the American Board of Psychiatry and Neurology (in child psychiatry if the client is a child)
Graduate of psychotherapy or psychoanalytic institute

Clinical psychologist

Master's degree in clinical psychology
State certification or license*
Ph.D., Psy.D., or Ed.D. in psychology
Member of the American Psychological Association
Diploma in clinical psychology from the American Board of Professional Psychology (ABPP, CL)
Graduate of psychotherapy or psychoanalytic institute

Psychiatric social worker

Master's degree (MSW) with two years' supervised clinical experience in social work
Certification or licensing by state and/or Academy of Certified Social Workers (ACSW, BSW, CSW, LICSW, RCSW, RISW)
Graduate of psychotherapy or psychoanalytic training program
Ph.D. or DSW in social work

Psychiatric nurse

Master's degree in psychiatric nursing (MA, MS, MN, MSN)
Certification by American Nurses Association
Graduate of psychotherapy training program

Psychoanalyst

Ph.D. in psychology, M.D., or MSW
State license as psychologist or physician
Certification by an accredited psychoanalytic institute

* Licensing laws, passed by various states, require competence in a particular field and restrict practice in that field to those who are licensed. Certification requirements are set by either the state or a professional organization (or both, in which case they are not necessarily the same), and attest to an individual's demonstrated skills. Note that practice is *not* restricted only to those who are certified. Licensing and certification for all the professions but doctors and nurses are relatively new, and therefore practitioners whose practice predates the laws may be licensed under a "grandfather clause," even though they may not meet all the present requirements (an older clinical psychologist might have only a master's degree, for example).

PSYCHOLOGISTS

The *clinical psychologist* is a psychologist who specializes in the study of abnormal human behavior in a clinical setting, and may have any of several degrees: master of arts (MA), master of science (MS), doctor of philosophy in psychology (Ph.D.), doctor of psychology (Psy.D.), or doctor of education (Ed.D.). The title "psychologist" is usually governed by state law and requires a Ph.D. or other doctoral degree with at least two years of supervised experience at a psychiatric hospital or clinic and the passing of an examination. Four years of graduate school and a one-year internship lead to a Ph.D. in clinical psychology or the newer, more practice-oriented degree of Psy.D.

In many states, the state psychological association, a branch of the American Psychological Association, sets standards and tests for certification of their members as accredited psychologists. The association requires a doctoral degree to join and currently has about sixty-six thousand members; nearly half of them practice in fields related to mental health. More than one-third are women.

Psychologists are trained in graduate schools, in special clinical psychology programs, and, since 1969, in schools of professional psychology. Some clinical psychologists have a diploma from the

American Board of Examiners in Professional Psychology (ABPP, CL). At present it is the only board in the United States that tests for competence in psychotherapy, and it requires passing examinations after at least five years of postdoctoral experience. Only about 14 percent of the psychologists who provide health care in the United States are board-certified.

Since 1975 there has been a National Register of Health Service Providers in Psychology, which lists all the psychologists licensed or certified in their respective states who have a doctorate in psychology and two years' supervised experience (one of them postdoctoral) in mental health services of some kind (not necessarily psychotherapy). Psychologists who desire additional clinical training can attend a training institute in psychotherapy or psychoanalysis.

Treatment by a clinical psychologist is covered by most insurance plans that include mental health coverage. In general their fees in private practice are lower than those of psychiatrists but higher than those of social workers.

Psychologists perform all kinds of psychotherapy—individual, family, group—according to their interests. They are more likely to be interested in behavior therapy (see Chapter 16) than psychiatrists are, since behaviorism was originally entirely within their discipline, but this is not necessarily true of all psychologists. They also still do psychological testing, the clinical application with which they first became associated, as well as school counseling and vocational guidance.

SOCIAL WORKERS

A social worker has completed four years of college and two years of postgraduate study in a school of social work, leading to a master's degree of social work (MSW). A *psychiatric* or *clinical social worker* is one who has concentrated on psychiatric casework, doing field work in a mental hospital, mental health clinic, or family service agency that provides guidance, counseling, and treatment for clients with emotional problems. Psychiatric social workers usually continue to work in one of these facilities, but some go into the private practice of psychotherapy.

The psychiatric social worker in a hospital or other inpatient facility maintains contact between patients and their families, serves as part of a treatment team (along with the psychiatrist, psychologist, nurses, and aides), helps the family understand and adjust to problems created by hospitalization, and supervises the rehabilitation of the patient after discharge. In a clinic the social worker usually sees clients and their families when they first come, and helps explain the clinic's resources. Then, depending on the clinic, the social worker either acts as a liaison with the family, giving counseling and guidance while psychiatrists or other professionals treat the client, or actually administers psychotherapy.

The National Association of Social Workers has a system of voluntary accreditation whereby members who have a master's degree in social work, two years of supervised clinical experience, and pass an examination are accredited as members of the Academy of Certified Social Workers (ACSW). Note, however, that not all ACSWs practice psychotherapy. About half the states license or certify social workers (certified social workers, CSW), the requirements for which tend to be similar to those for the ACSW. The National Association of Social Workers publishes a Register of Clinical Social Workers that lists those ACSW members who have had two years' postgraduate experience in clinical social work practice. Another organization, the Society of Clinical Social Work Psychotherapists, is comprised of trained therapists as well as certified graduates of master's or doctoral programs in social work. The National Registry of Health Care Providers in Social Work lists persons with all the training needed for an ACSW but with special emphasis on psychotherapy. They do not need to pass an examination, however. Such listing is voluntary and some well-qualified social workers simply never apply for it.

Those social workers who want additional training in psychotherapy or psychoanalytic work may acquire it through a program that accepts students without doctorates (many psychotherapy and psychoanalytic institutes do not require a doctorate). With or without this additional training, social workers in private practice perform various kinds of therapy—individual, couples, family, group. Whether or not health insurance covers treatment by a social worker depends on where you live. In 1976 California became the first state making social workers doing outpatient therapy eligible for private insurance payments provided the therapy was recommended by a physician (not necessarily a psychiatrist). To date eighteen other states and the District of Columbia have followed suit and now mandate reimbursement (and only a few require a doctor's referral).

Nearly three-fourths of the 120,000 licensed social workers in the United States are women. In private practice social workers sometimes charge lower fees than either psychiatrists or psychologists.

PSYCHIATRIC NURSES

The psychiatric nurse is a registered nurse (R.N.) who may or may not have special training in working with psychiatric patients. All nursing programs give some basic theoretical and practical experience in this area, usually including several months' work in a psychiatric inpatient unit. The registered nurse has completed either three years of training at the diploma level in a hospital-affiliated nursing school or a four-year college program with a nursing major, leading to a BA, BS, or BSN, and has passed state licensing examinations to become registered. Some states issue a special license for psychiatric nursing; in those that do not, it is performed by any general nurse. However, a nurse may become certified as a mental health specialist by meeting certification requirements of the American Nurses Association (a master's degree in psychiatric nursing; two years' supervised clinical experience, at least one of them postgraduate; passing of a written examination; documentation for competence as a clinician).

Nurses involved in mental patient care in state hospitals, general hospitals with a psychiatric service, and mental health centers often are ordinary registered nurses who receive on-the-job training in mental health care. Some hospitals also employ nurses who have graduated from two-year associate degree programs (usually offered by community colleges) or even briefer (twelve- to eighteen-month) training programs that qualify graduates to be licensed as practical nurses (LPN). These less highly trained nurses usually work under close supervision from registered nurses and other professionals. Some registered nurses take one to two years' additional graduate work to earn a master's degree in psychiatric nursing (MA, MS, MN, master of nursing, or MSN, master of science in nursing). These nurses often plan, carry out, and evaluate the nursing of psychiatric inpatients and also conduct training programs on the job for other nurses. Nurses may go on to a doctoral degree, but only a small percentage do so, and of these few do clinical work in mental health.

In the hospital or inpatient clinic, psychiatric nurses are directly involved in treatment, assisting with the administration of drugs and electroconvulsive therapy (ECT). They also may take patient histories, evaluate the current mental status of a patient, and coordinate treatment teams. Nurses also are increasingly practicing psychotherapy, principally as cotherapists in group therapy, although some may work as individual therapists under a psychiatrist's direction. Outside the hospital some psychiatric nurses have established a private practice in psychotherapy (individual, family, group, etc.).

Nurses may obtain additional training in psychotherapy at psychoanalytic training institutes that accept students without a doctorate. Although there is no state certification as such, some state nursing associations grant a certificate in psychiatric nursing for those who have met certain requirements, which may be quite demanding (a master's degree including at least three semesters of supervised clinical work, two years' postgraduate supervised experience in therapy, and a term of personal therapy). In some states psychiatric nurses are licensed to become individual mental health care providers, and therapy they perform is then reimbursable by a third-party insurer. More than 90 percent of all nurses in the United States are women, so someone looking for a male psychotherapist would do well to look among the other professions.

AIDES

The psychiatric aide, formerly called *orderly* or *attendant* and now occasionally called *mental health worker* or *mental health technician*, has in recent years assumed increased responsibility for inpatient care. Aides are found only in a private or public hospital or other inpatient facility, and their training ranges from very minimal (high school education with on-the-job training only) to fairly extensive (bachelor's or master's degree and special training). The first two-year college program for mental health workers in the United States was established in 1965, and several hundred such programs now exist. At present there is no special licensing or certification for aides, and their duties vary widely. Some act strictly as nurses' aides, doing work comparable to that of aides on medical and surgical wards in general hospitals. Others undertake some individual and group therapy, usually under supervision, and activity therapy such as art therapy, dance therapy, or music therapy; those participating in the last three usually have at least a bachelor's degree with a major in the relevant field.

CASE MANAGERS AND OUTREACH WORKERS

These individuals assist severely or chronically mentally ill persons, including the homeless mentally ill, to obtain the services they need to live in the community. Most chronically mentally ill persons need medical care, social services, and assistance from a variety of agencies, including those dealing with housing, Social Security, vocational rehabilitation, and mental health. Often such services are uncoordinated, so case managers provide a critical function in monitoring a person's needs and assuring that appropriate agencies become involved. In many instances they also act as advocates for the client. Case managers can be nurses, social workers, or mental health workers, and may be associated with mental health centers, psychosocial rehabilitation programs, or other agencies. They work in a variety of settings such as mental health centers, outpatient clinics, private and group practice, general hospitals, psychiatric hospitals, and prisons.

OCCUPATIONAL THERAPISTS

The occupational therapist (OT) usually works in a psychiatric hospital, general hospital, or day hospital, conducting programs involving work, recreation, and creative activities. OTs evaluate patients with respect to their abilities and emotional and/or physical handicaps. They have completed either a four-year college program with specialization in occupational therapy, leading to a BS, or a master's degree program in occupational therapy, which involves at least six months' supervised clinical experience. After obtaining either of these degrees, they may become registered (OTR) by passing an examination given by the American Occupational Therapy Association.

PSYCHOANALYSTS

A psychoanalyst is any person who has been trained in and uses
Freudian or Jungian psychotherapy or methods derived from them.
(See Chapter 15 for a fuller explanation.) There are several kinds of
psychoanalyst, depending on the individual's background and education: the M.D. psychiatrist, the Ph.D. psychologist, the college graduate (bachelor's or master's degree) with a major in psychology or a
related field. All three continue their education with three to four
years' training in a psychoanalytic institute that has state accreditation. There they usually are taught by practicing analysts in a program
of class study (twenty-five to thirty courses in all), personal psychoanalysis, supervised practice (called a *control analysis*), and experience in a clinic or hospital. Upon completing this program, they are
given a certificate by the institute declaring them qualified for the full-
time professional practice of psychoanalysis. Until 1988 the best
institutes accepted only M.D.s, but since then they have accepted all
qualified mental health professionals with at least a master's degree.

The majority of psychoanalysts in the United States are either
psychiatrists or psychologists with a doctoral degree. Most training
institutes for analysts will not accept candidates under the age of
twenty-five, so it is hard to find a certified analyst younger than thirty.
Psychoanalytic training is long and expensive, as is psychoanalytic
treatment.

A fourth category is the so-called *lay analyst*, who may or may not
have formal training and generally has neither licensing nor certification. A lay analyst may simply be anyone who goes into practice as an
"analyst."

COUNSELORS

Just as anyone may call themselves an "analyst" or a "psychotherapist," so anyone may hang out a shingle saying "counselor." Strictly
speaking, counselors are advisers, and of course you can always take
their advice or leave it. Nevertheless, someone in emotional distress
who is looking for help is, like any physically ill person, very vulnerable and thus more likely to take advice—especially advice they seek

and are paying for—than to ignore it. Therefore, it is important that you look into the credentials of whoever is described simply as a "counselor." Those in the counseling fields recognize the importance of maintaining standards of professional conduct and competence, and they increasingly have set up regulations for themselves.

MENTAL HEALTH COUNSELORS

A clinical mental health counselor provides professional counseling services, including psychotherapy, human development, learning theory, and group dynamics, to individuals, couples, and families. Mental health counselors render their services in private or group practice, a mental health center, or some other community agency. A clinical mental health counselor has earned at least a master's degree, and several years' clinical supervision are required before she can be certified by the National Academy of Certified Clinical Mental Health Counselors.

COUPLES AND FAMILY COUNSELORS

Couples, married or not, and families may be counseled by any of the professionals described so far who do individual and group therapy, that is, psychiatrists, clinical psychologists, psychiatric social workers, and psychiatric nurses. In addition, there are therapists who specialize in working with couples and families but who do not necessarily have the same credentials or training. Their professional organization is the American Association of Marriage and Family Counselors, which requires that its members have at least a master's degree in psychology, social work, or some related field, plus a year of supervised clinical internship, followed by three years of professional practice. Today many states have licensing laws for practitioners. (See also family therapy in Chapter 17.)

SEX THERAPISTS

Since about 1960 several specialized forms of couples counseling have developed. One is *sex therapy*, short-term psychotherapy that addresses itself principally to problems of sexual dysfunction—the inability to enjoy sexual relations to the fullest—experienced by one or both members of a couple. Because its very nature makes sex therapy readily open to abuse by the unscrupulous and/or unqualified, a person or couple considering it should take care to find a reputable practitioner. The American Association of Sex Educators, Counselors, and Therapists certifies therapists who hold at least a master's degree, and can usually recommend experienced, qualified therapists in various localities. In addition, you should ask any sex therapists you consider using about their training, which should include an advanced degree in social work, psychology, or medicine. (See also the section on sex therapy in Chapter 17.)

DIVORCE COUNSELORS

An even newer specialized form of family counseling is *divorce counseling and mediation,* which concentrates on the problems of couples and families who are faced with divorce. Divorce counselors address such questions as child support, alimony, property division, child custody, visitation rights, and co-parenting. They try to help separating couples reach amicable agreement on these difficult issues and seek to reduce the often bitter conflicts associated with them. The kind of counseling and therapy provided is quite flexible, ranging from counseling of individuals, couples, and couples with children, to group therapy for separating and divorced individuals, children and adolescents whose parents are being divorced, or people who are remarrying and becoming (or have become) stepparents.

There is no licensing or certification for counselors in this field. Practitioners generally have a background in social work or family therapy of one kind or another and usually work with consultants in law and child psychiatry. When they have a direct connection with an attorney, a conflict of interest can arise.

REHABILITATION COUNSELORS

A rehabilitation counselor helps individuals who have had physical or mental illnesses return to work, or, if they must change occupations owing to disability, to be trained for and to find new work. The counselor also helps clients obtain medical and mental health services they may need, as well as education. Because their principal focus is to return a person to gainful employment, which is regarded as important for mental health as well as economic well-being, they are sometimes called *vocational rehabilitation counselors.*

Most such counselors are employed by state rehabilitation commissions, which may assign them to mental health centers or other state-funded facilities, or by hospitals and rehabilitation centers. Their training includes four years of college and a two-year specialized master's degree program that includes the study of psychology, counseling techniques, community resources, and vocational and medical rehabilitation. Some rehabilitation counselors go on to obtain a doctorate in the field; the majority of these go on to work with the mentally ill.

The National Commission on Rehabilitation Counselor Certification awards a certificate (CRC) to those counselors who have completed master's-level training and have passed an examination.

EDUCATIONAL COUNSELORS

An *educational* or *school counselor* is usually a clinical psychologist (see above) who has either a master's degree or a doctorate (Ph.D., Ed.D., Psy.D.). They generally have special training in psychologic testing as well as in counseling youngsters in a school or college setting, which is where they are most likely to be employed. Some counselors address themselves to students' personal and family problems; others confine themselves to dealing with learning problems, educational and vocational choices, and related issues. Like other clinical psychologists, they usually must be licensed or certified in their state, or certified by the state psychological association. Those who are members of the American Psychological Association may apply for a diploma in counseling (ABPP,CO), which requires that they meet rather stringent standards. Some educational counselors work partly or entirely in private practice.

In the United States the services of educational counselors in the public schools are free. Moreover, at present public schools are required by law (Public Law 94-142, passed in 1975) to ensure that every handicapped child has a free, appropriate education. Here "handicapped" refers to children who are mentally retarded, seriously emotionally disturbed, physically handicapped in any way (impaired sight, hearing, speech, movement, etc.), or learning disabled. A child whose handicaps interfere with learning is legally entitled to certain diagnostic and treatment services provided by the school. Since the passage of this law, educational counselors have become increasingly involved in helping to assess children's abilities and performance by testing, and developing an individualized educational plan (IEP) for every youngster who has been determined as having "special educational needs."

In addition, there are still counselors who specialize in advising students on educational and career choices. Often called *guidance* or *vocational counselors*, they generally work within a school system. These counselors ordinarily have a master's degree in their specialty and are trained to administer and interpret psychological tests, as well as to be familiar with the requirements of various colleges and careers. Vocational counselors rarely are certified by the state but they may apply for professional membership in the National Vocational Guidance Association, whose members are required to have basic credentials. Some are certified through their state's department of education, although this certification usually is limited to counselors who also are certified teachers and therefore excludes those who do not have teacher certification. Insofar as their work is done in public schools, it is free of charge.

PASTORAL COUNSELORS

Priests, ministers, and rabbis have traditionally advised members of their congregations. People tend to trust their pastor with personal problems of a private nature, feeling that this person knows the family and will not betray a confidence. There is no social stigma on consulting one's pastor, nor is there usually a charge for doing so (but see below). Individuals with deep-seated religious beliefs may be wary of secular therapists who might challenge their beliefs. And, of course, many individuals believe in the healing power of prayer. For all these reasons, a member of the clergy often is the first person to be consulted about a specific mental health problem.

Informally the clergy have been mental health practitioners for hundreds of years. Traditionally they are present at many of the great emotional occasions of life: birth, marriage, serious illness, death. For unhappy events it is part of the clergy's job to comfort individuals and families going through difficult times.

Today many pastors receive formal education in counseling as part of their training, and those who are particularly interested in this aspect of their ministry usually take additional training, some of it quite intensive. For example, one pastor who was interviewed had more than a year of clinical pastoral education that included a six-month period of supervised work at a large state mental hospital. Some denominations operate a centralized pastoral counseling service in places where they have enough members to warrant it. Such a center offers specific programs and services to individuals and families in the congregations it serves, including short- and long-term counseling for individuals, couples, and families; evaluation and referral for those whose needs it cannot meet; and education and consultation for pastors who wish to enhance their counseling skills.

The problems people bring to a pastor range from murder and suicide to family problems (with children, spouse, elderly parents), alcoholism, drug abuse, and all the common forms of mental illness. Of the problems brought in, the largest category is family problems. The next most important group consists of spiritual problems, relating to such matters as belief in God and life after death. An estimated 80 percent of all problems brought to the clergy are handled by the clergy alone. Of the rest, about half are referred immediately, most often to a clinic or community mental health center, and the rest are subsequently referred to other therapists.

Most pastoral counseling is short-term, consisting of one or two sessions. Many pastors feel they cannot devote too much time to a few members of the congregation. One study indicates that the clergy spend about 6 percent of their time (two to three hours a week) doing counseling. Emergencies are referred immediately to a crisis center or hospital, and serious or long-term problems are referred to a community mental health center or individual mental health practitioner. Unlike others who make such referrals, pastors frequently follow up such cases and may continue to see individuals who are receiving treatment elsewhere, although usually on an irregular basis.

However, some pastoral counselors are licensed mental health professionals (psychologists, social workers, etc.) who also have a degree in religion, and who take on more serious problems and longer-term clients and charge the normal fees for their services. The clergy predominantly see members of their own congregation, but if they have the time they are occasionally willing to see outsiders, and if able, will nearly always give help or advice in an emergency.

The American Association of Pastoral Counselors is a professional organization that has set standards for training and certification of individuals and institutions in the field of pastoral counseling. Members must meet certain requirements for education, supervised clinical experience, and assessment of qualifications and professional competence by a committee of peers. There are three levels—member, fellow, and diplomate—with increasing requirements for each category.

Members must hold a master of divinity degree from an accredited theological school, have completed one unit of clinical pastoral education, and have done at least 375 hours of counseling (125 of them under supervision); fellows must hold an advanced degree (master's or doctorate) in pastoral counseling and have done at least 1,375 hours of counseling, 250 of them under supervision; diplomates must, in addition to these requirements, demonstrate ability to teach and supervise others in pastoral counseling, having supervised at least five trainees for 30 hours each, one-third of that amount under supervision. In addition, the association has set standards for pastoral counseling centers and other facilities providing training in the field. The association currently has approximately 3,000 members, of whom 550 are counselors-in-training.

Chapter

12

HOW TO CHOOSE AN INDIVIDUAL THERAPIST

YOU NOW know the basic qualifications behind the titles and degrees, but does that tell you how to choose a therapist? Not really. Rather, these tell you the minimum requirements—that a doctor went to an accredited medical school and is board-certified, that a social worker has at least a master's degree.

HOW *NOT* TO CHOOSE A THERAPIST

Do *not* go by whether the medical school attended is a prestigious one. Fine schools graduate incompetent therapists as well as competent ones.

Do *not* go solely by degrees, memberships, and the like.

Do *not* go by your friends, relatives, or neighbors, or at least take what they say with a grain of salt. They are not necessarily competent in judging whether or not a therapist is good.

Do *not* go by your county medical society. It is not a referral agency and can tell you little or nothing other than the names of licensed physicians in your area who practice psychiatry (most will give you three names).

Do *not* go by your local hospital. Staff privileges often are given to any applicant who is a licensed physician.

Do *not* go solely by a psychiatrist or psychologist you happen to know. He is inclined to favor those practitioners who have the same background or therapeutic approach as his own, and may overlook others, equally competent, who do not.

Do *not* go by the yellow pages (classified phone directory). In a large city or metropolitan area it may list both individuals and clinics under such headings as Psychologists, Psychotherapists, and Physicians (with the subgroups Psychiatrists, Psychoanalysts, Child Psychiatrists), but anyone can buy such a listing and the degrees listed after each name can be invented. There are perhaps one million unregulated lay therapists.

HOW TO GET NAMES

For names of reputable practicing psychotherapists in your area—without regard to their orientation or skill—you can call either the nearest branch of the Mental Health Association or the local professional societies for psychiatrists, psychologists, social workers, or psychiatric nurses. If you decide you want only certain ones of these categories, call only them. Note, however, that local medical societies and professional association chapters maintain referral lists of doctors looking for additional patients, and there is no screening for quality. Even doctors under investigation for malpractice may be listed until they are actually removed from membership, which does not occur very often.

You can also consult the directories of the various professional organizations, which all have a geographical listing so you can see who lives in your area. Psychiatrists who are board-certified are listed in the *Directory of Medical Specialties*; if not board-certified, they may still be listed in the *American Psychiatric Association Directory*. Psychologists are listed in the *American Psychological Association Directory* and the *National Registry of Health Service Providers in*

Psychology. Social workers are listed in the membership directory of the National Association of Social Workers or its *Register of Clinical Social Workers.* All these directories are available in large public libraries and university libraries.

A private or public mental hospital in your area, the psychology department of a nearby medical school, or the counseling service of a college or university also may give you names. However, they are likely to have a vested interest in recommending those practitioners whose background and orientation are similar to their own.

HOW YOU *SHOULD* CHOOSE

Your family doctor or your pastor may be able to recommend someone. With both you can be frank and ask what the outcome of their previous referrals to this practitioner has been. As indicated earlier, they tend to follow up, since they usually continue to see the person as a patient or parishioner and are likely to ask how they are doing.

If you have no family doctor, ask someone in the medical profession (doctor or nurse) to whom they would send one of their *own* family members who has a similar problem. Doctors and nurses usually are familiar with the best local practitioners.

Another good source is a person in the mental health field who has contact with many other mental health professionals but has nothing to gain from recommending one person over another. An ideal choice is a psychiatric social worker in a public mental health center or family service agency. In either case, politics is unlikely to play a role.

Do take into account the recommended practitioner's local reputation. Even if you don't take your neighbors' advice as gospel, when all four of the persons you talk to say that Dr. XYZ or Ms. ABC is wonderful and has helped so many people, chances are that he or she has something going that may help you. Also, if the name of one practitioner is mentioned by numerous sources, you just might try that person.

In all these instances it helps to tell your consultant a little about the nature of the problem. She then may be able to suggest a therapist who is very experienced or skilled with that kind of a problem (for example, depression, alcoholism, or phobias).

For a serious mental illness like schizophrenia, other families with

a sick member may be a good source of information. You can find them
through a local support group such as Alliance for the Mentally Ill,
which can be located either through the local Mental Health Association or the national office (see Appendix A).

These are ways to find a competent therapist, but there are three
other important considerations: *time, money,* and *compatibility.* The
best therapists often are the ones who are most in demand. Consequently, even if you can locate a highly promising individual, she may
be fully booked for some time. Nevertheless, it may be useful to see
such a person for a preliminary evaluation (one or two sessions), in
which you can determine if this therapist is worth waiting for (if you
are able to wait); or, if she will have no open time for many months,
maybe she can recommend a less busy colleague with similar characteristics and orientation.

Money is important. There is no point in locating a therapist who
costs more than you can pay or than your insurance can cover. Many
therapists make some provision for low-income clients—a sliding fee
scale, for example—but some will not or cannot (they have to live,
too). Depending on your financial circumstances, you may have to
abandon the person of your choice and opt for a clinic or other lower-
cost solution (see below).

Finally, the best-qualified and most highly trained therapist still
may not be the person best for you. You don't have to see eye to eye on
everything with your therapist, but you should feel comfortable in his
presence, believe he is listening to what you are saying and sensitive
to your feelings, and generally find this individual to be someone you
can talk to easily and trust. Much of this rapport will be evident in the
very first interview, which provides an opportunity for you to size
each other up and for you to ask questions about the therapist's education, professional affiliations, diplomas, and experience. Don't hesitate
to ask how long he has been in practice and if, in broad outline, your
problems are similar to those of other clients. Ask if he has had
personal therapy, and for how long. Psychotherapy is a profound
experience, and for insight/analytic/psychodynamic therapy, at least,
a therapist who has been through it may be better able to empathize
with clients who are undergoing it. (For more on insight therapy, see
Chapter 15; for how to evaluate treatments, see Chapter 22.)

YOU MAY NOT HAVE A CHOICE

Depending on where you live, the question of which practitioner to choose may be academic. In 1988, for example, New York State had 28.7 practicing psychiatrists and 45.6 psychologists for every 100,000 of its residents, while Mississippi had only 3.9 psychiatrists and 9.1 psychologists for every 100,000. A majority of the counties in the United States have *no* psychiatrist. Moreover, only a few hundred physicians each year are entering this specialty. In psychology, about 1,200 students are being awarded their doctorate each year, but not all of them enter the field of clinical psychology.

On the bright side, note that numerous studies have shown that psychotherapy is effective for a wide range of conditions, and that no one school of psychotherapy is better than the others, nor does the level of the therapist's professional training affect the outcome. However, if you cannot find a satisfactory (to you) private practitioner, or if you cannot find one you can afford, you may want to turn to a clinic (see Chapter 13).

Chapter

13

PROVIDERS OF TREATMENT: OUTPATIENT CLINICS

THE SAME kinds of mental health professional who work in private practice also work in clinics, and sometimes the same individuals divide their time between private and clinic practice.

A clinic is not the same as a *group practice*. A private practitioner works alone in treating clients, and some private practitioners join together in a group practice, which is basically an administrative and financial convenience for them; it does not affect your treatment. In private or in group practice, the therapist you see is the only person responsible for your treatment.

If you use a clinic, however, it is the clinic you pay, and it is the clinic that is responsible for your treatment, not the individual therapist. In mental health, as in medicine, the name *clinic* is used for a variety of facilities. Though it is basically set up to treat outpatients, a clinic may have provisions for inpatients. A clinic may be public or private; profit or nonprofit; charge lower, the same, or higher rates than private practitioners; be part of a hospital complex, university or other educational institution, social service agency, or mental health center, or be independent; represent a group of therapists specializing in a certain approach (behavior therapy, for example) or a special problem (such as alcoholism) or kind of patient (children only), or be eclectic (use many approaches); or be itself a school or institute for training psychotherapists. Other names for a mental health or psychiatric clinic are *guidance center* and *counseling service*.

The traditional clinic (which originally began as a facility for treating disturbed children) is based on a team approach. The team consists basically of a psychiatrist, psychiatric social worker, and clinical psychologist. In such a setup the psychiatrist directs the clinic and supervises psychologists and social workers who do therapy, and also gives some treatment directly. The psychologist performs testing and conducts individual and group therapy. The social workers also perform therapy and do social casework with patients and their families. Such clinics range in size from the basic team of three to several dozen or more professionals. However, as indicated above, many clinics do not follow this pattern.

In most clinics, a person seeking treatment is assigned to a therapist, which removes the privilege (or burden) of making a choice. Also, in many clinics either the therapist will have some supervision (especially if the clinic is a training institute or the therapist is relatively new to the profession), or there will be peer review, that is, staff meetings where cases are discussed. With peer review, the client has the advantage of having several professionals consider his problems, treatment, and progress.

The most common kinds of mental health clinic are the outpatient clinic of a mental hospital or a general hospital with a psychiatric service; the VA clinic; the clinic of a prepaid health plan (health maintenance organization, or HMO); a community mental health center; a family service association; a private clinic; a training institute; and a college or university clinic.

PSYCHIATRIC (MENTAL) HOSPITAL CLINICS

Depending on its size, such a clinic generally offers a wide range of services to adults and/or children, including individual, couples, family, group, and behavior therapy, psychopharmacology (administration of psychoactive drugs), vocational services, and evaluation and treatment of children's problems (in coordination with schools and other community agencies). Usually anyone can call to make an appointment at the clinic; one need not be referred by a physician, social agency, or psychiatrist. The initial appointment is with an "intake" person, usually a social worker, who evaluates the client and assigns him to a therapist. Medicaid and private health insurance usually cover some or all of the cost for such treatment. For persons not so covered, the clinic may adjust fees on the basis of ability to pay. Although a person is generally assigned to one therapist, a treatment team will periodically review the therapy and evaluate progress. Alcohol and drug dependence may be dealt with in a special clinic expressly set up for this purpose.

GENERAL HOSPITAL CLINICS

Depending on the area served and the size of the hospital, the psychiatric clinic of a general hospital offers a variety of services similar to those of the outpatient clinic of a mental hospital. If the hospital is a teaching hospital (associated with a medical school), the clinic staff may include a larger number of psychiatric residents who work under fairly close supervision. Some hospitals offer outpatient psychiatric care principally for inpatients who have been discharged, but most that offer any outpatient care make it more widely available. Some hospitals have walk-in clinics where anyone can make an appointment. In others a physician's referral is required. Many general hospitals now have a special program for treating alcohol and drug dependence.

VETERANS ADMINISTRATION (VA) CLINICS

Veterans Administration (VA) hospitals and outpatient clinics treat veterans who have service-connected mental disorders, and sometimes veterans with problems that are not service-connected (especially if the veteran cannot afford private care or if outpatient care is thought necessary to avoid hospitalization). Occasionally these services are extended to dependents (the veteran's family), primarily when the veteran in question will benefit from their involvement. Family members may be involved in couples or family therapy, and in some instances the veteran's spouse may be seen separately by a different therapist, for a limited time.

In larger population centers, VA clinics may offer a wide range of services. One large outpatient clinic offers the following: a *walk-in clinic*, which screens without prior appointment all new referrals for service for all programs, whether routine or urgent (crisis), schedules in-depth evaluation for candidates for diagnostic evaluation and therapy for all treatment programs, and serves as a crisis intervention unit (see Chapter 20); a *mental hygiene clinic* with numerous psychotherapy programs, including individual, couples/family, and group therapy, psychopharmacology (providing medication with psychoactive drugs) combined with supportive therapy, and adjunct therapy for medical problems combined with psychiatric problems; a *day treatment center* (see under partial hospitalization in Chapter 20); a *drug dependence center* for treating cases of drug abuse; a *center for problem drinking* for treating alcoholism; and a *compensation and examination section* that performs psychiatric evaluation on applicants for disability compensation and other veterans' benefits programs.

PREPAID HEALTH PLAN (HMO) CLINICS

All prepaid health plans, in which members make fixed regular payments that entitle them to certain services, must, by law, include a number of visits per year for psychotherapy. The law states that they must include "short-term (not to exceed twenty visits) outpatient evaluative and crisis intervention mental health services," although the nature of these services is not spelled out. Like a hospital clinic, an HMO provides a variety of mental health clinicians—psychiatrists, nurses, psychologists, social workers. However, anyone wanting to use their services must be referred by their primary-care physician (family practitioner, internist, or pediatrician) within that health plan. The primary-care physician thus screens out those persons who are thought not to require specialized psychotherapy.

Once a person is referred to the mental health department of the

HMO, she usually will first see the therapist assigned for treatment. Unlike either private or public care, in the prepaid health plan the insurer and provider are one and the same. Therefore, there is a strong economic incentive to provide high-quality care quickly and to prevent incurring the cost of either long-term care or hospitalization.

Typically all kinds of problems and illness are handled by the clinic itself, which offers individual, couples, and group therapy. Once the year's quota of visits is used up, the client must pay for additional visits, but the rate tends to be lower than that charged by private practitioners.

As with physical health, prepaid mental health care emphasizes preventive care and cost-effective treatment, and because it is performed in conjunction with primary health care, it encourages treatment of the whole person rather than of a specific problem. In the interests of keeping costs down, however, some HMOs may not provide a wide enough range of services, allow too few visits per year, and may not provide care of the highest quality. Critics of HMOs contend that only relatively healthy individuals are permitted to become members in the first place, thereby restricting their use to a small percentage of the population.

COMMUNITY MENTAL HEALTH CENTERS (CMHCs)

In 1963 Congress passed the Community Mental Health Centers Act, at the time considered a revolutionary action. The law provided $150 million in federal matching grants to create *local* services for psychiatric care—that is, a group of services, not necessarily all new or under one roof—coordinated to offer continuity of care for all kinds of mental illness within one's own community (or very nearby). The entire country was to be divided into catchment areas, each with a population of fifty thousand to two hundred thousand, and each served by its own mental health center. These were intended to replace state mental hospitals in caring for the seriously mentally ill. Originally two thousand centers were planned, but currently only about seven hundred are in existence.

In 1981 a shift in federal funding affected all CMHCs, forcing them to depend on other funding sources. Federal funds now go to the states. Most centers receive funds from their respective state, and many are run by the state's mental health department, sometimes as part of a state hospital. They also receive funds from local governments, grants, foundations, and other sources. However, after the withdrawal of direct federal funding, some clinics became multiservice mental health organizations, others free-standing outpatient clinics, and still others psychiatric units in a general hospital. Among the services they provide (which vary greatly from clinic to clinic) are inpatient services, outpatient services, partial hospitalization, emergency (twenty-four-hour) services, consultation and education, services for children, services for the elderly, screening, follow-up, transitional services, alcoholism and alcohol abuse services, and drug addiction and drug abuse services.

The principal purposes of the CMHCs were to keep clients and their treatment within the community, rather than send them off to a remote hospital or other facility, and to provide adequate services for all kinds of mental illness, for clients of all ages and all stages of illness, from diagnosis through treatment and rehabilitation. These goals were very ambitious, and few of the existing clinics met all of them. Indeed, critics point out that very few served those with serious mental illness (those who were in state and county hospitals). Most concentrated on therapy and counseling for marital and family problems, stress management, and similar lesser concerns.

Supporters hold that it is not really necessary for each service to receive equal weight in every mental health center. Each center serves its own catchment area, and needs vary, depending on whether it is a crowded ghetto in a big city, a thinly populated rural area, a well-to-do suburban area, or some other well-defined population. One mental health center in a large New England city, for example, has a catchment area with an exceptionally large number of elderly persons. Its services therefore include day care for disturbed elderly clients, with door-to-door transportation provided in both directions. Another mental health center about twenty-five miles west of this city principally serves nine small towns, with a fairly large school-age population (although its official catchment area grew to about twenty-five towns). It offers more extensive children's programs (about 25 percent of its services are child-oriented), including a therapeutic preschool program, outpatient therapy for children and adolescents, services for mentally retarded youngsters (and adults), a sexual abuse treatment program, and considerable consultation to schools and other agencies serving children.

Still another community mental health center serves eight hundred to nine hundred clients a month from fifteen towns. The majority of its clients (more than 75 percent) are adults, and, unlike many community health centers, the most prevalent problems it encounters are those of the chronically mental ill (schizophrenia, manic-depressive psychosis, or major depression) and those with a dual diagnosis (of mental illness and retardation, or mental illness and substance abuse). Consequently its outpatient and aftercare (following hospitalization) services are of paramount importance. They include residential treatment for clients who cannot live alone, respite services for the families of clients who live at home, day treatment and day activity programs (see Chapter 21 for a description), and a twenty-four-hour emergency service.

Not every community mental health center operates an outpatient clinic (some that once did no longer do so, owing to budget constraints or lapse of contracts with funding agencies). In those that do, a person who calls usually is connected with a member of the *intake* staff, who gathers initial information and forms an initial diagnostic impression. The client may be asked to fill out an information form, and is given an appointment with the first available clinician. The clinician will make an evaluation and present it at a staff meeting to the intake or case review committee. At that time an appropriate therapist or therapy group is assigned, based on availability, special skills, and experience with similar cases. This process may take anywhere from a few days to six weeks or so. If the problem is urgent, however, the intake worker sets up an immediate appointment. In an emergency a referral is made to the nearest emergency facility (if the center does not have its own). In some mental health centers all clients simply come to a walk-in clinic, where an appointment is made either at once (in an emergency) or for the near future (for evaluation).

All mental health centers have some connection or arrangement with one or more nearby hospitals should hospitalization be needed. Some centers actually started out as hospitals and were converted into centers that retain their own inpatient facility. Payment for services at a mental health center may be through Medicare, Medicaid, and/or private insurance plans. For those who have no insurance of any kind, there is a sliding scale of fees, based on ability to pay. In general the highest fees run much lower than those for private care (often only half as much or even less). In the center dealing mainly with the seriously ill, described above, the *average* fee is $2 an hour, and the scale slides down to no fee.

FAMILY SERVICE AGENCIES

The largest network of private, nonprofit social work agencies devoted to family problems in the United States and Canada are the family service agencies. There are approximately 315 such agencies, of which 235 are accredited members of the Family Service Association of America. Originally they were charitable organizations helping the poor, unwed mothers, children needing foster care or adoption, the aged in need of money or medical care, and so on. After World War II this focus changed, as direct relief was taken over by welfare departments and other government agencies. Today the family service agencies focus on assisting individuals and families under stress, and improving their personal and social functioning, as well as acting as agents for social change in areas of society that affect family life. In practice the agencies' main job has become counseling, although some continue to perform such services as providing homemakers, foster care, legal aid, day care, friendly visiting to the ill and lonely, aid to travelers, and so on. Not every agency provides all these services.

Since about 1965 a growing number of family service agencies— currently forty-five—have provided mental health clinic services. Although the agency staff always has (and continues to) consist primarily of trained social workers, the mental health clinics usually employ one or more psychiatrists and a number of clinical psychologists. The modes of treatment offered are similar to those of community mental health clinics and often are covered by health insurance.

Most clients learn of their local family service agency by word of mouth. Referrals are mostly through private social agencies or the schools, legal agencies (lawyer, court, police), a public welfare agency, or a physician or health-care agency. The problems most often brought by clients are marital (including divorce and single-parent family problems), parent–child problems, family violence, child abuse, and various other interpersonal issues. Adult personality adjustment is another major area of concern. Alcohol and drug abuse also are frequently encountered, often in clients who initially come in with other problems.

Most clients are seen on a short-term basis (fewer than six interviews), and many are dealt with by telephone or correspondence, but a small core of clients tends to be long-term, coming in weekly for six months or even several years. Basically, the family service agency provides therapy for depression, anxiety, and personality disorders. Its focus is on counseling of various kinds, as well as numerous special programs for particular groups such as the elderly, in its community. Clients who may require hospitalization, medication, or other intensive care are referred to the staff psychiatrist for evaluation and treatment. Some of the agencies take on the aftercare of discharged mental patients; others do not.

Anyone who telephones for help talks directly with a social worker. An appointment is either made at once or, if no one is available to see the person, a client is referred elsewhere. Some agencies have a waiting list; others do not. Usually a client continues to work with the social worker seen at the first interview, where an assessment generally was made. A therapy agreement may be formulated at subsequent sessions.

In addition to individual, couples, and family counseling, and group therapy, family service agencies may run workshops in career planning for women, assertiveness training, stress management, parenting, and similar topics of broad interest to the communities they serve.

Family service agencies are funded primarily by the United Way and sectarian federations. Some have endowments. They also receive donations and bequests, secure grants for special programs, and receive fees from clients for services. Fees charged are always based on income and ability to pay. Although in recent years budget constraints have curtailed some of their programs, they remain, with community centers, among the last providers of long-term, low-cost mental health treatment.

PRIVATE CLINICS

As explained above, a private clinic differs from a group practice in that the client pays the clinic rather than an individual therapist, and the clinic (not the therapist) is responsible for the treatment. Other than this basic characteristic, there is enormous variation among private clinics in practically every respect: size, cost, number and kinds of therapists, orientation (one approach, two, three, or many), and so on. Here are profiles of two private clinics operating in a large metropolitan area.

1. *Family Therapy Clinic.* The focus at this clinic, which has a professional staff of four psychologists, five social workers, and one psychiatric nurse, is largely on family therapy. It also offers individual, couples, sex, and group therapy, and one of the psychologists works with biofeedback therapy. The clinic conducts a training program for eight students, who are already professional therapists but want additional special training in family therapy techniques. The clinic's director is well known in this field. There is a special family therapy room with a one-way mirror and television camera whereby students may observe ongoing family therapy sessions. The students' input is brought up at staff meetings, so that a family may benefit from the expertise of a number of therapists at each meeting (although only one conducts the actual session). The average term of treatment is six to twelve months of weekly sessions.

About two-thirds of the clinic's clients are referred by other clients. The rest are referred by doctors, lawyers, school counselors, and pastors in the community. A client who calls for an appointment is assigned to a therapist and is seen within twenty-four hours. Most often the therapist who conducts the initial interview remains the person's therapist. Every client's treatment is periodically reviewed at the weekly staff meeting; both the therapist's written records and TV tapes of family interviews are used for this purpose. There is a twenty-four-hour emergency telephone service and crisis intervention, but this clinic usually does not handle severe disorders that require hospitalization, extensive medication, and the like.

The charges for therapy are comparable to current rates for private care in the community. The therapists at this clinic receive only 45 percent of the fee; the clinic takes the remainder for overhead, administration, and profit. The clinic is licensed by the state and therefore is eligible for Blue Cross and other health insurance coverage. If therapists at the clinic wish to lower their fees to accommodate particular clients, they may do so.

2. *Proprietary Counseling Center.* This clinic is a private busi-

ness corporation that owns and operates three facilities located in different suburban towns. One of the owners, a psychiatrist, serves as overall medical director. The largest of the three facilities has a staff of twelve, including two half-time psychiatrists; the next largest has a staff of ten, including two full-time child psychiatrists and one half-time adult psychiatrist; the smallest has a staff of six. The remainder of the professional staff are clinical psychologists (all with Ph.D.s) and social workers (with master's degrees). The average term of treatment at this clinic is only six and one-half hours, although the overall range is very wide, from one hour for some clients to several years for others. Clients find out about the clinic through physicians, advertising in the yellow pages, word of mouth, and various community agencies (schools, the police, social agencies). The clinic treats all kinds of mental illness except psychotic individuals requiring hospitalization and mentally retarded people requiring long-term treatment (although it does evaluate children for mental retardation).

A client calling for an appointment talks to the receptionist, who either sets up an appointment with one of the clinicians or has a clinician return the call. The first interview usually takes place within a week to ten days of the initial call, but emergency treatment can be provided, on a daily basis if the client is in crisis.

Often the person conducting the first interview becomes the ultimate therapist. The clinic holds regular staff meetings at which all current cases are discussed. A case is always brought up after the initial interview, so that the proposed treatment plan can be reviewed, and usually at the end of treatment or after three months (whichever comes first).

All kinds of psychotherapy are offered: individual, couples, sex, and group therapy. There are two kinds of group therapy, short-term goal-oriented therapy (parenting, divorce, single-parent, etc.) and long-term therapy. About 10 percent of the clients receive psychoactive drugs as part of their treatment. Individual therapy tends to be of the psychoanalytic, insight-oriented type, whereas family therapy focuses more on interpersonal problems.

The principal emphasis at this clinic is intensive, short-term treatment to avoid hospitalization or long-term care. Consequently its clients pay far less, even though the actual hourly rates are comparable to those for private care within this community.

TRAINING INSTITUTES

A training institute is basically a profit-making corporation that employs staffs of therapists schooled in a particular kind of therapy, most often that developed by a particular therapist whose theories and techniques have become well known. In addition to providing therapy, such an institute serves to train more therapists in its particular method. The training is, in effect, an apprenticeship; it consists mainly of doing therapy under supervision. The quality of such institutes and the therapists they employ varies widely, from highly competent and reputable to downright incompetent and shoddy. Similarly, the rates vary, from relatively low as compared to private care to just as high or higher.

Training institutes vary in the kind of psychotherapy they provide. Those that give advanced training are apt to prefer clients who are willing to commit themselves to long-term therapy. Psychoanalysts, for example, spend four to ten years obtaining postgraduate training at places like the New York Psychoanalytic Institute or the William Alanson White Institute. Consequently, a trainee therapist at such an institute may be quite experienced, but a client may be expected to remain in treatment for a number of years. Other clinics, however, may provide little or no supervision for their trainees and indeed seek out therapists with little experience or inferior qualifications who are willing to work for lower fees (a saving not necessarily passed on to clients).

In some respects, therefore, the training institute is as mixed a bag as the private clinic, and it is wise to check carefully the credentials of any therapist assigned to you at such a facility. The Family Therapy Clinic described above is in part an institute, since it trains students in family therapy, but it employs many nontrainee therapists as well. Further, it does not confine itself to a single approach, treating individuals as well as families, and combining insight-oriented therapy with behavioral, client-centered, and other methods.

COLLEGE AND UNIVERSITY CLINICS

Most colleges and universities provide some mental health services. Depending on the size of the institution, the service may range from a counseling center staffed by a single part-time social worker or psychologist, with a consulting psychiatrist on call, to a full-scale clinic staffed by psychiatrists, psychologists, nurses, and social workers. In the case of the latter, found primarily at large state universities, the staff may also be affiliated with the university's medical school and teaching hospital.

Generally, the psychiatric service cooperates closely with other college counseling centers, including the health service (infirmary) and academic counseling, but the usual rules of confidentiality apply, and records are not made available from a counseling service to a psychiatric service, or vice versa, without the student's permission.

In a fully staffed college mental health service the director is usually a psychiatrist but may be a psychologist or social worker. Counseling services ordinarily are run by psychologists, and social workers may belong to either the mental health or the counseling staff. Psychiatrists often serve as consultants to counseling services.

Students usually are seen without any charge beyond the regular health fee, at least for the first few interviews. Most schools, however, must limit the psychiatric services they provide, and if students need more extensive help they may be referred to either a private therapist or a public clinic. When neither of these alternatives is available (which may be the case in a small town), the college psychiatrist and mental health staff must function as best they can with whatever help they can get from counseling services, academic advisers, and the students' family physicians.

Here is a profile of the mental health service of a small private college with 1,200 students, located about half an hour's distance (by train or car) from a large Middle Atlantic city. The staff consists of four part-time mental health professionals and a consulting psychiatrist, collectively the equivalent of one and a half full-time professionals. They consist of the director, a clinical psychologist (with Ph.D.) who does some therapy; a social worker with a master's degree (who is enrolled in a doctoral program) who sees students ten hours a week; a doctor of psychology (Psy.D.) who provides six hours a week; a fifth-year clinical psychology intern at a nearby medical school who provides fourteen hours a week; and a consulting psychiatrist who gives two hours of consultation every other week. At least one of these staff members is available to students at all times on weekdays. In addition, the college medical center provides an immediately responsive emergency on-call system with backup hospital care, consultation, and psychotherapy and counseling of the kinds most often sought by students. The health center can reach a mental health staff person by telephone or in person within a few minutes at all times.

The most frequent service sought by students at this college is individual help with personal emotional problems. Some are in crisis but most are not. The number of interviews provided varies. Sometimes one or two sessions to offer guidance and support are sufficient to get a student through a temporary crisis. More often students are seen for a short term of brief psychotherapy once a week, the average term of treatment being six sessions. Approximately 15 percent of the students make use of the service in this particular college every year, although 8 to 10 percent is the norm in most schools (regardless of size).

College and university mental health services as a rule are available only to the students enrolled at the institution (sometimes also to faculty and other staff members), a highly restricted population. Only in the case of very large clinics at state universities are they sometimes open to the public as well.

Chapter

14

SELF-HELP AND
SUPPORT GROUPS

THE REGIONAL calendar of a small-town weekly newspaper serving a dozen neighboring New England communities recently listed the following under the heading "Organizations":

Bereaved Parents Support Group, meets first and third Mondays of every month;

Northeast Singles, Inc., hosts ballroom dancing every Sunday;

Project HIRE, funded by M____ Home Care Corporation is registering persons fifty-five years and over who are seeking employment; many excellent full- and part-time openings;

Methodist Church of M____ runs drop-in center; topics include alcohol use;

Jewish Family and Children's Service is offering a four-session discussion group for engaged couples called "Surviving the Wedding";

Feingold Association of B____ alley, a support group for parents of hyperactive children, C____ chapter meets second Monday of each month;

Widowed Outreach Program is seeking volunteers for one-to-one out-
reach program, six-month commitment expected, six-hour training
program given;
Support group for cancer patients of D____ Hospital;
Single Fathers' discussion group;
Women's support groups sponsored by A____ women's cooperative;
D____ Hospital's Geriatric Team offering support group for family
members caring for a person with Alzheimer's disease, meets
Tuesdays;
Alcoholics Victorious, meets every Wednesday;
Veterans of the armed services will find help for drug dependency at
B____;
Anorexia Nervosa Aid Society offers support services for anorexics,
bulimarexics, and their families, ongoing workshops;
Children of Single Parents, Inc., meets Saturday mornings.

These were but one week's listings in an area that, as it happens, has
two community mental health centers and two general hospitals, each
with a psychiatric service, not to mention a state hospital and a large,
prestigious private mental hospital. But numerous communities that
lack more formal services, or that include individuals who cannot use
them owing to lack of funds, or individuals who oppose the established, traditional ways of dealing with mental illness, have set up
many self-help groups. Sometimes the groups are founded and run by
dedicated persons who want to help others and provide a place to go
and someone to talk to. Some of them are professionals, but frequently
they are people with relatively little formal training who simply wish
to fill a need. Most often they are people who themselves have coped
with a particular problem and feel they are uniquely qualified to help
fellow sufferers.

The self-help movement has been expanding rapidly in recent
years. There currently are perhaps half a million groups in the United
States alone. Underlying self-help and support groups is the basic
theme, "You are not alone." Self-help groups have been organized to
help people through the entire range of life crises: infertility, single
parenthood, loss of a child, widowhood, a chronic health condition,
addiction, mental illness. There also are many groups who serve those
with caregiving responsibility, such as the parents of the mentally ill
and children of the elderly.

Perhaps the best known of the self-help groups is Alcoholics Anon-

ymous (AA), which was begun in 1935 in Akron, Ohio, and became so
successful that today there are some seventy-four thousand local AA
groups worldwide, with an estimated total membership of more than
1.6 million. Two other groups formed about the same time were the
American Association of Retarded Children and the United Cerebral
Palsy Foundation, which serve not only as support organizations for
those afflicted with these disorders but also as fund-raising and
research-supporting bodies.

One of the first self-help programs for mental patients was founded
by Dr. Abraham A. Low, a Chicago psychiatrist. He believed that
mutual support was essential to his own patients and in 1937 expanded this idea into Recovery, Inc., a lay-directed self-help organization for formerly hospitalized mental patients. Currently Recovery
has more than one thousand chapters throughout the United States,
Canada, Ireland, and Puerto Rico, which welcome anyone with emotional problems, whether or not they were ever hospitalized (see
Appendix A for the address). Like Alcoholics Anonymous, it uses a
directive, inspirational method of group therapy led by members who
use Low's book, *Mental Health through Will-Training*, as a source of
guidance. Although nonsectarian, the groups have a religious tone.

HOW THEY WORK

Today self-help groups function across America, meeting the needs of
people in a variety of situations and problems involving health, mental stress, addiction, social welfare, and rehabilitation. They differ in
many respects but tend to have certain basic features in common: they
are made up of individuals who share certain symptoms or have
undergone a similar experience; they generally offer a face-to-face or
phone-to-phone fellowship network that is available without charge;
they are likely to be self-governing and self-regulating, emphasizing a
community of interests among the members rather than positions of
authority within their organization; they advocate self-reliance and
require a high sense of commitment to other members; they often have
a clear-cut code of beliefs and practices that include rules for conducting meetings, entrance requirements for members, and ways of dealing with those who "backslide"; they usually are funded by donations

from members and friends rather than requiring membership fees or relying on government support or foundation grants.

One of the great strengths of the self-help movement is that those who initially come for assistance stay on to help others. This process of helping others appears to be highly therapeutic. Although some mental health professionals believe there is potential danger in the approach, with untrained individuals taking on problems that confound the experts, many regard them as a valid extension of professional treatment that also helps provide for those who cannot or will not get assistance from more conventional health-care sources. Many physicians refer patients to one or another such group; Alcoholics Anonymous says that about 20 percent of its members are so referred. Certainly self-help groups are less expensive than conventional therapies, and they also are much more personal, informal, and peer-motivated in their approach, with members openly sharing their own experiences and disclosing their private feelings to each other.

There are self-help groups for alcoholics, their families (Al-Anon), families with brain-damaged children, child abusers and potential child abusers, children with learning disabilities, parents of Down's syndrome children, the retarded, families with children who have alcohol, drug, or other behavioral problems, compulsive gamblers (Gam-Anon), manic-depressive individuals, drug addicts and their families, people with phobias, ex-psychiatric patients, suicidal persons, compulsive eaters, compulsive self-medicators, runaway children and their families, and just about any other problem one can think of.

One that has become increasingly important in recent years is Narcotics Anonymous (NA), founded in 1953 in southern California by a group of drug addicts. Until the mid-1970s it grew slowly and gradually, but thereafter its growth exploded. Currently there are fourteen thousand registered NA groups worldwide, and an additional two thousand hospitals and institutions where meetings are held. NA does not focus on addiction to a single drug, because many of its members have used more than one. Rather, it focuses on the entire problem of addiction, which it approaches in much the same way as AA approaches alcoholism. In addition to groups for addicts, there are groups for their families (Nar-Anon and Families Anonymous). For addresses, see Appendix A.

A group founded by a former mental patient who also spent time as a street (homeless) person in New York is the National Mental Health Consumers' Association, which has grown to more than five thousand members and three hundred chapters nationwide. One of the most effective support groups for family members of the mentally ill is the National Alliance for the Mentally Ill (NAMI), which is also an important advocacy group on the local, state, and national levels. (See Appendix A for addresses.)

Although some of the self-help groups were founded by mental patients opposed to the medical establishment, many if not most mental health professionals believe that they are extremely beneficial in helping people develop more effective coping strategies for dealing with their day-to-day problems.

HOW TO FIND ONE

Is there a self-help group appropriate for you or for the person you are trying to help? If so, how can you find one? Your family doctor may know of some groups, as may your local county and state medical associations, or your county and state mental health boards. Your local mental health association may sponsor some mutual support groups. In Canada, this information is obtainable from Health and Welfare Canada. You may also be able to get up-to-date information by contacting the National Self-Help Clearinghouse (see Appendix A).

Chapter

15

GIVING HELP—PSYCHOTHERAPY 1: FREUD AND HIS DESCENDANTS

THE TREATMENT of mental illness, like that of physical illness, is directed both at relieving symptoms and at eliminating their causes. Even though mental health professionals frequently cannot identify the causes or predict accurately what treatment will work best in a case, mental illness often can be treated very effectively.

Three principal kinds of treatment are in current use: *psychotherapy*, essentially a process of talking over one's problems with one or more other persons from whom one receives comfort, support, advice, and/or instruction; *somatic therapies*, also called *organic therapies*, which are administered to a person's body in order to induce changes in feelings and behavior, and which include inducing seizures (convulsions) by means of chemicals or electricity, changing the body chemistry by means of exposure to light, diet (adding some nutrients, eliminating others), psychoactive drugs, or other chemicals, and sometimes, in extreme cases, brain surgery; and *hospitalization*, which involves a drastic change of environment and social relations.

These treatments are used alone or in conjunction with one another. Most often the mildest forms of mental illness are treated with psychotherapy alone. If the symptoms cannot be relieved satisfactorily, psychoactive drugs may be added to the treatment (or, the reverse procedure may be used, drugs being given first to relieve symptoms sufficiently so that a person is able to talk over problems with a therapist). For more severely ill persons, hospitalization may be necessary, and for certain acute or intractable disorders, physical treatment—electroconvulsive therapy (ECT) or even brain surgery—may be undertaken. This chapter and Chapters 16 and 17 describe the principal kinds of psychotherapy.

Psychotherapy in nearly all of its forms is basically an interview process. In one way or another it involves talking over your problem. For the individual with underlying medical problems or active hallucinations, severe disorientation, or other symptoms of being out of touch with reality, no form of psychotherapy *alone* will be of much use. Indeed, it may even be harmful in that it delays more effective treatment.

But the symptoms you or your relative or friend are experiencing, you are told, are often helped by psychotherapy. What kind is for you? There is a bewildering array of therapies to choose from—four hundred and fifty, according to one recent count—and each one has its advocates. Psychoanalysis tries to root out problems at their very source. Behaviorists sometimes succeed in relieving clients of symptoms in just a dozen one-hour sessions. Family therapists suggest that help is ineffective unless those closest to the client are also involved. Certainly it would help to know what kinds of therapy there are and how they differ from one another. Although psychiatry is the only medical specialty that has no genuinely accepted treatment guidelines, some 75 percent of clients do improve as a result of therapy.

FREUDIAN PSYCHOANALYSIS

The ancestor of modern psychotherapy is Freudian psychoanalysis. Although rarely used in its pure form today, some of Freud's ideas underlie many (although not all) of the therapies that are available.

Sigmund Freud (1856–1939) decided that the human mind consists of three areas: id, ego, and superego. The *id* is the area of instincts, inborn, unconscious biological forces and drives that blindly seek to be gratified. The *ego* is the area of rational thought and adaptive behavior. The *superego* is the area of checks and restraints, the voice of conscience and the source of guilt feelings, gradually acquired. Because of their very nature, the id is frequently in conflict with the ego and superego.

The most basic of human drives, said Freud, is the *sex drive*. Suppose, for example, that you, a successful middle manager on your way up to an executive position in your firm, interview a very attractive person, X, for a job opening. X is well qualified for the job and is, on your recommendation, hired. You now find yourself strongly attracted to X and have reason to believe the feeling is reciprocated. *But*, your career would suffer if you became involved with a fellow employee, especially one who is under your supervision. So says your ego, the rational part of you. Further, X is married and has three children, and you, too, are living with someone to whom you are firmly committed. An affair with X would not be fair to X's spouse or to your lover. So says your superego, your conscience. But X is very attractive and has even made some advances. How can I resist? says your id.

This conflict is, of course, on a conscious level, that is, you are fully aware of your feelings. And it will be resolved one way or another. Either you will give in to your strong impulses, with or without subsequent feelings of remorse and guilt, or you will restrain yourself, with or without subsequent regret. Such conflicts can be temporarily troublesome but they rarely cause deep psychic distress.

However, most conflicts between id and ego (and/or superego) as Freud conceived them are *unconscious*. Something is bothering you, perhaps so much that you can't function properly, but you have no idea what it is. Suppose, for example, that X originally had a choice between two jobs. Firm A offered a higher salary, a longer vacation, and better opportunities for advancement. But the person who interviewed X, and who would be his boss at Firm A, bore a striking physical resemblance to X's father. Though X is an ambitious man, he nevertheless took the job offered by Firm B, for less money and vacation but with better benefits and a more conveniently located office. In fact, those are the reasons he gave his wife for his choice, telling her this would give him more time to spend with the family. The reality was that throughout his childhood X felt he could never please his highly critical father, and unconsciously he was afraid that he would not be able to please a boss who looked just like Dad. X thus sacrificed a better opportunity on account of an unconscious, neurotic fear.

Freud believed that the sources of psychic distress inevitably lie in the past, which includes all experiences from birth on. Indeed, he shocked his colleagues by advancing the idea that the sex drive is present from birth. He went even further, saying that repressed sexual feelings, from as far back as infancy (though more often from early childhood), are the source of most adult neuroses.

Freud had a broad definition of sexuality, to be sure. He saw it as any biologically motivated form of sensual gratification, which takes different forms during the various stages of a person's life. For approximately the first two years of life, he said, an infant's principal source of "erotic" satisfaction is *oral*, the pleasure derived from sucking on breast or bottle. The second stage, during approximately the next two years, is *anal*, directed toward control of elimination (toilet training) and the sense of accomplishment it affords.

There follows, during the fifth and sixth years of life, the *phallic* phase, in which pleasure centers around the genitals. This period roughly coincides with a child's sexual interest in the parent of the opposite sex. Freud calls this stage the *Oedipal* stage, after the Greek tragic hero who unwittingly killed his father and married his mother. During this period every boy has an unconscious incestuous desire for his mother, ordinarily expressed in the wish for more physical displays of affection, cuddling, and the like. As a result the child begins to regard his father as a rival whom he wishes to displace (also unconsciously).

By this age, however, a boy has learned enough of society's rules to know that the gratification of these unconscious desires is forbidden. He therefore begins to feel guilty for having them and to fear that his father will punish him, specifically by taking away his sex organs; Freud called this fear *castration anxiety*. It must be emphasized that Freud believed these stages occur in everyone's development, not just in those who later become neurotic. Further, though some children may be quite explicit about their wishes—in one household where the father was leaving on a business trip, his six-year-old son offered to take his place in Mom's bed—they are not consciously aware of them or their meaning.

In a girl the Oedipal stage (which some authorities call the *Electra* stage, after a Greek tragic heroine who helps her brother kill their mother) takes a somewhat different form. A girl suffers from *penis envy* (rather than castration anxiety) because she lacks what Freud regarded as a highly desirable organ. She blames this condition on her mother and turns to her father for love and gratification.

In both sexes, said Freud, the Oedipal conflict is resolved normally when the child begins to identify with the parent of the same sex. In the example above, when the little boy's offer was turned down, he responded, "Well, don't worry, I'll take care of Mom while you're away." In Freudian terms, he was beginning to identify with what he saw as the father's protective role. The final stage of development, according to Freud, is the *genital* stage, which characterizes normal adults.

When the Oedipal conflict is not satisfactorily resolved, said Freud, or when development is arrested at any of the pregenital stages, neurosis results. But because these processes are unconscious—the child is not specifically aware of what is going on at the time—they are repressed (buried, forgotten). As a result, neuroses in later life are not easily or directly traceable to their early sources. It is the job of psychoanalysis to discover these sources, to dig out material that has been repressed, which, Freud believed, is chiefly sexual in nature.

There are two principal avenues for this discovery. One is the present-day workings of the unconscious mind, which are more freely expressed at night, that is, through *dreams*. Every dream, said Freud, contains symbols of those parts of the id that the ego and superego will not permit to surface. The second means is a process called *free association*, the seemingly random statements that emerge when a person says whatever comes to mind in whatever order the thoughts occur. The association of ideas one after another is not consciously controlled, and it often enables one to recall events, ideas, and feelings that have long been forgotten (or, in Freudian terms, *repressed*).

Dream interpretation and free association are the two principal tools of Freudian psychoanalysis. Moreover, the mechanics of analysis are set up so as to encourage one to bring up as much unconscious material as possible. The person being analyzed, called the *analysand*, is asked to lie down on a couch and say whatever comes to mind. The analyst usually sits behind the couch, more or less out of sight. For the person being psychoanalyzed, this position is intended to make it easier to relax and talk about anything at all—fantasies, daydreams, distant memories, night dreams, as well as day-to-day happenings and rational ideas.

The analyst says little and plays a largely passive role, in order to encourage *transference*, that is, the analysand begins to direct toward the analyst both positive and negative feelings that originally were directed toward someone else. For example, if a girl regarded her mother as a harsh, punishing person, as a grown woman she might transfer this feeling and react as though her analyst were harsh and punishing. Further, if she knows few actual details about the analyst, it is easier for her to transfer such feelings and so bring them into the open. For this reason the analyst usually says very little.

Even though analysands understand the ground rule of saying whatever comes to mind, they cannot always do so. Some thoughts may seem too embarrassing, some memories too painful, or sometimes one simply draws a blank. The Freudian term for such blocking is *resistance*. In such instances the analyst usually does intervene and tries to help discover the reason for a particular blocking. Also, periodically the analyst points out connections between seemingly different events, feelings, reactions, or other occurrences in the analysand's life that are not recognized. Except for these interpretations, and dream interpretation, the analyst does little of the talking and takes care to remain noncommittal. Since so much depends on the analysand's talking, it is clear that successful psychoanalysis calls for a relatively intelligent, articulate person.

Classical psychoanalysis as just described is expensive and time-consuming. It ordinarily requires four to five visits to the analyst per week, each visit lasting about fifty minutes. The total period of time ranges from three to six years or longer. At the rate of $100 (or more) per visit charged by analysts in private practice, the total cost would come to at least $18,000 per year. Since health insurance rarely covers more than a fraction of this cost, few individuals can afford psychoanalysis.

Psychoanalysis is also hard work, for both analysand and analyst. Its ultimate goal is not just the relief of painful symptoms but a major change in personality so as to lead to better overall adaptation. To be genuine and permanent, such a change can be achieved only after one has surmounted emotional obstacles and acquired *insight* into one's behavior and feelings. It is not enough for the analyst to point out otherwise unrecognized relationships between experiences, memories, behavior, or emotional responses. Nor is the analysand's intellectual understanding of such relationships enough. An insight must be accepted on a detailed emotional level; only then will it begin to change feelings and behavior.

For example, Nancy J., 45, finds that she is always very upset—sometimes to the point of hysterics—when she has to pack for a trip. During analysis she remembers that the feelings evoked by packing resemble her anxiety at the age of five, when her soldier-father left for wartime duty overseas and she helped her mother pack the family's belongings to move to another city. Her mother, preoccupied with her own worries about her husband, was not, at the time, sensitive to her daughter's fears and did little to reassure her. This insight, although perfectly valid, does not change Nancy's anxiety about packing. Only many weeks later, after she has relived the experience a number of times, with a revival and neutralization of the old feelings surrounding the original incident, can she begin to cope better with her distress over departures and separations. This process of incorporating an insight is called *working through,* and it is slow and usually painful. (Freud called it bringing unconscious, id material under conscious, ego control.)

ANALYTIC/INSIGHT/PSYCHODYNAMIC PSYCHOTHERAPY

Partly because of the high cost, partly because the long and arduous training required for analysts greatly limits the number available, and partly because few therapists today agree with Freud in all details of his theory and method, many other kinds of treatment have been developed. In general, those therapies based on the idea that emotional problems have their origin in unresolved psychological conflicts of the past, and that symptoms are best relieved through working out these conflicts and acquiring insight, are called *analytic* psychotherapy, *insight* therapy, or *psychodynamic* therapy.

These therapies differ from classic Freudian therapy in a number of ways. They do not necessarily regard the prime cause of distress as a sexual problem that was not resolved in early childhood, nor do they consider the sex drive the single most important instinct. They try to facilitate the working-through process with more active participation by the therapist. Rather than delving into the distant past for every detail that can be recalled and relived, they set as their chief goal the relief of those symptoms that strongly interfere with present-day normal life processes; thus, they try to help clients learn how to handle their distressing situations, without necessarily removing their underlying cause. Although in general these therapies are more superficial than classical psychoanalysis, they often are very helpful, especially to individuals suffering from neuroses or from disturbances triggered by environmental changes.

The schedule of visits is less intensive and shorter than in classic analysis, and the couch is seldom used. Normally the client sits facing the therapist (often across a desk), although if this posture proves too threatening the chairs may be turned at an angle. Free association is used; dreams also are interpreted, although less than in classic analysis. In general the therapist is more active, both in directing the choice of subject matter and in deciding how long a subject should be pursued. Some therapists even offer advice or make specific suggestions on how to handle ongoing situations that are difficult for the client.

Although the psychotherapist is less careful about remaining noncommittal, transference still takes place. Indeed, some authorities feel that such therapy works mainly when client and therapist like and respect each other, and that the precise details of what goes on during therapy sessions have less importance than a positive relationship.

Whereas drugs such as tranquilizers and antidepressants are little used in classic analysis lest they hamper free association and block dreams, they often are used in conjunction with insight therapy to relieve anxiety and depression. Also, whereas classic analysis is provided only by a highly trained psychoanalyst (see Chapter 11), analytic psychotherapy may be conducted by a psychiatrist, psychologist, social worker, or other professional, and it is widely available in community mental health centers and clinics as well as in the traditional private office.

Because of its focus on specific problems, insight therapy does not take nearly as long and therefore is less expensive than classic analysis. One or two visits per week for a period of two or more years is typical. And finally, although like classic analysis it is rarely used alone for severe mental illnesses, such as schizophrenia or manic-depressive illness, insight therapy often is used in combination with other treatments (drugs, electroconvulsive therapy, a hospital setting) for patients recovering from an acute psychotic or depressive episode.

SHORT-TERM "FREUDIAN" THERAPY

Several offshoots of Freudian analysis have become increasingly widespread. Objecting to the exceedingly long-term therapy called for by classic analysis, although not disagreeing with any of its basic tenets, Franz Alexander and his associates at the Chicago Institute of Psychoanalysis developed a short-term therapy called *intensive short-term analytic therapy* (or *Chicago School therapy*). Unlike classic analysis, the therapist takes a strongly directive role in the client's free association, attempting to lead to those past experiences that appear to be directly connected to the present-day troublesome symptoms. By reviving these painful memories, the client is relieved of the emotional pain associated with them, a process called *catharsis-abreaction*. This process replaces the more tedious, drawn-out working through of insights and focuses on material affecting the specific neurotic symptoms, which are thereby relieved. Therapy involves considerable flexibility. Whereas clients who are intensely anxious may be seen daily, other, less anxious persons may do well on a weekly basis. The couch may be used for some and not for others. In general, the therapy is tailored to meet what the therapist sees as individual needs.

Another confrontational version of insight therapy is *short-term dynamic therapy*, developed by Habib Davanloo of Montreal. This therapy depends on unlocking the unconscious with high-level confrontation. In doing so, therapists are better able to reach the root of whatever is actually causing a client's depression, anxiety, phobia, or other disorder. The therapist is necessarily very active, incessantly probing and challenging the client, and pointing out problem behavior rather than waiting for the client to identify it. In back-to-back sessions that sometimes last as long as five hours (especially for the first evaluation session), the therapist presses the client to look deeper and deeper into the source of his feelings, until the client and therapist arrive at a so-called breakthrough—the point at which sadness, anger, fear, or resentment, long suppressed, can pour out. Short-term dynamic therapy is conducted in eight to thirty sessions and is said to work best for individuals who have identified a particular problem.

Although based on Freudian psychoanalysis, short-term dynamic therapy rejects free association. Rather, the therapist directs the course of conversation and badgers the client into bringing up painful experiences. There is no transference, either. A video camera is used to tape sessions, allowing the client and therapist to review the course of treatment.

Critics point out that these techniques can raise a client's anxiety to intolerable levels, and further, that a few dozen sessions of such therapy are insufficient to change maladaptive behavior patterns of many years' standing. However, for individuals to be accepted for this form of treatment, they must show, in two evaluation sessions with two different therapists, that they can tolerate the anxiety generated by this technique; those who cannot are referred to other therapies.

Proponents, on the other hand, claim that approximately 70 percent of clients treated do benefit significantly. Six months after treatment ends, clients are invited back for the first of several follow-up meetings in which they view randomly selected segments of their sessions on tape and discuss the treatment, its effect on their lives, and their current feelings. Certainly one benefit of this approach is the short time it takes, and consequently the much lower cost than psychoanalysis. (See also short-term anxiety-provoking therapy, described in Chapter 16 under Short-term problem-oriented therapies.)

FREUDIAN OFFSHOOTS

Two of Freud's most brilliant associates in Vienna during the early 1900s were Alfred Adler and Carl Jung. Each went on to develop his own theories and methods of psychotherapy, which to some extent are still practiced today.

Alfred Adler (1870–1937) developed the theory that people are directed less by the sex drive than by feelings of inferiority, which drive them to compensate by striving for superiority and power. When such striving is blocked, neurosis results. Later Adler expanded this view, saying that tensions generated in parent–child and sibling relationships can also give rise to neurosis. *Adlerian therapy*, which can be conducted by a psychiatrist, psychologist, or other professional, calls for twice-a-week sessions for a period of several years. The Adlerian therapist takes a more active, directive role than the Freudian analyst, helping the client uncover the original experiences that led to feelings of inferiority and fostering the development of greater self-assurance.

Carl Gustav Jung (1875–1961) also thought that repressed sexual urges alone could not account for neurosis. Rather, he believed that the individual unconscious is a combination of unique personal elements and common racial (cultural) elements. Each individual inherits patterns of conflict common to the race. In order to understand a neurosis, therefore, one must go back not only to one's own infancy but to the infancy of one's race. *Jungian analysis* involves much less free association and a great deal of dream interpretation, since Jung believed that dreams reveal much of the "racial" or "collective" unconscious. The Jungian therapist plays a more active role than the Freudian analyst, and the couch is not used much. Jungian therapy also is shorter, usually consisting of one session per week for three of four years.

Two others in Freud's circle who broke with him and founded their own schools of therapy were Otto Rank and Wilhelm Reich. Rank (1884–1939), whose method is called *will therapy*, said that a patient's quest for treatment expresses his instinctive will to live. He believed that the true source of neurosis is the birth trauma, the shock all human beings experience when they are thrust from the womb. In therapy, the Rankian analyst, who takes a quite active role, leads the client to reexperience the trauma of birth. This time, however, this shocking experience is cushioned by the therapist's love and support for the client. The ultimate goal is to strengthen the client's will and independence. Rank was one of the first to suggest that short-term intensive therapy is effective, and Rankian therapy lasts no more than a few months. However, it has fewer followers than other analytic therapies.

Wilhelm Reich (1877–1957), on the other hand, took Freud's emphasis on the sex drive one step further, saying that this all-important drive, rather than being channeled in other directions, needs to be liberated. In Reich's view an all-powerful *orgone energy* (also called the *Radix*), flows through the body, gradually building up a charge akin to an electrical charge. Therefore, it must periodically be discharged. If sexual feeling is suppressed, there is no healthy discharge of energy, and neurosis results. One major symptom of such suppression is chronic muscular tension. It is the job of therapy to relieve such tension, through special breathing exercises and massage, in order to free the body (and hence the mind) of crippling inhibitions. *Reichian therapy*, also called *vegetotherapy* and *orgone therapy*, was one of the first kinds of body therapy. However, it, like other body therapies (described in Chapter 16), is considered by many to be of dubious validity.

INTERPERSONAL THEORIES

Two other schools of insight therapy differ from both Freudian analysis and the therapies just described in that they place less emphasis on the inner workings of the mind and unconscious drives and more on people's relations with one another. How one gets along with others is, for one thing, far more readily observable than unconscious urges are.

Karen Horney (1885–1952), who was trained as a Freudian analyst in Berlin and came to the United States in 1932, first taught at two Freudian institutes and then, in 1941, set up her own clinic in New York. Freud's views on women in particular led her to formulate her own theories. Horney could not go along with the idea that women's lack of male genital organs accounted for all of their emotional problems. It is not instinctual sex drives repressed in childhood that cause neurosis, concluded Horney, but the insecurity children feel when the family does not make them feel strong and confident. The basic human drive is the search for security. When it is threatened, a person experiences anxiety. Anxiety leads one to move in one of three ways: toward people (socialization, dependence); away from people (detachment, independence); and against people (hostility, aggression). It is the goal of therapy to produce a healthy balance among all three.

Horneyan (or *Hornevian*) *therapy* involves three sessions per week over a period of several years. Both free association and dream interpretation are used, but the Horneyan therapist takes a stronger, more directive role than the Freudian analyst.

Horney's friend and colleague, Harry Stack Sullivan (1892–1949), also considered interpersonal relations more important than inborn instincts. Sullivan maintained that people seek both physical satisfactions and security, which he defined as a sense of feeling accepted. Your concept of yourself, he said, comes from how you think others react to you. When your perception of these reactions is faulty—for example, when you think everyone in a group hates you—neurosis results. The goal of therapy is to help you see such distortions.

Like Freud, Sullivan traced human development through a series of stages, but rather than defining them in terms of the sex drive (oral, anal, etc.) he defined them in terms of the principal personal relationships at each stage. Thus, in infancy, relations with the mother or mother-substitute are of prime importance. A constantly angry or anxious mother can communicate anger or anxiety to her child, who will then bring this reservoir of unhappiness to later relationships.

Sullivanian therapy, also called *interpersonal psychotherapy,* is centered in the Washington (DC) School of Psychiatry and the William Alanson White Institute in New York City. Its techniques are similar to Freudian analysis except that the search is focused on childhood experiences. Also, it is important that therapist and client form an intense relationship, with the therapist playing a very active role. The therapist listens to the client's problem and asks a great many questions about the client's past. During this process an intense relationship is established through which the therapist becomes the object of the client's interpersonal relations (and distortions). Then, by explaining how these distortions operate and teaching the client to replace them with healthy reactions, the therapist can relieve the client's neurotic symptoms. (See also short-term interpersonal therapy, described in Chapter 16 under short-term problem-oriented therapies, for a newer therapy based on Sullivan's ideas.)

Sullivan himself was one of the few psychotherapists who had some success in treating schizophrenia, but his descriptions of such cases indicate that his success may have been as much a result of his own clinical and interpersonal skills as of his particular methods.

Erich Fromm (1900–1980), schooled in Germany in the analytic technique of Freud, was another founder of the William Alanson White Institute and practiced psychoanalysis. He became very influential through his writings, which dealt with subjects ranging from the alienation of the individual to the sanity of society. In clinical practice he modified Freudian technique considerably, directly confronting clients with their problems, dynamically engaging them with relevant insights, and working actively toward understanding.

Chapter

16

GIVING HELP—PSYCHOTHERAPY 2: NEWER INDIVIDUAL THERAPIES

BECAUSE OF Freud's basic premise that the key to neurosis lies in the sufferer's past, the therapies based on his theory tend to be past-oriented. Clients try to understand their present behavior and feelings in the light of past experience. However, several kinds of therapy concentrate instead on the present-day symptoms, problems, feelings, and behavior of the client.

Although these therapies differ from one another in many ways, they all are inclined to be more practically oriented. Whereas insight psychotherapy considers self-understanding the ultimate goal, from which growth, self-control, and self-esteem will come, these newer therapies tend to be more directly supportive, and the therapist plays a more active role in helping the client deal with emotional distress and problematic life situations. Indeed, in some the therapist is quite active, giving advice, speaking openly, and making no attempt to hide or neutralize her own personality.

FOCUS ON THE HERE AND NOW

Among the most radically different from Freudian therapy in this respect is William Glasser's *reality therapy*. Glasser saw the individual ego as the mediator between a person and the world around her, its general functions being to protect the individual and fill her needs. The basic cause of emotional disturbances is impaired ego function, so it becomes the therapist's job to restore adequate ego function. The reality therapist deliberately seeks to become involved with the client and to win respect as a reliable authority. Once the client does respect the therapist, the latter proceeds to convince the client that moral and responsible behavior are more desirable than neurotic patterns. In effect, the therapist tells the client to shape up and get well.

Cynics point out that Glasser's approach makes the therapist simply a purveyor of conventional values and conformity. In practice, however, this approach has proved successful with some adolescent delinquents, as well as with persons suffering from a single definable symptom, such as a nervous tic, or a bad habit, such as smoking. The underlying causes of neurotic behavior are not even considered relevant by the reality therapist; only the behavior itself is treated, primarily through a positive therapeutic relationship. (See also behavior therapies, below.)

CLIENT-CENTERED THERAPY

Another here-and-now approach is Carl Rogers' *nondirective* or *client-centered therapy*, which is based on the idea that every individual has his own way of seeing both self and world. The basic drive of all human beings is self-actualization, that is, realizing their potential for growth and development. To promote this, Rogerian therapy concentrates on building the client's sense of self-worth. The therapist is permissive and nondirective, allowing the client to say anything at all, no matter how unimportant or childish it may seem, and expressing empathy for whatever feelings are revealed. In this way the client is free to explore his feelings, acquire deeper understanding, and reorganize his view of things in general.

The nondirective therapist makes no interpretations and offers no suggestions. For example, suppose Mary complains that her husband was late to dinner twice during the previous week without apology or explanation. The therapist might say, "You feel you deserve more consideration," or "You feel your efforts are not appreciated." Mary presumably then feels free to talk more openly about her marriage and her feelings about related issues.

The nondirective therapist may point out things that the client is not aware of, such as, "You always smile when you are telling me how angry you are," or "You generally face me when you talk, but whenever you mention your father you turn away from me." But the therapist does not give specific advice, praise or blame any action or idea, or suggest areas that should be further explored. All responsibility for the course of the therapy is left to the client. The therapist does not, on the other hand, remain silent or conceal details about her own life; in fact, such details may deliberately be revealed if it is thought they will encourage the client to talk more freely.

Rogerian therapy is usually conducted by clinical psychologists rather than psychiatrists, in clinics and mental health centers (as well as in private practice). Some of its techniques have been adopted by therapists specializing in other kinds of therapy, as well as by teachers, the clergy, guidance counselors, and administrators in many lines of endeavor.

EXISTENTIAL THERAPY

Existential therapy also aims at a kind of self-realization. Based on existential philosophy and developed mainly by Rollo May in the United States and Ludwig Binswanger and Medard Boss in Switzerland (where it is called *Daseinanalysis,* from the German words *Da sein,* meaning "being there"), it holds that awareness of being is the essence of existence, and that the individual exists principally in relation to other people and things. The goal of existential therapy, which uses a variety of techniques—talk, free association, dream interpretation—is to help the client understand his potential. This process requires a great deal of empathy on the therapist's part. Indeed, the therapist is so deeply involved that she also expects to be changed by the relationship. Again, the emphasis is on the here-and-now rather than on some past source of problems.

GESTALT THERAPY

Gestalt therapy, developed by Frederick (Fritz) S. Perls (1894–1970) and others, also is directed toward immediate experience rather than the past. The source of neurosis is thought to be faulty perception, a kind of fragmentation of reality in which a person sees neither himself nor the world accurately. In contrast, the healthy individual is a well-integrated whole (in German, *Gestalt*), fully aware of both self and environment. The goal of therapy, therefore, is to help restore whatever parts are missing until the client is fully aware of his own feelings and interactions with others.

Though it cannot be directly inferred from the theory behind it, the process of Gestalt therapy is different from the therapies described so far. The client is encouraged to talk, but only about current feelings and situations. He is also encouraged to use nonverbal communication—to act out some of the situations and feelings in dramatic fashion. Gestalt therapy often is conducted in group settings; sometimes five or six clients get together with a therapist for an entire weekend of activity.

The Gestalt therapist plays a very active role, prodding the client to express feelings, ideas, bodily sensations, perceptions of the immediate environment (treatment room), and the like. The client may be asked to dramatize a particular situation. For example, suppose Martha is very frightened of the therapist, who now asks her to act out her fear. She sits first in one chair and, as Martha, says, "You make me very nervous. I'm afraid that you won't like me when you find out what kind of person I really am." She then moves to another chair and speaks for the therapist: "I am here to help you. You must tell me what you are feeling at this very moment." If Martha is angry at being made to feel afraid, the therapist may ask her to express her anger, by shouting, or by hitting the chair that is made to represent the therapist, or some similar means. Since Gestalt therapy involves vigorous interaction of therapist and client, it often becomes highly emotionally charged, and therefore it is not considered suitable for a severely disturbed person who could not tolerate such intensity.

BEHAVIOR THERAPIES

A number of therapies—both individual and group—have been developed to treat mental illness by, in effect, correcting maladaptive
behavior. They differ from analytic (insight) and client-centered therapies in that they generally are less concerned with increasing clients'
self-knowledge and self-awareness than with changing their behavior
as a means of preventing or treating their illness. Behavior therapists
use procedures that bring about learning, their implicit assumption
being that one can *learn* to replace maladaptive behavior with new,
adaptive behavior. (They do not, however, attempt to treat severe
psychoses such as schizophrenia or manic-depressive disorder in this
way alone, although they may use some procedures in conjunction
with other treatment.) Behavior therapists sometimes treat the body as
well as the mind, as in teaching clients relaxation techniques, but
their methods, unlike those of some body therapies (see below), are
endorsed by the American Psychological Association and other reputable professional groups.

The origins of behavior therapy, also called *behavioral therapy* or
behavior modification, lie in the learning experiments of Ivan Pavlov,
B. F. Skinner, and others, and their extension into the clinical area by
Joseph Wolpe and other practitioners. Pavlov, a nineteenth-century
Russian physiologist, found he could teach dogs to salivate in response to a bell rather than the actual presence or smell of food, thus
establishing what came to be called a *conditioned reflex*. Skinner, a
twentieth-century American psychologist, found he could change the
behavior of rats by reinforcing desired behavior with a reward and
negatively reinforcing (deterring) undesired behavior by either withholding food or by giving an electric shock, a method that came to be
called *operant conditioning*. Versions of both methods are used by
present-day behavior therapists.

Just as Pavlov taught animals to respond automatically to a different
stimulus (a bell instead of food), so can a therapist teach a client to
establish a desired reaction to replace an unwanted behavior. Suppose, for example, that Wanda, the young woman who suffers from
agoraphobia and experiences anxiety attacks almost anywhere outside her own house, decides to see a behavior therapist. The first step
in treatment probably will be teaching Wanda to put herself into a

state of deep muscle relaxation whenever she feels the slightest anxiety. Two or three sessions may be devoted to teaching her how to induce relaxation throughout her whole body, muscle group by muscle group, until she can do so at will, both in the therapist's office and at home.

Other methods of inducing deep relaxation are transcendental meditation (see below) and *autogenic training*, that is, using passive concentration to create an inner sense of warmth, heaviness, and tranquility, also learned progressively like deep muscle relaxation. Some therapists teach their clients to control the physical manifestations of anxiety—pounding heart, sweaty palms, and so on—by means of *biofeedback,* a method of exercising control over normally involuntary physical functions by means of feedback (information) concerning those functions. With biofeedback, clients can be taught to control their heart rate, blood pressure, peripheral body temperature, and salivation.

SYSTEMATIC DESENSITIZATION

While Wanda is being taught relaxation, she and the therapist also construct a series of anxiety-arousing situations, each of which is more frightening (to her) than the next. The therapist then will ask Wanda to relax completely and to imagine the first situation, which produces the mildest level of anxiety. If she can pretend to experience this situation without panicking, or is able to eliminate her anxiety by relaxing, the therapist proceeds to the next situation, and so on, up to the most anxiety-provoking one (in Wanda's case, perhaps, returning to the supermarket where her first attack of panic took place). If Wanda experiences anxiety at any point, the therapist stops and backtracks to a less threatening situation.

In addition to deep relaxation, a client may be taught to imagine a very pleasurable experience—for Wanda, perhaps a family party staged by her children. Whenever she feels anxiety, then, she not only induces deep relaxation but also pictures herself in this very happy situation, thus replacing her anxious feelings with pleasurable ones. In cases where the client fears specific objects, such as dogs or snakes, *modeling* might be used. Rather than imagining contact with the feared object, the client observes a fearless person (either the therapist or someone else) coming closer and closer to the feared object, and gradually is encouraged, under the model's guidance, to do the same.

This entire process is called *systematic desensitization*. It continues until the client can experience in her mind the entire spectrum of frightening situations without experiencing anxiety. Next, Wanda will be asked to do the same outside the therapist's office, gradually exposing herself to each slightly more frightening experience, but retreating at once and practicing deep relaxation at the first sign of anxiety.

A rather different technique is *intense exposure therapy*, also called *flooding* or *implosion*. Here, instead of gradually exposing Wanda to ever more frightening situations, the therapist tells her to imagine the very worst possible experience, for example, being lost in a large crowd in a strange city. Films and tapes depicting such situations are shown to her to make her feel even more anxious. Such "overloading" is intended to collapse her phobic reaction entirely. It is not understood how this technique works to eliminate phobias, but it can be very effective.

ASSERTIVENESS TRAINING

Assertiveness training is a form of conditioning that has been effective particularly for individuals suffering from extreme anxiety in social situations. It uses role-playing or behavior rehearsal to teach a person to express his views and wishes more effectively in various situations. An assertive person acts as if he believes in his own self-worth and is not threatened by criticism or disagreement. Assertiveness training does not attempt to go into the causes of low self-esteem but simply teaches a client to respond assertively more often.

Although assertiveness training can be performed on an individual basis, it is frequently carried on in a group format, with members of the group practicing assertive behavior with one another. This form of conditioning has been extended beyond clinical uses to, for example, individuals who simply wish to improve their negotiating ability in a business setting but are not eager to change their behavior in other respects.

AVERSIVE CONDITIONING

Aversive conditioning involves the repeated use of an unpleasant or painful stimulus, such as administering an electric shock to a client, or withdrawing positive reinforcers, such as words of praise or candy, whenever undesired behavior occurs. For example, a man with strong sexual feelings for preadolescent girls might be shown pictures and films of such children in various stages of undress. Whenever he exhibits signs of sexual arousal, he is given a shock. In time, it is hoped, he will come to imagine the pain of the shock whenever he is inappropriately aroused and therefore will curb the feeling and any temptation to act on it. Today aversive conditioning is most often used in conjunction with techniques that establish and reinforce desired behavior, described as operant conditioning.

OPERANT CONDITIONING

Operant conditioning is based on the idea that behavior is influenced by its consequences, a notion subscribed to by any parent who has ever rewarded a child's good behavior with a hug or a treat. The behavior therapist calls it *positive reinforcement*. When the desired behavior is complicated or the client seems unable to produce it, *modeling* may be used as a teaching tool.

More elaborate forms of operant conditioning have been devised in mental hospitals and other institutions where, it has been found, even extremely disturbed or profoundly retarded individuals may respond to a system of rewards. Some hospitals use a program called a *token economy*, in which patients are "paid" for good behavior with such privileges as watching television, receiving special food, or gum, or extra time outside. In a school—residential or otherwise—good academic work or effort may be rewarded with candy, toys, or extra recess time. *Negative reinforcement* simply consists of withholding the extra privileges.

Such systems may work very well, but they have been criticized on a number of counts. For one thing, in hospitals and prisons they are open to abuse, privileges being withheld unfairly. For another, in this form of behavior control authorities decide what is desirable behavior and what is not. Prisoners who are rewarded or punished may disagree with the values of the authorities, inevitably causing considerable resentment and undermining the effectiveness of the technique.

The therapy contract described in Chapter 22 is used by some behavioral therapists as an intrinsic part of the treatment—so-called *behavioral contracting*. In such instances the contract specifies the client's obligations to change her behavior, in exchange for the therapist's responsibility to provide some desired reward, such as a privilege or special attention. Behavioral contracts can be effective in institutional settings as well, between a hospital patient and a staff member, or child and teacher, with the former agreeing to perform certain tasks without prodding (getting dressed, attending meals/ remaining in one's seat, completing assignments) in exchange for desired privileges (extra food, later bedtime/longer recess, a small gift).

Behavior therapy generally begins, as other therapy does, with an assessment based on the client's history and stated problems, as well as direct observation and quantification of the actual behavior. The behavior therapist rarely inquires into the reasons for problems: Why do you become frightened in a crowded place? Why do you punish yourself by overeating? Rather, the therapist is likely to ask specific questions concerning the circumstances under which the client behaves undesirably: What were you doing when you became anxious? Who was with you? How often does this happen? The problems then are defined in a concrete way, and the goals of treatment are established.

What disorders lend themselves best to behavior therapy? The greatest success has been with focal phobias (fear of snakes, dogs, high places, crowds, etc.), obsessive-compulsive behavior (incessant handwashing, for example), and substance abuse of various kinds (food, tobacco, drugs, alcohol), as well as with specific problems such as stuttering, and head-banging and other forms of self-injury among severely retarded, autistic, and/or brain-damaged children. Behavior therapy alone has been less effective for depression and other mood disturbances.

Behavior therapy is practiced more by psychologists than psychiatrists, and also by social workers and other mental health professionals. For information about practitioners in your area, you can contact the Association for Advancement of Behavior Therapy (see Appendix A). Similar information may be available through the psychology department of a nearby college or university, or through your local community mental health center or mental health association.

COGNITIVE BEHAVIOR THERAPIES

The early behaviorists concentrated on modifying the overt behavior (that is, observable actions) of experimental animals and, later, of human clients. Beginning about 1960, however, a number of therapists began to regard patterns of thought and expressed feelings (called *cognitions*) as much a part of behavior as overt actions, and similarly subject to modification. Cognitive behavior therapy represents a combination of cognitive psychology, which emphasizes that thoughts influence behavior, and behavioral psychology, which focuses on specific methods to change behavior. Thus it uses the methods of behavior therapy—desensitization, operant conditioning, aversive conditioning, imagery, modeling, behavior rehearsal—to modify what a client "says to himself" or how he "sees himself" before, during, and after overt behavior.

The first important cognitive behavior therapist was Albert Ellis, whose approach is called *rational-emotive therapy*. Ellis maintained that our emotions are caused and controlled by our thinking. A disturbed person is one who has adopted irrational and illogical ideas that lead to and perpetuate emotions that give rise to neurotic actions. In rational-emotive therapy, the therapist helps the client discover what she is internally "saying," to question its rationality, and to substitute more rational and realistic "self-talk." In effect, the client is directed to "think positive," to become assertive, and to set sensible goals for getting ahead and enjoying life.

The author of several self-help books, notably *A Guide to Rational Living* (1961), Ellis believed that certain irrational assumptions made by many individuals lead to profound anxiety or depression. Among them are (1) it is vital that practically everyone I know loves me and approves of me; (2) I must be extremely competent in every undertaking in order to be worthwhile; (3) certain individuals are inherently bad and they should be punished; (4) if things don't go exactly as I wish them to, it is catastrophic; (5) people have little or no control over their sorrows or upsets; (6) it is better to avoid certain difficulties and responsibilities; (7) it is better to depend on others and I need someone strong on whom I can rely; (8) every human problem has a single perfect solution, and it is disastrous if this solution is not found.

For example, David R., 40, is out nearly every night of the week doing community volunteer work. He coaches a Little League team, leads a Scout group, serves on three town boards, and takes charge of several charity fund drives. His job during the day as a bank loan officer is very demanding, and he often must bring work home. Further, at work he becomes very upset whenever he has to turn down a loan application. David begins to develop several distressing symptoms—insomnia, shortness of breath, and finally a bleeding ulcer. After the ulcer has been treated, his family doctor suggests that David see a therapist, and the one he recommends is a rational-emotive therapist. The therapist soon discovers David's underlying behavioral problem: He cannot say "No." David has always wanted everyone to like him and approve of him. What people think is terribly important. The therapist points out that it is more important to think well of oneself than to be a friend to everyone, which isn't possible anyway. Through assertiveness training, role-playing, modeling, and other techniques the therapist gradually helps David accept this view.

Similar to rational-emotive therapy is *cognitive therapy*, developed by Aaron T. Beck in the 1960s to treat depression. It, too, is based on the idea that one's moods and emotions are determined primarily by how one construes the world (thinks). These thoughts, or cognitions, are developed from early experience, but tend to be applied whether they are appropriate or not. Thus a person who has little self-esteem may readily develop depression; a person who anticipates personal harm may develop anxiety and phobias; a person who habitually mistrusts others may develop paranoia.

Beck's treatment for these misperceptions is behavioral in approach. For example, the cognitive therapist might lead a depressed client like Jane, the widow, through a series of easily accomplished tasks that clearly demonstrate her mastery and competence. He may then help her to identify the specific thoughts she has that make her feel depressed. Suppose Jane greeted a friend on the street who did not see her and passed by without response. To Jane, already sad, this appears to be a devastating rejection and makes her feel that no one likes her. The therapist will ask her to examine this interpretation, perhaps by asking how many telephone calls from friends she has received in the past two weeks, to indicate that some people do in fact like her enough to call.

One of Beck's classic cases is that of a profoundly depressed college student who believed she was lazy and stupid even though she had a straight A average. Whenever she got an A, she told herself that the class was easy, the grade was an accident, or the teacher felt sorry for her. With help she learned to interpret her grades more positively and to recognize that the source of her deep-seated depression was her own misinterpretation of events.

Cognitive therapy usually consists of weekly sessions for a period of three to six months. It appears to work best for clients with depression, anxiety, phobias, and obsessive-compulsive disorder. It requires the ability to differentiate reality from fantasy and consequently is not suitable for persons undergoing a psychotic episode. It also is not considered very useful for disorders of substance abuse (alcoholism, drug addiction).

During the 1970s, some cognitive behavior therapists broadened their approach so as to teach clients not only to deal with specific current problems but to prepare them to deal with situations that might come up in the future. The therapists wanted to teach their clients so-called "coping skills," providing them with a prospective defense for dealing with future stress. Clients were taught broad self-relaxation, to be used whenever they faced problems that might cause physiological arousal (sweaty palms, pounding heart, muscular tension) and also were taught to substitute positive "self-statements" for the habitual anxiety-producing ones that were associated with stress.

For example, as a client who had experienced one or more phobic reactions in the past you would be instructed to follow a series of procedures: Assess the reality of this new frightening situation; control any negative thoughts or self-statements; acknowledge the fact that you are aroused (frightened); "psych yourself up" to confront the situation; cope with whatever intense fear you might experience (you're intensely frightened, true, but this object can't really hurt you, nor can the feeling of intense pain, which will soon pass); and reinforce (congratulate) yourself for having coped successfully with this stress. This approach is called *stress-inoculation training*. To the extent that its strategies succeed in avoiding future breakdowns, they represent a form of preventive treatment. (See also Chapter 25.)

SHORT-TERM PROBLEM-ORIENTED THERAPIES

Several other methods of psychotherapy have been developed to treat specific disorders in a relatively brief time (weeks or a few months instead of many months or years). They tend to use a variety of techniques borrowed from other kinds of therapy and they are essentially pragmatic.

One such therapy is *short-term anxiety-provoking therapy*, or *STAPP*. Developed by Peter E. Sifneos in the 1960s, it is grounded in Freud's ideas of unconscious conflict, but in marked contrast to the many years required for classic psychoanalysis, it usually entails a total of eight or nine fifty-minute sessions. The basic approach is to make clients confront their troubling feelings, relate them to past events, and work out the current problem. The therapist plays a very active role, asking leading questions, pointing out similarities, and so on.

The client is first asked to select a single emotional problem he wants to overcome. The therapist, through skilled interviewing and history-taking, looks for a formulation of the emotional conflicts underlying this problem and concentrates on those conflicts alone, using anxiety-provoking questions to stimulate the client to examine areas of difficulty and to help him become aware of feelings, experience the conflicts, and learn new ways of dealing with them.

For example, Karen B., 27, is planning to be married in two months to a man she has been living with for three years. She suddenly finds herself terribly anxious about the wedding and goes to an outpatient clinic. The intake clinician she sees suggests STAPP. At her first interview she tells the therapist of her anxiety, which she finds especially troubling because until now her relationship with her boyfriend has been excellent. After getting a full description of her present situation, the therapist asks Karen to describe her general history and any occasions in the past when she felt very upset and anxious. In the next few sessions he raises questions that Karen might find too threatening to bring up herself, such as, "Is your father jealous of your fiancé?" or "Are you afraid that your marriage, like that of your parents, will end in divorce?" After six weekly sessions, Karen determines that it is her parents' bad marriage and bitter divorce that is making her frightened. The therapist helps her separate her own situation from theirs, and to discover that she has tested her relationship with her fiancé sufficiently over the past three years to know that they get along well together.

Another therapy is *short-term interpersonal psychotherapy (IPT)*, a form of brief (twelve to sixteen weeks) treatment that has been used primarily for treating depression. Grounded in the interpersonal theories of Harry Stack Sullivan (see Chapter 15), it is based on the idea that depression occurs in an interpersonal context, that is, a person's relations with others. These relationships account for the onset of symptoms. Therefore, treatment, which can be used alone or in conjunction with psychoactive drugs (antidepressant medication), focuses on resolving the client's immediate difficulties in his important relationships with others (close family, close friends, work associates). The therapist is active (in making suggestions, pointing out contradictions, and so on), supportive, and nonjudgmental. Definite limited treatment goals are set during the first three sessions, which focus on one or two specific problem areas, such as grieving over a loss, marital conflicts, or difficulty in relationships with co-workers. First developed by Dr. Gerald L. Klerman, IPT has evolved since about 1970 from the experience of the New Haven-Boston Collaborative Depression Projects. Dr. Klerman and his associates have developed a program for training experienced therapists (psychiatrists, psychologists, social workers) in the method, and have written a manual outlining the concept, techniques, and strategies of IPT.

Who benefits from such short-term therapies? They tend to work best for a person who is able to state the presenting problem, is genuinely eager to do something about it, is willing to accept personal responsibility for difficulties, and is able to tolerate some anxiety, anger, and frustration. They are particularly helpful for a client with acute symptoms that occur in reaction to a life crisis—changing schools, marriage, job-hunting, a new baby. They usually are not suitable for a person with a chronic psychotic condition, such as major depression, manic-depressive psychosis, or schizophrenia.

SEX THERAPY

Sex therapy is a specialized form of problem-oriented therapy that is used to treat sexual dysfunction in men and women. Sexual dysfunction is defined as any disturbance or disorder that frequently or always prevents a person from engaging in satisfying sexual intercourse, and it arises anywhere in the three-stage cycle of sexual response, desire—arousal—orgasm. The most common forms of sexual dysfunction are impotence and premature ejaculation in men and failure to reach orgasm in women.

Sex therapy differs from marital and couples therapy in that its goal is limited to relieving sexual dysfunction. For this purpose it employs a combination of prescribed sexual experiences that the clients use at home to modify the immediate causes of their problem. Typically a couple is asked to learn first to caress one another to evoke pleasure without thought of completing the act of intercourse, and to perform other actions designed to relieve performance anxiety and excessive self-observation, two common sources of difficulty.

Sex therapy can be undertaken by one partner alone but usually requires the participation of both. Most therapists begin with a detailed history of the clients' sex life and give a thorough explanation of the anatomy and physiology of the sex organs and of sexual response. Present-day techniques of sex therapy are based on the work of William Masters and Virginia Johnson, who, about 1960, formed a clinic for treating couples in a series of daily sessions over two weeks. Their work has since been modified by Helen Singer Kaplan and others. The therapy is usually time-limited and fairly short-term (typically twelve to fourteen sessions held weekly or semiweekly) but the exact procedure depends on the individual clinician, who may adapt it to each couple. Therapy is usually terminated when the sex difficulty has been resolved—in effect, when the symptom has been cured, its immediate causes modified, and the clients have enough insight to prevent recurrence. Not all such treatment is successful, of course. Sometimes one or the other partner is found to have an underlying problem that requires individual treatment, or the entire relationship between the partners is pathologic. In other cases the clients may simply give up and either seek relief through some other treatment or decide to live with the problem.

Its very nature makes sex therapy readily open to abuse by unqualified and/or unscrupulous practitioners, and because it is a relatively new field, standards for licensing are not well established. Sexual contact *with* a therapist is *never* a legitimate part of treatment. The best way to find a reputable practitioner is through the American Association of Sex Education, Counselors, and Therapists, which will provide names of qualified and experienced therapists in your area.

HYPNOTHERAPY

Hypnotherapy means treatment involving hypnosis, a mental state of heightened concentration and suggestibility, characterized by altered perception and memory. Its first reported use in modern times was by Franz Anton Mesmer (1733–1815), a German physician who practiced what he called "animal magnetism." Although the sensational aspects of hypnotism soon led to its dismissal and condemnation by physicians and scientists, it continued to intrigue individuals interested in the human mind, particularly Sigmund Freud. Today hypnotism is still used as a form of entertainment, but it also is useful as a form of anesthesia in dentistry, childbirth, and surgery, for the relief of intractable pain from cancer and other disorders, and in psychotherapy of various kinds. In therapy it is used to recover long-buried memories that are brought to consciousness while a client is in a hypnotic state (trance); to help induce deep relaxation in clients undergoing systematic desensitization (see above); and to discourage clients from overeating, compulsive gambling, smoking, and other forms of abuse. In general hypnotherapy is thought to be most effective when used as an adjunct to other therapy.

The techniques for inducing hypnosis vary, but initially they usually involve some procedure to focus the client's attention, inducing her to concentrate solely on the therapist. Exactly what happens in hypnotism is not completely understood. There appear to be several levels of trance: light, moderate, and deep. A hypnotic trance is characterized by extreme relaxation and heightened susceptibility to suggestions, but it does not involve giving up one's will or being controlled by someone else. Hypnosis cannot be performed without the subject's full cooperation. In this sense, it has been suggested, all hypnosis is in fact self-hypnosis, and the practitioner is only a guide.

While a client is in a trance, the therapist may suggest new ways of behaving and thinking that eliminate an undesirable behavior or habit, or bring recall of a forgotten event that became the source of anxiety of neurosis. Many clients can learn to hypnotize themselves and thus supplement and reinforce the therapist's efforts. In therapy, hypnosis tends to be used in short-term forms of treatment, often involving only four to six sessions.

Not everyone can be hypnotized. Some subjects are more susceptible than others, and those of a resistant frame of mind will succumb only slowly, if at all. Moreover, hypnotherapy is not completely without risk; on rare occasions a trance brings out latent violence, in the form of a psychotic outburst or a physical attack. Because it is not totally understood, hypnotism is open to abuse by inadequately trained practitioners. Both the American Medical Association and the American Psychiatric Association have published standards for treatment by hypnosis, pointing out the dangers of inappropriate use in clinical situations where it is contraindicated. It requires careful evaluation of clients, their problems, and their total life situations, and is

most effectively used by someone well trained in psychological and
physiological processes. If hypnotism is suggested as a form of treatment for you, your relative, or your friend, it is wise to check carefully
the credentials and experience of the therapist before agreeing to the
procedure.

BODY THERAPIES

A number of therapies use what is sometimes called a *holistic* approach, regarding the mind and body as an inseparable whole. None of
these therapies has to date been endorsed by a reputable body of
professionals, such as the American Psychiatric Association, and all
should be viewed with caution, if not skepticism.

Reich, who developed orgone therapy (see Chapter 15), observed
that physical tension often was a symptom of mental distress and tried
to get clients to release pent-up emotions by deep breathing and laying
hands on contracted muscles. His pupil, Alexander Lowen, went
further, saying that emotional problems are always expressed in muscular tensions that "bind up" one's energy so that it cannot be discharged. His system of *bioenergetics* is supposed to get the client back
together with his body, and help him enjoy the life of the body to the
fullest. The client must first undress, so as to reveal the body completely. A variety of breathing and other exercises are employed to
release tension. For example, a woman who cannot express her feelings may be instructed to move her body more freely—to jump up and
down, or to kick her legs. Then massage and other physical contact
between therapist and client (ranging from touching all the way to
sexual intercourse) are used to break down what Lowen considered
the conflict between a person's desire for and fear of body contact.
This kind of therapy has never been endorsed by any professional
organization and is readily open to abuse. If anyone recommends it for
you, get a responsible second opinion before undertaking it.

Rolfing, named for its inventor, Ida Rolf (1896–1979), is a method of
body reorganization through deep massage. Also called *structural
integration*, it is based on the idea that the body's muscles literally
absorb psychological trauma, which makes them stiff and rigid. By
massaging various muscles, allegedly the trauma stored in each is
evoked, allowing the client to confront long-repressed feelings. Mas-

sage is sometimes combined with guided fantasy, a system of conscious attempts to remember oneself at various early ages, through which one is then supposed to reexperience the painful incidents of the past. Rolfing is usually performed by a kind of physiotherapist who applies pressure to various muscles in a prescribed sequence; occasionally the process is physically painful. The standard term of treatment is a series of ten one-hour sessions, which makes it one of the shortest-term therapies available.

Similar in basis but different in practice is Arthur Janov's *primal therapy*. Janov believes that the source of emotional problems is the denial of a child's basic (primal) needs—for food, warmth, physical contact—by his parents. The child realizes through such deprivation that his parents do not love him, a realization that Janov calls "the primal trauma." Allegedly all neuroses are a response to this trauma. The goal of therapy is to release the "primal pain" by addressing its sources, one's father and mother. Therapy thus consists of reliving the experience of primal pain and responding to it in an uninhibited way, by screaming, kicking, crying, and the like. It usually is begun with a period of twenty-four hours spent in total isolation in order to weaken the client's defenses. It is followed by an intensive three-week course of individual therapy, with daily sessions that last several hours each, during which the therapist tries to get the client to express the deepest possible feelings toward his parents. This course may be followed by a period of group therapy in which each individual's primal pain is further explored and expressed.

TRANSCENDENTAL MEDITATION

A very different route to relieving tension—both physical and emotional—is that of various Eastern meditative practices, ranging from yoga to Zen and other kinds of Buddhism, with or without the aid of mind-expanding (psychedelic) drugs. (Such drugs, which include LSD, marijuana, and mescaline, induce hallucinations and, sometimes, psychotic states.) Transcendental meditation is a form of inducing a trance state; it was introduced to the West in 1959 by Maharishi Mahesh Yogi.

Meditation has its basis in religion and is much older than any of the other therapies described. Its goal is the attainment of a different state of consciousness, in which the self, the subject and center of ordinary experience, ceases to exist as a separate entity. Instead, the meditator perceives herself as an integral part of the rest of the world. Thus meditation is sometimes described as "losing oneself." To practice meditation, one focuses on a single subject and, sometimes, repeats a single word or phrase called a *mantra* in some systematic way. This rhythmic repetition allegedly exerts a hypnotic effect on the mind, leading to trance. Insofar as it employs various breathing and body exercises to induce concentration and a kind of special awareness, it is related to the body therapies.

Meditation is essentially nonverbal. Naming thoughts and feelings is discouraged; rather, the goal is to concentrate so that ordinary ideas and images lose their usual verbal meaning. Strictly speaking, meditation is not a psychotherapy at all, since we defined psychotherapy as an interview process. It does, however, alleviate some of the tensions associated with various neurotic disorders, and in general it is not incompatible for use in conjunction with other forms of therapy. It also can be and is used by persons not suffering from any particular psychic distress but who are seeking spiritual fulfillment, or looking for a simple means to reduce ordinary, everyday tensions.

ACUPUNCTURE

Long used to treat both physical and mental illness in the Orient, where it has the same status as Western medicine, acupuncture is being increasingly used in the United States and other Western countries to treat a wide variety of disorders. Acupuncture is based on the idea that illness, injury, and the pain and discomfort they cause are disturbances in the body's natural flow of bioelectric energy, called *chi*. Therefore treatment is directed at correcting obstructions, imbalance, or other adverse changes in the paths of that flow, and thus restoring the body's natural balance. The pathways have been mapped as a system of more than two dozen *meridians* passing over more than eight hundred points associated with specific body organs or functions. The method of treatment involves the insertion of hair-thin needles of surgical steel to stimulate the specific points thought to be associated with the problem being treated. The needles remain in place for ten minutes to an hour at a time. They are carefully sterilized and are so fine that they rarely cause bleeding or pain beyond that of a pinprick or tingling sensation. Sometimes heat or electrical stimulation is applied via the needles, and the treatment may also involve special herbal remedies and Oriental massage. Usually a series of treatments, five to twenty on the average, is required. The cost is relatively low, about $20 to $25 per treatment.

Acupuncture is said to alleviate anxiety and depression. In recent years it has increasingly been used to help treat nicotine, alcohol, and drug abuse, both to relieve withdrawal symptoms and to lessen the stress of doing without these substances. Research suggests that needles inserted at certain points can trigger the release of endorphins, which are natural pain relievers. (See Chapter 27 for more about brain chemistry.)

In some states acupuncture is regulated by licensing; in others, it is not regulated, and in still others it is illegal, or may be practiced only by a physician or a chiropractor working under a physician. To find a competent practitioner in places where there is no licensing, consult the national professional organization, the American Association of Acupuncturists and Oriental Medicine (see Appendix A). In order to protect against infection, make sure the needles used have been properly sterilized, or request the use of disposable needles (some acupuncturists keep a separate set of needles for each patient).

FEMINIST THERAPY

Feminist therapy is an outgrowth of the women's movement of the 1960s and 1970s and represents a reaction against male-dominated psychiatry (some 75 percent of American psychiatrists are men) as well as against the theories of Sigmund Freud and others insofar as they pertain to women's "appropriate" roles and sexuality. Feminist therapy incorporates the basic beliefs of feminism, or women's rights, in the approach to treatment. In theory, feminist therapists may be either male or female, but in practice nearly all are women. They do not use any special therapeutic method; rather, each uses whatever mode of psychotherapy she prefers but adapts it to feminist thinking.

Among the ideas most feminist therapists subscribe to is that the traditional role of women as subordinate to men, passive and powerless, should be replaced so that they are—and feel they are—active, equal, and independent. Another central belief is that a therapist should not behave as an authority figure who dominates, intimidates, or patronizes the client. Rather, she should help the client overcome her own feelings of helplessness and dependency, and encourage her assertiveness. To this end feminist therapists often try to avoid technical language, give the client free access to her own records and files, and encourage the client to set her own goals for therapy (rather than rely on the therapist to set them for her).

PSYCHOTHERAPY FOR CHILDREN

Many of the modes of psychotherapy described in this and the previous chapter have been adapted and used for children and adolescents. In addition, some methods have been developed specifically for treating disturbed youngsters.

One such technique is *play therapy*, which originally was used mainly by therapists with a psychoanalytic orientation but today is used by therapists of diverse backgrounds. Most children under the age of ten or twelve are not sophisticated enough to be able to talk about their problems to a therapist. Indeed, most young children are not able to sit still long enough to hold a half-hour conversation with a grown-up. Just as conversation is the natural social activity of the adult, play is the natural activity of the child. During a play therapy session the therapist and child play together, usually with any toy or game chosen by the client from a collection made available by the therapist. Play, it is believed, allows children to display anger, fear, anxiety, and other feelings, and to act out fantasies and conflicts. The equipment varies, but there are nearly always dolls and household toys to allow children to act out family relationships and everyday occurrences; soldiers, guns, and other weapons to express aggression; and drawing materials, paints, and clay for less structured means of self-expression.

The analytically oriented therapist uses play therapy to try to understand the symbolic meanings of a child's play in order to clarify the symptoms and underlying pathology. The client-centered Rogerian therapist uses play therapy to allow a child to communicate thoughts and feelings in a comfortable way, and to create a permissive, nondemanding environment in which the child feels accepted and comes to accept his own feelings. Play therapy is used less often by behavior therapists, who rather focus on reinforcing actual behavior in an ordinary setting, although they may play a game with a child as a form of positive reinforcement.

Psychotherapy for children involves the parents to varying degrees. Some therapists like to see the parents in separate sessions as frequently as they see their child. Others rarely bring the parents into therapy, except to report on progress. Still others may use family therapy—with both parents and the child and siblings present—for some sessions, as well as individual therapy with the child. (Family therapy is discussed in the next chapter.) And some behaviorally oriented therapists scarcely work with the child at all but rather instruct parents and teachers in carrying out a reinforcement system of their design.

Although mental illness in children—even quite young children— has been recognized and treated for some time, it is only relatively recently that psychiatry has undertaken the *treatment of infants*. However, some serious illnesses, such as autism, appear quite early in life. Further, infants who have been subject to abuse, sexual or otherwise, or other traumatic events may well require treatment.

Most often such treatment involves taking the baby to a therapist mainly for purposes of observation and evaluation. The parent(s) and/ or principal caregiver must necessarily be involved as well, and perhaps be instructed in how to deal with the baby. Developmental psychologists have, through a series of rigorous studies, determined that a child's feelings grow in a predictable, orderly fashion from birth. Most infants are born with the capacity for pleasure, surprise, disgust, and distress. By the age of six to eight weeks they can feel joy, by three to four months anger, by eight to nine months sadness and fear, and by twelve to eighteen months tender affection and shame. By the age of two they can perceive pride, and by three to four years, guilt. Although these ages are average for these feelings, and individual babies vary, it seems clear that an infant who fails to develop these feelings within a reasonable time or otherwise is not thriving may be having problems. (See also the section in Chapter 25 on preventive care for the very young.)

Chapter

17

GIVING HELP— PSYCHOTHERAPY 3: GROUP THERAPIES

SINCE ABOUT 1950 group therapies have become increasingly popular. There is no one kind of group therapy. Rather, such therapies range from analytical (insight) psychotherapy, which focuses on the problems of individuals but in a group setting, to encounter groups and various kinds of marathon, which offer very concentrated, intense, and brief terms of therapy. Among the individual therapies that have been used in a group setting are Horneyan, Adlerian, Sullivanian, rational-emotive, existential, Gestalt, and bioenergetic.

From the standpoint of cost per session, group therapy is decidedly less expensive than individual therapy. On a per-person per-session basis, it is one-third to two-thirds less expensive. Thus a $100-per-hour psychiatrist would charge about $35 to $50 per person for each group session (see page 88). However, depending on numerous factors—the problem, the group members, the therapist, the method(s) used, and so on—group therapy may not be as worthwhile as individual therapy.

In conventional group therapy, six to ten clients meet, usually once a week for one and one-half hours, with one or two (or more) therapists. (If there is more than one therapist the treatment may be called *conjoint therapy*.) The makeup of the group may be either homogeneous or heterogeneous in terms of age, sex, and kinds of problems. The role of the group leader(s) may vary from very neutral to very active.

CANDIDATES FOR GROUP THERAPY

Group therapy can be undertaken alone or in conjunction with individual therapy. Some therapists invite their clients to join a group after a period of individual therapy, and sometimes a client continues individual therapy, too, with the same or with another therapist. This treatment is sometimes called *combined psychotherapy*.

Since group therapy is used even for extremely disturbed patients in mental hospitals, it would seem to be appropriate for anyone interested in psychotherapy. However, outside a hospital or other setting where there can be very close supervision, group therapy is neither desirable nor suitable for everyone, and for some individuals it may be actively harmful. Who should *not* be in group therapy?

- A person who is managing, with difficulty, to get along but who is close to a serious breakdown; such a person needs more intensive individual treatment.
- A person who is unduly distressed by the ills of others; hearing about the other group members' problems week after week can be overwhelming.
- A person who crumbles under criticism; to such a person even a mildly negative comment by another group member may be devastating.

Further, some individuals may so disrupt or hamper the functioning of a group that it is unwise for them to participate. Among these are:

- A person who wants to monopolize the leader's attention all or most of the time

- A person unable to share his ideas or experiences, and thus is unable to contribute to the group
- A person extremely insensitive to the feelings of others, who therefore frequently makes wounding remarks and is unable to listen to what others are saying
- A person who becomes explosively angry

A skilled and experienced group leader usually screens prospective members very carefully, but even the best leader can make mistakes. If you are considering joining a group, or group therapy has been recommended for you, it is wise to find out as much as you can about the group. In your individual meeting with the group leader—and a group leader nearly always sees each prospective member for at least one session to learn the person's history, evaluate his problems, and define goals—you can and should ask the therapist about her background (training and experience) and about the makeup and goals of the group, how long it is expected to meet (for a month, several months, a year or more) and whether during that time members will leave and be replaced by new members, how active the therapist will be in group meetings, and any other questions that seem important to you.

Because the interaction of group members sometimes is hard to perceive while it is actually going on, some therapists find it useful to videotape group sessions. Playing back portions of the tape, either to individual members or to the entire group, makes it possible to review exactly what happened and enables individuals to see how they behave in a group setting. If the therapist does videotape your group, you may want to know what happens to the tapes, in order to preserve confidentiality. Often such tapes are not stored at all, but are used, erased, and reused, which avoids the need for legal release forms and preserves privacy.

Note, however, that group members, unlike the therapist, are not legally bound to respect confidentiality. Therefore, what is said in a group does not have the same confidentiality value as a comment made to an individual therapist.

Who *should* consider group therapy? As indicated above and further described below, there are many different kinds of group therapy, and groups have been used to treat a huge variety of problems, ranging from chronic severe mental disorders such as schizophrenia in long-term institutionalized patients to individuals coping with alcoholism and drug abuse. Some mental problems seem to lend themselves more readily to group therapy than individual therapy. Among them are:

- The shy, lonely person who is very dependent and in fact very isolated. The group process makes him realize there are others in the same boat. This approach is very useful for some adolescents.
- The person in individual therapy who has become overdependent on the therapist. Group therapy forces her to share the therapist's attention with the other members and fosters a greater degree of independence.
- A person who has trouble getting along with others. The group may focus on the precise sources of the difficulty and teach ways to overcome them.
- Persons with a problem seen as unusual or shameful: an embarrassing phobia, addiction to alcohol or drugs, obesity. A group made up of individuals with this same problem can offer mutual emotional support.
- Couples with marital difficulties. Groups made up of married couples experiencing problems can benefit from observing each other's interactions in a group setting. Also, with more than one couple present, the therapist is in less danger of being drawn into the role of judge between two warring individuals.

If you are interested specifically in some form of group therapy, you may be able to obtain the names of practitioners in your area from the American Group Psychotherapy Association (see Appendix A).

Insight group therapy can take several forms. It may focus primarily on the individual members and how they react to the group setting, or it may address itself to the group as a whole and let individual problems arise as they may. For example, consider a therapy group in which one person, Tony, tends to dominate meetings. Whenever anyone brings up an issue, he offers his opinion or brings up a similar event in his experience. Today Laura is trying to tell the group about her difficulties with her teenage daughter, and Tony, who has no children himself, constantly interrupts her. John tries to stop Tony so that Laura may talk, but he is ignored.

If this group is concentrating on individuals, the group leader, Phyllis, might stop Tony and suggest that he is interrupting Laura for several reasons. She might point out that he feels uncomfortable unless he is the center of attention; he cannot just sit back and listen. Also, Laura seems to find John attractive, which might remind Tony of his childhood, when his mother seemed to favor his younger brother. On the other hand, if this group is one in which the collective process is in focus, Phyllis might point out that here Tony was bossing the meeting and giving Laura a hard time, but the other members of the group, except for John, were doing nothing to stop him. They were sitting back and allowing these events to take place, even when they had nothing to gain (and something to lose, in terms of time, attention, etc.) from their inaction.

PSYCHODRAMA

A commonly used technique in group therapy is borrowed from psychodrama, invented by Jacob L. Moreno (1889–1974). Some members of the group act out a particular situation or issue, while the rest of the group acts as an audience. After the "performance," everyone is asked to make comments and offer interpretations of what they have observed. Thus Laura might be asked to play the mother, John would play her teenage child, and Tony would play Laura's husband. First Laura might express anger at her child for always staying out much later than her curfew and refusing to help with household chores. John might respond that he thought "mother" was always picking on him. And so on. John, although playing the role of Laura's child, inevitably will reveal some of his own background (perhaps his own experience as a teenager), which makes the drama helpful for analyzing his feelings and behavior as well as Laura's problem. Other psychodrama techniques include *role reversal* (next John might play the parent and Laura the child) and the *mirror method* (Laura sits back and observes while some other group member acts out her role).

FAMILY THERAPY

Family therapy is a specialized form of group therapy, usually involving a single family. It was developed in the 1950s, growing out of the treatment of mentally ill children and their mothers, a focus that expanded to family processes, that is, all the relationships within a family. Today most people see a family therapist when they have problems involving their marriage or one or more of their children. Children over the age of eight usually can participate in family therapy. When no children are involved or the basic problem is a marital one, it is usually called *marital* or *couples therapy*.

Family therapy may be analytically oriented, concentrating on the conflicts each individual has with other family members, or it may use any or several of the other individual or group psychotherapy approaches described above. It may be the only method of treatment or it may be combined with other treatment, one or more members of the family also receiving individual therapy and/or being engaged in other group therapy.

The underlying theory of family therapy—no matter which of the various techniques of group therapy is used—is that a family is a system or group that has definite functions, among them survival, security (safety of its members), economic viability (having enough money to live on), identity (who belongs and who doesn't), power and control, and affection and intimacy. A family's behavior becomes maladaptive (emotionally ill) when it emphasizes some functions at the expense of other, equally important ones, or if the parents' leadership function is impaired.

For example, in one family certain members (the parents) may consider identity so important that they do not allow their children to have friends but insist they come straight home from school and limit their social life to members of the family. In another family making money and acquiring property may become so important to the parents that they spend little or no time with or energy on their children other than buying them expensive clothing and toys. In still another family the father might withdraw from all disciplinary, decision-making, and other functions that would normally involve agreement with the mother, leaving her to perform all these duties yet covertly undermining her decisions. In all these cases the relations among family members may readily become distorted, so that there is a trend toward recurring crises, and eventually one or more of the family members may break down.

There are three main approaches to family therapy. The *insight-awareness* approach is basically insight therapy adapted to the family, that is, observation, clarification, and interpretation are used to foster understanding. The therapist listens to the family, keeps a "therapeutic distance," and tries to form a therapeutic relationship with family members. It is essentially individual insight therapy practiced in the presence of other family members.

The second approach is *strategic-behavioral* (also called *systems, communications,* or *structural*). It focuses on patterns of behavior and attempts to change them for the better. The therapist plays a far more active role, sometimes assigning specific tasks both in and out of the treatment sessions, manipulating mood, focusing on specific symptoms, interrupting repetitive behavior patterns to point them out, explain them, and prescribe certain behaviors.

The third approach is the *experiential-existential,* in which the emphasis is on what the therapist sees and what family members perceive and feel. The therapist may act either as a role model or as an advocate for the family members, and the overall goal is to change the ways family members experience and react to each other. It is to some extent the counterpart of Gestalt therapy applied to a family.

A number of specific techniques have been developed and/or used by family therapists. Among them are:

- Family tasks, in which the therapist assigns tasks to be performed during or between sessions, for example, undertaking an outing that includes all the family members, or instructing a husband and wife to discuss a family secret.
- Paradoxical prescription/intention (also called *symptom scheduling, negative practice,* or *reverse psychology*), in which symptoms are made more intense and/or more frequent so as to demystify them; for example, a couple who constantly argue may be told to argue about which restaurant they will go to *before* dinner, so they can enjoy their meal without arguing once they get there.
- Coaching, in which the therapist directly coaches family members in their various interactions during a therapy session.
- Home visiting, where the therapist goes to the clients' home, school, church, etc. and meets the individuals and agencies that influence their lives.
- Guided fantasy, in which the therapist helps a family member share his personal fantasies with other family members.
- Family sculpture, in which the therapist asks one or all of the family members present to create, at a given moment during the therapy session, a physical representation of their relationships by arranging their bodies in space.

- Psychodrama and role-playing (see above).
- Video- and audiotaping of a therapy session, with an immediate playback to help family members see how they interact and communicate, both verbally and nonverbally (through gestures, facial expression, etc.).
- One-way mirror, used in a number of ways: by the therapist, who leaves the family in the treatment room and observes them through the mirror; by one of the family members leaving the group and observing the others; or by one of a pair of therapists (co-therapists), with one remaining in the room and the other observing.
- Weekend family marathon, where one or several families get together for eight to twelve hours of intensive encounter (see also encounter groups and marathons below).
- Multiple family group therapy, where several families meet together.
- Network therapy, in which the family, friends, and all other individuals who have any bearing on a person's problems meet together in three to six biweekly, four-hour sessions at the client's home (there may be as many as forty-five persons at such a meeting).

How Family Therapy Works

Even if not all the family members agree to enter treatment together, a family therapist may want to see all of them for a single session, for purposes of evaluation. This first meeting can reveal a great deal about the family, just in the way they enter the room and sit down—who sits with whom, who speaks and who listens, who smiles and who frowns, and so on. The therapist can take note of how the members talk to each other, what they choose to talk about, what they choose to avoid, and what they reveal through body language (gestures, posture).

Suppose, for example, that Harry and Mary H., the couple in their thirties described in Chapter 2, decide they must do something about eight-year-old Mark's tantrums, and their pediatrician suggests they see a family therapist. At the first session, Harry, Mary, Mark, and nine-year-old Judy attend; Harry's two children from his former marriage, who visit him every other weekend, have refused to come. Mary leads the way into the room, followed by the children and then Harry. She walks briskly; he drags his feet. She sits in the chair nearest the therapist, the children stand very close to her, and Harry takes the chair nearest the door. Already some of the interactions of this family are evident. It is Mary who has come for help and seeks an ally in the therapist. The children align themselves with their mother, and the father remains in an alien position, near the door, as though he were ready to walk out any time (and, you may recall, he has actually walked out on the family several times earlier).

In the course of therapy, the H. family and their therapist will focus on defining the causes of problems, improving communication among family members, learning to cope with stress, and involving the children in this and other processes. If most or all of the family members remain in the group, therapy is sometimes called *conjoint family therapy*; if it is decided that this family will benefit from meetings with one or more other families, it becomes *multiple family therapy*; and if a team of professionals—not just one or two family therapists but perhaps a psychologist to test and evaluate Mark, an individual therapist to treat Harry separately, and a social worker who sees Mary alone—is brought in, it is called *multiple impact family therapy*.

Family therapy tends to be relatively short-term, typically consisting of weekly hour-long sessions over a period of six months to a year. It is appropriate for a wide range of disorders, but especially when interpersonal conflicts in the family strongly affect one or more of the members. It is also considered very useful in treating children, on the theory that a shift in parental relations and parent–child relations can free a child from anxiety and reduce her need to act out parental and family problems in maladaptive behavior.

When is family therapy *not* appropriate? According to Dr. Nathan W. Ackerman, one of the experts of family therapy:

- When the family is about to break up anyhow, and it is too late to stop the process. Then, however, divorce mediation (see Chapters 11 and 25) might ease the breakup for parents and children).
- When one parent has a severe mental disorder, particularly severe paranoid delusions, or is determined to behave destructively.
- When one or both parents cannot be honest because deeply rooted deceit makes family therapy useless.
- When a deeply held religious, cultural, or economic belief of the family is opposed to this form of intervention. The family members must *want* to change things for the better, or change cannot take place.
- When one or more of the family members has extremely rigid de

fenses that, if broken down, may trigger a crisis—a psychotic episode or physical assault.
- When one or more members has a disease or other disability of a progressive nature that rules out their participation.

SPECIALIZED FAMILY THERAPY

Family therapy has also been adapted for specific problems, such as alcoholism. Such an approach tries to look at the family as a whole as well as focusing on one member's addiction. Sometimes one or more family members are unwittingly contributing to the addict's behavior pattern, which may be revealed in a therapy session or two. An outpatient program might involve seeing the family once a week for eight to twenty weeks. Rehabilitation centers employing family therapy techniques often invite patients' families, relatives, or close friends to "family weeks," which combine therapy with educational sessions. At one such center relatives spend a week taking part in therapy groups during the morning while patients are meeting in separate groups. In the afternoon, patients and family members work together in groups led by counselors. This center also tries to involve all patients and their families in a two-year period of aftercare, which includes weekly family therapy sessions as well as participation in Alcoholics Anonymous, Al-Anon, or Alateen (alcoholic self-help groups).

Not all alcoholics benefit from a family therapy approach. Many do not have families, or their families' patience has been thoroughly exhausted so that they do not want to become involved. However, when it works, family therapy helps motivate alcoholics to come for treatment, helps them to focus on family relationships, and helps to keep them from returning to old patterns after they have stopped drinking.

TREATING CODEPENDENCE

An issue that has come to the forefront in recent years, especially publicized in popular literature, is so-called *codependence*. According to this view, an individual close to a person suffering from chemical dependency may be unwittingly contributing to that dependency, as well as suffering from self-destructive behavior patterns. The self-help group Al-Anon has long recognized the importance of helping individuals who are close to alcoholics, and similar help for those close to drug abusers is increasingly becoming available. In some cases where a family member is found to be codependent in a self-destructive way, he may be advised to seek separate treatment from the family group, either in a special therapy group or individually.

GERIATRIC FAMILY THERAPY

Another kind of family therapy focuses on the elderly and their families. Originating with elderly psychiatric patients who were hospitalized, it focuses on the special problems encountered by such patients and their families. Therapists have discovered a number of common themes in such families, among them problems with loss, chronic illness and death, and the insistence of children that their parents move elsewhere or enter a nursing home.

In one case, for example, it was discovered through a session with all the close relatives that a woman who had been repeatedly admitted to psychiatric wards had an underlying reason for her many "illnesses." Her husband had just retired and wanted to go to Puerto Rico to visit relatives. His father had died while making a similar trip, and the woman, knowing her husband would not travel while she was hospitalized, felt that if she remained "ill" she could keep him from dying. When her delusion was uncovered, the therapist and family members could begin to convince her that he would be all right even if she were not ill. The goal of such geriatric family therapy, which should become more widespread with the increasing number of elderly persons in the population, is to help families reorganize when the basic structures and relationships change.

TRANSACTIONAL ANALYSIS (TA)

Transactional analysis is a technique developed in California in the early 1950s by a Canadian-born psychiatrist, Eric Berne (1920–1970). Berne maintained that our social needs are as important as our biological drives (hunger, sex, etc.), and that we all have a basic need for love and recognition. The human personality has three basic aspects, or *ego states:* parent, child, and adult. Unlike Freud's superego, id, and ego (see Chapter 15), to which they are roughly comparable, Berne's states are directly observable in behavior. The *parent* is essentially critical and judgmental; the *child* is a leftover of childhood, dominated by intense feelings; the *adult* is the rational decision maker, responding to real-life situations and mediating between parent and child. When either child or parent dominates the way we behave toward others—what Berne called our *social transactions*—our behavior is maladaptive.

The child and parent express themselves by means of "games," repetitive behavior with hidden meanings. For example, "kick me" is a "game" played by the child that asks for the very rejection that is feared.

Although TA can be an individual therapy, it more often is carried on in groups. In TA groups, the members interact and confront one another, and the leader explains and interprets the "games" they are playing. Often TA is combined with other techniques, especially role-playing and psychodrama. The therapist, whose background may range from advanced training in psychiatry or psychology to a few months' training in TA alone, is very active, as are all the group members. Everyone is encouraged to clarify points, intervene to discuss a member's behavior, confront a passive member, point out contradictions, and so forth. If you are specifically interested in TA, you may obtain the names of practitioners in your area from the International Transactional Analysis Association (see Appendix A).

ENCOUNTER GROUPS AND MARATHONS

The basic purpose of encounter group therapy is to overcome emotional alienation and isolation by means of intimate encounters with others. Also called *T-groups* (for training groups, referring to training mental health professionals in methods of group therapy), and *sensitivity groups*, they tend to be intensive in nature and short in duration. The first important encounter group was formed in the 1960s at Esalen Institute in Big Sur, California. It consisted of ten to fifteen persons who met in several sessions over a short period, ranging from several days to several weeks. One encounter form is the marathon, consisting of a single long session that extends over a day or a weekend, in which both verbal and nonverbal contact (confrontation, hugging, massage), as well as various structured exercises, are used. Honest and open communication is stressed. Participants are encouraged to pay close attention to their feelings and to their bodies, and to obey such rules as "Fight when it feels right," "Take off your clothes if it feels useful," and "If possible express yourself physically rather than verbally."

Many mental health professionals schooled in more traditional methods regard encounter groups as expensive hoaxes, useless for permanent accomplishment of any kind and potentially harmful to individuals in need of effective treatment for mental disorders. One element common to nearly all such groups is direct confrontation. For example, a group member who makes a statement such as "I'm really nervous when I'm with someone who's bigger than I am" may be asked to repeat that statement individually to every person in the group. This tactic can be very threatening to some individuals.

Another frequent criticism is that such groups tend to be run by persons with little or virtually no training in mental health. The same criticism applies to another kind of group therapy—that of the peer *self-help groups* described in Chapter 14—but in this case the members all have had experience with the same problem (alcoholism, drug addiction, recovery from mental illness, or whatever) and consequently are less likely to cause serious harm.

ECLECTIC THERAPY

We have described the most important modes of psychotherapy currently being practiced, and even these represent just a fraction of the total (there may be as many as four hundred and fifty different methods and schools in the United States alone).

In actual fact, most are variations of a handful of major approaches. *Psychodynamic* therapies build on Freud's insights into emotional conflict and tend to lean heavily on the interaction between therapist and patient. *Cognitive* therapy aims to correct distortions in thinking associated with emotional problems. *Behavior* therapy concentrates on unwanted behavior itself rather than underlying, deep-seated causes of such behavior. Cognitive and behavioral techniques often are used in combination. *Systems* therapies focus on relationships of the entire family in treating one of its members.

Some therapies, as has been indicated, are more suitable for certain disorders than others, and some should never be undertaken by certain individuals. Nevertheless, it would be difficult to choose a therapist by orientation or method alone. However, we are *not* suggesting you should do so (see the section on how to choose a therapist, Chapter 12); rather, method should be just one factor in your choice. Further, one recent survey of 710 therapists indicates that 53 percent consider themselves *eclectic*, which means they draw on the theories and techniques of a variety of schools and try to adapt them to the unique needs of each client.

Here is a profile of one therapist who describes herself as eclectic. Dr. P. holds a master's degree in counseling and a doctor of education degree (Ed.D.) in psychology. She began her career as a high school teacher, found herself spending an increasing amount of time counseling students, and returned to school to obtain advanced training. She has been in private practice for six years, and performs individual, couples, family, and group therapy. As a clinical psychologist, she cannot prescribe medication, so she uses a psychiatrist she knows well as a backup. However, she prefers to avoid the use of medication on a long-term basis. The clients she sees, on the average of once a week each, have disorders ranging from alcoholism to depression, personality disorders, and various neuroses. She usually refers persons with active schizophrenia and other psychotic conditions to other clinicians.

Dr. P's formal training was principally in client-centered therapy (see Chapter 16), but in her practice she takes a much more active role than the traditional nondirective therapist. She draws on analytic insight therapy, using dream interpretation and guided fantasy,* and in group therapy she frequently uses psychodrama (see above). A strong believer in "the whole person," she advises her clients on diet, exercise, and recreation, maintaining that a healthy body makes for a healthy mind. The average term of treatment with Dr. P. is one year. Clients do not enter into a formal treatment contract with her but she emphasizes frequent reevaluation of the direction of treatment.

There still is considerable variation among eclectic therapists. Some

---

* Guided fantasy is a technique in which the therapist describes some imaginary situation to the client—"You are entering a large room full of strangers," for example—and asks the client to enlarge on this theme, in as much detail as possible. Originally used by Freud, this method to foster insight is now employed by therapists from various schools, including behavior therapists.

combine elements from just two schools of therapy. Others take elements from numerous kinds, or any in which they have had some experience and training. Attempts have been made to establish a more integrated approach, and to adapt those elements of any therapy that best meet the specific needs of each client.

Eclectic therapy thus would seem to have advantages in that it can draw on any or all schools of thought. In practice, however, many therapists today who say they belong to one school or another would freely admit their debts to other theories and methods. Moreover, the experienced therapist of any persuasion tends to recognize her limitations and, if honest, will admit that not every client will be helped.

The very multiplicity of theories and therapies indicates at least two important realities. First, the state of understanding of mental illness—indeed, of mental activities in general—is still too primitive to enable anyone to say that any one of the theories of personality now in existence is correct. Human personality is so complex that no simple theory can be formulated for any but its most gross aspects, and some theories are inadequate even in that respect. Second, for a psychotherapy to become popular, it must help some people. The element that seems common to psychotherapies (and also to treatment by faith healers and witch doctors) is that of a reliable, authoritative person who is presumed to understand the mysteries of the illness and whom the troubled person trusts for help.

Which mode of psychotherapy is right for you? As the Russian playwright Anton Chekhov said, "Where there are many remedies, the disease is incurable." That is partly true of psychotherapy, in that a person is seldom "cured" of his illness. But many people *are* helped (one large study says 75 percent of clients, no matter what the school of therapy). In Chapter 22 we discuss how you can tell if psychotherapy and other forms of treatment are helping you, or your relative or friend.

Chapter

18

GIVING HELP—TREATMENT
WITH PSYCHOACTIVE DRUGS

THE SOMATIC or organic therapies treat a person's body in order to bring about changes in emotions and behavior. They include inducing seizures by means of chemicals or electricity; changing the body chemistry through diet, drugs, or other chemicals, or exposure to light; and brain surgery. The most widespread somatic therapy used today is the administration of psychoactive drugs.

WHAT ARE PSYCHOACTIVE DRUGS?

The use of drugs to alter mental states was common among ancient and primitive peoples, who discovered various natural substances that would induce hallucinations. The modern clinical use of drugs to alter mood and behavior began about 1950 and revolutionized the treatment of mental illness. For the first time, violent patients could be

COMMONLY USED PSYCHOACTIVE DRUGS

	Generic Name	Brand Name
Antianxiety drugs (minor tranquilizers or anxiolytics)		
	alprazolam	Xanax
	chlordiazepoxide	Librium
	clorazepate	Azene, Tranxene
benzodiazepines	diazepam	Valium
	lorazepam	Ativan
	oxazepam	Serax
	prazepam	Centrax, Verstran
antihistamines	hydroxyzine	Atarax, Vistaril
beta adrenergic blocker	propranolol	Inderal
other	buspirone	Buspar
Sleeping medications		
benzodiazepines	flurazepam	Dalmane
	temazepam	Restoril
	triazolam	Halcion
antihistamines	diphenhydramine	Benadryl
	hydroxyzine	Atarax, Vistaril
Antidepressant drugs (mood elevators)		
	amitriptyline	Elavil, Endep
	clomipramine	Anafranil†
	desipramine	Norpramin, Pertofrane
tricyclics	doxepin	Sinequan, Adapin
	imipramine	Tofranil, Imavan
	nortriptyline	Pamelor, Aventyl
	protriptyline	Vivactil
tetracylics	maprotiline	Ludiomil
serotonin re-uptake inhibitors	fluoxetine	Prozac
	trazodone	Desyrel
monoamine oxidase inhibitors (MAOI)	phenelzine	Nardil
	tranylcypromine	Parnate
other	buproprion	Wellbutrin
Antimanic drugs (mood stabilizers)	lithium carbonate	Eskalith, Lithane

COMMONLY USED PSYCHOACTIVE DRUGS (continued)

	Generic Name	Brand Name
anticonvulsants	carbamazepine phenytoin valproic acid	Tegretol Dilantin Depakene
Antipsychotic drugs (neuroleptics)		
phenothiazines	chlorpromazine fluphenazine perphenazine thioridazine trifluoperazine	Thorazine *Prolixin, Permitil Trilafon Mellaril Stelazine
thioxanthenes	chlorprothixene thiothixene	Taractan Navane
butyrophenones	haloperidol	*Haldol
others	clozapine loxapine molindone	Clozaril Loxitane Moban
Anti-obsessive-compulsive drugs		
serotonin re-uptake inhibitors	clomipramine fluoxetine fluvoxamine	Anafranil† Prozac Faverin†

* Available as long-lasting injection.
† Awaiting FDA approval, expected by 1991.

reliably controlled instead of having to be locked up or put in physical restraints like straitjackets. First tested on a large scale in 1954, the antipsychotic drugs made it possible to reduce the hospital population in some areas by as much as 75 percent. It is impossible to estimate how many suicides have been prevented by antidepressant drugs, or how many manic-depressive individuals have been able to lead useful lives since their mania has been controlled by lithium carbonate.

Like most powerful chemical agents, psychoactive (also called *psychotropic*) drugs are a mixed blessing. Some are addictive, causing a person to become physically and/or psychologically dependent on them. Some have side effects serious enough to make them either a treatment of last resort or quite unusable in certain individuals. Some are widely prescribed by numerous kinds of practitioner—family physicians, internists, gynecologists—to patients for whom they are of little or no benefit. Their use then can represent a form of drug *abuse*. In an emergency the wrong drug can cause considerable harm; for example, an antipsychotic drug given to a person delirious because of drug withdrawal can dangerously lower the blood pressure. Different individuals react differently to psychoactive drugs, so the proper dosage can be difficult to determine. Furthermore, practically every reputable clinician encounters some individuals who are "hooked" on one or more drugs that are not helping them at all, and that may be hindering other more appropriate treatment.

Perhaps the most serious problem of all is that after decades of using them, no one knows for sure exactly how or why psychoactive drugs work, or if they will be effective in any particular patient. For example, antidepressants are ineffective in an estimated one out of five cases, and they always take several weeks to take effect. Nevertheless, despite these drawbacks, the psychoactive drugs are undeniably valuable in treating not just the most severe mental illnesses but also some less serious but distressing disorders, lending support to the theory that all mental disorders—minor as well as major—are basically due to biochemical derangements of the brain. As with any treatment, the risks must be weighed against the benefits. More often than not, the benefits of these drugs do outweigh the risks if they are administered under competent medical supervision, and for serious mental illness—schizophrenia, major depression, and manic-depressive psychosis—they are the principal means of controlling symptoms.

What should you do if a physician suggests a psychoactive drug for you, your husband, or your friend? As indicated earlier, it is vital to have a medical checkup before undergoing any physical or chemical treatment. Further, be sure the mental health practitioner knows your medical history, particularly with regard to allergies and adverse drug reactions. If you regularly take other medications of any kind—whether they are over-the-counter remedies or prescription drugs—be sure the prescribing physician knows about them, lest they be compounds that can interfere with the new drug's action or that the new drug will interact with them. Finally, be sure to ask about possible side effects, restrictions on your activities or diet while taking the drug, and, if you are a woman of childbearing age, the effect of the drug on pregnancy and breast-feeding. Also ask how long a drug's influence persists; in some cases it may not be flushed out of the body for a week or more after it has been discontinued.

There are four main classifications of psychoactive drugs, based on their major uses: antianxiety drugs (minor tranquilizers, anxiolytics); antidepressant drugs (mood elevators); antimanic (mood-stabilizing) drugs; and antipsychotic drugs (major tranquilizers, neuroleptics).

ANTIANXIETY DRUGS (TRANQUILIZERS)

The principal antianxiety drugs, also called *minor tranquilizers* or *anxiolytics*, are the benzodiazepines, which include alprazolam (Xanax), chlordiazepoxide (Librium), and diazepam (Valium). Although these compounds were discovered in 1933, it was only in 1960 that one of them, chlordiazepoxide, was found to have a calming effect on wild animals, and thereafter began to be used in human patients.

The antianxiety drugs have four principal effects: They sedate, they combat anxiety, they relax muscles, and they act against convulsions.

The benzodiazepines are long-acting drugs, remaining in the system long after they are taken. The individual drugs vary in how fast they are eliminated from the body, some taking as little as five to ten hours and others thirty-six to two hundred hours (for half to be eliminated). Since these drugs can make one drowsy and lethargic, anyone taking them should be cautious about driving, operating machinery, or undertaking other activities requiring alertness and good coordination. Also, these drugs enhance the effects of alcohol, so that even a small amount of liquor can be intoxicating. Therefore, alcohol and other depressants should not be taken while on these drugs and for several days after they are discontinued.

The benzodiazepines frequently are prescribed by doctors other than psychiatrists. In fact, alprazolam (Xanax) currently is the fourth most frequently prescribed of all drugs in the United States. To some extent these drugs are addictive. Abrupt withdrawal from any of them has been known to cause seizures, an effect that is avoided if the dosage of the drug is reduced gradually. They also can cause depression or deepen an already existing depression.

Another drug, meprobamate (Equanil, Miltown), developed in 1954, was formerly widely used against anxiety. However, its principal effect is sedative (calming) and hypnotic (combating sleeplessness due to anxiety and tension). Its side effects are similar to those of the benzodiazepines, and if it is used over a long period it can be addictive.

SIDE EFFECTS OF BENZODIAZEPINES

Warning signs of overdose: call for emergency help

Mental confusion
Severe drowsiness
Severe weakness
Slurred speech
Staggering

Serious side effects to report to physician promptly

Continuing mouth ulcers or sores
Mental confusion or depression
Hallucinations
Skin rash or itching
Sore throat and fever
Unusual excitement, nervousness, irritability, insomnia

The *barbiturates* have been used as sedatives and sleep inducers since 1912. Today the mildest of them, *phenobarbital,* is sometimes still used to provide daytime sedation or to control epileptic seizures. Some of the stronger ones—amobarbital, secobarbital, pentobarbital—are occasionally used as antianxiety drugs. For this use, however, they are less effective and have more side effects than the benzodiazepines, several of which are better suited for this purpose (see sleeping medications in the table for psychoactive drugs). Also, they are addictive.

A newer antianxiety drug approved in the mid-1980s is buspirone (Buspar), which has less of a sedative effect than the benzodiazepines and also does not interact with alcohol as they do. Some side effects (dizziness, nausea, headache, nervousness) have been reported among a small percentage of patients. There also appear to be none of the withdrawal symptoms associated with benzodiazepines when buspirone is discontinued. More specifically targeting anxiety symptoms, buspirone does not have the muscle-relaxant or anticonvulsant effects provided by other tranquilizers. Also, it is quite slow to take effect, requiring a week to ten days to produce signs of improvement and three to four weeks to reach a peak effect. Currently it is considered useful mainly for long-term anxiety and to treat anxiety in patients who cannot tolerate the benzodiazepines.

Other antianxiety drugs include one of the antihistamine (antiallergy) drugs, hydroxyzine (Atarax, Vistaril), and propranolol (Inderal), a drug useful against hypertension (high blood pressure) and certain heart conditions but which is associated with numerous side effects (fatigue, dizziness, insomnia, hallucinations, and, especially, depression).

ANTIDEPRESSANTS

There are two main kinds of antidepressant, tricyclic antidepressants and monoamine oxidase inhibitors. In addition, newer medications are being developed, and some older central nervous system stimulants are occasionally still used against depression.

The tricyclic antidepressants were discovered in 1958 by a Swiss psychiatrist, Ronald Kuhn, who was looking for a compound effective against schizophrenia. Instead he found one that relieves depression; from it imipramine (Tofranil) and related drugs were developed. Antidepressants appear to work by enhancing the action of a group of neurotransmitters called the trigger amines (epinephrine, norepinephrine, serotonin), which are believed to be central in regulating moods. The tricyclics, so called because of their three-ring chemical structure, modulate their effects, especially that of norepinephrine (see Chapter 27 for more about neurotransmitters).

The benefits of antidepressants often are not felt for two to five weeks after beginning treatment. They help an estimated 40 to 70 percent of patients substantially. However, they do not work in every case, and even when they are effective their side effects sometimes are severe and hazardous enough to make it necessary to discontinue them. They can cause such unpleasant symptoms as dry mouth, drowsiness, blurred vision, sweating, dizziness when standing up, rapid pulse, tremor, urinary hesitation, and constipation—all of which often disappear after a few weeks' use or when the dosage is lowered.

They also can give rise to more serious symptoms, such as low blood pressure, cardiac arrhythmias (irregular heartbeat), and seizures in epileptic patients. Sometimes switching to a different compound helps. Nevertheless, they must be used with extreme caution by persons with glaucoma, epilepsy, prostate gland enlargement, asthma, kidney disease, liver disease, or heart disease. For this reason some doctors recommend taking a baseline electrocardiogram and checking blood pressure before beginning the drug, especially in elderly patients. Long-term use of the tricyclics may cause a craving for sweets and a consequent weight gain. A large overdose (ten to thirty times the normal daily dose) is lethal, so depressed patients usually are given only small amounts at a time.

Tricyclics will add to the effects of alcohol and sleeping pills, and stomach problems may occur if alcoholic beverages are consumed while taking them. They also may cause drowsiness and may inhibit alertness, so reactions to them should be considered before driving a car, using machinery, or doing other tasks that require alertness for safety.

Tricyclics are not addictive but they should be discontinued gradually to avoid agitation, nightmares, and insomnia. Once the symptoms of depression subside, a daily maintenance dose—the minimum needed for a response—may be continued for three months, after which the dose can be gradually reduced. If symptoms do not recur, the drug can then be stopped. If they do recur or a serious depression recurs within two or three years, long-term maintenance may be considered. Many patients take tricyclics continuously for ten or more years without ill effects. Tricyclics may be used in combination with an antianxiety drug. In recent years some of them have been found effective for obsessive-compulsive disorder as well.

TRICYCLIC ANTIDEPRESSANTS

Serious side effects to report promptly to physician

Blurred vision or eye pain
Confusion
Fainting
Hallucinations
Irregular heartbeat
Problems urinating
Seizures
Shakiness
Skin rash and itching
Sore throat and fever

The second main category of antidepressant are the *monoamine oxidase inhibitors (MAOIs)*, which work by increasing the concentration of available neurotransmitters (by preventing their metabolism by the enzyme monoamine oxidase). Soon after these drugs were introduced, it was discovered that they cause some individuals to develop severe hypertensive reactions and cerebral vascular accident (stroke). Further, since the newly developed tricyclics seemed to work very well for many depressed persons, the MAOIs were for a time abandoned. Then it was discovered that patients taking MAOIs who avoid foods high in tyramine—a chemical compound present in many foods but particularly concentrated in red wine, aged cheeses, pickled herring, and other fermented foods—are less likely to have an adverse reaction. Tyramine, it appeared, causes too great a release of the neurotransmitter norepinephrine, which in turn can cause not only hypertension but severe headache and cardiac arrhythmias. A similar response can be triggered by substances present in many over-the-counter cold and hay fever remedies (nose drops, sprays, antihistamine preparations), as well as some local anesthetics, which therefore also must be avoided.

Monoamine oxidase inhibitors should not be taken by persons with a history of liver disease, congestive heart failure, or a previous blood clot or hemorrhage in the brain, or persons with adrenal disorders or epilepsy. Anyone considering the use of an MAOI should first provide the physician prescribing it with a complete list of prescription and over-the-counter drugs that are already being taken or might be taken, lest some of these react adversely with it.

Side effects of the MAOIs include dizziness, insomnia, and impotence. Despite these and the potential hazards, MAOIs may be extremely useful in cases of severe depression that, unlike the typical major depression, are accompanied by anxiety attacks, phobias (especially agoraphobia), oversleeping, overeating, irritability, and other atypical symptoms. Usually, however, practitioners prefer to give tricyclic antidepressants an extensive trial before they prescribe MAOIs.

IF YOU TAKE AN MAOI FOR DEPRESSION

You must avoid

Aged cheeses or cheese products
Aged, pickled, or dried meat or fish, especially herring
Pods of broad beans (fava beans, etc.)
Yeast extract or tablets
Red wine*
Nasal decongestants in the form of nose drops, cough drops or cold remedies†
Diet pills of any kind
Any other medications unless your physician approves them specifically

* Occasional single cocktail, two to three ounces white wine or one or two bottles of beer are permitted.

† Permitted cold remedies: aspirin, acetaminophen (Tylenol), guaifenesin (Robitussin cough syrup), cepylpyridinium (Cepacol gargle).

The newer antidepressants, introduced in the past twenty years, differ from the tricyclics in chemical structure and sometimes also in how they affect brain activity. Among them are maprotiline (Ludiomil), a tetracyclic—that is, it has a four-ring chemical structure—and trazodone (Desyrel) and fluoxetine (Prozac), which primarily affect the neurotransmitter serotonin. These drugs work against depression about as well as the tricyclics but have different side effects. Maprotiline causes dizziness upon getting up and seizures; fluoxetine causes weight loss (instead of weight gain) but may also produce agitation and nausea. Trazodone has been known to cause priapism (persistent and often painful penile erection). Fluoxetine has been found effective against obsessive-compulsive disorder as well as depression, but allegedly it occasionally contributes to aggressive and even suicidal tendencies.

Another class of drugs used against depression are psychostimulants (central nervous system stimulants) such as dextroamphetamine (Dexedrine). They work by stimulating the release of neurotransmitters that in turn are activated by the release of norepinephrine. After a time, however, they can deplete norepinephrine and cause either depression or a psychotic episode similar to schizophrenia. They also are addictive and subject to abuse. However, they sometimes are used for a short time in the early stages of treatment (until the tricyclic being prescribed has time to take effect). They also sometimes are used for older patients or those with a physical illness who cannot tolerate the tricyclics.

ANTIMANIC DRUGS

The principal antimanic drug in use is lithium carbonate, a compound that was first used against mania in 1949 in Australia by Dr. John J. Cade and began to be commercially produced in the United States in 1970. Until then the same antipsychotic drugs (see below) were used for both schizophrenia and manic-depressive psychosis. Lithium, however, proved more useful as a maintenance drug, that is, one given over a long period of time after the manic episode had ended, because it appears to prevent subsequent mania and also prevents depressive episodes. Since lithium takes five to ten days to take effect, initially an antipsychotic drug may be used along with it to control mania. Long-term use of lithium can cause enlargement of the thyroid gland (goiter), which, however, returns to normal size when the drug is stopped.

The administration of lithium requires periodic monitoring of its concentration in the blood to keep it at safe and effective levels in the body. Minor side effects of the drug are stomach upsets (mild nausea, diarrhea), increased thirst, muscular weakness, fatigue and a dazed feeling, and fine tremors of the hands or mouth; all these usually subside as the dosage is adjusted. Possible long-term side effects include weight gain, hand tremors, severe thirst, and frequent urination. Toxic levels of the drug are marked by sluggishness, drowsiness, slurred speech, a coarse tremor, muscular twitching, vomiting, and severe diarrhea. These must be reported promptly since they can lead to seizures, coma, and even death.

Despite its possible dangers, lithium succeeds in controlling an estimated 70 percent of cases of manic-depressive psychosis. It also helps many schizophrenics, sometimes working when antipsychotic drugs alone do not. Before beginning treatment, a physical examination should be made that includes laboratory studies of electrolytes and blood urea nitrogen, a urinalysis, and an electrocardiogram; some physicians advise repeating these tests every six months while the drug is being used.

Stopping lithium suddenly can be risky, causing irritability, anxiety, insomnia, or even a psychosis. It is believed that most patients who stop taking lithium will resume experiencing manic symptoms, even after many years of maintenance.

Some patients cannot tolerate lithium, or should not take it owing to conditions such as pregnancy (it can harm the fetus) or breast-feeding. Some of the anticonvulsant drugs, used mainly to prevent epileptic seizures, can be an effective treatment for mania. Some authorities believe they work especially well for patients who experience extremely rapid mood swings. They include carbamazepine (Tegretol), phenytoin (Dilantin), and valproic acid (Depakene).

They, too, are not free from side effects. Carbamazepine may cause drowsiness, double vision, dizziness, nausea, and vomiting when the drug is begun. More serious side effects are depletion of white blood cells, aplastic anemia, hepatitis, and heart problems.

ANTIPSYCHOTIC DRUGS

The antipsychotic drugs, or *major tranquilizers*, are used to treat serious psychiatric disorders, principally schizophrenia, acute mania, and acute confusional states. They produce a state of emotional quiet and indifference, technically called *neurolepsy*, and are therefore also called *neuroleptics*.

The various antipsychotic drugs differ in potency, effectiveness, and side effects. All of them act by blocking the effects of the neurotransmitter dopamine, which, it is believed, is how they inhibit psychotic symptoms. The more they block dopamine, the more effective they are. The most common side effects are dry mouth, constipation, blurred vision, and drowsiness, all of which tend to diminish or disappear after a few weeks of use. Some persons also experience a dystonic reaction, a stiffening of muscles on one side of the neck and jaw; this can be reversed almost immediately by administering a minor tranquilizer or anticholinergic drug—trihexyphenidyl (Artane), benztropine (Cogentin), or another—of the type used to control the symptoms of parkinsonism. More serious common side effects are restlessness, stiffness and diminished spontaneity, slurred speech, and tremors of the hands and feet. These symptoms are sometimes helped by giving another medication along with the antipsychotic or by switching to a different compound. Oversensitivity to sunlight, fainting on arising suddenly, and weight gain also may occur.

Another serious side effect seen in persons who take these drugs in high doses over a period of several years (as chronic schizophrenia patients sometimes do) is tardive dyskinesia, a syndrome of uncontrolled repetitive movements of the tongue, mouth, jaws (grimacing or chewing movements, for example), and sometimes of the limbs. The older the patient, the greater the susceptibility to this condition. It appears to be permanent—symptoms do not go away when the drug is discontinued—and while no complete cure has yet been found, it sometimes can be countered by using anticholinergic drugs of the kind used against parkinsonism, which has very similar symptoms. These drugs, however, have side effects of their own and therefore cannot be used routinely. Most authorities believe it preferable to lower the dosage of the antipsychotic drug or change to a drug with less pronounced side effects. Some authorities feel that anticholinergic drugs should be used only during the first three to five months on maintenance antipsychotic medication.

The anticholinergics are so called because they mostly produce their effects by blocking the neurotransmitter acetylcholine. Side effects include drowsiness, dizziness, blurred vision, weakness, loss of muscular coordination, nausea and vomiting, constipation, numbness of fingers, dry eyes, dry mouth, and decreased digestive activity. Digestive complaints must be reported promptly to a physician, lest they develop into life-threatening paralytic ileus (nonfunctioning of the intestine).

The principal antipsychotic drugs in current use are the phenothiazines, which include chlorpromazine (Thorazine), thioridazine (Mellaril), and trifluoperazine (Stelazine), the thioxanthenes, and the butyrophenones, including haloperidol (Haldol). The most recently developed of them is clozapine (Clozaril), approved in 1989, but for use only after other therapies have failed (because of potential life-threatening side effects).

The antipsychotics work mainly by blocking the receptors of the neurotransmitter dopamine, and some also block the action of another neurotransmitter, serotonin. They usually relieve such distressing symptoms as thought disturbances, delusions, hallucinations, and agitation. Some individuals require a daily maintenance dose for many months or even years; without it they relapse and need to be rehospitalized. Others seem to be able to stop the drug after a year or two without relapse. In most cases, those schizophrenics who respond to antipsychotics immediately do better in the long run.

Antipsychotics are given in tablet or liquid form, or are injected into a muscle. They usually may be taken once a day, but fluphenazine (Prolixin) and haloperidol (Haldol) are also available in a long-acting form that can be injected every one to four weeks. The initial effects usually are felt within forty-eight hours.

About 70 percent of patients with schizophrenia are helped by these drugs, about 25 percent improve slightly or not at all, and 5 percent get worse. The results with long-acting injections, which ensure that the drug is really being taken, appear to be even better in preventing relapse. (Schizophrenics often stop taking their prescribed medication, either because they dislike the side effects or because they are so much improved that they believe they no longer need it.) If one type of drug does not work, another of the major types might be tried. When one drug does work, it will probably be effective again in

BEHAVIORAL SIDE EFFECTS OF PSYCHOACTIVE DRUGS

Side Effect	Description	Possible Misdiagnosis	Drug(s) Responsible
Aggressiveness	Increased assaultiveness, combativeness, hostility	Behavior disorder	Benzodiazepines (minor tranquilizers)
Akathisia	Involuntary motor restlessness, e.g., constant pacing	Increase in severity of illness	Antipsychotics
Akinesia	Muscle weakness, lack of expression		Antipsychotics
Carbohydrate craving	Increased appetite, especially for sweets	Depression	Tricyclic antidepressants
Dystonic reaction	Sudden onset of tonic muscle spasms affecting any body part	Conversion reaction	Antipsychotics
Impaired sexual function	Inability to achieve/maintain erection; inability to achieve orgasm	Psychogenic impotence	Antipsychotics, tricyclics, MAOIs
Incontinence	Bedwetting, spontaneous urination during day	Behavioral regression	Benzodiazepines, antipsychotics, MAOIs, lithium
Mania	Increased energy, overconfidence, buying sprees, euphoria and/or irritability, pressured speech, decreased need for sleep	Hyperactivity, behavioral disorder	Tricyclics, MAOIs
Tardive dyskinesia	Involuntary movements of muscles of lips, tongue, jaw, and upper body parts	Stereotypes, other mannerisms	Antipsychotics (long-term use)

WARNING SIGNALS OF RELAPSE (SCHIZOPHRENIA)

Sleep difficulties
Irritability
Restlessness
Less or more talkative
Changes in usual behavior
Poor concentration

a relapse, so it is important to keep records of what drugs have been used and their results.

There are two basic methods for determining the proper dosage for effectiveness, which varies considerably among individuals. One approach is to begin with a low dose and increase it very gradually, until the symptoms are under control. The other approach, called "loading," is to begin with a high dose in order to control psychotic symptoms quickly and then decrease dosage gradually until the minimum needed to control the symptoms is found. This method is somewhat chancier and is used only when the risk of the illness is greater than the risk of serious side effects.

DRUGS THAT INTERACT WITH ALCOHOL

Antialcohol preparations (Antabuse)
Use of alcohol with this medication results in nausea, vomiting, headache, high blood pressure, and possible erratic heartbeat; it can result in death.
Antidepressants (Elavil, Tofranil, etc.)
Alcohol may cause an additional reduction in central nervous system functioning and lessen a person's ability to operate normally. The combination of alcohol and the MAO inhibitors can cause a high blood pressure crisis, potentially life-threatening.
Antipsychotics (Mellaril, Thorazine, etc.)
Alcohol may cause additional depression of central nervous system function that can result in severe impairment of voluntary movements (walking, using one's hands, etc.). The combination can also cause a loss of effective breathing function and can therefore be fatal.
Sedative hypnotics (Nembutal, etc.)
Alcohol further reduces central nervous system function, sometimes to the point of the loss of effective breathing (respiratory arrest) or consciousness (coma). This combination can be fatal.
Antianxiety drugs (minor tranquilizers; Valium, Librium, etc.)
Alcohol will cause reduced central nervous system function, especially during the first few weeks of drug use. The result is decreased alertness and judgment that can lead to household, automotive, and industrial accidents.

PSYCHOACTIVE DRUGS AND THE ELDERLY

According to an article in the *New York Times*,* Dr. Mary S. Calderone, a highly respected and sophisticated physician, suffered two
and one-half years of debilitating and often humiliating misery, including extreme sleepiness, loss of balance, memory problems, weakness, difficulty concentrating, depression, malaise, and lassitude.
Many would regard these symptoms as normal for a woman in her
eighties and none of the practitioners she consulted could find a
reason for them. Nevertheless, Dr. Calderone took matters into her
own hands and decided to stop taking—one by one—the drugs, both
prescription and over-the-counter, that she had been using regularly.
Within forty-eight hours of discontinuing one of them, she began to
feel normal again. That drug was amitriptyline (Elavil), a tricyclic
antidepressant prescribed in a small nightly dose years earlier to help
her sleep.

The doctor's story is much like that of hundreds of thousands of
older people who suffer adverse reactions to common drugs. Some
studies show that 10 to 15 percent of hospitalizations among the
elderly are due to drug reactions. Moreover, once they are hospitalized
or admitted to a nursing home, the elderly are given more and more
medication to control symptoms that may have been drug-induced in
the first place.

There are several reasons for this problem. First, the majority of
elderly persons have at least one chronic health problem and most
have several that require medication. Consequently they are far more
susceptible to adverse reactions from the *interactions* of medications
they are taking. Sometimes one drug will cancel out the benefits of
another, sometimes it will enhance the action of another, and sometimes a drug for one condition will adversely affect another health
problem.

Second, with age the body's ability to metabolize and excrete drugs
declines as the efficiency of the liver and kidneys lessens. The result
can be a harmful *buildup* of a drug that is being taken in normal doses.
Also, body composition changes with age, which affects the way
drugs are distributed in the body. With less muscle and more fat

---

* In the Personal Health column by Jane E. Brody, *New York Times*, November 10, 1988.

tissue, water-soluble drugs may become more concentrated in the bloodstream, and fat-soluble drugs may accumulate. The brain and other organs also grow more sensitive, leading to oversedation or unstable blood pressure and dizziness from what would be normal doses for a younger person.

Finally, some drugs are not appropriate for the elderly. For example, diphenhydramine (Benadryl), an antihistamine, is often used as a mild sedative, and it is the active agent in several over-the-counter sleeping medications (Sominex, Nytol). But this drug is not appropriate for the elderly because of its strong anticholinergic effects, which often cause dry mouth, constipation, problems with urination, drop in blood pressure, sedation, mental confusion, and impaired mental function.

Does this mean that the elderly cannot use psychoactive drugs? Not at all. Mentally ill elderly persons can benefit from the same medications that help younger patients. However, they are more likely to have adverse drug reactions, and so the dosage and monitoring of prescriptions must be more constant and more cautious.

The testing of drugs, resulting in recommended dosages, is often done on young people, who may tolerate larger doses or even have radically different responses from those of the elderly. Also, many elderly patients add to the problem by not following prescription instructions precisely, either forgetting to take a drug or taking it more often than they should. All these issues point to the need for greater care, on the part of the prescribing physician, the patient, and concerned relatives or other patient representatives.

DRUGS FOR ATTENTION DEFICIT HYPERACTIVITY DISORDER (ADHD)

Three kinds of central nervous system stimulant—the amphetamines (Dexedrine, Benzedrine, etc.), methylphenidate (Ritalin), and pemoline (Cylert)—have been used to control hyperactivity in children. Although in adults they act as stimulants, in children they tend to have a calming effect, enabling them to sit still longer and concentrate better. It is not known why the drugs work in this way, and they do not work for all children. About 10 to 30 percent do not improve. Their effectiveness should be carefully monitored by parents and teachers, and examination by a physician at frequent intervals also is important in order to assess the effects of the treatment and to make sure there are no serious side effects. The most common side effects are sleep difficulty (insomnia), loss of appetite, weight loss, and rapid heartbeat—similar to the side effects of these stimulants in adults. They also may slightly retard body growth. These effects usually can be eliminated by reducing the dosage or discontinuing the drug.

Although amphetamines and methylphenidate can be addictive, when these drugs are properly monitored youngsters have not been found to become dependent or abusers. Pemoline is nonaddictive and need be given only once a day but it also is less effective and takes two to eight weeks for its effect to become apparent.

Some patients with ADHD respond to tricyclic antidepressants. In a test of desipramine (Norpramin) 68 percent of adolescents with ADHD showed improvement. The main side effect is sleepiness.

ANTIALCOHOLISM DRUGS

The drug disulfiram (Antabuse) is a very potent agent that, when taken alone, is innocuous. But when it is taken in combination with alcohol, it produces a painful and frightening reaction that includes nausea and vomiting, drop in blood pressure, rapid and irregular heartbeat, and severe headache. Drinking any alcoholic beverage within twelve hours of taking the drug will cause this reaction. The intensity and duration of the reaction vary, depending on the amounts of the drug and alcohol in the system, but one to three hours is typical. It is extremely unpleasant and can be life-threatening if the doses involved are very large.

Disulfiram must be taken on a daily basis in order to ensure a reaction. At first it may cause drowsiness, fatigue, headache, skin rash, and other reactions, but these usually disappear within a week or two. A person considering the use of disulfiram should be carefully checked by a physician; it should not be used (or only with extreme caution) by persons suffering from disorders that predispose them to cardiovascular complications (particularly diabetes and liver, kidney, or thyroid disorders), and it should be avoided entirely during pregnancy. Disulfiram also enhances the effect of tricyclic antidepressants and can lead to toxic levels of these medications.

Disulfiram is useful for alcoholism in two ways. First, its effects last ten days, so that a person cannot change his mind rapidly and take a drink, but must wait until the drug is out of the system. Further, stopping the drug generally means that he intends to resume drinking. Thus the drug is a useful test of a person's seriousness about giving up alcohol. An alcoholic who really wants to stop is likely to recognize the "crutch" value of the drug in helping to stop drinking and usually is willing to take it. A person who is unsure about stopping usually is unwilling to take it and tends to resume drinking soon.

Alcoholics Anonymous, the largest network of alcoholic self-help groups (see Chapter 14), opposes the use of disulfiram and other drugs on philosophic grounds, maintaining that inner strength alone is effective in keeping a person from drinking.

MEDICATION FOR DRUG ADDICTION

The principal "antidrug" drug is methadone, a synthetic narcotic that has been widely used as a treatment for heroin addiction since the mid-1960s. This drug induces a generalized feeling of contentment rather than heroin's precipitate rush and euphoria. It eases the physical pain of withdrawal from heroin and reduces cravings for it. Methadone is, however, addictive, inducing both psychological and physical dependence on it. Available only through prescription, it is, despite its critics, being made available to addicts through methadone clinics established entirely for that purpose. Although not a cure, it has helped an estimated 20 percent of heroin addicts in the United States by offering a legal alternative to heroin as well as the possibility of a productive life.

Methadone appears to have little effect on addiction to cocaine or "crack," which became a major form of drug abuse in the 1980s. Among drugs being tested and showing some promise in treating such addiction is buprenorphine, a pain reliever that appears to reduce the cravings for both heroin and cocaine (many users are addicted to both). At this writing the anticonvulsant carbamazepine, the parkinsonism drug bromocriptine, and the antidepressants desipramine and imipramine are among the medications being tested for specifically combating addiction to cocaine.

* * *

In summary, although psychoactive drugs still are an imperfect treatment in that it is not known exactly how or why they work, and prescribing them still may proceed on something of a trial-and-error basis, they are the primary treatment for the most serious mental illnesses. Unfortunately many individuals suffering from these disorders do not like to take drugs. They do not like to depend on them, and they may be distressed by their side effects. Yet discontinuing medication nearly always leads to a revival of symptoms, often to the point where a person must (again) be hospitalized.

In the case of less serious disorders, which in time often respond to one or another kind of psychotherapy or counseling, medication may be very useful to control distressing symptoms sufficiently so that psychotherapy has a chance to work. In such cases there often is no need to continue medication for more than a matter of weeks. Here, however, the decision as to whether or not to use drugs is more open to disagreement. Psychiatrists, who are physicians and may write prescriptions, often are more likely to favor medications than psychologists and social workers, who are not physicians. Although it certainly is not true of all individuals, to some extent the answer you get may depend on whom you ask. (See also the section evaluating somatic therapies, including drugs, in Chapter 22.)

Chapter

19

GIVING HELP—
OTHER SOMATIC THERAPIES

LIKE DRUG treatment, most other somatic therapies for mental illness are carried out by physicians, principally psychiatrists and neurosurgeons. The chief exceptions are treatment with vitamins and other nutritional therapy, which, if it does not involve a prescription drug, can be administered by anyone, phototherapy, and acupuncture, described in Chapter 16.

At the risk of being repetitive, we emphasize again that anyone considering medical treatment for mental illness should first have a physical checkup. Further, whoever prescribes treatment for a mental disorder should know the results of this checkup and be acquainted with the person's medical history, especially with respect to allergies, drug reactions, and chronic conditions such as high blood pressure, heart disease, or diabetes. Before you decide to accept any medical treatment for mental illness, ask about the possible side effects of the treatment. Should you avoid certain substances (alcohol, foods, other medications) while undergoing treatment? Will there be any expected side effects or lasting aftereffects?

If, after discussing the treatment with your doctor, you have any doubts about a therapy that is being recommended, by all means get a second opinion, preferably from a physician who has no professional connection with the doctor who prescribed the treatment.

"SHOCK" THERAPY

"Shock" therapy is a method of changing brain activity by chemical or electric means. In the late 1920s a Viennese psychiatrist, Manfred Sakel, observed that an overdose of insulin given to a drug addict appeared to lessen his withdrawal symptoms. Sakel then began to treat schizophrenic patients with insulin, which in large doses produces profound hypoglycemia (low blood sugar) and coma.

Insulin coma therapy (ICT), also called "insulin shock," was introduced at a number of American mental hospitals in the 1930s. Patients first were given large doses of insulin to reduce their blood-sugar level and induce coma; after an hour or so they were revived with large doses of glucose (sugar). Although insulin therapy does appear to benefit schizophrenic patients in particular, it is a fairly elaborate procedure that requires a specially trained staff, and the method has been largely abandoned in the United States, mostly because other chemical therapies work as well or better and are much simpler to administer. However, it is still widely used in some other countries.

In the mid-1930s a Hungarian psychiatrist, Ladislav V. von Meduna, discovered that injections of camphor brought on convulsions, and that many schizophrenic symptoms seemed to disappear after such a convulsion, or seizure.* The results with camphor injections were very uncertain, and often a patient underwent not one but a series of seizures. Another drug, pentylenetetrazol (Metrazol), proved to be more reliable. However, this drug caused the patient to have a terrible sensation of impending death just before onset of the seizure, so its use was strongly resisted by patients.

---

* A *seizure* is a sudden pattern of electrical discharge of a network containing about one hundred thousand brain cells. Exactly where in the brain this discharge occurs and how widely it spreads determines the seizure's clinical manifestation. Uninhibited spread throughout the brain is a *grand mal seizure*; the occurrence of such seizures spontaneously is a disorder called *grand mal epilepsy*.

Convulsions also can be induced by means of inhaling flurothyl vapor, a procedure in which three to four respirations are forced into the lungs by means of an oxygen bag. The effects are similar to those of bilateral electroconvulsive therapy (see below), although with somewhat less memory loss and somewhat more post-treatment confusion. Many patients also develop nausea, vomiting, and dizziness immediately after treatment, and since the method is slightly more cumbersome than electroconvulsive therapy, it is not used as often.

ELECTROCONVULSIVE THERAPY (ECT)

In 1938 two Italian psychiatrists, Ugo Cerletti and Lucio Bini, who were searching for a cure for schizophrenia, used electricity to induce a grand mal seizure in a disturbed patient. The patient's condition improved, and in subsequent years the procedure became a common treatment for a variety of mental disorders, both in Europe and America, particularly since it did not evoke nearly as much resistance from patients as chemically induced seizures. (Interestingly, electrical therapy had been practiced as long ago as the first century, when ancient Roman physicians used the shock of electric eels on patients with severe, intractable headache.)

With the development of psychoactive drugs, the use of electroshock therapy (EST) or electroconvulsive therapy (ECT), as it often is called, declined considerably, and at the same time doubts arose as to its safety and effectiveness. A 1978 survey conducted by the American Psychiatric Association revealed that about one-third of its members had reservations concerning ECT. The treatment continued to be used, although its use declined between 1975 and 1980. Thereafter it began to be used increasingly. It is presently regarded as very helpful for patients with a major depression who either are not helped by or cannot tolerate (because of heart disease or some other physical condition) antidepressant medications. Some practitioners believe its use is overregulated because the law has not kept pace with changes making the procedure safer, and therefore some who might benefit from ECT do not receive it.

Persons undergoing ECT first are injected with a short-acting anesthetic, and then a muscle relaxant to prevent the sudden muscular contractions that, in the early days of ECT, occasionally caused broken bones or chipped teeth. An electrocardiograph (ECG) may be used to monitor heart rhythm, and an electroencephalograph (EEG) to monitor brain waves. Oxygen generally is administered from the time the patient falls asleep until spontaneous breathing resumes. Electrodes are attached to the head, and an electric current is applied for a fraction of a second. The intensity is 5 to 103 joules (1 joule is equivalent to 1 watt-second), or just enough to cause a brain seizure that can be traced on an EEG.

The patient regains consciousness within a few minutes but may continue to be groggy and confused for a time. Normally ECT is given in a series of treatments, usually three a week for two to four weeks. The principal side effect is memory loss. Patients often do not recall either the treatment itself or any events immediately before it; some lose recollection of events during the entire two- or four-week period of treatment. Some also find it difficult to retain newly learned information for a time after treatment.

It has been found that it is the seizures that cause clinical improvement and the amount of current that influences memory loss. Therefore, research has been directed at finding a way to induce a grand mal seizure—one that affects both hemispheres of the brain—with the smallest possible amount of electric current. One way is to apply the stimulating electrodes so as to deliver current to only one side of the brain—the nondominant hemisphere. (It has been known since the times of the ancient Babylonians that the right hemisphere of the brain controls the left side of the body, and the left hemisphere the right side.) For a right-handed person, therefore, the electrodes are placed so as to elicit a seizure on the right side of the brain, which controls the left (nondominant) side of the body. This so-called *unilateral* (one-sided) technique reduces loss of memory (of both past events and newly acquired information) and also reduces the confusion immediately following treatment. It is not definitely known whether it is as effective as bilateral (both sides of the brain) treatment or whether a larger number of treatments is required for the same effect.

How and why ECT works are unknown. Some authorities believe it stimulates the brain cells in certain critical areas to produce neurotransmitters (see Chapter 27) that the brain cells for some reason had been failing to produce. Whatever the mechanism, there is no doubt that ECT will often relieve a major depression in the 20 to 30 percent of patients who do not respond to drug treatment or for whom drugs are considered unsafe. An estimated 90 percent of such patients experience improvement provided that enough ECT treatments (six to eight) are given. One rule of thumb used is that very improvement. If ECT helps after four or so treatments, it is continued. If no relief at all is experienced by then, it usually is stopped.

At first glance, ECT may seem to be an extreme and frightening procedure, and in the past there were some settings in which it was overused. However, it appears to be both safe and effective, and the tendency toward using it inappropriately has been reversed.

What should you do if ECT is recommended for you, your severely depressed relative, or your friend? Unless immediate intervention is essential, as it may be if the person is actively suicidal, more conservative treatment might first be considered. (It should be noted that a determined person may commit suicide despite strong precautions and virtually constant supervision, but once ECT has been begun suicide is extremely rare.) If there is no state of emergency, however, and there is time to use other treatments, antidepressant medication might be tried. If it is decided to use ECT, a medical history should be taken and a complete physical examination performed, including routine blood tests, urinalysis, chest x-ray, and for patients over forty or those with a history of heart disease, an ECG. No individual suspected of having a brain tumor or intracranial bleeding should undergo ECT unless that condition has first been ruled out. Under such conditions ECT can cause serious injury or even death. This, however, is the only physical contraindication to ECT. Also, one should not take anything by mouth for six hours before treatment (the usual precaution when general anesthesia is administered).

It is advisable to find a practitioner who has wide experience with the treatment, and a setting where it is often performed (usually a hospital). ECT frequently is done on an outpatient basis, but if it is, a relative or friend should be available to take the patient home (about one hour after awakening). If this cannot be arranged, patients should remain in a recovery area until they have been examined and cleared for release in their own care by the physician. Relatives should be warned to keep a patient who is confused or has suffered memory loss immediately after a treatment away from normal social contacts until adequate functioning resumes. Further, patients should not try to conduct business or legal affairs until their confusion and amnesia have disappeared.

After a course of ECT, those patients who can tolerate and continue to receive antidepressant medication for a time tend to have fewer relapses. Without such medication, about one-fourth may experience a relapse into profound depression within six months (some studies indicate a smaller percentage, and others a larger one).

Are there any indications for ECT other than a major depression? In manic-depressive psychosis, about 10 to 20 percent of patients in the manic phase do not respond to either lithium or antipsychotics. For such patients, who are in an acute manic phase characterized by overactivity to the point of exhaustion, ECT given twice a day for two or three days may control the overactivity. At that point they may either be given lithium, or ECT may be continued at the normal rate of three times a week until the course of treatment (six to ten treatments) is complete.

In schizophrenia, ECT is occasionally effective with patients who are not responding to antipsychotic drugs, although the rate of success is less than that with either depression or manic-depressive disease. The course of treatment usually is longer—ten to fifteen or more treatments—and is most effective in those cases of acute schizophrenia where the onset has been rapid and recent (during the first six months of the illness) and where the symptoms are either paranoia (persecution delusions) or catatonic excitement. It is used much less for this purpose in America than in Europe.

ECT does *not* work for persons with organic psychoses, neuroses, personality disorders, or senile dementia. It probably should not be used in conjunction with antipsychotic drugs (described in Chapter 18).

ECT is covered by medical/surgical insurance. Those who have no insurance can expect to pay between $100 and $600 for a course of six treatments.

NUTRITIONAL THERAPY

Treatment of mental illness with large doses of food supplements, such as vitamins (*megavitamin therapy*) and trace minerals, has been used since the early 1960s. Large amounts of such vitamins as B_1, B_6, B_{12}, C, and E have been used for patients with schizophrenia, on the theory that most (some say 60 percent or more) schizophrenics have hypoglycemia (low blood sugar). To date this finding has not been verified by reliable independent investigators. Hypoglycemia is said also to appear in hyperactive children, autistic children, and the mentally retarded. (Genuine hypoglycemia is relatively rare. It is caused by the body's inability to metabolize sugar properly and is diagnosed by means of a glucose tolerance test, which should be a six-hour test to ensure accuracy; it is treated with a diet high in protein and low in sugar.)

The name *orthomolecular psychiatry* was coined in 1968 by Nobel Prize-winning chemist Linus Pauling, who defined it as "the provision of the optimum molecular environment for the mind, especially the optimum concentration of substances normally present in the body." By the optimum (best) molecules Pauling means megavitamins (huge doses of the above-named vitamins) as well as protein concentrates and supplements of certain trace minerals, such as zinc. Another idea is that schizophrenics have too much blood histamine, which responds to zinc and manganese supplements.

A related theory is that food allergy plays a role in many mental disorders. Supporters of this notion insist that certain foods must be avoided, particularly cereals (wheat, rye, oats, barley, etc.), sugar, dyes and other food additives, and any particular foods that cause an allergic reaction in the individual being treated. In addition, vitamin and mineral supplements are given. This therapy may be used in conjunction with psychoactive drugs, but in exceedingly low doses. Treatment is said to be required for varying periods, from a few months to a lifetime; the end is determined by withdrawing nutritional supplements after the patient has been free of symptoms for a long period.

Nutritional therapy has had its most fervent support among parents of children with learning disabilities and hyperactive behavior. Their symptoms are said to be reduced or to disappear entirely when their diet is free of all foods containing chemical additives (colorants, flavorings, preservatives) and when essential nutrients are added that may have been lacking. The principal proponent of this regimen was Benjamin E. Feingold (1900–1982), a pediatric allergist who wrote two books and many articles in scientific journals.

The popular belief that sugar causes hyperactivity in sensitive youngsters has not been verified. A controlled double-blind experiment with hyperactive children showed that sugar either did not alter the children's behavior at all or slowed them down somewhat. Possibly hyperactive children eat more sugar because they have such high metabolic rates that they need extra calories, that is, hyperactivity causes them to eat more sugar rather than the sugar causing hyperactivity. Continued research concerning sugar intake and child behavior is proceeding, but at this writing there is no conclusive evidence of a connection.

Vitamin therapy as such is not dangerous, provided it does not involve those vitamins—A and D—where large doses can actually cause serious damage. However, the claims of vitamin therapists have not been substantiated according to accepted scientific standards, and their studies have never been duplicated by independent, unbiased researchers. Many mental health professionals regard both theory and practice in this field as worthless. They point out that giving and withholding food are potent weapons with respect to young children, that the very careful attention required by a special diet may itself be what a hyperactive child benefits from, and that many hyperactive youngsters outgrow their hyperactivity in time. Therefore, it is impossible to tell if improvement is caused by a change in diet.

Supporters, on the other hand, claim that American health practitioners traditionally know little and care less about nutrition, that the American diet is loaded with "junk food" containing few nutrients and numerous chemicals, and that our understanding of the connections between diet and brain activity is very limited.

What, then, should you do if nutritional therapy is recommended for you or your child? If a thorough medical checkup reveals no medical condition that contraindicates a change of diet, it may do no harm to try it, at least for a time. The principal drawback of nutritional therapy is that it may not help. Moreover, it may delay seeking treatment of a condition that will respond to other therapies. Given these factors, and the lack of reliable evidence concerning its effectiveness, it seems unreasonable to rely on nutritional therapy alone.

OTHER PHYSICAL THERAPIES

Hydrotherapy consists of using warm water baths, usually given in a hospital, to calm disturbed individuals. The patient is placed in a tub of warm water at a carefully maintained temperature and is covered with a sheet so that only her head remains out of the water. In order to maintain the temperature, an attendant must remain nearby. Hydrotherapy is rarely used in America today, since tranquilizers and other drugs calm most individuals more reliably, but it is still used in Europe.

Modern *sleep therapy* was invented in 1922 by a Swiss psychiatrist, Jakob Klaesi, who used drugs to induce long periods of sleep, as much as a week at a time. Patients were roused only for feeding and toilet use. It, too, is believed to be a very old treatment, used intermittently since ancient Egyptian times. Today it is rarely used in America but occasionally is used in Europe.

Kidney dialysis, regular treatments on an artificial kidney machine, was put into use in the late 1970s to improve symptoms of schizophrenia in persons who had no kidney disease. The treatment was based on the idea that some forms of schizophrenia are caused by either an excess or a defective form of endorphins or enkephalins, opiate-like molecules in the brain, and that the artificial kidney filters out these substances. An expensive procedure, dialysis was not found to be of particular benefit for this purpose and has largely been abandoned.

Phototherapy for individuals who suffer from seasonal depression —*seasonal affective disorder*, or *SAD*—appears to be quite effective. This disorder seems to be related to an abnormal circadian rhythm of the secretion of the hormone melatonin. Under normal conditions the pineal gland secretes melatonin at night and not during the day. In winter, as the days grow longer, some individuals begin to suffer from depression, withdrawal from social activities, sleepiness, and weight gain. By exposing them to intensive bright light for three to five hours a day (patients simply sit close to bright fluorescent lights), simulating the same exposure they would experience during a thirteen-hour spring day, their symptoms are relieved, usually within two to four days of treatment. By selecting the right time for such light exposure, it also is possible to treat certain sleep disorders.

Acupuncture is described in Chapter 16.

BRAIN SURGERY

Human skulls found in ruins testify to the fact that long before men and women learned how to record events in writing, they attempted to cure diseases of the brain and/or mind by means of surgery. These efforts were confined to *trephination*, the simple act of boring a hole in the skull in order to let out the evil spirits or blood or pus or whatever was thought to be causing a problem. The actual content of the skull—the brain—was inaccessible to surgeons until the nineteenth century.

The first brain operation in which a surgeon knew where to look for disease inside the skull was performed in London in 1884, and this occasion marked the beginning of modern brain surgery. However, the mortality rate for such operations remained astronomically high until the mid-twentieth century, when the need to treat traumatic head wounds inflicted on the battlefields of World War II, the Korean conflict, and the Vietnam War spurred the development of increasingly successful techniques and procedures. While these have been of enormous benefit to persons whose mental illness is caused by brain tumors, blood clots, or other lesions that can, sometimes, be successfully repaired, they have had little effect on the many others whose mental illness has no definite organic cause. Nevertheless, surgery attempting to cure functional (nonorganic) disorders has been used, and sometimes it has even succeeded.

The term *psychosurgery* was invented to define surgical procedures that are undertaken not to correct visible brain lesions, such as repairing a wound or removing a tumor, but rather to produce behavioral change. One kind of such surgery was introduced in 1935 by Nobel Prize winner and neurosurgeon, Egas Moniz. The procedure he developed, *leukotomy* or *frontal lobotomy,* involves cutting nerve fibers that run from the frontal lobes of the brain to the deeper limbic system, portions that are associated with the ability to experience emotion. It was widely used in the 1940s and early 1950s to treat uncontrollably violent and other mental patients, and it did indeed make them less troublesome. However, it often induced in them a state of total mental apathy, so that they stopped caring about or reacting to anything at all. In effect they became emotional vegetables.

Because of its drastic results, which are irreversible, and the simultaneous development of psychoactive drugs that, in most cases, control violent patients more safely, psychosurgery was used much less in the United States from the late 1950s on. About 1970, however, there was renewed interest in it as more sophisticated surgical techniques were developed and as some patients were found to experience undesirable side effects from long-term use of certain drugs. Indeed, surgical techniques have been greatly refined, so that less brain tissue is damaged and the risk of personality changes is decreased. However, in about 25 percent of cases it results in no improvement.

These issues, and also the experimental use of psychosurgery in some patients, occasionally even in hyperactive children, caused growing concern about its misuse. Consequently, the National Mental Health Association in 1973 issued a statement maintaining that psychosurgery was still to be classified as experimental and should not be used except in those instances where (1) a patient is in such great distress from a mental disorder that he, by choice, elects to have such surgery; (2) all other alternatives have been considered or adequately tried according to the patient, the patient's family, and at least two reputable physicians, one of them a psychiatrist; (3) the procedure has been reviewed and approved in writing by at least two independent neurosurgeons; and (4) the patient's own lawyer is present when any final decision to operate is made.

Those who favor or engage in psychosurgery today are a distinctly small percentage of mental health professionals. Most are conservative neurosurgeons who only operate in response to desperate appeals from patients and their families. The majority of mental health professionals take a very cautious position regarding psychosurgery and would not consider its use except in very rare instances.

If someone suggests that surgery is appropriate for you, your relative, or your friend, by all means seek at least a second opinion from another physician, preferably a psychiatrist but perhaps also from another neurologist. In any case be sure it is a physician whose practice is in no way connected to the physician who proposed surgery.

Chapter
20

GIVING HELP—HOSPITALIZATION

EVERY YEAR more than 1.7 million Americans become patients in psychiatric facilities. Currently it is estimated that at any one time, some 347,000 hospital beds in the United States are occupied by mental patients.

Being hospitalized for mental illness may still seem, to most people, a very frightening alternative. But today's inpatient care is a far cry from the "snakepit" conditions that were the norm as recently as 1940. To be sure, there is a small core of psychiatric patients who are hospitalized for life, for whom no treatment of any kind has been effective and who therefore have become permanent residents of the so-called "back wards." Such wards exist mainly in state and county mental hospitals because, given the costs of hospitalization of any kind, even a very wealthy person's financial resources cannot keep up with the cost of private care for more than a limited time. In 1955 there were an estimated 559,000 chronic patients in public mental hospitals; during the next thirty years this number declined to fewer than 117,000.

THE HISTORY OF ASYLUMS

Hospitalization for mental illness has been with us for a long time. Mental patients were hospitalized by the Arabs in the eighth century at Damascus, and again in the tenth century at Basra, in both instances in general hospitals. There is mention of a hospital devoted exclusively to mental patients at Mandu, in India, about the year 1000. The Turks had hospitals that admitted mental patients in various centers throughout the thirteenth century, and in Europe, St. John's Home in Ghent admitted mental patients, along with vagrants and paupers, in 1191. In Europe the insane at first were admitted along with the physically ill into shelters or hospitals. The first European hospital exclusively for mental patients was opened in 1409 in Valencia, Spain.

In America during colonial times, public provision for the mentally ill took the form of poorhouses, workhouses, and jails. In these settings they were treated no better than criminals and often worse, since their keepers regarded them as no different from animals and subjected them to humiliation and torture. The first American mental hospital opened in 1773 in Williamsburg, Virginia. In 1793 Philippe Pinel removed the chains from inmates of Bicêtre, a mental hospital in Paris, and began a new era in treatment of the mentally ill in Europe and America.

The nineteenth century saw a spate of "moral reformers" who aroused public indignation over inhuman conditions in institutions. The reformers attributed mental illness to an underlying social disorder and regarded the mentally ill as victims of forces beyond their control who deserved philanthropic treatment. From these humanitarian convictions arose the cult of asylum, a haven of safety and good treatment. Dorothea Dix, one of the principal leaders of the reform movement, traveled across the nation to encourage governments to establish or enlarge state mental hospitals, and her personal efforts led to increases in institutional services to the mentally ill in twenty different states.

In 1847 Congress passed a bill that provided aid for the development of public mental institutions run by state and local governments, but President Franklin Pierce vetoed it. Despite the lack of federal support, a system of institutions soon spread across the nation. In 1810 only a few eastern states had private asylums. By 1850 there were state care facilities throughout the northeast and midwestern states, and by 1860 public institutions operated in twenty-eight (of the then thirty-three) states.

Because mental illness was believed to result from social and economic ills, it made sense to isolate the mentally ill from those forces in the community that had caused their illness. The asylums therefore were located in remote rural areas. Visits from family and friends, and other forms of outside contact, were discouraged. Rather, life in a well-ordered environment was supposed to restore the ill to normality. Therapy consisted of a highly structured life, with meals and all other activities following a rigid schedule. Repetitive and simple chores, usually farming and workshop crafts, occupied the day, the performance of work being considered therapeutic. It was assumed that with this regimen patients would recover from their illness and rejoin the labor force.

Most patients, however, were not "cured." Some recovered (spontaneously, no doubt) but most remained in asylums, becoming chronic patients. The asylums continued to grow, and by the end of the nineteenth century they had become huge, overcrowded institutions. Staffing was inadequate, and patients who could not work simply did nothing at all. Treatment was negligible or nonexistent. The abuses of institutional care began to come to light, and horror stories of cruelties reached the public, but no practical alternative to institutionalization presented itself for many years. The superintendents and other asylum employees had a vested interest in the existing system and argued that the public needed protection from dangerous mental patients, who not only might become violent but might somehow infect others with their disease. Their custodial treatment, they argued, represented a necessary service to the community.

This legacy still taints the popular view of mental hospitals and in fact lies behind the movement for deinstitutionalization that began in the 1950s. Its supporters argued that institutions made people worse, not better. Moreover, this more recent "reform" movement could address itself to long-term and chronic mental patients who, thanks to the development of psychoactive drugs in the late 1950s, now constitute a relatively small percentage of cases. Hospitalization for mental illness today can be as brief as twenty-four hours, and the average hospital stay for most mental patients is well under one month.

WHO SHOULD BE HOSPITALIZED?

Although not everyone in crisis needs hospitalization, most who are hospitalized are indeed undergoing a crisis. As we saw in Chapter 4, a person likely to commit suicide or presenting a threat to others needs constant supervision, at least for a short time, and that can best be provided in a hospital.

A person who needs to be kept away from alcohol or drugs similarly may need constant supervision for a time.

A person unaware of his own illness, either unable or unwilling to cooperate in treatment, or whose illness has become worse despite treatment, may require the intensive care available only in a hospital. A person in need of treatment or tests that are better or more safely performed in the hospital, or a person who has physical needs (special diet, physical rehabilitation) or other illness requiring special medical treatment is best off in a hospital.

A person whose home setting is contributing to the illness or is undermining, in one way or another, the effectiveness of treatment may be at least temporarily removed from that setting by means of hospitalization.

A person whose illness has made it impossible to function independently may have to be hospitalized. In fact, it is this category of patient that accounts for the majority of very long-term or chronic inmates of mental institutions.

Finally, a person whose illness is thought to respond to milieu therapy—that is, a healing environment provided by means of interaction with other patients and a multidisciplinary professional staff—is hospitalized so that an intensive course of such treatment can take place.

INPATIENT FACILITIES

Up to about 1950 the only facilities that admitted seriously ill mental patients were state or county mental hospitals and Veterans Administration mental hospitals, supplemented somewhat by private mental hospitals (some of which were prohibitively expensive). Today about half of those hospitalized for mental illness still use these facilities, and the other half go to a general hospital with a psychiatric service. The principal reason for this change appears to be the use of psycho-active drugs. Until they came into use, a person ill enough to require hospitalization usually had symptoms that made him very difficult to manage; today the worst symptoms often can be controlled with medication.

As a rule, in order to devote some of its space to psychiatric patients, a general hospital must have a hundred or more beds. However, some smaller hospitals (with fifty or so beds) may have a psychiatric unit if there is sufficient demand. Currently about fifteen hundred general hospitals in the United States have psychiatric units of one kind or another, ranging from a fully staffed service comparable to that of a full-scale psychiatric hospital to just a few beds set aside for mental patients. They represent about 30 percent of the nation's mental health facilities. Of the large hospitals (with five hundred or more beds), 75 percent have an inpatient psychiatric unit, usually a fairly well staffed one. Still, in less densely populated areas—in Idaho or Montana, for instance—it may be hard to find a general hospital that admits mental patients.

Another major change generated by the use of psychoactive drugs is the much shorter duration of hospitalization. About 85 to 90 percent of all mental patients leave the hospital within a few weeks, and many leave even sooner. The median length of stay in county and state mental hospitals has dropped from eight years in 1956 to less than one month.

Most authorities today agree that a long-term stay in the hospital—one of years—may do more harm than good. Over time the hos-pitalized patient becomes more and more passive, lethargic, and de-pendent. The long-stay patient is likely to show less and less interest in her surroundings, withdraw from social contact, begin to neglect personal grooming, and rely wholly on others to make decisions and provide for needs. Even if patients must eventually be readmitted—and a great many are—current thinking holds that it is better for them to be released as soon as possible, even only temporarily, rather than to remain in the hospital for a long period.

Most general hospitals admit only patients who are in crisis or who will stay for a foreseeable short time, ranging from a few days to a few weeks. Those who do not recover in that time often are referred elsewhere for extended care, frequently to a state mental hospital or a

VA mental hospital, although some patients are referred to private mental hospitals.

Further, many general hospitals accept only voluntary patients, that is, patients who are not hospitalized by means of certification or commitment (see Chapter 26 for a discussion of these legal terms), even though a gradually increasing number are providing locked wards to accommodate involuntary patients. Private mental hospitals, of which there are close to three hundred free-standing ones in the United States, generally accept both voluntary and involuntary patients, and, depending on the individual hospital, may or may not accept patients for long-term care. County and state mental hospitals take mostly involuntary patients, both short- and long-term.

The most common disorders for which a patient goes to a county or state hospital are schizophrenia and alcohol or drug dependence; the main diagnoses in private mental hospitals and general hospitals with a psychiatric service are schizophrenia, depression, and alcohol and drug abuse.

CRISIS INTERVENTION: BRIEF TREATMENT

One of the more dramatic innovations of the past forty years is the brief treatment unit or crisis intervention center, to which patients are admitted for twenty-four hours to one week in order to obtain help during a difficult period. The underlying theory of such treatment is that rapid and appropriate intervention at a critical time can prevent the development of maladaptive behavior leading to more serious illness and thus avoid the need for more extensive treatment. In addition, it is hoped that the prompt resolution of a crisis can help promote healthier adaptive patterns for the future.

Crisis intervention often may be handled on an outpatient basis, provided a qualified professional is able and willing to commit a large block of time to the individual in need. Unfortunately this is not always the case. Many hospital and community health center emergency services consist of a twenty-four-hour telephone service that arranges for immediate referral, but rarely is there a trained person available at all times to stay with a suicidal person or help someone deal with acute alcohol withdrawal symptoms. Most individuals needing such supervision are referred to an inpatient unit, which may be part of a community mental health center but more often is part of a general hospital.

Although the precise regimen varies from hospital to hospital, the general approach to crisis treatment is essentially the same. The length of hospitalization is limited to as brief a time as possible, as little as twenty-four hours and rarely more than seven days. From the start, the patient is encouraged to plan for discharge, often actually being informed that he will not be permitted to stay in the hospital beyond a certain time. Treatment is intensive, and usually involves individual therapy at least once a day. Psychoactive drugs are pre-scribed as soon as possible to relieve symptoms, and the family, friends, and, if necessary, social agencies are involved at once in order to set up the supports that will be needed after discharge.

The treatment plan is formulated quickly, the immediate—and sometimes the only—goal being to find a solution to the immediate problem that precipitated the crisis. For example, a woman who be-came suicidally depressed upon learning that her only child was incur-ably retarded might be treated with electroconvulsive therapy (ECT), which tends to work faster than antidepressant drugs; her husband would be called in for counseling, to help her cope after discharge; and a temporary hospital stay for complete evaluation might be set up for the child, to begin when the mother was discharged so that she would not have to care for the child at home immediately.

Hospital units for brief treatment tend to be highly flexible in their procedures. There may be a daily patient and staff meeting to plan the day's activities and to review each patient's progress, but other sched-uled activities are held to a minimum. The transition to home life might begin with giving patients a pass to go to work during the day for several days but returning to spend the night in the hospital, or making short visits before actually spending a whole day at home. Patients are encouraged to take as much responsibility for themselves as they can.

The patient is discharged when the acute symptoms of distress are under control and there appears to be enough support to allow her to survive at home. If symptoms do not subside enough, or if the home situation remains problematical, a patient may be referred for further hospital care, either in a longer-term unit at the same hospital or in another facility. Often the staff of the crisis unit will follow a patient for some time after discharge, remaining available to provide support and perform therapy if needed.

The team format is standard in most hospital psychiatric units, that is, a team of professionals, including a psychiatrist, psychologist, social worker, nurse, and aide, is assigned to each patient for evaluation and treatment. In crisis intervention this approach is considered virtually essential, because so much work must be done in such a short time. Often several teams are enlisted: one to work with a patient, another with the patient's family, and perhaps still another with the appropriate social agencies. Because of time pressure, many of the activities—meetings with family members, therapy sessions, and so on—must take place during evenings and weekends rather than being confined to the ordinary hours of the work week.

The goal of brief treatment is to provide temporary relief of symptoms and to enable an individual to return to normal activities as quickly as possible. It appears to work well for persons with a temporarily serious or suicidal depression, or for those experiencing a mild manic episode. It is less (sometimes not at all) effective for very severe illnesses, such as a severe schizophrenic reaction, psychotic depression, or full-blown mania, or for the confusion and other symptoms of organic brain disease. For these disorders it usually takes more than a week to control symptoms. However, brief treatment may be very useful for a patient with chronic schizophrenia whose symptoms are normally controlled by medication but who has experienced a mild to moderate increase in symptoms owing to some unusual life stress or to discontinuing medication.

INTERMEDIATE TREATMENT: ONE TO FOUR WEEKS

Critics of short-term intervention units maintain that they tend to concentrate entirely on the life events that sent a person to seek emergency help and pay no attention to an underlying illness. Such short-term units, it is held, take too great a risk by discharging very disturbed and/or suicidal individuals before they are ready, or they may force a person to make important life decisions without taking time to consider the alternatives and long-term implications.

A somewhat longer term of inpatient treatment may be provided. In a general hospital an "intermediate" term usually means more than one week and up to one month; in psychiatric hospitals it may mean four to eight months. Again the treatment plan is made as quickly as possible, and a treatment team is assigned to the patient, but there is less pressure on returning a person to the community quite so fast.

Here is a profile of a 211-bed general hospital, nonprofit and private, that offers both brief and intermediate care. Although the average stay for patients is eleven days, some stay only one day and others have stayed for nine weeks or longer. (The latter tend to be patients with anorexia or elderly patients who are too disturbed to be admitted to a nursing home and for whom no other appropriate facility can be found.)

This hospital serves as the main inpatient facility for a nine-town area in eastern Massachusetts. It has thirty-one beds devoted to psychiatric (including alcoholic) patients, and is about to open a separate twenty-two-bed addiction unit. It accepts any patient aged fifteen or older, unless the person is uncontrollably violent or considered a danger to self or others; such patients are immediately referred to the acute-care unit of a nearby state mental hospital or a private mental hospital.

The psychiatric unit's staff consists of twenty-five full-time counselors and nurses, as well as two staff psychiatrists, a part-time psychologist, two full-time social workers, one occupational therapist, alcohol specialists, and a part-time unit teacher (to instruct nurses). Most patients are admitted to the unit straight from the hospital's emergency room; some are referred by the police, the community mental health clinic, a physician, family member, themselves, or some other source. There is no waiting list, and no one must wait more than twenty-four hours to be admitted. Each patient has an attending physician and also is immediately assigned to a "key person," that is, a particular nurse or counselor who is in contact with the patient's family, physician, outside agencies, and the patient, on a daily basis if necessary. Also, a physician performs a thorough physical examination within twenty-four hours of admission.

Treatment is begun almost at once and is quite intensive. It includes individual therapy, where the major thrust is to restore the patient to functioning well enough to leave the hospital. There also are milieu groups that include all the patients in the unit as well as the staff and meet five times a week. (Milieu therapy is further described below.) Further, where it is appropriate there may be couples and/or family therapy, and some patients with acute depression are given ECT (described in the previous chapter). The patient, staff, and physician together devise an individual treatment plan.

Although there are no locked doors, each patient requires her physician's approval for leaving the unit floor and, even with such approval, is expected to inform her key person when leaving and to sign out and in at the nursing station. Medications must be specifically prescribed by the physician and are distributed in the medication room. Visiting hours are liberal, but no visitors are allowed during the scheduled milieu group meetings or during two smaller group therapy meetings. In addition, some day patients participate in the program.

This hospital always refers patients who are being discharged to some form of aftercare, usually to the community mental health center. In fact, a member of the treatment team, most often a nurse, actively follows the patient into the aftercare program and coordinates case aides and other support. This service, performed to prevent rehospitalization, is an unusual one—few hospitals provide it—and, it is believed, is the main reason why this hospital has such a low rate of return patients; its readmission rate is 30 percent, a figure that includes alcoholic patients, who typically have a 75 percent or higher return rate.

In contrast, another general hospital, with 305 beds, serves a fifteen-town area. It has twenty-three beds in its psychiatric unit and is about to get fifteen more for a substance abuse unit. It accepts patients aged fourteen and older and the average length of stay is only 9.46 days. It presently accepts voluntary patients only but is applying for involuntary status, meaning it will provide a locked unit. It also provides day or night care for patients who are being discharged but are not ready to leave the hospital entirely.

Because of the brief average length of stay, governed to a large extent by insurance-coverage constraints, the staff tries to accomplish as much as possible in a very short time. Within two or three days of admission diagnosis and medication are established, as well as some sense of what a patient will require in aftercare.

One innovative strategy is a treatment contract, in which each patient soon after admission outlines and clarifies the goals of treatment, that is, exactly what is to be accomplished during the hospitalization. This contract is read and discussed and modified in twice-a-week group meetings with other patients and their assigned key person—in this hospital a registered nurse assigned upon admission to coordinate the treatment and afterplans. (See the accompanying sample treatment contract on page 226.)

HOSPITALIZED PATIENTS' RIGHTS

These are the basic rights of every patient at Emerson Hospital.*

EQUALITY OF CARE
You can expect to be treated with consideration and with respect regardless of your race, sex, religion, national origin, or the source of payment for your care.

EMERGENCY TREATMENT
You have a right to prompt, life-saving treatment in an emergency, regardless of your ability to pay.

COMPLETE INFORMATION
You have a right to be fully informed about your treatment and a right to consent to or decline such treatment. For example, a patient suffering from any form of breast cancer has the right to complete information on all alternative treatments that are medically viable.

PRIVACY
You are entitled to privacy during the rendering of medical or any other kind of care, to the best of our capacity. At all times you can expect that your privacy and dignity will be respected.

CONFIDENTIALITY
You can be sure all your records and communications about you will be kept confidential to the extent provided by the law.

IDENTIFICATION OF STAFF
You have a right to know the name and specialty of the physician (or any other person) responsible for your care or the coordination of your care. You also have the right to know the affiliations of the physician and any affiliations of Emerson Hospital with educational institutions or other health-care facilities as these may be related to your care.

THE RIGHT TO SAY "NO"
You may refuse to be examined, observed, or treated by students or anyone from the hospital staff who is not involved with your treatment. Even so, you will receive our very best care—whether it be psychiatric, psychological, or medical/surgical care and attention.

You may also refuse to serve as a research subject, or you may refuse any care or examination when the primary purpose is educational or informational rather than therapeutic or diagnostic.

ACCESS TO YOUR MEDICAL RECORDS
You may ask to inspect your medical records and may even request a copy for yourself. We will ask you to pay for copying expenses.

EXPLANATION OF YOUR BILL

You may ask for an itemized bill and an explanation of each item. In addition, you may receive a copy of any bill or statement of charges to any insurance company or third-party payor. If you wish, you may also receive information we have about financial assistance and any free care that may be available.

COPY OF REGULATIONS

You have a right to obtain a copy of any rules and regulations of the hospital that apply to your conduct as a patient.

YOUR RESPONSIBILITIES

Along with the rights and privileges of being a patient, there are also some responsibilities. We ask that you respect these responsibilities so that we can do our job of giving you the best possible care.

- Please keep your appointments. When unable to do so, notify us promptly.
- When we ask, do provide us with accurate information about your medical history, present condition, medication, and other pertinent facts about your health.
- Please follow all instructions given for your care. Ask questions whenever you do not understand the instructions or cannot comply with them.
- Please follow hospital regulations and be considerate of the rights of other patients as well as those who serve and care for you.

QUESTIONS?

If you have any questions or problems concerning your care or your rights as a patient, let us know. Your nurse or physician are always ready to discuss your concerns.

In addition, a patient representative—whose only job is to listen to you—is available to talk with you about your rights or any questions or problems you may have. This person is your representative, a well-trained volunteer who is interested in your rights and well-being and who will try to make your hospital stay as pleasant as possible.

Please feel free to consult with the patient representative. Dialing extension 345 (from 8:30 A.M. to 5 P.M.) will put you in touch.

* Concord, MA. In addition, Massachusetts Law, Chapter 214 of the Acts of 1979, known as Patient's Bill of Rights, is available upon request.

```
                    TREATMENT CONTRACT*

        PATIENT:   Mary Smith
        WEEK OF:   June 15, 1990
     PROBLEM #1:   Overwhelming depression. Can't do any-
                   thing (get out of bed, get dressed, etc.).
 LONG-TERM GOAL:   To return to normal functioning as a house-
                   wife and schoolteacher.

SHORT-TERM GOALS:
              A:   To tell a staff member when I'm feeling so
                   low that I want to do away with myself.
              B:   To get up in morning, get dressed, wash,
                   and go to breakfast.
              C:   To take my medication.
     PROBLEM #2:   I feel worthless, good for nothing. I hate
                   myself. I deserve to be miserable.
 LONG-TERM GOAL:   To feel better about myself, and get back my
                   confidence so I can function at home and at
                   school.

SHORT-TERM GOALS:
              A:   To take part in group meetings, especially
                   the assertiveness group.
              B:   To make a list of all the positive, good
                   things I can say about myself.
              C:   To meet my assigned nurse daily and talk
                   over my feelings.
     PROBLEM #3:   My marriage is breaking up, and my kids
                   blame me for it.
 LONG-TERM GOAL:   To cope with my grief over the breakup and
                   make plans for a new life and new goals.

SHORT-TERM GOALS:
              A:   To keep a journal of my sad feelings when-
                   ever they come up.
              B:   To go to couples counseling with my hus-
                   band and the social worker.
              C:   To have short visits with the kids and talk
                   over what happens at them with my nurse.
```

* Developed and used at WalthamWeston Hospital, Waltham, MA. It is filled out by patients
themselves. Mary Smith is a hypothetical patient hospitalized for major depression.

MILIEU THERAPY

Psychotherapy (individual, couples, family, group) and somatic therapies (medication, ECT) can readily be performed on an outpatient basis, but hospitalization offers several forms of treatment that require use of the hospital setting. One is *milieu therapy*. *Milieu*, a French word meaning "environment," refers to a patient's surroundings, which consist not only of the physical surroundings but all the individuals with whom the patient comes in contact (other patients as well as hospital staff) and the planned activities (therapy, meals, recreation, etc.). All these elements are part of the treatment. Milieu therapy consists of active efforts directed toward getting a patient involved with others, including the assumption of some responsibility for others, in the hope of making the patient ultimately responsible for herself.

Although very short-term hospitalization in a crisis unit can include milieu therapy, there may not be time enough to establish relationships with all the other patients and staff. The main focus is on getting better fast so as to get out of the hospital. Intermediate-term hospitalization usually involves milieu therapy, often in a quite intensive form.

In the first general hospital described above, the psychiatric unit has three single rooms but the remaining rooms are doubles (and one has four beds), since complete isolation is discouraged. Meals are served in a common dining area; there also is a small kitchen adjacent to it, where patients can prepare snacks.

A schedule of each day's activities is posted in the dining area, and patients are encouraged to participate in unit activities unless their individual treatment plan conflicts. Community group meetings are held for an hour each Sunday and Tuesday morning, attended by all the patients and much of the staff. Individual problems and concerns may be discussed during these gatherings, and patients are encouraged to share their ideas and feelings. Small group meetings are held on four other mornings, and attendance at these is required as well. In addition, alcohol group meetings, run by the special alcohol counselors, are held every weekday, and although they are specifically recommended for patients with alcohol-related problems, other interested patients may attend, too. Intensive, 9-to-5 addiction treatment is also available.

North 5 Patient Milieu*

Time	Sunday	Monday	Tuesday	Wednesday	Thursday	Friday	Saturday
7:00							
8:00	Breakfast	Breakfast	Breakfast	Breakfast	Breakfast	Breakfast	Breakfast
8:45		Check-In	Check-In	Check-In	Check-In	Check-In	
9:00		O.T. Eval. Group					
10:00 / 10:15		Fitness	Fitness	Fitness	Fitness	Fitness	
11:00	Community Meeting	Small Group	Community Meeting	Small Group	Art Therapy	Small Group	Small Group
12:00	Lunch	Lunch	Lunch	Lunch	Lunch	Lunch	Lunch
		O.T.		Dessert		O.T.	
1:00		Group →		Preparation →	Writing Group	Group →	
2:00							
3:00							

228

4:00		Relaxation/ Assertiveness Group	Transition/ Discharge Group		Family Issues	Community Meeting	
5:00	Dinner	Dinner	Dinner	Dinner	Dinner	Dinner	Dinner
6:00				Dessert and Family Meeting →			
7:00	NA				AA(EH)		AA(EH)
7:30		AA Pickup	AA Pickup	AA Pickup		AA Pickup	
8:00	Addictions Education	Addictions Education	Addictions Education	Addictions Education		Addictions Education	Addictions Education
8:30	Wrap Up	Wrap Up	Wrap Up	Wrap Up	Wrap Up	Wrap Up	
9:00							
10:00							
11:00	Closing Time	Closing Time	Closing Time	Closing Time	Closing Time	Closing Time	Closing Time

*Emerson Hospital, Concord, MA.

The occupational therapy program offers a variety of activities. An activity/task group focuses on a craft or project designed to help develop concentration and attention span, increase self-esteem through the successful completion of projects, and perhaps also develop a hobby interest or skill to be used after discharge. A weekly family-issues group focuses on typical family problems and behavior patterns. One afternoon a week a dessert-planning meeting is held, and the dessert decided on is prepared by patients, with some help from staff, the following evening. Patients may invite relatives and friends to this event, which is followed by a group meeting for patients and their families, where common problems can be discussed.

Other activities are a five-times-a-week exercise group, a weekly relaxation-assertiveness group, and art therapy. Also, outings to sports and cultural events outside the hospital are organized periodically by patients and staff, and patients may sign up to perform various chores in the unit on a weekly basis.

An essential idea underlying milieu therapy is that all staff members participate in the treatment, not just the physician or the individual therapist or group therapy leader, but nurses, aides, social workers, art therapists, and so on. This function is facilitated in the meetings where anyone may express an opinion, describe any problem, and propose solutions. Patient groups and patient government organizations give the patient a strong voice in decisions, and open, easy communication with the staff is stressed. This therapy is in marked contrast to the older approaches to hospital care, where the patient's activities were chosen and directed by the staff much as a small child's are by the parents, encouraging a dependency that serves as little preparation for life after discharge.

Another form of treatment requiring an institutional setting is *social learning therapy*. It is based on the principles of operant conditioning (see under behavior therapies in Chapter 13), and a comparative study of its use over a decade among chronic mental patients indicates it can be very successful. In contrast to milieu therapy, in which patients are held responsible for their own behavior, social learning therapy tries to teach new and desirable behavior by demonstration, prompting, direct instruction, and the use of a token economy. Patients receive tokens, which they can later redeem for rewards, whenever they behave appropriately (get up in the morning, dress themselves, attend meals and assigned activities, etc.). Undesirable behavior, on the other hand, is ignored entirely if possible and is never rewarded.

PRIVATE MENTAL HOSPITAL VERSUS GENERAL HOSPITAL

A private mental hospital offers the same kinds of short-term and intermediate care as a general hospital, although, as noted above, the interpretation of "short" and "intermediate" tends to be longer. In addition, it may offer long-term care, for a period of a year or more. Few patients can afford long-term private care, and for most it is not an option. Admission to a private hospital may be either voluntary or involuntary (commitment), whereas many general hospitals accept only voluntary patients. Many private hospitals do not accept children, but some have special child and adolescent programs. In general hospitals children may be admitted, but sometimes to the pediatric service rather than to a psychiatric unit (as is the case with both above-described general hospitals).

In the private mental hospital every staff member is to some extent trained and experienced in caring for mental patients; in a general hospital the nursing staff may rotate among the different departments. In the mental hospital a therapy team such as that described above is the rule, whereas general hospitals cannot always assign one. A private mental hospital may have either an *open staff*, in which case a patient's own psychiatrist may continue to treat him during hospitalization, or a *closed staff*, where certain physicians work for the hospital on a salary basis or in partnership and only they can treat patients hospitalized there. With the latter, a private psychiatrist who is not a member of the staff must refer the patient to another psychiatrist on the staff who will take over the treatment. Most general hospitals have open-staff arrangements. Private hospitals that admit adolescents often have a school program with certified teachers that is an integral part of the treatment program.

About 70 percent of the 340 American private mental hospitals are proprietary, that is, they are operated for a profit. Monthly fees are high—currently up to $12,000 a month or higher. Compared to nonprofit private mental hospitals, the proprietary ones tend to have fewer beds, higher rates of patient turnover, shorter lengths of stay, and lower expenditures per patient day. The typical general hospital psychiatric unit has about thirty beds; the typical private mental hospital has about eighty beds, although some hospitals are smaller and others are much larger. Although some people disapprove of profit-making facilities in the health-care field, contending they are more interested in making money than in providing quality care, others believe that they are filling a large gap, providing psychiatric services where previously there were none, and that their profits come from increased efficiency rather than from poor-quality or decreased treatment.

Private mental hospitals tend to concentrate on inpatient care, although many provide outpatient treatment as well. General hospitals with a psychiatric service often have outpatient clinics, and some also have twenty-four-hour walk-in emergency service, partial hospitalization (see below), and other services.

A stay in a mental hospital—public or private—is likely to involve more restrictions on a patient's activities than a stay in a general hospital. There may be regulations regarding the use of the telephone, for example, or no telephone privileges, and rules concerning relationships with staff and other patients. There also may be a system or privileges that are extended or denied, such as, for example, the privilege of walking freely about the hospital grounds. (See the accompanying example of a privilege system.)

PRIVILEGE SYSTEM IN A MENTAL HOSPITAL

Definition of Privileges

STAFF TWO TO ONE—A patient may leave the hall accompanied by two staff members.

STAFF ONE TO ONE—A patient may leave the hall accompanied by one staff member.

PATIENT ESCORT—A patient may leave the hall accompanied by another patient who is responsible for him.

GROUP ESCORT—A group of patients may leave the hall for a specified activity accompanied by a staff member.

MUTUAL ESCORT SYSTEM—Two patients may go to a designated place, each being responsible for the other.

FAMILY ESCORT—A patient may go to a specified area accompanied by a designated member of his family.

DESTINATION PRIVILEGED—A patient may go unaccompanied to a specified "locked supervised area." Staff on the patient's hall and staff in the "locked supervised area" keep each other informed of when the patient is expected to leave and arrive at either location.

CALL BACKS—A patient may go unaccompanied to any specified place, but must call his hall on arrival and again when he is ready to leave to report his next destination.

LIMITED GROUNDS—The patient may go unaccompanied to limited areas on hospital grounds as specifically prescribed.

FULL GROUNDS—A patient may go anywhere within the designated patient areas of the hospital by himself.

FULL TOWNS—A patient may take trips to town freely by notifying the charge nurse of his intended departure and return.

OVERNIGHTS—The patient may leave the hospital for one or more nights, as prescribed.

STATE AND COUNTY MENTAL HOSPITALS

It is rare to gain admission to a public mental hospital by simply walking in and asking to be admitted. Though each of the fifty states has its own laws, most require some form of commitment or certification. Further, as a result of the deinstitutionalization policies that have become the predominant public mental health outlook since the 1970s, it has become much harder to get into a public mental hospital. Deinstitutionalization has resulted in drastically cutting the public mental hospital census. Just between 1965 and 1980, 358,000 patients left public mental hospitals. In 1987 only 112,000 patients remained in them.

Those who remain in state and county hospitals tend to be the most incompetent, violent, or suicidal—a danger to themselves and/or the community—and also those most resistant to treatment. The majority of them suffer from schizophrenia or manic-depressive psychosis and are a danger mainly to themselves. Of necessity this patient population reduces the feasibility of group therapy, for one thing. Yet public hospitals are by law required to provide treatment, not just custodial care. Sometimes the only therapy that is carried on, other than medication, is a minimal form of the milieu therapy described above.

Among the greatest problems of public mental hospitals are the shortage of staff and the difficulty of recruiting competent staff. The reasons are logical: The patients are hard to treat, there are too many of them, and mental health professionals tend to find better pay and more satisfying work in the private sector. Many public hospitals therefore resort to hiring foreign physicians, who may be well trained and willing to work but whose knowledge of the English language and of American customs may be quite limited, and who therefore cannot communicate well with patients. In the end, staff shortages may drive

even the best-intentioned staff members to overmedicate patients and/
or put them in seclusion too frequently.

A state or county hospital admits patients requiring either short-
term acute care or long-term care. Usually a program of intensive
treatment is begun soon after admission in order to discharge the
patient as soon as possible. Those who do not respond within a
reasonable time become chronic or long-term patients and receive
much less treatment of any kind.

Intensive treatment includes the use of drugs, ECT, and group psychotherapy. Individual psychotherapy is rarely performed because
there are not enough therapists to go around. There usually are recreational and occupational therapy programs as well, which often depend heavily on the services of volunteers recruited from the
surrounding communities. About 90 percent of the patients are discharged within a few months. However, the rate of readmission—the
return of previous patients through the so-called "revolving door"—
can be discouragingly high, as much as 80 percent in some institutions. Much of the reason for this recidivism is that few are ready to
live in the outside world on their own, without supervision for taking
needed medication, yet there are few settings where they can go.

The outlook for improvement in a state or county hospital depends
a great deal on the hospital's ability to provide intensive treatment for
a sufficient period of time. Since most of these facilities are under-
staffed, they generally cannot do much for very long.

Most state hospitals are situated away from community population
centers. They consist of a group of buildings that can house fifteen
hundred to five thousand patients. Owing to deinstitutionalization,
many are now half-empty, and many others have closed. Patients live
either on wards or in "cottages" that house twenty-five to one hundred
patients each. Only about one-third of the nation's state mental hospitals have facilities for children. They either house children with
adults or in a separate unit or wing. Although a few state hospitals
bring in teachers to provide schooling for child patients, most do not.

With increasing pressure to discharge those that can leave, and to
prepare more patients for such discharge, the best of the public hospitals are giving group classes on living problems (how to cook, shop,
wash clothes, etc.), and some have group apartments on their grounds
to serve as a transitional home for those who are scheduled to leave
the hospital.

Since it is the states that are largely responsible for public institutions serving the mentally ill, it is they who are to be praised or blamed for the quality of this service. In 1988 a publication jointly issued by the Public Citizen Health Research Group, a consumer advocacy organization, and the National Alliance for the Mentally Ill, representing mostly the families of seriously mentally ill patients, rated the state programs for care of the seriously mentally ill. Included in this assessment were county and state hospitals, outpatient care, rehabilitation services, and housing with various levels of support for patients who cannot live entirely on their own. Interestingly, the five states ranked highest—Rhode Island, Wisconsin, New Hampshire, Maine, and Vermont—are far from the richest in per capita income. The accompanying table shows the standards used for their assessment (see pages 236 and 237).

VETERANS ADMINISTRATION (VA) HOSPITALS

Both VA mental hospitals and VA general hospitals with a psychiatric service include some of the best facilities of their kind. Unfortunately they often limit admissions to veterans with service-connected disorders. If the hospital has a free bed and a veteran cannot afford other care, he may be admitted with a mental disorder that is not service-connected. Dependents (the families of veterans) are not admitted, but they may be involved in the treatment on an outpatient basis when it is judged to be beneficial to the veteran. There are about 168 VA hospitals in the nation; of these 24 are primarily psychiatric hospitals, and most of the rest have psychiatric units. Both give the same kinds of care as other mental hospitals and psychiatric units, but on the whole they are adequately staffed and well equipped, and able to provide intensive treatment for as long as necessary. Their services to veterans are free, paid for by tax dollars.

ALCOHOL AND DRUG TREATMENT CENTERS

There currently are six thousand to ten thousand alcohol rehabilitation centers in the United States, including inpatient and outpatient facilities, both hospital-based and free-standing. Most provide

STANDARDS FOR PUBLIC HOSPITALS*

Minimal Acceptable Care	Ideal Care

1. Quality of staff

Applicants screened for valid credentials, criminal history, prior allegations of patient abuse, etc.

Initial and in-service training for specific duties and responsibilities.

Utilization of only fully trained and licensed professionals (none practicing on restricted licenses).

Adequate job stability and salaries to attract and keep good employees.

Job advancement partly based on quality of patient care, not just administrative skills.

Applicants screened by patients and families for warmth, empathy, other personality traits considered important.

Intensive, ongoing training programs at all levels.

Jobs viewed as so appealing that private-sector professionals eager to apply.

Job advancement influenced by evaluation by patients and families.

2. Quantity of staff

Sufficient number of all professional and paraprofessional staff to ensure good care.

Staff not shifted to unfamiliar wards because of shortages; no overtime and double shifts; same staffing on weekends as weekdays.

3. Quality of treatment

Individual treatment plan formulated with help of patient and family (if willing).

Skilled use of drugs, including trial of available ones, minimum maintenance doses, monitoring of side effects.

Regular screening for tardive dyskinesia.

Complete initial diagnostic assessment, including neurological, psychological and laboratory examinations. Assessment on readmission as indicated.

Good medical and dental care.

Patients treated with dignity and respect.

Seclusion and restraint used only when needed, for brief periods, mostly on admission wards.

Specialized programs for dual diagnosis (e.g., schizophrenia and mental retardation), substance abuse, psychiatric

Annual written review and evaluation of treatment plan goals and achievement with patient and family.

Use of blood levels to measure antipsychotic and antidepressant drug use.

Specialized diagnostic tests (such as MRI) when indicated.

Specialists available in nearby medical center.

Relationship between staff and patients such that visitor can't tell which gets more respect.

Low total hours of seclusion and restraint; staff prides selves on calming disturbed patients without using them.

STANDARDS FOR PUBLIC HOSPITALS* (continued)

Minimal Acceptable Care	Ideal Care
patients with legal charges, and special needs (e.g., deafness, impaired vision).	
Children and adolescents separated from adults, and continued schooling while hospitalized.	
Begin postdischarge planning on day of admission; involve patient and family.	Continuous treatment team; same staff cares for patient whether inpatient or outpatient (except in rural areas where distances too great).
Case manager, where used, assigned when patient enters hospital.	
Patient education regarding illness, avoiding relapse, medication, living skills, etc.	Formal classes with educational credits available.
Patients' legal rights protected by patient advocate; access to legal assistance.	Allegation of patient abuse by staff automatically investigated by committee including members from outside hospital.
When hospital or guardian assigned as representative payee, maximize use of funds for patients' use and needs.	

4. *Environment*

Minimal Acceptable Care	Ideal Care
Maximum four persons per room with partitions for privacy.	Individual rooms.
Clean bathrooms with guaranteed privacy (e.g., shower curtains).	Separate baths attached to individual rooms.
Evidence of personal effects in bedroom.	Personal effects from home for long-stay patients.
Common living areas decorated with rugs, lamps, pictures, etc.	Common living areas resemble a home.
Leisurely, noninstitutional dining with attention to individual food needs.	Flexible dining schedule in small eating units.
Exercise, occupational therapy, recreational therapy, and other regularly scheduled activities.	Special activities, e.g., weekly wine party for those with no alcohol problems.
Patients have own clothing that fits and is kept separate for each patient.	Clothing of patients indistinguishable from that of staff.
All fire and safety regulations for hospitals or nursing homes are met.	

* Adapted from *Care of the Seriously Mentally Ill: A Rating of State Programs*, 2nd ed., 1988, by E. Fuller Torrey, Sidney M. Wolfe, and Laurie M. Flynn, a joint publication of Public Citizen Health Research Group and the National Alliance for the Mentally Ill. Used by permission.

twenty-eight days of intensive treatment and nearly all refer patients to Alcoholics Anonymous and insist on complete abstention. They cost anywhere from $6,000 to $24,000 for the twenty-eight days. Rehabilitation centers are state-licensed but do not need accreditation from the Joint Committee on Accreditation of Hospitals.

The severely alcoholic person must first recover from acute intoxication and withdrawal, a process called *detoxification*. It usually takes place in a medical facility, either on an inpatient or an outpatient basis, because of the severe physical reactions that detoxification can entail. During this period the patient is given medication to ensure safety and reduce discomfort, and is put on a nutritious diet supplemented with high-strength vitamins. At the same time, any related health problems are treated, among them gastritis, malnutrition, dehydration, and cirrhosis of the liver. Most treatment programs also offer individual therapy, along with group and/or family therapy, by therapists specifically experienced with addiction.

Inpatient care is offered by public and private hospitals, special detoxification centers, residential care facilities, and some alcoholism clinics, and is considered necessary for individuals suffering from acute intoxication or serious related medical problems. For those with early symptoms of alcoholism, outpatient treatment, usually provided by a local alcohol treatment clinic and including medical treatment, psychotherapy, and vocational guidance, may be sufficient. Either after or concurrent with treatment, patients are urged to participate in the self-help program of Alcoholics Anonymous (AA; see Chapter 14).

Some *chemical dependency* programs treat drug abusers together with alcoholics, in the belief that addiction is the same illness no matter what substance is involved. See, for example, the accompanying weekly schedule for inpatients of the addictions treatment program at one general hospital. Although under the general aegis of the psychiatric unit, addictions patients are treated in separate therapy groups of their own. The only difference between treatment for alcoholism and narcotics addiction is that patients with the latter participate in Narcotics Anonymous (NA) rather than AA.

Inpatient narcotics programs range from four-day programs to year-long ones. The shortest-term ones are generally based in a special hospital ward, attract mainly those who can afford only a short hospitalization, and are principally for detoxification only. They are permanently effective for only a tiny minority who proceed to longer-term treatment. One such program, a four-day one in Baltimore, treats nearly two thousand addicts a year. Nearly 75 percent of its patients are on welfare and relatively few are "cured."

The most popular form of addiction program is a month-long one that consists of detoxification, individual counseling, group therapy, and faithful attendance at Narcotics Anonymous meetings after discharge. Most of these centers, of which the best known is the Betty Ford Center in Rancho Mirage, California, do not accept Medicaid and are quite expensive. A free-standing (non-hospital-based) nonprofit clinic currently costs about $5,500 for thirty days; a similar program operated by a profit-making hospital can cost up to $1,000 a day.

The longest-term program is provided in a so-called *therapeutic community*, a highly structured communal home that relies on strict discipline and encounter group confrontation to effect the rehabilitation of hard-core addicts. It appears to be the most effective treatment for those who stay for the entire *year* of treatment, but the requirements are stringent and many leave within the first two months. Addicts must be detoxified (off drugs) before they are admitted, and must, of course, remain drug-free. At first they are assigned menial tasks and gradually they take on increasing responsibility as they earn more privileges. Some therapeutic communities do not accept pregnant women, individuals with a history of violence, or anyone with a serious mental illness such as schizophrenia. Among the oldest therapeutic communities is Phoenix House, founded in 1967 and headquartered in New York; it operates treatment centers in other cities as well. Another is Second Genesis, based in Washington, D.C. The program currently costs about $15,000 per year.

In recent years, with the alarming increase in narcotics abuse among younger and younger individuals, a number of drug treatment centers specifically for children and adolescents have been established. Some require residence at the center for a time, usually ranging from four to ten weeks; others do not. One such program is Straight, a private program for patients in their early teens to early twenties. It was founded in 1976 in Florida and has expanded to a number of localities. During the first treatment phase of sixty-five to seventy-five days, youngsters live with the family of another youngster in the program who is involved in a later stage of treatment. They may not receive mail or phone calls, and may see their parents only on the center premises. During this period youngsters receive intensive group therapy and must remain drug-free, behave properly, and demonstrate a positive attitude. They may then live at home during the

Addictions Treatment Program (ATP)
Patient Schedule*

	Monday	Tuesday	Wednesday	Thursday	Friday	Saturday	Sunday
	8:00 – 8:15 A.M. Reflections						
	8:15 – 9:00 A.M. Breakfast						
	9:00 – 9:30 A.M. Community Mtg.	9:00 – 9:50 A.M. Community Contract Set	9:00 – 9:30 A.M. Community Meeting	→	9:00 – 9:50 A.M. Community Contract Eval.	9:00 – 9:30 A.M. Community Meeting	→
	9:30 – 9:55 A.M. Intro to Transition Group		9:30 – 9:55 A.M. Step Series #1	Education		9:30 – 10:30 A.M. Patient Speaker	9:30 – 10:30 A.M. AIDS Ed. & Film
	10:00 – 11:00 A.M. Group Therapy				Psycho-drama Group ATP	10:45 – 11:30 A.M. Music	10:30 – 11:30 A.M. AA Meeting Hospital
	11:00 – 12:00 Lunch	Physician's Rounds		11:00 – 12:00 Medical Consequences			
	12:00 – 1:00 P.M. Lunch	Conference Time/Free Time					
	1:00 – 2:00 P.M. Education	Step Series #3	Discharge Planning	Step Series #2	1:00 – 2:00 P.M. 12-Step Film	1:00 – 3:00 P.M. Film/ Discussion	1:00 – 2:00 P.M. Music/Exer.
	2:15 – 3:00 P.M. Body/Mind	2:00 – 3:00 P.M. Film	2:00 – 3:00 P.M. ATP Film	Assertiveness Training	Body/Mind		2:00 – 3:15 P.M. Cooking

240

3:15 – 4:15 P.M. Expressions	Psychodrama Group	Education	Family Issues	Expressive Arts ATP	Free Time	3:30 – 4:30 P.M. Arts & Crafts
4:30 – 5:00 P.M. Exercise	↑					↑
5:00 – 6:00 P.M. Dinner	↑					↑
6:00 – 7:00 P.M. Study Group	Consequences	↑	↑	Relapse Prevention	6:00 – 7:45 P.M. N.A. Hospital Meeting	Living Sober
7:00 – 7:30 P.M. Free Time	7:15 – 8:00 P.M. Men's/Women's Group	Free Time	Community Meeting	Study Group		7:30 – 8:30 P.M. Activities
7:30 – 9:00 P.M. Alumni Group	↑	See calendar: AA/NA (Closed Meetings)		↑	Program Process Group	†
9:00 – 9:30 P.M. Wrap-up				↑		↑
10:00 – 10:30P.M. Relaxation Group	↑					↑

* Waltham‑Weston Hospital, Waltham, MA.

† Sun. eve. 7:30 – 8:30 P.M. "Family Group" (relatives & friends). Patients do not attend. *Supervised visit* at conclusion.

next rehabilitation phase. Treatment at Straight takes about one year and currently costs about $11,000. In most cases insurance covers only a small portion of the cost; some employee assistance programs may cover more.

Like many programs for young people, Straight views dependence on alcohol, cocaine, and other drugs as a family rather than an individual problem. Separate sessions for parents are held that focus on chemical dependency as a family illness. Not every program takes as strong a stand, but patients' families are necessarily more involved in addiction treatment when the patient is a minor.

RESIDENTIAL FACILITIES FOR CHILDREN

Children and adolescents who need hospitalization for severe mental illness can be placed either in the psychiatric or the pediatric unit of a general hospital or in a psychiatric hospital. The former, however, may accept children only for short-term care, and may exclude some categories of illness entirely. Private mental hospitals often do not accept any children, and the majority of public mental hospitals have no facilities for them. Sometimes children are admitted to the latter, but they then are placed together with adults, which is rarely desirable. Some private psychiatric hospitals do deal primarily or exclusively with children, but they are few and far between. They also are expensive. The average cost for a child or adolescent is currently about $17,000 for the average stay (fifty days).

Another kind of facility for mentally ill children is the *residential treatment center (RTC)*, which provides long-term care in a protected environment for children and adolescents who are too disturbed to function at home or in school. These centers usually provide schooling (either in the center or in the community) and various forms of therapy, especially milieu therapy. They tend to be small, rarely accommodating more than fifty youngsters, and they, too, are few in number—about three hundred in the entire nation—compared to the need for them.

Originating as an outgrowth of orphanages, residential treatment centers are run by various agencies, usually private but often with the help of some public funds. Some are a unit within a psychiatric hospital. In these a psychiatrist usually supervises and directs treatment, carried out by nurses, social workers, psychologists, and educators. Others are free-standing and rely less on regular physician care and more on mental health workers especially trained to work with children. Most children remain in a center for no more than one or two years; some stay a considerably shorter time. Some RTCs accept autistic or psychotic children; others do not.

Another residential facility, principally for adolescents, is the *group home* or *group shelter*, which provides a supervised living arrangement for disturbed youngsters. Frequently funded entirely or partly by the state, such homes generally are affiliated with a community mental health center or a mental hospital.

Because of the shortage of twenty-four-hour residential facilities for severely mentally ill children, it may be easier to find a special day-care center or day school that caters to such youngsters. These facilities provide psychiatric treatment and schooling similar to those of residential centers but the patients return to their own homes for the night. Some day programs are part of a community mental health center. Day schools are more likely to be private schools specializing in the care of emotionally disturbed children, often along with mentally retarded and learning-disabled youngsters.

NURSING HOMES

Nursing homes, also called *extended care facilities*, are used as mental health-care facilities primarily for elderly persons with mental illness (either alone, or, more often, in association with physical illness), for middle-aged and elderly persons suffering from Alzheimer's disease or dementia from other causes (see Chapter 7), and for elderly patients who must leave a public mental hospital but still require considerable round-the-clock supervision and care.

The elderly vary tremendously in their response to drug treatment, far more so than younger people, and they tend to suffer frequent and severe side effects. The simultaneous presence of several physical and mental disorders may necessitate using several medications, which can complicate the picture. Consequently it is much more difficult to control psychiatric symptoms in the elderly by means of drugs.

Today more than 2.3 million Americans reside in nursing homes. About 90 percent are over age sixty-five and fully half have been diagnosed as "senile." The majority rely on Medicare and Medicaid to cover most or all of the cost of their stay. More than three-fourths of American nursing homes are proprietary, that is, in business to earn a profit. They represent a $55 billion industry, an amount expected to double by the year 2000. Some of them give excellent care; many others do not.

Basically three kinds of nursing home accept patients with mental illness: intermediate care, skilled nursing, and extended care. *Intermediate-care nursing homes*, which represent the majority of all nursing homes, are supposed to give nursing supervision and such personal care services as help with eating, bathing, dressing, and walking. Therapy and other services may be provided, but in reality many such facilities offer little more than custodial care. Medicaid may reimburse the cost of intermediate care completely; Medicare does not cover it at all.

A *skilled nursing facility* must provide round-the-clock nursing and preventive care, rehabilitation, therapy, and other services as needed. Skilled-care facilities are covered by Medicare (for a limited time) and Medicaid—although some are covered only by Medicaid— and are eligible for accreditation by the Joint Commission on Accreditation of Hospitals. An *extended-care facility* is supposed to supply round-the-clock skilled nursing and medical supervision; it is intended to serve as an extension of hospital care on a long-term but not necessarily permanent basis. It is covered by Medicare and by some private health insurance plans, and is eligible for accreditation by the Joint Commission on Accreditation of Hospitals. In addition, numerous private insurance firms offer long-term-care insurance, with widely varying coverage and prices.

Medicare coverage eligibility depends on the illness. Physicians must periodically certify that a patient needs a given level of care or Medicare will not pay for it. (See Chapter 24 for more about Medicare and Medicaid.)

To locate a nursing home for an elderly mentally ill relative, ask your relative's physician, rabbi or pastor, a local family service agency, the local board of health (which checks to see if local homes comply with the health code), a local Social Security office, your community or state council on aging (or elderly affairs), or senior citizens' organization (they may have first-hand knowledge of local homes). Two national organizations to contact (for information and also for making specific complaints about a home) are the American Health Care

Association, for proprietary (profit-making) homes,* and the American Association of Homes for the Aging, for nonprofit homes (see Appendix A for addresses). Ask for the names of *licensed* facilities that are eligible for the kind of reimbursement on which you or your relative will be relying.

Each state has its own licensing requirements. Most states require regular inspection of a home by the Department of Public Health, as well as by local bodies that make sure it meets sanitary codes, fire ordinances, electrical codes, and other safety requirements. It is wise to see these licenses, which indicate that the home meets some minimum safety standards.

There are some excellent guides on how to select a nursing home. Every one of them urges you to visit the home for at least an hour or two and look it over from top to bottom, including not only bedrooms and toilets but halls, lobby, dining room, kitchen, activity rooms, and grounds. Note particularly how the staff members treat patients (kindly, politely), how patients look (clean, dressed, not in obvious distress), and the appearance of the food (try to time your visit during a meal). See the administrator personally and ask her detailed questions concerning medical and nursing services (is there a physician?), activities (is there physical therapy? occupational therapy?), rules, licensing, eligibility for Medicaid and Medicare, extra charges if any, and so on.

Your state office of elderly affairs or human services or welfare may issue a brochure or guidelines to investigating local nursing homes. *Nursing Home Care,* published by the U.S. Department of Health and Human Services is available for a modest price from the Superintendent of Documents, U.S. Government Printing Office, Washington, DC 20402.

CHOOSING A HOSPITAL

Let's assume that you or your relative needs to be hospitalized. Frequently hospitalization is arranged by your doctor, but sometimes one doesn't have a doctor or the doctor offers several hospitals from which

* Write them for a free copy of *Thinking About a Nursing Home?* which includes a list of state nursing home associations.

to choose. In that case it certainly is desirable for the patient and her family to take part in the decision.

Length of stay, costs and insurance coverage, and the age and legal status of the patient all are factors that limit choices. As indicated above, some hospitals do not offer long-term treatment, many will not admit patients unless they have hospitalization insurance or can demonstrate their ability to pay, and many do not accept children at all. Unless a person is legally committed it is unlikely that she can be admitted into a state hospital, where charges are based on ability to pay. Most often, the only facilities among which one can choose for a voluntary admission will be either a general hospital or a private mental hospital.

Ideally a hospital is a therapeutic community where the patient is protected from outside influences that have contributed to her illness, where therapy of many kinds is available, including appropriate recreational and occupational therapy, and where she may receive attention from a variety of competent and concerned specialists. In practice this protective environment may be prisonlike, with locked rooms, the use of physical restraints, and rigid rules to which all patients must conform. Moreover, you cannot judge from appearances alone. Repression can take place in an attractive setting, too.

Staffing can also be deceptive. A high ratio of staff to patients can look wonderful on paper, but what is the reality? For example, in one state hospital thirty-four employees were assigned to a unit of fifty-eight acutely ill patients: twenty on the day shift, seven on the evening shift, and another seven on the night shift. The day employees were eleven therapy aides, only four of whom were actually there; two psychiatrists, one of whom left daily at noon; one treatment team leader; one nurse; one social worker; and a practical nurse, psychologist, and rehabilitation specialist, who also were not there (they had resigned six months earlier and still had not been replaced). The evening shift consisted of six aides and one practical nurse, and the night shift of seven aides. Since no registered nurse was on either of these shifts, any emergency arising between 4 P.M. and 8 A.M. had to be handled on a catch-as-catch-can basis by a nurse management team that was responsible for several hundred other patients as well. As pointed out before, state hospitals have severe staffing problems, so this situation is not altogether surprising. However, the staff on paper was a far cry from the staff present in the hospital.

What, then, should you look for in selecting a hospital? At the minimum, the hospital should have a *license*, which means it reports to the state department of health. You can ask to see a copy of the Department of Mental Health inspector's last report, which should be on file in the administrator's office.

If possible, the hospital should be *accredited* by the Joint Commission on Accreditation of Hospitals, which means it has been inspected by the commission, has filled out an extensive questionnaire, and undergoes a very thorough survey every three years. The survey focuses on patient care and services, as well as general environment safety, staff quality, and administration. Most hospitals that have it display their JCAH accreditation. About half of state mental hospitals and three-fourths of private psychiatric hospitals and general hospitals are accredited.

Another question concerns the patient's legal status. In most general hospitals a patient can leave the hospital any time he wishes to, whether or not the staff agrees, provided a paper is signed releasing the hospital from any responsibility. In some psychiatric units of general hospitals and in most mental hospitals (public or private) a patient must give notice before leaving, and if the staff disagrees, the patient's departure may be delayed for several days.

Ultimately, your most important questions concern the hospital's quality of care, which is harder to judge. For a general hospital, which might be your first choice for a case requiring either short- or intermediate-term care, consider the hospital's *reputation* in the community. Is it well regarded? Is the psychiatrist in charge well qualified and competent (some believe this is *the* crucial question)? Here you can rely on the opinion of local doctors not directly concerned in mental health care, as well as psychiatrists and other mental health professionals.

What *kinds of treatment* are available? If individual therapy is given, how often and for how long, and by whom? If there is group therapy—and there generally is—how often do groups meet and how large are they? Is milieu therapy part of the regimen? It is in most hospitals today, so if not, you should find out why not. Is there occupational (activity) therapy? If so, what kinds of activities are available? Do they seem appropriate for the patient for whom you are inquiring? You can ask all these questions over the telephone, when you also should inquire about the *number of beds*, the *kinds of accommodation* (ward, semiprivate room, how many beds per room), and any limitations on *length of stay*.

Who will be treating the patient? Is there a *treatment team*? Is there an individual *treatment plan* for each patient? Does the patient know what it contains, and can he request changes in it once it is made? Does the professional staff meet to discuss each patient's progress or lack of it? How often? A treatment plan is not just a schedule of activities. Rather, it states specific goals for a patient that are to be reached (it is hoped) in a specified time. Since these goals involve the patient's behavior and/or symptoms, he should know precisely what they are. (See the treatment contract earlier in this chapter.)

What is the *overall goal of treatment* for you or your relative? Is it to bring the patient through a current crisis, or to prepare him for discharge and care as an outpatient? When does the hospital expect to discharge the patient? Are there plans for both discharge and after-care? In a good hospital the goals for treatment are set during or almost immediately after the patient's admission, and a treatment plan is devised almost at once. Treatment actually begins on the day of admission, and so should a plan for discharge.

These questions may seem like an enormous number to ask, and indeed there may not be time to get every answer in the critical period when a decision must be made. However, many of them can be raised with the referral source, and if admission can be put off for a day or so, as it often can, a great deal can be learned over the telephone if you are persistent and patient.

Most hospitals publish a brochure for patients and their families that lists the names of the chief administrators and gives basic information about clothing, mail, telephone, laundry, visiting hours, and the like. Be sure to ask for such a brochure and read it carefully. It may answer some of your questions in advance, so that you can reserve the others for telephone or personal inquiry.

Upon admission, ask *who will be in charge* of the patient's treatment—who is the person to ask the many questions that may arise in the course of hospitalization? Is this person the same one who will be in touch with the patient's family? If not, whom should family members call to inquire about progress? Are there restrictions on *visiting*? Is visiting ever prohibited?

How does the hospital deal with a violent or disruptive patient? Is *seclusion* used, and if so, for how long, and how often? Seclusion means confining a patient in a special room, usually containing only a mattress, in order to calm her down. It is rarely used in general hospitals, since they tend to refer unruly individuals elsewhere, but it is frequently used in both private and public mental hospitals. Generally there are strict rules on how seclusion is to be used; find out what they are.

During admission you should ask exactly what hospital care is included in the published rates and what is extra. Even if the hospital will be paid through Blue Cross or some other insurance plan, ultimately you are paying and you should know exactly what you will get.

Treatment in a general hospital tends to be more expensive than in a private mental hospital, since the latter usually does not need to maintain much special medical equipment, laboratories, operating rooms, or the like. Some psychiatric hospitals are very expensive indeed, but as a rule they are less expensive than a general hospital. Treatment in a general hospital usually is almost fully covered by standard insurance plans like Blue Cross for a certain period of time, most often sixty days; it also is covered by Medicaid and Medicare. Treatment in a private mental hospital may be covered in part by such private plans, but usually for a shorter time, and most private hospitals do not accept Medicaid patients.

A good private mental hospital is likely to have more staff available for treatment. Individual therapy may be given as often as three times a week; group therapy may be conducted by more highly trained therapists. Or it may not. The variation among private hospitals is enormous in every respect: cost, quality of care, staff-to-patient ratio. Some private hospitals refuse certain kinds of patient—the psychotic, the drug abuser, the alcoholic. Others specialize in certain disorders. There is an Association of Private Psychiatric Hospitals that requires its members to meet certain standards, but some very good hospitals simply do not choose to belong to it. Accreditation by the Joint Commission on Accreditation of Hospitals, however, is a must.

IF YOU CAN'T FIND A HOSPITAL

Psychiatrists usually have admitting privileges at one or more hospitals and they somehow can make room for their patients who need to be hospitalized. But suppose you or your relative is seeing a clinical psychologist or social worker for therapy, and a crisis arises requiring hospitalization. Usually your therapist will have connections enabling admission, either directly or through your local community mental health center. In an emergency something can nearly always be found.

Sometimes, however, it is hard to find a hospital bed nearby. To cope with this problem, the same psychiatrist who founded a therapist-finding service (described in Chapter 10) also established a computerized "bed-finder" service, used by crisis teams, mental health centers, individual practitioners, and the hospitals themselves (when they don't have room for someone who needs admission fast). The service keeps track of bed availability in twenty-two hospitals in a given metropolitan area, including both private psychiatric hospitals and general hospitals with a psychiatric unit. In making a referral, numerous factors are taken into account, including the patient's age and sex, insurance status, need for medication, and whether the admission is voluntary or involuntary (for the latter, it must be to a locked ward). For practitioners who want to avoid making perhaps several dozen phone calls, such a service fills a real need.

Chapter

21

LEAVING THE HOSPITAL:
AFTERCARE AND REHABILITATION

LACK OF support and follow-up treatment after being hospitalized for mental illness can, and often does, lead to a relapse, which in turn can lead a patient right back to the hospital. For many individuals an appointment once or twice a week with a therapist is not enough, at least not at the beginning, during the initial period of recovery and adjustment that follows discharge. Where the hospital stay has been very brief, and the focus of treatment has been on controlling the worst symptoms, with no time taken to deal with or even investigate possible underlying problems, *aftercare* of some kind is even more important.

Ideally, planning for discharge should be part of the overall treatment from the start. Merely instructing a patient who is being discharged to visit the hospital outpatient clinic (or community mental health clinic) once a week is not enough. The patient may never get there. Preferably the same therapist should be available for treatment after discharge. When that is not possible, and often it is not, some other arrangement for follow-up therapy should be made. If at all possible, the patient should have some say in the choice of the new therapist and arrange to meet him *before* discharge.

PARTIAL HOSPITALIZATION

In addition to normal twenty-four-hour hospitalization, some mental health centers and hospitals provide *day care*, where patients come to the facility to spend a certain number of hours every day but return home at night, or *night care*, where patients work or attend school during the day and return to the facility for the night. Partial hospitalization is a loosely used term, for some programs provide evening and/ or weekend care. The facilities provide individual and/or group or family therapy, as well as activities judged to be therapeutically useful, in a safe, controlled atmosphere. They are intended to serve either as a transition between the hospital and the community (that is, a form of aftercare for patients leaving the hospital) or as alternatives to full-time hospitalization.

Here is a description of a day-care program run by a community mental health center. This program serves clients from three suburban towns. Transportation is not provided; the clients must get to the program on their own.

Approximately twenty-two clients per day use the center. Each is assigned to a staff person to plan the individual's daily schedule and to reevaluate it every three months. The schedule consists of therapeutic groups—a setup similar to the milieu therapy practiced inside the hospital. Most clients come either for certain groups or for the full day (9:30 A.M. to 3 P.M.). All of them receive additional therapy, either at the mental health center clinic or privately.

The average stay in the program ranges from six months to a year. Clients usually begin the program on a part-time basis, and then leave it in stages when departing for a job or school. The staff is multidisciplinary, including a half-time psychiatrist, a psychologist, occupational therapists, social workers, nurses, and students of nursing, occupational therapy, and social work.

Clients range in age from eighteen to eighty or older. Most have problems that have been diagnosed as severe: schizophrenia, manic-depressive psychosis, major depression. The majority are young adults who are learning to lead independent lives. There also is a group of women, which fluctuates in size, who are dealing with problems of middle age: departing children, reentry into the job market, separation, and divorce.

The cost of attending this day-care program is usually covered by medical insurance (up to $500 for Blue Cross), Medicaid, and other plans. A person paying for the service entirely out-of-pocket in 1989 would be charged $52 per day.

The schedule (see the accompanying table) consists of therapeutic groups that are either task-oriented (that is, they work on specific group projects, such as meal preparation) or verbally oriented (engage in verbal group therapy); some groups do both. There is a daily community meeting attended by everyone present that day. The medications group (nearly all the clients receive psychoactive drugs) discusses kinds of medication, why one takes certain drugs and not others, increases and decreases in dosage, side effects, and so on. The skill-building group undertakes individual projects designed to examine what skills a client has, what tasks can be performed, the level of concentration, the need for supervision, and so forth. The healthy eating group prepares lunch one day a week. On other days clients either bring a bag lunch or go out to local restaurants. Every client is expected to attend the activities and groups listed on her schedule, and is asked to plan appointments and personal errands outside program hours. Clients are not supposed to take naps while attending the program, unless there is special staff approval.

Who might need a part-time hospital?

- A person who needs more treatment than visits to a psychiatrist or other mental health professional can provide but who does not require full inpatient care. Suppose Mary H., who has been quarreling constantly with her husband and whose children are showing signs of disturbance, becomes acutely depressed by her situation and finds it increasingly difficult to meet the normal day-to-day demands of her family. She is spending more and more time sleeping. A day hospital program, where she can receive therapy and support while her children are in school, may be a valuable alternative for her; full-time hospitalization might not be necessary for her treatment needs and would also have the disadvantage of disrupting the family to a much greater extent.
- A person whose illness is under control but who is not ready to

Week's Schedule in a Day-Care Program

Time	Monday	Tuesday	Wednesday	Thursday	Friday
A.M. 8:30					
9:00					
9:30	Coffee	Coffee	Coffee	Coffee	Coffee
10:00	Comm. mtg.	Comm. mtg.	Comm. mtg	Comm. mtg.	Comm. mtg.
11:00	Medication group	Healthy eating	Current events	Skill bldg.	Arts & crafts
	Newspaper	Other's point of view	Ind. Living	Taking care of yourself	Open verbal
12:00	Lunch	Lunch	Lunch	Lunch	Lunch
P.M. 12:30	Recreation	Recreation	Recreation	Recreation	Recreation
1:00	Outing	Art therapy	Medication group	Social club	Women's group / Movement
2:00	→	Work exploration	Prevocational	→	Communications
2:30	→	→	→		→
3:00					

resume work or school. For example, suppose Donald's schizophrenia has been brought under control with medication but he is not ready to return to college. He continues to live at home and is enrolled in a day-care program for adolescents, some of whom attend a special school. This school offers a computer course that he finds interesting, and in the structured environment provided along with daily group therapy and numerous therapeutic activities, he might improve enough to reenroll in college by the next semester.

CAREER REHABILITATION

Not all day programs are as good as those described. Particularly for adolescents, a day hospital where watching television is the main activity of the day and the clients, who are treated like patients, sit around drinking coffee and smoking cigarettes, becomes tedious, especially for those who attend for several years on end. With this in mind, the Boston University Center for Psychiatric Rehabilitation embarked on two innovative programs. One, a *continuing education program*, is aimed at helping students choose a career goal and develop and implement a career plan in order to enter or reenter the work force in the occupation of their choice, with the level of support they need to succeed.

This project was actually undertaken in order to develop a model program that could be replicated at other colleges and universities throughout the country. A four-semester program, in which students first tried to determine what they like to do and what they are good at doing, narrowed down the appropriate possibilities among the hundreds of different occupations, determined the qualifications and credentials students needed for their chosen career, and then planned how to take the first step toward that career. At this last stage students determine the supports and skills they need. One returning to school might need a typewriter or help in paying tuition, as well as test-taking and other study skills. In the program's first three classes, twenty-seven of the forty enrolled completed all four semesters, eight dropped out, and five left but hoped to return to finish. Of those who finished, one entered a one-year legal-advocate program and another started a two-year medical technician course. Some went straight on to jobs; one became a letter carrier for the postal service and another a live-in counselor in a group home for mentally retarded adults.

Another program started by the same center was a *supported employment program* on the university's campus. Such programs already exist in some areas, but they are not widespread, nor do they accommodate many individuals. Indeed, most of those currently existing are for retarded adults, who either work in a state-supported sheltered workshop or, if they are able, are "outposted" to work for a bank, store, or other business willing to hire and train them. Owing to lingering prejudice, all too few employers are willing to hire mental patients, but it is hoped that such programs will grow.

One former community mental health center, which is now a closed-referral facility (meaning that its clients are referred mainly by state agencies), has a number of programs designed to integrate people with mental illness, retardation, and/or serious family problems into the community. One is an adolescent day program for youngsters who were hospitalized for psychiatric problems that offers group therapy, health education, and prevocational and educational training. Another is an adult day-activity program that includes social activities, work training, and trips for adult psychiatric patients.

RESIDENTIAL AFTERCARE

With massive deinstitutionalization, thousands of patients were discharged from state and county hospitals in which they had lived for years and found themselves with no place to go. The National Institute of Mental Health estimated in one study that 38 percent of them were referred to no aftercare facilities at all.

Many, if not most, long-term chronic patients have no families to which to return, and they cannot manage life on their own in the community. Some have been institutionalized too long to remember how to shop, cook, do laundry, and perform other simple tasks of everyday life. Some are still too disturbed to behave reliably. Consequently many of them join the ranks of the homeless. One California VA hospital reported that 79 percent of its applicants in a three-week period were homeless individuals who had previously been in mental institutions. Not only is this true for patients discharged from public institutions: General hospitals, owing to insurance constraints, can treat patients only until they are no longer psychotic and then must discharge them. Not all have families or can live alone.

In practice there are residences with varying levels of care and supervision. Unfortunately there are far too few of them to accommodate those who need them. Community residences called *halfway houses* and *quarterway houses* serve either as transitional steps between the hospital and the community or as alternatives to full-time hospitalization.

Quarterway houses often are sections or wards in a mental hospital that serve as a transition to discharge, encouraging skills in everyday living. Halfway houses often are located in the community but have an on-site staff and programs. They tend to serve younger, more vocationally able patients who have retained ties within their community.

There also are *long-term residences* based in the community. They tend to have more staff than halfway houses and are intended for persons who may stay more than a year (as opposed to those who use the halfway house as a transitional living arrangement). Those nursing homes that are extended-care facilities (see above) may be used as a form of aftercare, but more often they serve as a substitute for long-term hospitalization, particularly for elderly patients.

EXAMPLES

The community mental health center that serves nine towns, described in Chapter 13, runs a traditional halfway house with a staff of two and beds for twelve adults; four of those are in a separate apartment in the house, to prepare its residents for still more independent living. It also runs a house for elderly chronic patients who are moving out of a large state hospital, along with staff members who have helped them prepare for this move (some have spent forty years in the hospital). This house is within an elderly complex that includes both independent living and nursing home care for those who will eventually need it.

A large prestigious private mental hospital in the same area runs five community residences: a twenty-four bed facility for anyone in psychiatric treatment who is at least seventeen years old and has a bona fide program to attend during the day (a job, school, day hospital); a seventeen-bed residence for persons twenty-one or over with chronic psychiatric problems who do not require hospitalization but cannot live in the community without special supervision; two five-bed units for recovering alcoholics who have been discharged from the hospital's own inpatient alcoholism program; and an eight-bed residence for younger adolescents (fourteen to nineteen) who are enrolled in a hospital treatment program and its special high school but who do not need inpatient care.

This hospital's residential programs are among the very best obtainable. They are small, comprehensive, and rarely available elsewhere. More common are the group homes or shelters for adolescents (see above), but they, too, are limited in size and number, and there may be a considerable waiting period before one can get in.

A variety of other residential aftercare programs have sprung up, ranging in quality from very good to abysmally bad, and varying greatly in how much and what kind of supervision are provided: professionally trained supervisors, untrained supervisors, staff living in-house or coming in daily, weekly, or less. One kind is the *cooperative apartment* or *house* where the occupants help one another, both emotionally and in running the household. During the week they may attend a day-care program, or perhaps hold jobs or attend school; evenings and weekends they are on their own, without supervision. The cooperative apartment usually is either leased by a mental health agency or by a related nonprofit corporation, and/or their leases are shared with the tenants. The tenants live in groups of two to five. They pay their own rent, share in household chores, and have professional supervision, with crisis intervention available.

Another alternative is the *supervised apartment*, where staff members of the sponsoring organization live in a building containing several such apartments and provide supervision, therapy, and other forms of support. In rural areas, *work camps* may serve those persons who cannot yet survive in independent housing but do not need a full-scale institution. Such camps generally function as working farms, with daily chores and work, and supervision available as needed.

These arrangements require a level of independence that some discharged patients cannot undertake. For them a *foster home* may be found with a family in the community, or they may go to live in a *licensed community boarding house* (in some places called a *board-and-care home*). Foster care, based on a centuries-old program in Gheel, Belgium, involves placements that are run by a nonclinical caretaker, who provides housing for one to four persons. Often such persons are elderly or mentally retarded. Other necessary services are provided in the community, foster care being essentially custodial in nature.

Private (proprietary) facilities consist of hotels (welfare or single-room occupancy) or homes for adults. Usually they provide neither relief from social isolation, since there are no common activities in which the occupants can join, nor appropriate rehabilitation or treatment. The latter two arrangements, unfortunately, are open to abuse by untrained and unscrupulous providers. Although some private homes and boarding houses provide a genuinely homelike atmosphere and family-style activities, many others are dreary, dismal places where the family or boarding-house operator has no interest in the occupants other than the rent and board they pay and may in fact treat them abusively.

Providing for deinstitutionalized mental patients remains a major problem in many places, and in some inner-city areas, a disgrace. Community resistance often forces residences to be established in run-down or undesirable neighborhoods, creating, in effect, an "ex-mental patient ghetto." Funding is limited, and local regulations for obtaining funds and establishing housing alternatives can be very cumbersome; at one point forty-seven separate steps to obtain approval from various bodies were required in one state.

The best housing, where residents are treated with dignity and warmth, has a maximum of ten to twelve persons in a single facility. Ideally a person can be moved to a residence with more or less supervision, depending on her current needs. Furthermore, housing should be integrated with other important activities, such as employment.

Those ex-patients who are lucky enough to find good housing still may need psychosocial rehabilitation to manage the tasks of day-to-day living: transportation, grooming, shopping, personal hygiene, banking, and so on. To cope with these problems, the National Institute of Mental Health set up a Community Support Program (CSP) that began in 1977 with federal grants to twenty states to promote the development and coordination of the necessary services described: housing, income, employment, social life, counseling, medical care, safety. In the next decade this program was expanded to include all fifty states. Most CSP programs utilize a *case manager*, an individual specifically designated to coordinate services for one patient and to ensure that the patient's needs are met.

THE CLUBHOUSE

The CSP program is not richly funded nor does it always work perfectly. Another model for combining housing, socialization, and rehabilitation is the *clubhouse*, the name given to centers such as Fountain House (New York City), Horizon House (Philadelphia), Threshholds (Chicago), Rose Garden (Rockford, Illinois), Council House (Pittsburgh), Hill House (Cleveland), Fellowship House (Miami), and Portal House (Los Angeles). It was Fountain House, begun in 1948, that became a model for the others, and in the next two decades more than one hundred and eighty clubhouses in thirty-eight states were patterned after it. Beginning as a social center, the clubhouse usually is allied with housing, sponsoring apartments, halfway houses, and the like, and also employment programs. Ideally it works closely with the local state or county hospital to assure a smooth transition from hospital to clubhouse. (A similar program can be carried out by a mental health center, for example, the house for elderly patients run by the community health center that is described above.)

A vocational rehabilitation program, including a series of gradually increasing responsibilities with guidance and supervision, helps those who may be able to work. Some patients progress to a transitional employment program, at first part-time. Job-sharing, with two patients hired for one position, may be used. The clubhouse enlists the support of local businesses and civic organizations and uses funds from a variety of sources—county, state, and federal.

Such programs are not only humanitarian but cost-effective. Studies have shown that they decrease the rehospitalization rate of their members considerably, and hospital stays cost far more than their relatively modest outlays.

Chapter

22

IS IT WORKING? HOW TO EVALUATE TREATMENT

How CAN you tell if the treatment you have gone to so much trouble and expense to obtain is any good? Is it helping? Is it making you worse? Or is it neutral, a virtual stalemate (and therefore a waste of time and money)?

Again, there is no easy answer. Even in cases where the goal of treatment is limited and obvious—to remove a particular symptom, such as impotence—and the method of treatment is very specific, as it usually is in sex therapy, you may end up being able to enjoy sexual relations more but discover that you have a whole set of new problems.

There are some clear-cut instances where certain treatments are a waste of time. Psychoanalysis and insight-oriented individual or group therapy will not help the psychotic person suffering from schizophrenia or manic-depressive disorder *unless* the psychosis is being controlled with medication—and perhaps not even then. But suppose you don't like your therapist. Should you change to another? What if you start having trouble sleeping and have bad dreams about issues brought up in therapy? Does this mean you are getting worse? Or suppose the medication you have been given to make you feel less tense and anxious is leaving you too groggy to do your work at the office? Or your therapist keeps asking you about past events when you really want to talk about your present problems? What if your therapist makes sexual advances? Or suppose your therapist never says much of anything and your sessions are increasingly taken up by long silences? Does this mean you are finished, that you have gone as far as you can go?

TREATMENT GOALS

To a large extent your judgment of whether or not your treatment is effective depends on what you expect it to accomplish. Do you want to be rid of troublesome symptoms? If so, exactly what symptoms are you talking about?

In your very first interview with a therapist, whether it is a private practitioner who has been recommended or the intake person at your mental health clinic, you will probably be asked just what brought you (or your relative or friend) here. If no one does ask, you should certainly bring it up yourself, and without delay. Says one psychiatrist:

> When I see a person, I am most concerned with how he functions, usually in a major area of life. People usually come to me with a problem for which they—or someone else—wish to have help. I suppose if they came to me and said, "How am I doing? Do I need help?" I would try to assess what they were doing with their lives in terms of how they were functioning at work, what they were achieving in relation to their potential, how they were getting along with others (harmoniously or in conflict), how much they were suffering subjectively, how confident they felt, how much they were able to do what they wanted, how they were facing their problems, and so on.

During your first session the therapist—any therapist—is looking you over, trying to assess just what is the matter and what can or should be done about it. You may know that help of some kind is needed, or you may simply be responding to someone's recommendation (that of your doctor, perhaps, who can find no organic cause for your frequent stomach upsets). In that case, you may be seeing the therapist in order to find out if she thinks therapy is indeed the right course of action for you. That in itself is an appropriate goal—to find out if therapy is indicated—and some authorities suggest it should be the very first goal for everyone. In other words, the decision to be evaluated in order to find out if therapy is needed and the decision to enter therapy with a particular practitioner are two separate matters.

The process of assessing symptoms was discussed in Chapter 2. The therapist (or intake person) will (or should) obtain from you a history of the present problem, a detailed past history, including some family history, and take account of your present mental status in order to come to some conclusions about your condition. At a clinic this initial interview becomes the basis for choosing a mode of therapy and a therapist for you (the client rarely has much choice, at least not initially), or, if no appropriate therapist is available or no appropriate treatment is given there, for referring you elsewhere. With a private individual therapist (or one who is screening you for membership in a therapy group) the first interview becomes the basis for an initial diagnosis.

It is at this point that you should ask some questions. We are assuming that you have already inquired, before even coming to the first interview, about this therapist's fees and whether or not he has time to take you on. (See Chapter 12 on how to choose a therapist.) If for some reason you have not obtained this information, now is the time to ask. Let us assume, however, that you already know you can afford this therapist (or your insurance covers it adequately) and he does have time to take another client. Essentially you are now determining how compatible you find him.

ASK YOUR POTENTIAL THERAPIST:

1. What do you think my problem is?
2. How do you propose to help me?
3. How do you feel about working with me?

First, you may want to know the therapist's training and background, and general philosophy of treatment. Does he use one method
exclusively or primarily? Is this method proposed for your problem?
Has he had experience with this kind of problem, and if so, what were
the results? Does he agree that your problem is . . . , or does he believe
it is really something else (and if so, what)? What does he consider the
primary goal of treatment? Approximately how long might it take to
achieve this goal (six months, a year, three years)? The response to this
last question may well be that it is too early to tell, but ask it anyhow;
you certainly will want to bring it up again some time.

A variety of other issues may be of special concern to you, so feel
free to ask about them. Among them are:

- May you telephone the therapist? Is there any special time for doing
  so? Does he ever discuss therapy issues on the phone, or schedule an
  emergency interview if you need it?
- What provisions does the therapist make for vacations and/or out-of-
  town trips? Is there someone who covers?
- Do you have to pay for a canceled (by you) appointment? How much
  notice is required to avoid payment?
- Does the therapist prescribe medication or have it prescribed by a
  consulting physician? If so, what if any precautions are taken (concerning side effects, allergic reaction, etc.)?
- How does the therapist feel about using ECT?
- How does the therapist feel about getting a second opinion? Is he
  agreeable to consultation should the need arise?
- Is the therapist willing to draw up a treatment contract (see below)?
- If after a time the fee becomes too burdensome and continued ther-
  apy is indicated, is the therapist willing to adjust the fee?
- Is the therapist willing to see one or more members of your family
  (once, occasionally, or as the need arises)?
- Has the therapist ever been in personal therapy?

In the end, however, what is most important is your overall impression of this person, in whom you may be confiding some intimate
details of your life. Does he seem to understand what you are saying?
Does what he says make sense to you?

An elaborate research study of the interpersonal skills of an effective therapist came up with three particular characteristics: accurate
empathy, nonpossessive warmth, and genuineness. In terms of how

well clients respond to treatment, the ideal therapist, according to this study, is a person who can really understand what people are saying, who can readily get on someone else's wavelength (accurate empathy). Moreover, this person has a genuine liking and concern for others, accepting them with all their faults and foibles (nonpossessive warmth), and is able to convey that feeling to them. Finally, the ideal therapist is not a phoney. He does not pretend to know everything, or to be superior to his clients. He is not defensive about his own shortcomings, and does not feel threatened when you ask questions about his background and orientation.

In another, less formal study, twenty-three psychotherapists were asked what *they* consider important in choosing their own therapists. The qualities mentioned again and again were "warmth," "liking," "caring," and "support." They looked for someone who would give them a feeling of being "approved," "appreciated," "respected." They rejected therapists whom they described as "cold fish," "too distant," and "ungiving."

Against these criteria, how does your therapist measure up? It may take more than one interview for you to make these judgments, or it may take some time and thought after the first interview. There is no need to decide immediately, or to schedule another appointment at once. If you are not sure, say so—feel free to tell the therapist about your hesitations and reservations—and say you will think it over and make another appointment if you decide to proceed.

If you do think this person is right for you, you may want to propose drawing up a treatment contract or plan that will spell out the goals of treatment and some kind of timetable for achieving them.

THE THERAPY CONTRACT

Strictly speaking a contract is a promise or set of promises whose performance the law recognizes as a duty and for breach of which the law gives remedy. The therapy contract is a more flexible agreement. Rather than intended to be legally binding, it establishes an explicit mutual understanding and accountability between client and therapist. It defines the agreed-on goals of therapy and the basic ground rules: when and where therapy will take place, and for what fee. It does not guarantee results. The stated goals may or may not be ful-

SAMPLE THERAPY CONTRACT*

I, Jane Doe, hereafter referred to as CLIENT, agree to join with Mary Jones, hereafter referred to as THERAPIST, every Tuesday evening at 7:00 P.M. until 7:50 P.M. beginning October 2, 1990 until November 20, 1990. During these eight fifty-minute sessions we will direct our mutual efforts toward the following goals:

1. Relieving my chronic headaches.
2. Explaining to my satisfaction my frequent temper outbursts at my husband.
3. Exploring the possibility of my returning to work.

I agree to pay $90 per session for the use of Therapist's resources, training, and experience as a psychotherapist. This amount is payable within thirty (30) days of each session.

If I am not satisfied with the progress made in attaining the above-named goals, I may cancel any and all subsequent appointments for these sessions provided that I give Therapist three days' notice of my intention to cancel. In that event I am not required to pay for sessions not met. However, if I miss a session without such forewarning I am financially responsible for that missed session. The only exception to this arrangement is unforeseen and unavoidable accident or illness.

At the end of eight sessions Therapist and Client will agree to renegotiate the terms of this contract. We include the possibility that stated goals will have changed during this period. I understand that this agreement does not guarantee that I will have attained all my goals in full in the stipulated time. However, it does constitute an offer on my part to pay Therapist for access to her resources as a psychotherapist and her acceptance to apply all those resources in good faith.

I further stipulate that this agreement become part of the medical record, which is accessible to both parties at will but to no other person without my written consent. Therapist will respect my right to maintain the confidentiality of any information communicated by me to Therapist during the course of therapy. In particular, Therapist will not publish, communicate, or otherwise disclose, without my written consent, any such information which, if disclosed, would injure me in any way.

| _____ | _____ | _____ |
| Date | Signature of Client | Signature of Therapist |

---

* Adapted by permission from _Through The Mental Health Maze_ by Sallie Adams and Michael Orgel. Courtesy of Health Research Group, Washington, DC.

filled. They may even be changed in the course of the therapy. But at the very least a written contract makes the client decide on his priorities—why therapy is being undertaken and what it is intended to accomplish—and it makes those priorities clear to the therapist.

A contract may take several sessions to draw up, a time during which your goals can be clarified. The therapist will provide input, too. Some of your goals may be unrealistic, or they may not be ambitious enough. A problem that was years in the making, a habit you have had for a long time, may take more than a dozen sessions of therapy to understand and change.

The therapist will learn a great deal about you in the formulation of the contract, and, conversely, the therapist's reactions will tell you a good deal. Not all therapists will react favorably to a contract. Some may feel it limits therapy too much to certain issues at the expense of other, equally important ones. Others may find it puts too much responsibility in the hands of the client, whom they may judge to be too disturbed to make rational decisions. Still others may feel it presupposes a certain approach to treatment on their part, with which they may not agree. Even a therapist not opposed to the basic idea of such a contract might feel that for a client to think through problems and feelings enough to formulate a contract is too much to ask. In some cases no doubt it is, but even if it can't be done at once, it might be done after a few sessions when, with or without medication, the client could be feeling well enough to begin sorting out goals.

A good therapy contract is flexible. It allows for changing goals at all times, even within the period of the contract. After all, one of the basic purposes of therapy is to get a new, informed perspective on your feelings and behavior. This often results in a redefinition of goals and even of the problems that brought you to a therapist in the first place.

The basic elements of the therapy contract are:

1. Names of each party to the contract.
2. Dates of the beginning and end of the agreement.
3. The length of each therapy session.
4. The goals of the sessions (stated as specifically as possible).
5. The cost per session and when payable.
6. The definition of the therapist's services.
7. Provisions for cancellation of the contract and of any sessions.
8. Renegotiation at the end of the stipulated period.
9. Allowance for changing goals.

10. Definition of the nature of the services; no guarantee of results; guarantee of good faith.
11. Establishment of access to medical records; guarantee of records' confidentiality and their content and use of any information therein.

WHAT ABOUT GROUP THERAPY?

Although the above-described therapy contract and the accompanying sample contract are designed for individual therapy, there is no reason why it could not be adapted for group therapy as well. Here, however, unless the group can agree on a set of general goals and expectations that apply to all members, each group member would have to state her specific goals and make them known to the others.

As indicated in Chapter 17 in the general description of group therapy, most group leaders hold at least one individual meeting with a prospective member in order to determine whether or not that person will fit into the group. It is the time, as we noted, for you to ask about the therapist's background, the makeup and goals of the group, how long it will meet, and how members enter and leave the group. In addition, you may consider your first session or sessions with a therapy group as a period of evaluation similar to the first interview or two with an individual therapist. Some groups actually have a trial period of a set number of sessions during which a new member may decide whether or not the group is appropriate for her, and the group decides whether the new member will fit in.

What should you be considering in evaluating a therapy group? Here you must take into account two factors: the group members and the group leader. Are the other members very different from you? If so, are they *too* different—in background, education, goals, life-style—for you to understand and help each other? What kind of help are the others seeking? Is it very similar or very different from what you need? For example, some groups function principally in a low-key, supportive fashion, allowing members to talk about their own special concerns and problems with little attempt on anyone's part to work on solutions.

In contrast, another kind of group may use psychodrama, role-playing, and a variety of techniques to hasten the process of individual change. Is the group leader active or does he sit back and let the group run itself? In an insight-focused therapy group the leader may in effect be conducting individual therapy with the members in turn, rather than using the presence of other members in a constructive way. Or, if the approach is client-centered nondirective counseling, the leader may say little or nothing during meetings, even allowing the group to bog down in trivial or irrelevant conversation. Does the leader attempt to draw out a shy person and curb an overtalkative one?

Although beginning sessions with a group can be an alarming experience, making the newcomer feel as shy and anxious as a child on the first day of school in a new town, you should make an effort to learn as much as you can about the group and its leader in order to decide whether or not this group is indeed the right place for you to seek help.

IS YOUR THERAPY WORKING?

The immediate effect of any psychotherapy is a sense of relief. You have taken a giant step ahead. You have looked around and found someone who, you think, will be able to help you. You feel less anxious and unhappy just because you are seeing someone, and are comforted by the very process. Even more than most physical illnesses, mental illnesses are sensitive and responsive to care, at least initially. This response is the psychic counterpart of the placebo effect, when the very fact of a relationship with a therapist brings some relief from pain and discomfort.

After this initial period, however, things may change. If you have decided on a very brief period of therapy, such as six or eight sessions of STAPP (see Chapter 16) or a couple of months of cognitive therapy, you will soon be expecting positive results of a more permanent nature. Some of the goals you set forth originally should begin to look attainable, or begin to give way, perhaps, to somewhat different goals. From the example shown in the sample therapy contract, Jane Doe's headaches may be less intense or less frequent, and she may begin to make some connections between her outbursts at her husband and his habit of bringing home work every night and every weekend. These are signs of progress.

Sometimes, however, the initial period of relief is followed by a period of getting worse. You find yourself becoming more anxious, especially during the hours just before each session, or you find yourself unaccountably depressed. Does it mean your therapy is making you worse? It may indeed be working in just this way, forcing you to face some truths about yourself that you would rather avoid. Or it may mean that you are not making much progress after all, that your high hopes of improvement are not being fulfilled.

When is it the fault of the therapist? Here are a few early-warning signs that you may be on the wrong course:

- You find yourself frustrated by the method of therapy being used; you don't want the therapist to turn around every question you ask with, "What do *you* think?" but to give you a straightforward answer, even if that answer is simply, "I don't know."
- You are rambling on about this and that, and the therapist is not directing you in any way; for example, you know you have some serious hangups about sex but can't find a way to bring them up and consequently avoid the subject week after week.
- You have been given antidepressant medication and it is not working at all, but the therapist refuses to consider changing the dosage or trying a different drug.
- You are anxious before each session, *and* you feel dissatisfied and depressed afterward.
- The therapist has been late for three of the past four sessions and has made no offer to make up the time owed to you.
- The therapist frequently interrupts your session in order to take a phone call or talk to her secretary.
- You are not sure if the therapist is really listening to what you say; she tends to forget what happened in the previous sessions, and twice has obviously mixed you up with another client.
- When you express some doubts about your treatment the therapist flatly says you are experiencing resistance (see below for more about this) and refuses to discuss the matter further.
- The therapist suggests she can help you resolve your sexual problems by means of direct practice with the therapist. *Sex with a therapist is never therapeutic.*

SEX WITH A THERAPIST

"Sexual misconduct by psychiatrist," blasts a page-one headline. In recent years sexual abuse has made sensational news stories with increasing frequency, yet it is still believed to be one of the most underreported of crimes. Sexual abuse by physicians is not a rarity, nor is sexual abuse by therapists. Psychotherapy is a clinical relationship that is charged with emotional intimacy and trust, so when a therapist abuses that trust by indulging in sexual contact with a client it seems even more disturbing.

In one recent case a therapist who holds both an M.D. and a Ph.D. from respected universities was sued by several women alleging sexual misconduct. Three of them alleged they were abused after they were given drugs—in two cases the drug MMDA ("Ecstasy"), a derivative of mescaline and a close relative of LSD that has since been banned. Both the Hippocratic oath, taken by all physicians, and the code of ethics of most professional organizations prohibit sex between therapist and client, in the belief that the therapeutic relationship brings with it an emotional taboo similar to that associated with incest. People who come to therapists are vulnerable, and often they have a fantasy of an older, wiser person helping them. These feelings exaggerate the power imbalance already present in a therapeutic relationship, rendering the client vulnerable to exploitation.

Despite these strictures, studies indicate that as many as 6 to 10 percent of therapists admit to having some sexual contact with a client. Even this figure may be low because some therapists will not admit to such conduct even in a confidential questionnaire. Thus, although the number of malpractice suits against psychiatrists and complaints to ethics committees and licensing boards has increased in recent years, most experts believe that only a tiny fraction of such cases ever come to public attention.

State regulation of therapists has done little to prevent the problem. A few states have made sexual misconduct within psychotherapy a serious crime. In Massachusetts, one of the states with the highest per capita number of psychiatrists and psychologists, any sexual contact is legal unless it involves rape or the use of drugs (at this writing new legislation is being considered). It also is possible for a psychiatrist whose license has been revoked for sexual misconduct to start a practice as an unlicensed psychotherapist the very next day, in Massachusetts or in almost any other state. Moreover, those who are disciplined for sexual misconduct rarely serve a prison term or even face criminal trial.

One major problem of passing legislation to correct this situation is that psychiatrists, even though they often hear of sexual abuse by others from their own patients (in one survey 65 percent of respondents had heard of such events), feel that reporting it to the state would violate the confidentiality on which successful psychotherapy depends. However, there is no reason they could not urge the victim of abuse to report the psychiatrist, and then give her the emotional support needed to follow up on the situation.

ARE YOU STALLED?

You as a client are entitled to know the basic assumptions and methods of treatment undertaken, and to make sure that you and the therapist share the same goals for you. If you feel more upset during the course of therapy, it may be because you are confronting upsetting issues for the first time, or it may be because therapy is not dealing with important issues. The best way to distinguish between these is to discuss your doubts with your therapist, and without delay. Moreover, they should be fully discussed, and not dismissed with a brief, "That's resistance; you'll soon get over it," or some similar statement.

The same tack should be taken if your therapy gets into a rut. You may have heard of one or another person whose "analysis" or "therapy" drags on and on and on—for five years, ten years, even longer. There are some cases where clients must stay in therapy simply to avoid getting worse, rather than to get better, but they are not the general rule. Most of us would not even consider therapy unless we want it to have more positive results than that, and in a reasonable time. Therefore, if week after week you are bringing up the same material and nothing in your life is changing as a result of therapy, it's time you did something about it.

If you are truly stalled, probably the best thing to do is to ask for another opinion, that is, a *consultation*. It may involve bringing a consultant to sit in on your therapy session, or it may mean seeing a consultant separately. In either case your therapist certainly should allow the consultant to see your records (with your permission), so as to have as much information as possible on which to base an opinion.

RESISTANCE

Remember, however, that therapy is a profound and sometimes painful experience. In order to overcome neurotic symptoms you must sometimes reexperience anxiety, you must remember painful events from the past, and you must give up cherished fantasies to look at the truth.

Paradoxically, you may feel worst about your therapy when it actually is working best. Though you think you want to change for the better, long-lived habits are not easily given up, even if they have caused you suffering. Most people are afraid to make major changes, and rather than understand or even acknowledge their fear, they find it easier to become angry with the therapist or complain about the treatment. Indeed, they may find it hard to express their anger at all (difficulty in expressing feelings directly is often what brings clients to therapists in the first place), and so their genuine *resistance* to change is not brought out in the open. Instead, they refuse to talk about anything important during their sessions, they arrive late or cancel appointments, or they decide abruptly to end therapy.

How can you distinguish between your own resistance and a genuine dissatisfaction with your therapist? Resistance usually comes after a period during which some good things have been accomplished, when some of your goals have begun to be attained. If you examine your dissatisfaction carefully, do you find it resembles negative feelings you have (or had) toward other important individuals in your life? Is your gut reaction one of fleeing? A "yes" to either question is a sign of resistance. If you really are not sure, the best thing is to force yourself to discuss your reluctance with your therapist. An experienced therapist has undoubtedly encountered resistance before and is likely to know ways of helping you to overcome it.

Perhaps the answer is not to look for instant or constant improvement, since therapy is likely to work in fits and starts. Instead, look for new understanding, a progressive awareness of feelings and memories, relief from distress, improved ability to deal with everyday matters. Therapy is a voyage of self-discovery, and as with other travels

you must sacrifice some of the comforts of home and familiar surroundings and put up with some discomfort in order to experience
new adventures. Just be sure that the journey is in the right direction
for you, and that if your goal, for example, is a happy marriage no
longer marred by your temper tantrums, it is not diverted to someone
else's goal for you, such as revising your sex life or rearranging your
career. If, after careful consideration, discussion with your therapist,
and perhaps seeking a second opinion, you then find your therapy is
not working for you, the sensible action is to terminate it.

WHEN IS THERAPY FINISHED?

Again, if your goal is a simple and objective one, such as overcoming
impotence, its achievement is easily determined and your therapy can
be terminated. For more subjective goals, such as having more satisfactory and comfortable relations with others, or being able to sustain
an intimate relationship, the end is harder to determine. It is probably
easiest to define it as the time when the effort and cost of therapy seem
greater than the likelihood of further improvement.

The very process of giving up therapy and the therapist can be
difficult. After all, you are giving up a person you like, and who you
believe likes you. Moreover, if this person has helped you, you probably have a sense of gratitude as well, along with admiration and other
warm feelings. To a large extent one's feelings of dependency on the
therapist are related to the kind of therapy. In very short-term treatment and in behavior therapy, the relationship between client and
therapist is less close and less emotional. Moreover, behavior therapy
focuses on symptoms, not personality, and when the symptoms of
illness are removed the treatment is finished.

In psychoanalysis, on the other hand, the treatment is of an intense
and long-term nature, and the relationship of analyst and client inevitably becomes very close. Termination of this relationship therefore is
an important phase of therapy, which might take months to accomplish. In other forms of therapy it is basically the client who decides
when it is time to quit, although under normal circumstances it
doesn't make sense to terminate against the therapist's advice.

The time of termination often revives some of the very symptoms
that brought a client to treatment. One client may experience an

anxiety attack after having had none for six months; another will have nightmares; still another, whose profound depression had lifted, will again have intolerable feelings of sadness. However, the final sessions frequently can be a very useful therapeutic period during which clients, faced with the idea that this is their "last chance" to sort things out, often bring up deep concerns that they had never been able to talk about before.

Often those who find it hardest to terminate treatment are individuals who have had severe problems coping with separation and loss. The "loss" of the therapist revives the feelings of desolation and abandonment caused by earlier losses in their lives. If they can make the appropriate connections between their feelings about earlier loss and the ending of therapy, they may in the end gain a lasting sense of balance.

Even when a client is ready to end treatment, and the treatment has been successful in that the maladaptive behavior has ended, it does not mean that the person will never again need therapy for mental illness. New problems come up, and new difficulties arise. In the study of twenty-three psychotherapists cited above, twenty had themselves been in treatment with more than one therapist. This treatment was by no means continuous. Rather, at different times in their lives, for different reasons, they sought the help of another therapist. Further, a survey of graduates of one of the best psychoanalytic training institutes found that 55 percent of its graduates had additional therapy after completing their training analysis.

What does that signify for the much larger population of nontherapists? It means simply that a "once and for all" attitude, the idea that once therapy is done one is necessarily "cured for life," is unrealistic and inappropriate. Relieved of this burden, the approach can be more practical, with the overall focus on current problems. Once those problems are solved, of course, there is no guarantee that new problems will not arise, any more than one can be sure one will never again get bronchitis or pneumonia.

If this discussion of evaluating therapy seems inconclusive, don't despair. If you genuinely like your therapist, and feel he likes you, chances are you are being helped. In the end, the most important factors probably are not the method used, but your faith in the therapist, your expectation of being helped, and the encouragement and supportiveness of the therapist—these ingredients are known to be effective. And, in the last analysis, some authorities point out, you may never really know what helped you. Numerous studies show that the disorders for which people generally seek psychotherapy are self-limiting, and that as often as not they will improve in time (two years is the period usually quoted) *without* treatment. We are not suggesting that you put up with disabling symptoms and allow them to disrupt your life for many months in the hope that they will go away, but we are pointing out that you need not agonize unduly over whether or not your therapy is exactly right.

EVALUATING SOMATIC THERAPIES

Psychoactive drugs are used in one of two ways: on a short-term basis, to bring severe symptoms under control so that a person can benefit from psychotherapy, which will be the main form of treatment; or on a long-term basis, to control a severe chronic mental disorder, such as manic-depressive disease or schizophrenia, for which medication is the principal form of treatment. Some mental health professionals are opposed to using medication for anything but psychosis—severe mental disturbance. They maintain that medication simply removes the symptoms, not their causes, and therefore cannot be effective in the long run. Others maintain that one cannot separate symptoms from causes—the symptoms *are* the illness. Whichever point of view your mental health professional subscribes to, it is important to remember that psychoactive drugs are powerful agents, and their use should be carefully monitored. In other words, no one should continue taking the same drug for many months, or take a drug prescribed for someone else, or alter the dosage one is taking, without periodic evaluation by a competent physician. (In practice, prescriptions for such drugs frequently are for limited amounts of the drug and are nonrenewable.)

How can you tell if the drug prescribed for you or your relative or friend is the right one? It would seem that if a medication modifies or eliminates the symptoms for which it is being given, and does not give rise to other undesirable symptoms, you can say it is effective. Unfortunately it doesn't always work that way. Antidepressants, for example, may take as long as four or five weeks to make a person feel less depressed. If a medication does not work within that period, it still may not mean it is the wrong drug; it may mean simply that the dosage is too low, which in turn may mean you have to wait another two or three weeks, during which a higher dose is taken, to see if it works. If it does not, a different antidepressant might be tried. Obviously this process is time-consuming and cumbersome, which is all the more distressing because the person taking the drug continues to suffer until it takes effect.

A drug may help the symptoms for which it is taken, but may give rise to unpleasant (or, less often, dangerous) new symptoms. The minor tranquilizers can make you feel drowsy and lethargic; the tricyclic antidepressants can cause blurred vision, constipation, and dry mouth; the antipsychotics can cause all these symptoms and also appetite increase and weight gain; and lithium carbonate may cause stomach upsets, incessant thirst, muscular weakness, and mild tremors. (See Chapter 18 for more detailed descriptions.)

All such side effects should be reported to the physician. Some can be eliminated by lowering dosage or changing to a different drug of the same family. Others may be unavoidable. In any case, whenever there are side effects, the decision must be made as to whether the drug's benefits outweigh the undesirable effects. If you are lucky, your medication will work perfectly, without side effects. If you are typical, however, you will have to make a decision as to which is the lesser evil: the illness or the drug's effects. Further, there is always a degree of uncertainty about the future of both the illness and the drug's effects. The best possible guess must be made, but if the guess is wrong you usually can change your mind.

Why, might you ask, don't physicians who prescribe these drugs know what to expect, and if they do, why not inform their patients? The answer here is that different individuals respond very differently to psychoactive drugs. Some of the results and side effects can be readily foreseen, but many physicians believe it is foolish to warn patients of discomforts that they may never actually experience, lest fear keep them from taking medication on a regular basis.

If you are truly concerned about the effects of a drug on you or your relative or friend, ask your physician. If you don't get a satisfactory answer, either ask another physician or go to your local library and look up the drug in one of the several excellent up-to-date guides that are readily available. The *Physicians' Desk Reference* (commonly called *PDR*), revised annually, lists drugs by manufacturer, generic name, and brand name, and describes dosages, precautions, and adverse reactions; a recent edition should tell you everything you want to know. The American Medical Association also publishes patient medication instruction sheets for most drugs. Get one from the prescribing physician.

Although it is not possible to determine with certainty which, if any, of the drugs available will be most useful to a particular individual, the potential benefits should be greater than the potential side effects or risks.

ELECTROCONVULSIVE THERAPY (ECT)

There is even more disagreement regarding the use of ECT than there is about psychoactive drugs. Its use has been violently opposed by groups of ex-patients, and in some states, notably California, it cannot be used without the approval of a special state board. In America today it is used almost exclusively to treat severe depression, either when antidepressants do not work or for some reason are not tolerated, or to help a severely depressed person faster than drugs are likely to work. In Europe it is also used for schizophrenia.

The effectiveness of ECT usually can be judged by the end of a complete course of treatment, that is, six to eight applications over a period of two to three weeks. Some clinicians, however, discontinue ECT if no improvement begins by the fourth treatment. Concerning side effects, the most troubling of which is loss of memory, they tend to be much milder with unilateral ECT (applied only to one side of the brain; see Chapter 19 for further explanation), although unilateral ECT may be less effective than bilateral ECT.

EVALUATING A HOSPITAL

Given the high costs of hospitalization, you may not have much choice of where you, your relative, or friend can go for inpatient care. Nevertheless, you should have some criteria for differentiating good care from bad.

Good hospital care begins at the time of admission, when the patient arrives. Well-handled procedures include explaining the hospital routine from the very start, but only giving as much information as the patient is able to absorb (some patients arrive for admission in acute distress; trained personnel are sensitive to this). If papers must be signed, they should be adequately explained. Whoever accompanies the patient to the ward or room should introduce him to staff members there and provide a little general orientation. It should be made clear from the start which individual will be primarily responsible for the care of this patient, and that information should be shared with the family member or other person accompanying the patient to the hospital.

As was pointed out in Chapter 16, the majority of hospitalized patients today—especially those who go to a general hospital rather than a psychiatric hospital—remain there for a relatively short period of time, typically ranging from one to four weeks. In the case of serious illness—and if it is not serious, why hospitalize the patient?—intensive treatment is needed to effect a recovery in that time and prevent (or try to prevent) a recurrence of the illness. What you should look for, therefore, are signs of such intensive care, as well as ongoing preparation for being discharged from the hospital:

- What is the place of drugs in the patient's treatment?
- Will ECT be used?
- Will there be individual psychotherapy? How often and for how long?
- Will there be group therapy? How often? How large a group?
- Is there milieu therapy? Regular ward meetings? Are they led by a skilled staff member?
- Is there occupational therapy? Of what does it consist?
- What facilities are there for recreation?
- How much access does the patient have to staff members? Are nurses and aides available for casual talk with patients?
- Is there a set schedule for patients' activities or are they left to their own devices?
- What, if any, preparation is made for discharge and aftercare? (See the accompanying illustration of one hospital's discharge plan.)

For longer-term care, the same questions apply. Even if your relative or friend is in a long-term facility, typically a state or county hospital, you can assess the overall conditions and, if necessary, work for change. (Living quarters can be improved, and recreation equipment of various kinds provided; volunteer contributions, either of time or of material things, can be enlisted and encouraged.)

Patient Discharge Plan*	

Discharged to: Home_____ Other_____ Social Worker   Telephone
At Home Services: None____ See Below____

Agency/Address	Service/Equipment Requested	Frequency
Contact Person/Telephone		Date
Agency/Address	Service/Equipment Requested	Frequency
Contact Person/Telephone		Date

Date_____Time_____A.M./P.M. Discharged Via_____
Accompanied by_____Referral Forms____Prescriptions Given____
_____

Medications					
Name	Dose	Time	New	Old	Special Instructions/Side Effects

RESTRICTIONS ON ACTIVITY LEVEL (Stairs, lifting, driving, etc.)	FOLLOW UP ARRANGEMENTS What: When:
	Physician:
	PT:
	Lab:
	Tests:
	Diet:
	Instructions:
Treatments	Symptoms to Report to Doctor

I understand the above plans that have been arranged for me.
Patient/Patient Representative
_____ R.N._____

* Emerson Hospital, Concord, MA.

The basic ingredient of good hospital care, however, lies not in the facilities but in the staff. Sheer numbers alone do not ensure a good staff, although a larger staff is more apt to provide more care. It is both the amount and the quality of their contacts with patients that make the difference. Some warning signs of poor staff are:

- Staff members are not seen much. (In many hospitals psychiatric staff members wear street clothes rather than uniforms, so do not be misled, but they usually wear name tags to identify themselves.)
- Staff members are talking and interacting mostly with one another (at the nurses' station, for example) rather than with patients.
- Staff members do not know patients by name.
- Staff members do not show proper respect for the patient (treat patient as a child—"This medicine is doctor's orders, that's all you need to know about it"; call patients by their first names but expect themselves to be addressed more formally; talk about a patient in his presence as though he was not there or could not understand).
- Staff members show impatience and try to hurry patients through routines, medication, and so on.

If you yourself are the patient, it is not always possible to evaluate hospital treatment with any objectivity. If you can, have a family member or close friend help you make such assessments. If visiting hours are too limited—to an hour or two a day—that in itself is a sign that the hospital may want to avoid such scrutiny. Another bad sign is a constantly groggy and drowsy patient. Although high doses of drugs may be necessary to give relief from acute symptoms, some hospitals routinely use them to keep patients from being troublesome and to make them easier to manage. If your friend or relative seems totally "out of it" over a long period of time, it bears investigation.

EVALUATING CHILDREN'S PROGRAMS

If a particular program has been recommended for your emotionally disturbed child, either in a special class in a regular school or in a separate school for "special needs" children, you certainly should evaluate it. What should you look for?

Again, the most important factor in any such program is staff, and the single most important quality, most experts agree, is *warmth*. Do

PATIENT EVALUATION OF CARE*

TO OUR PATIENTS:

We are interested in your opinions about our service and ask that you take a few minutes to answer the following questions. Your views will assist us in our continuing efforts to provide the highest possible level of care.

o Were you ____ admitted directly to the unit, or ____ admitted through the E.R.?

o The ADMITTING PROCESS was

    courteous　　　　　 ____ excellent　 ____ good　 ____ fair　 ____ poor
    efficient　　　　　　 ____ excellent　 ____ good　 ____ fair　 ____ poor

o Did you receive adequate information/orientation about what to expect during your hospitalization?

                     ____ yes　　　　 ____ no

o The NURSING CARE was ____ excellent　 ____ good　 ____ fair　 ____ poor

o The KEY COUNSELING was

                     ____ excellent　 ____ good　 ____ fair　 ____ poor

o The SOCIAL WORK SERVICE was

                     ____ excellent　 ____ good　 ____ fair　 ____ poor

o The GROUPS were　　　　 ____ excellent　 ____ good　 ____ fair　 ____ poor

o The OCCUPATIONAL THERAPY was

                     ____ excellent　 ____ good　 ____ fair　 ____ poor

o The PSYCHIATRIST CARE was

                     ____ excellent　 ____ good　 ____ fair　 ____ poor

o DISCHARGE AND AFTERCARE PLANNING were

                     ____ excellent　 ____ good　 ____ fair　 ____ poor

o Your MEALS were　　　　 ____ excellent　 ____ good　 ____ fair　 ____ poor

    Were you on a special diet? ____ yes　　　　 ____ no

o The CLEANLINESS OF THE UNIT was　　　　 ____ excellent　 ____ good　 ____ fair　 ____ poor

o What helped you most was:

o What you would change if you were in charge:

o Other comments:

* Given to patients being discharged from Emerson Hospital, Concord, MA.

you get a sense of warmth from the teachers, a feeling of their connecting with the children? Do they know how to talk to the children in ways that bring out feelings? Do they *listen* to the children?

Other questions to ask are:

- Are classroom goals and limits clearly set and shared with the children so they understand what is considered appropriate behavior? Ideally there is a disciplined approach, but one that is not too rigid to respond to individual needs and situations.
- What happens when a child blows up? Are there experienced staff members who can work with a child whose behavior becomes unmanageable in the classroom? There should be skilled "crisis intervention" until a child can regain enough control to rejoin the group, not just sending the child to isolation or to the principal's office for punishment.
- Is getting along with others stressed as part of the curriculum? Social relations is an important element of education, and skilled teachers can help children improve communication, develop assertiveness, handle embarrassing situations, and learn how to make friends.
- Does the program reflect an awareness of a child's need to build self-esteem?
- Is there time during the day, both formal and unplanned, for children and teachers to talk together about important questions and issues?
- Is there teamwork among the staff who work with children? Are there regular opportunities for talking things over between classroom teachers and other professionals, such as social workers, psychologists, reading specialists, art therapists, and others involved in the program?
- Is there good communication with the parents? Are they enlisted as allies in the program, or viewed as uninformed laypersons or even enemies?

EVALUATING A NURSING HOME

The same standards used to pick a nursing home in the first place (see under nursing homes, in Chapter 20) apply to evaluating the care your aged relative is getting. Is your relative clean and does she look cared for? Are activities available? Is there physical therapy? Is there a physician always on call? Many if not most residents of nursing homes will have complaints about the food and other matters. Try to be there once or twice at mealtime to see if there is enough food and if it is adequately prepared and served.

One major problem in many nursing homes is the tendency to overprescribe and misuse psychoactive drugs. As pointed out in Chapter 18 (under the heading, psychoactive drugs and the elderly), most nursing home residents take medications for one or more chronic illnesses, making for a greater likelihood of unfavorable drug interactions. One recent study showed that nursing home residents were prescribed an average of 8.1 different drugs and received an average of 4.7 different drugs during a single month. Nearly two-thirds were prescribed at least one psychoactive drug, and one-fifth received two or more psychoactive drugs. Almost one-third received a sedative/ hypnotic drug. Further, the psychoactive drugs prescribed were not always suitable for the diagnosis; antidepressants were given to patients who had no diagnosis of depression, antipsychotics to nonpsychotic patients, and so on.

Consequently, if you have a relative in a nursing home, and especially if you notice that your relative seems to be acting strangely (too sleepy, too nervous, suddenly confused, etc.), arrange a meeting with the doctor and nurses in charge of her care, and find out what medications are being prescribed. List them, along with the purpose of each, the possible side effects, and the dosage. Ask if the most appropriate drug is being used and if it is being administered as prescribed. When you visit, check that this procedure is actually being carried out and report any new or worsened symptoms you observe to the caretakers.

Chapter

23

THE ROLE OF THE FAMILY

Suppose you have a close relative, a sister or a husband, a parent or a child, who is being treated for mental illness. What, if anything, can you do to help? The answer depends very much on a number of factors: the severity of the illness, how it is being treated, and the nature of your relationship (parents, for example, have certain responsibilities toward a young child). Is your husband seeing a behavior therapist once a week for treatment of anxiety, for example, or is he seeing a psychoanalyst five days a week over a period of years? Is your relative's problem a mild depression, or is it schizophrenia for which he has been hospitalized one or more times? Is your severely depressed elderly mother receiving electroconvulsive therapy (ECT) on an outpatient basis? Your role depends a great deal on the circumstances.

IF YOUR CHILD IS SEEING A PSYCHOTHERAPIST

Depending on the nature of the problem and the orientation of the therapist your relative's therapist may or may not want to involve you in the treatment. There is only one exception: When the client is a child, the parents (or guardian) are nearly always involved to some extent.

Some child therapists see one or both parents on a frequent and regular basis, as often as once a week (in addition to the child's sessions). Others prefer to see only the child but confer with the parents on a regular basis. Still others believe therapy is a private matter between therapist and client, and that the child's feelings of trust will be violated if they share specific information with the parents, but they do keep in touch with them.

Whatever the situation for you and your child, after a few months you will no doubt have a sense of how the child is responding to treatment, and you will be able to evaluate its effectiveness to some extent. Since you in part are responsible for the decision to enter treatment at all, and presumably are paying for it as well, it makes sense to reinforce the therapist at home in whatever ways you can, and to follow whatever advice the therapist may give you in dealing with your child. Of course, if the therapist's advice seems inappropriate, you should talk it over before taking any action, and, if you continue to find yourself in disagreement, you probably will want to seek another opinion.

IF YOUR ADULT RELATIVE IS IN THERAPY

Suppose, however, that the relative seeing a therapist is an adult in your household. What, then, is your role?

Anne, 23, shared an apartment with her cousin Frances, 27, who was divorced. The cousins had grown up together in the same small town and both now worked in a distant city. Unhappy about a number of matters, Frances had been seeing Dr. Green, a psychoanalyst, three times a week for about four months. She told Anne little about her treatment except that she had been given some pills to take when she felt upset. Formerly quiet and shy, Frances now began to behave quite differently. Several nights she went out and came home extremely late. She would not tell Anne much except that she had gone by herself to "a few bars" and, from something Anne gathered, she did not remember much about what had happened. She mentioned the name of one bar, however, which Anne knew was in a very rough neighborhood, down near the docks. Extremely concerned about her cousin, Anne nevertheless did not want to alarm Frances's mother, a widow in poor health, who lived a thousand miles away.

What should Anne do? In this case, which is a true story, Anne decided to telephone her cousin's analyst, telling him of her concern. He was not easy to get hold of, and when she finally reached him he was difficult to talk to. Anne said she was worried about her cousin's behavior. Dr. Green made no comment. Anne said she was sure Frances was drinking too much when she went out, possibly getting drunk and blacking out, and she was concerned for Frances's safety. Dr. Green again made no comment. Finally Anne bluntly asked him what she should do. Dr. Green said he could not even tell her if Frances was his patient or not without her explicit permission. He suggested that she might wish to inform her cousin's mother, and then he hung up.

Anne was not sure she had done the right thing in calling. She told Frances about it afterward, and her cousin was furious, telling her to mind her own business. Nevertheless, in this situation she had done what she could. She had expressed her concern, both to her cousin and to the therapist. She also had provided the therapist with information about Frances's behavior that he otherwise might not have had, and that was relevant to the treatment. (If he was prescribing medication, he should certainly know whether or not she was combining it with alcohol.)

THEY'RE GETTING WORSE

This case points out one of the common difficulties of living with a person being treated for mental illness. Whether the illness is a mild neurosis or a full-blown psychosis, the symptoms are not only unpleasant but at times they appear to become worse during the course of treatment. The husband in therapy who is in the process of reliving some early conflicts with his mother may come home and accuse his wife of behaving "just like mother," when in reality she has only unwittingly reminded him of a painful early conflict.

It may be even more serious. There have been instances where a spouse in treatment has, in reliving old sexual conflicts, acted them out in the present, either by seeking affairs outside marriage or by behaving differently in the marital sexual relationship. Therapy nearly always introduces tensions into family life, particularly when the treatment involves reexperiencing suffering. During these periods the family member in therapy may occasionally feel and act worse than ever, becoming increasingly moody and demanding at home.

What can family members do then? If they can tolerate the behavior, realizing that it is temporary, that may be the best solution. If they are able to respond to false accusations and displaced anger (anger directed at them when it is really aroused by someone else) with a statement such as "That's not really true; maybe you'll see it differently one day," that also may be helpful. But if the tensions generated become intolerable, it may be wise to ask permission of the person in treatment to see his therapist (perhaps jointly) to discuss these problems, or even to obtain a consultation oneself from a different mental health practitioner.

At best the family's role is supportive. Listening to and sympathizing with the person in treatment, encouraging him to continue treatment, to keep scheduled appointments, to take medication that is prescribed—all these can be very useful. Indeed, one's family is usually a chief source of support, warmth, and love. Family members are in the best position to help one another, knowing each other more intimately than anyone else.

At the same time, the very closeness that makes it easy to help also makes it difficult, because when you are emotionally involved it is hard to be objective. Love and concern can blind you to the realities. A loving relative may be unable to see an illness for what it is. A father may make constant excuses for his daughter when the parents of other children and teachers complain about her behavior, reacting defensively rather than recognizing a real problem. The wife whose husband refuses to go out and is withdrawing from everyone may explain that he always has been quiet and shy and simply doesn't want to make an effort.

A similar problem is overprotectiveness. The woman who returns from a brief hospitalization for depression may find her family on tiptoe and whispering, as well as taking over all her normal household tasks for her. Yet most therapists would agree that the sooner normal activities are resumed, the better.

A direct and open line of communication with the therapist can prevent such problems. If you don't know how to behave with an ill family member, and you are afraid you may somehow make her get worse, ask the therapist's advice.

COMMUNICATING WITH THE THERAPIST

Anne's phone call to her cousin Frances's analyst took place in the mid-1950s. Today such a doctrinaire approach as Dr. Green's, who wanted no contact with his patient's relative, is far less common. Most therapists, including traditional psychoanalysts, are willing to maintain open lines of communication with the client's family. They realize it is useful to have, from time to time, a factual account of the client's activities and behavior—what she did, said, undertook. However, they are apt to want a straightforward account, not the family's opinions, views, or arguments, which reflect mainly their own concerns.

You certainly should be able to check on your relative's progress by calling the therapist periodically. That does not mean you should call after every appointment, or once a week, or even once a month. It makes sense to know what is happening in terms of improvement (or lack of it), but there is no reason to make a nuisance of yourself, or to violate the client's right to privacy by asking about details. If you are in doubt as to when to call, ask the therapist and/or your relative.

Some therapists actively involve family members, at least with some of their clients. For example, the husband of Wanda, the young woman who experienced anxiety attacks whenever she left the house, might be advised, as her therapy progresses, to accompany her halfway on a neighborhood errand and wait at the halfway point to accompany her home again. Or the sister of Jane, suffering from profound depression after her husband's death, might be told specifically to talk to Jane about her loss and to relate it to her present forgetfulness and sadness.

On the other hand, it is unwise for family members to play the role of therapist on their own. You may believe in your heart of hearts that what your teenage son Joe really needs is to get together with the other kids at ballgames and parties and learn to have a good time, not realizing that his social withdrawal is such that it is hard for him even to eat dinner with the rest of the family. Or you may, being a person who basically disapproves of drugs and other "artificial props," sympathize with Uncle Frank when he complains that the side effects of the antipsychotic drug his psychiatrist prescribes are terrible. The reasonable course of action for you, however, is to encourage him to continue the drug.

LIVING WITH A DEPRESSED RELATIVE

Perhaps the most important thing a relative can do is to be sure the depressed person seeks treatment. Depression in particular destroys self-esteem and confidence, and family and friends can help the depressed person feel more worthwhile in a number of ways. You can acknowledge, first, that your relative is suffering and in pain. At the same time, point out distorted negative thinking *without* being critical or disapproving. Above all, show that you care, respect, and value the depressed person. Don't blame your relative for the condition. Don't criticize, pick on, or put down this person, exacerbating her poor self-image. Rather offer kind words and pay honest compliments.

You also can help by keeping the depressed person busy and active. Depression itself leads to apathy and inactivity. Gently prod your relative, especially if you see signs of withdrawal. Depression also arouses feelings of guilt, so do not compound such feelings by blaming the individual for the symptoms.

Depression frequently arouses anger in others. You may be tempted to become impatient and tell your relative to snap out of it. Realize that she can't, and she needs your support.

LIVING WITH SCHIZOPHRENIA

Again, the most important contribution of family and friends is to make sure that their relative with schizophrenia seeks and continues treatment, especially with regard to taking prescribed medication. When your relative makes strange or completely false statements, based on bizarre beliefs or hallucinations, do not go along with them or make fun of them. Rather, acknowledge that while things may seem that way to him, you do not see them the same way and do not come to the same conclusions. Humor, especially sarcastic humor, is hard for a schizophrenic person to understand. Intense emotion is also to be avoided. Many schizophrenics like to be around others, but they also need time and space to be alone. An atmosphere of calm confidence is important. Predictable, simple routine helps to counteract hallucinations, delusions, and sensory overload. Do take a positive approach and encourage your relative to regain whatever abilities he can.

Living with someone who has a serious and chronic illness can be very difficult. Consider joining a family support group such as those of the National Alliance for the Mentally Ill. They offer mutual support and education on the subject of psychiatrists, living problems, housing, finances, and patient advocacy. Their most important function is to provide a forum for sharing common experiences and problems. (See Appendix A for addresses.)

LIVING WITH ALZHEIMER'S

Many Alzheimer's patients continue to live at home for months or years before their disease progresses to the point of requiring round-the-clock care. The burden on the family caretaker(s) can be considerable. In general, specialists say that planning can ease that burden somewhat. With this progressive mental illness, where in effect your relative's brain is deteriorating, you cannot expect any improvement but must adapt to the patient. If your relative begins to wander about at night, you might have to get door locks or camouflage doors. Get rid of scatter rugs to minimize falls, and close off access to stairs. Unplug the stove, and install an ignition lock on the car. If the patient makes incorrect or false statements, do not try to contradict him. Even if your relative accuses you of stealing his money or possessions, ignore the accusation. Try rather to respond to the person's feelings, not necessarily the content of the words. Accusations of theft may mean your relative is upset about losing things or forgetting things.

Do arrange for respite care. If you have no family members or friends who can relieve you on a regular basis, try to arrange for some form of paid respite care: aides who come to your home, an adult day-care center, or short-term (overnight or several days' worth) institutional care (usually in a nursing home). Also join a local Alzheimer's support group, through which you can get more information about the course of the disease and what to expect, as well as respite care and other assistance in your area.

THERAPY FOR THE FAMILY

Suppose life with your ill relative has become intolerable. You and/or the other family members are miserable. You may want to learn to cope with these stresses by considering family therapy. Some family therapists believe that when any individual is ill the entire family is necessarily involved; some even hold that it is the family that really is ill, and the "sick" person just happens to be the one who is most openly expressing that illness. Not all family therapists agree with this idea, but most will focus on understanding how the family members interact with one another. In this process they may be very helpful in indicating ways of adapting to the tensions generated in connection with the family member who is in psychiatric treatment and who is changing a formerly stable family equilibrium. In the case of a serious illness especially, what has been called the "blame-and-shame syndrome" is particularly painful. Family therapy that encourages expressing beliefs, fears, and feelings helps mitigate the tendency to blame one another for causing the illness.

Such therapy may be conducted with or without the patient present, and with all or part of the family involved. Appropriate goals for such treatment might be learning how the family members' behavior affects the patient and vice versa, agreeing on what they may expect of the patient in terms of functioning, determining how much responsibility they should take for the patient, and deciding in advance what they should do if the patient has a severe relapse.

A school of thought that evolved in England in the 1960s holds that certain family characteristics, summarized as "high" *expressed emotion (EE)*, are likely to cause schizophrenic patients to relapse. For example, very critical, hostile, or intrusive behavior by family members becomes too stressful for the patient. However, families can be taught to employ better coping methods. Considerable research has been done about EE, which is said to affect eating disorders and other psychiatric illnesses as well. Opponents of this theory, on the other hand, believe that the undesirability of overcritical and emotionally overinvolved behavior is self-evident, and that the principal cause for relapse is failure to take prescribed medication, which leads to the recurrence of psychotic symptoms. The most important thing families of schizophrenics can do, therefore, is to ensure compliance with medication. Family therapists can, however, help by educating family members about the disease, referring them to support groups, and sharing information about the patient in appropriate two-way communication. There are support groups for all the serious illnesses and for relatives of patients with alcohol and narcotics addiction (see Appendix A).

Suppose either you cannot find a family therapist or the other members of the family do not wish to see one. You might then consider individual counseling. Should you go to your relative's therapist or to someone else? The choice may not be yours. Some therapists, particularly those who are psychoanalytically oriented, will not treat close relatives at the same time. However, if your relative's therapist is of this persuasion, and seems to be competent and effective, she might be able to recommend a different therapist for you to consult, one with whom she can cooperate. Other therapists, of course, have no objection to treating several members of the same family, individually or together.

VISITING YOUR HOSPITALIZED RELATIVE

Whether your relative is in the psychiatric unit of a general hospital or in a private or public mental hospital, you most likely will want to (or feel you should) visit. Some years ago "no visitors" was a common rule in mental hospitals, particularly those treating children (whose illness often was blamed on the parents, who therefore were discouraged from visiting) and those concentrating on analytic treatment (where it was feared that visits from the real-life figures in a patient's early childhood conflicts would delay or otherwise upset the treatment). Today, the focus of most hospitals is on returning the patient to home and community as quickly as possible, and visits from family and friends are seen as a means of retaining close contact with home life. Consequently, visiting hours tend to be quite liberal, and in some hospitals, like the general hospital described in Chapter 13, special provisions are made for family members to share a dessert with the patient and to engage in group meetings with other families and patients.

Leonard Cammer, a psychiatrist, has given excellent advice to families visiting hospitalized patients. Among the points he makes are:

- Keep your visit short. A brief congenial visit is less likely to put a strain on you or the patient.
- Don't bring along your anxieties or grief over the illness, but rather try several topics of conversation to find one of mutual interest.
- Talk about things at home but do not unnecessarily relate disturbing news; if you must, emphasize the positive aspects. (Yes, Mary did bang up the car last week, but no one got hurt, and the insurance adjuster says most of the damage is covered.)
- Bring a small gift if you wish, but make sure it is not something forbidden by hospital rules. (Usually that includes anything that is a potential weapon and any medication—even aspirin—or alcoholic drink; even if your relative is reliable, other patients there may not be.)
- Do not become too involved with other patients, bringing them gifts or gossiping with them. A friendly greeting is fine, but you are there to visit your relative, and you don't know what you are getting into if you become involved with others.
- Listen sympathetically to your relative's complaints (about the food, service, nurses, etc.), but do not act on them until you have verified their accuracy. Your relative's perceptions may be distorted.
- Do be alert for signs of physical illness in your relative. Even in the best hospitals, these are sometimes inadvertently overlooked.
- Respect your relative's privacy; don't discuss her with other patients or visitors.
- Encourage your relative to cooperate with her treatment; listen if she complains about it, but don't undermine it by expressing your own doubts openly.
- Leave gracefully. Don't watch the clock, but give the patient something to look forward to, such as, "Let's save this topic for my next visit."

Whatever you do or say during your visits, remember that, for better or worse, you represent a part of the real world, the world to which your relative will be returning when she leaves the protective environment of the hospital. Therefore, make her exposure to that real world a gentle one, but at the same time don't try to be something or someone you are not. Act yourself, and express your love and concern with warmth.

AFTER HOSPITAL DISCHARGE

Though it may seem that the brief hospital stays encouraged nowadays represent a less drastic upheaval than long-term hospitalization, remember that anyone ill enough to have been hospitalized at all has been through a traumatic experience, whatever its duration. Moreover, the end of your relative's hospitalization rarely means that he is "cured" and will need no further treatment. Rather, he is convalescing.

It is unrealistic to expect the newly discharged patient to return to normal activities and behavior immediately, but you can play an important role in speeding up that return. During the first days at home, he may be easily upset, and too much stress will exacerbate that situation. What is too much stress? The National Mental Health Association, in its booklet, *Helping the Mental Patient at Home,* suggests you avoid the following:

- Early mixing with too many people. It takes time to get used to crowds and social gatherings, so don't push. Go slowly.
- Constant watching. If the patient's quietly occupied, don't keep checking; it isn't necessary and may make him nervous.
- Threats and criticism. Don't threaten him with a return to the hospital, and don't nag.

You also can be of practical, positive assistance. You can help get your relative to therapy appointments and whatever other forms of aftercare (such as partial hospitalization, see Chapter 17) may have been recommended. You can help make sure he continues taking prescribed medication regularly. You can help intercede on his behalf with school authorities or employer, as well as with other family members and friends. You can help ease social commitments. You also can help with health insurance and social agency contacts. And you can continue to be a source of emotional support and encouragement, praising his progress toward normality and helping him see in perspective any failures or setbacks that may occur.

SPECIFIC PROBLEMS

The specific problems family members may encounter with a newly discharged patient vary with the seriousness of the illness. Some may be very temporary and easily dealt with. For example, the depressed person's lack of appetite may in a few weeks respond to antidepressant medication. In the meantime, you can encourage eating by offering favorite foods in small (not overwhelming) amounts and by ignoring the leftovers on her plate (don't nag).

Other problems also may be temporary but harder to deal with. For example, many of the antipsychotic drugs used for schizophrenia diminish sex drive, causing lack of desire in women and retrograde ejaculation and impotence in men. Thioridazine (Mellaril) appears especially prone to have this effect. (Sometimes, however, these effects are due to the illness rather than the drug.) Sexual inadequacy not only upsets a marital relationship but is terribly detrimental to self-esteem. As your husband's sex partner, what can you do? Certainly you should bring up the problem with his therapist, for both of you need a thorough explanation and reassurance in order to be patient during this period. Sometimes an adjustment in medication is indicated. Occasionally the opposite is true and the patient acts in a promiscuous manner, either in a halfway house or some other setting. The family then may need to investigate if their relative—especially if it is a woman—is being taken advantage of or is trading sexual favors for food, cigarettes, or some other privileges.

Your schizophrenic relative may no longer be actively delusional or hallucinating, but may still distort reality to some extent. For example, he may accuse family members of causing the illness, of undermining the treatment, or otherwise making his life miserable and recovery impossible. This kind of accusation is hard to take, especially when family members are already bending over backward to help their relative recover. Arguing is unlikely to help. About all you can do is point out that it is the illness that is making him see things in this way, and that when he gets better things will seem quite different.

Other common problems are failure to care for personal needs (bathing, grooming), inability to handle money, social withdrawal, suicide threats, and persistent strange habits (talking to oneself, for example). Violent and aggressive behavior is associated mainly with patients with paranoid schizophrenia who go off their medication or with alcohol or narcotics abusers. Most often such behavior is preceded by threats, which should be taken seriously and be assessed by their psychiatrist.

Frequent weepiness and long crying spells also are hard to cope with. When weeping represents a normal grief reaction, of course, it is to be encouraged. Some individuals cannot cry for many months after losing a loved one and then find it a great relief to do so. But if the weepiness is inappropriate, you may want to try to stop it. One psychiatrist suggests an interesting technique for doing so: Place yourself directly in front of your weeping relative and, rather than asking her to stop crying, insist that she faces you and looks into your eyes. If your relative complies, the tears will most likely stop, since it is virtually impossible to keep on crying while looking straight at another person. You may have to repeat the procedure several times, but it may be well worth trying to induce your relative to stop this waste of energy and instead try to talk about what is so painful.

Suppose your relative decides to make a major life change. Your son, for example, decides to move into an apartment with his girlfriend, or your wife decides she wants another baby. If your relative has been severely ill—with a major depression or with schizophrenia, for example—it is wise to persuade those involved to postpone such a change. Often, as people's emotional health changes, their views of the desirability of making a major change also alter. Moreover, major life changes seldom are necessary on an emergency basis. It is better to wait.

Any major life change represents a stress, and stress may exacerbate a mental illness, or trigger a relapse. If the proposed change is a new baby, presumably the person's mate has some voice in the matter. But suppose your grown-up son insists on moving out of your house to his own place. If you cannot persuade him to wait a while, there probably is not much you can do but go along with his decision. If you can indicate that you want him to succeed in spite of your opposition, your support may minimize the stress.

Perhaps the hardest decisions to make on a day-to-day basis are those affecting your relative's independence. How much is he able to decide, or to do? You must try to strike the very difficult balance between over- and understimulation, the balance between being included in normal family activities (ranging from ordinary meals to outings and visiting) but not being forced to take part beyond his ability, the balance between companionship and privacy, between freedom and structure.

In the hospital most patients are on a strict schedule, and to return home to total freedom can be very difficult. Most individuals do better with some structure—meals at definite hours, waking and sleeping at certain times. Most also need some privacy, a room to which they can withdraw. Only if such withdrawal becomes persistent or excessive should it be a cause for concern.

Although your relative may not be able to return to work or school immediately, he should be encouraged to take on as many appropriate household tasks and errands as possible. Helping with household chores is an excellent means for patients to show readiness for more independence. Questions of responsibility and independence are best handled by an open discussion of what is expected, what is fair, and what the patient needs to do to achieve more independence. It may be useful to include his social worker, counselor, or case manager in such a discussion.

For some chronically ill persons, living away from home in a halfway house or other supervised setting may be best for both patient and family. There need be no guilt or blame concerning such a solution. After all, most adults who are not mentally ill also prefer to live independently rather than with parents and siblings, coming home simply to visit.

WHAT TO TELL THE CHILDREN

How do you deal with the return of a hospitalized relative to a household with small children? If the person is the children's mother, presumably the children have been told something to explain her absence. Preferably it was the truth, that Mom was ill and needed to be taken care of in a hospital to get better. Upon discharge, if she is well enough to take full charge of the children, she can explain again to them why she was gone. If, as may well be the case, she is not yet ready to take on her former child-care role, some kind of help will be required, ranging from a babysitter a few hours a day to a full-time mother substitute.

Whether the relative is the mother, father, or someone else, the person's behavior may for a time be different or unusual. This behavior should be explained to the children as being part of the illness, and in fact most children are able to accept this explanation. Some of the behavior may be very frightening to a child: a father who, after ECT (shock treatment), does not remember some recent event, or an older sister, usually very gentle, who suddenly has outbursts of rage. Even if a child does not ask what's wrong—perhaps especially if the child doesn't ask—a simple explanation should be offered.

Remember, too, the great propensity of young children to assume guilt. When their parents quarrel or separate or divorce, it is common for children to believe it is their fault. When a family member, especially a parent or sibling, is mentally ill and acts peculiar, it is just as common for children to worry that the illness is caused by something bad they did (or thought, or wished). Other questions they may ask, or be afraid to ask, include: Is it catching? Will I get this illness, too? Can I tell anyone (my friends) about it? Can I have friends over to play?

Frankness about the symptoms and openness about unusual behavior will make it easier for everyone concerned. Children accept a great deal. Moreover, they like to be included, so call on them to help. A newly discharged relative may find it easier (less demanding and less threatening) to talk with a child than with an adult. On the other hand, don't allow a child to become too intensely involved in the relative's symptoms, to be dangerously close to aggressive outbursts or to be involved in a compulsive behavior pattern. Should that happen, it is up to an adult to intervene and to protect the child. On the whole, however, the presence of a mentally ill person in the household, while it is hard on family members, can be a maturing experience for the children. Many families find their ability to adapt to this stress—and it is a stress—far greater than they realized.

WHAT TO TELL THE NEIGHBORS

Tell the neighbors the truth, although you may not want to give them all the details. For others to accept a person's mental illness, you yourself must accept it. At the same time, you must balance the needs of other family members. The family cannot revolve around the one ill member exclusively, nor should everything be done for that one person. It is important to accept the illness and whatever limitations it imposes. One's expectations must be adjusted so as to be realistic.

You also can help lift the stigma of mental illness by telling your neighbors the facts. The portrayals of the mentally ill in the media often show aggression and violence, confusion, and unpredictability as the main characteristics. Only a fraction of mentally ill persons are in fact violent or commit crimes of any kind. You can assure them that your relative is not dangerous and that they have nothing to fear.

FAMILY SUPPORT GROUPS AND ADVOCACY

As has been mentioned, to deal with specific illnesses such as schizophrenia and Alzheimer's a support group can help family members by lending moral support and specific advice based on personal experience with practitioners, hospitals, medication, coping methods, and the like. Such support is immensely valuable. There is no substitute for the sharing of common experience. Many support groups supplement this private information exchange, which takes place either in large group meetings or in smaller "sharing" meetings, with a newsletter, issued more or less regularly, to disseminate relevant information.

The National Alliance for the Mentally Ill (see Appendix A), which was formed in 1979 by eighty local self-help groups of families, now has more than nine hundred affiliated groups and seventy-five thousand members, covering all fifty states and the District of Columbia. It serves individuals and their families who have schizophrenia, major depression, manic-depressive psychosis, and other disabling brain diseases. One recent meeting of a local NAMI support group was attended by the mother of a daughter variously diagnosed as depressive, manic-depressive, and schizophrenic, who lives at home but attends a day program; a couple whose daughter, currently in a private halfway house, has both alcoholism and manic-depressive disorder; a woman whose son, now age twenty-eight, became schizophrenic at seventeen, and after numerous treatments has been in a state hospital for the past two years; a man whose wife had become ill five years earlier following the birth of their daughter, received dozens of diagnoses, was given lithium and suffered toxic effects, and finally was diagnosed and effectively treated for temporal lobe epilepsy; and a man whose twenty-two-year-old son is both mentally ill and addicted to marijuana, despite numerous admissions to a private hospital and a drug rehabilitation program. They exchanged advice and information about financial arrangements (what to do when insurance runs out), about several hospitals, and about a special support group being formed for the young children of mentally ill parents. They also discussed a program the group had begun the previous year for regular inspection and monitoring of the local state hospital, which has had very positive effects on both staff (who welcome their interest) and patients (they have raised money for a new television set and are looking for a small computer for patient use).

Advocacy for the mentally ill is much needed and takes numerous forms. Interviews with radio and television hosts and the press help dispel some of the common myths and fallacies concerning serious mental illness. On the local level members urge businesses and other organizations to undertake supported work programs for those patients who can begin or resume employment. They encourage the establishment of group homes and other housing for the mentally ill who cannot live on their own but would prefer to stay in or near their own communities. They monitor community mental health centers. On the state and federal levels they help educate legislators and lobby for legislation and budgeting, including the allocation of more tax dollars for research into the causes and cures of mental illness. They also try to raise private funds for this purpose. For families who have experienced the devastating effect of serious mental illness, the opportunity to do something positive can be extremely therapeutic.

Chapter

24

PAYING FOR TREATMENT

BILLIONS OF dollars a year are spent for mental health services in the United States. These sums represent only the direct cost, that is, the actual money spent for mental health services, including treatment, facilities, research, and training. They do not include the indirect cost, mostly in terms of lost productivity due to disability, estimated to be many billions more.

Who pays for all this? In the United States, every taxpayer pays a share. Federal, state, and local taxes contribute a good proportion of every dollar spent (half or more). Thus, even if you yourself never need mental health services of any kind, you are paying some part of their cost. (In Canada taxpayers are responsible for a much larger share, since National Health Insurance pays not only for hospital psychiatric treatment but for unlimited outpatient psychiatric care.)

WHO CAN AFFORD TREATMENT?

Practically every American can afford some mental health treatment, but the kind and amount available depend to a large extent on ability to pay. In a true emergency it is unlikely that treatment will be denied to a person who cannot demonstrate ability to pay for it, but it can happen. A long-term mental illness can be very costly. If it afflicts a family's principal breadwinner, savings, unemployment insurance, and other assets may be decimated. If it afflicts a parent with young children, alternate child-care arrangements may need to be made. For either short-term or long-term health care, choices may be limited by funds and insurance coverage.

Approximately 90 percent of all working Americans have some form of employer-sponsored health insurance that covers some mental health care. As a rule such policies provide far less coverage for mental illness than for physical illness, and most coverage is limited to hospitalization and inpatient care. Even so, an estimated 30 percent of employers' health-care dollars are spent for mental health and substance abuse treatment.

When policies are employer-connected, they may be lost if a person loses her job or is unable to work. Public insurance is available for the elderly, the poor, and the chronically disabled, but the laws governing the various benefits and the agencies administering them are extremely complicated and constantly changing.

PRIVATE INSURANCE PLANS

Private or commercial insurance policies are issued by the nonprofit organization Blue Cross and Blue Shield and by various large insurance companies. The subscribers include employers, labor unions, other groups, and individuals. The costs of these policies and the benefits they confer vary greatly and depend on many factors, including where you live (since hospital costs and practitioners' fees vary from region to region) and your own health history. As a rule group plans are more generous than individual ones.

Chances are that you or your relative has one of these policies, or possibly has coverage through the policy of a spouse or parent. Your first step should be to find out exactly what the policy covers. If you don't have the brochure explaining coverage, ask for it at your place of employment, from the union steward or personnel director. If they don't have it or your policy is an individually issued one, call or write the insurance company directly. When you do get it, and to do so may take some persistence on your part, read it carefully to see if it covers, in full or in part, the following services:

- Diagnostic consultation (evaluation or assessment)? If so, in practitioner's office or only in hospital? By a psychiatrist only? By a psychologist? Other professional? Does it include psychologic testing?
- Treatment for any nervous or mental disorder, regardless of previous illnesses?
- Office visits to a psychiatrist? Psychologist? Other professional?
- Electroconvulsive therapy (ECT) in the hospital? In the doctor's office?
- Anesthesiologist assisting doctor with ECT?
- Hospitalization in psychiatric unit of general hospital? Full or partial cost of room? For how long?
- Hospitalization in mental hospital? Full or partial cost of room? How long?
- Cost of prescription drugs?
- Nursing care? In hospital? At home?
- Partial hospitalization? Day care? Night care? Halfway house? Residential treatment center?
- Transportation to and from places of treatment?
- Rehabilitation therapy after hospitalization? Physical therapy? Vocational rehabilitation?

The typical private insurance plan allows a total of $500 per year for outpatient psychiatric care and approximately sixty days for hospitalization in a general hospital and thirty days in a mental hospital, even though general hospital care is roughly twice as expensive as care in a mental hospital (as noted earlier, the latter needs less elaborate facilities and equipment). Some plans are limited as to the number of psychotherapy visits, or impose a lifetime dollar limit, such as $15,000. That amount scarcely allows two months' stay in a private mental hospital.

Most states now allow licensed clinical psychologists to bill insurance companies directly for outpatient therapy, and some also allow licensed social workers and psychiatric nurses to do so. Other clinicians only are reimbursed if they work in a hospital or under the direct supervision of a licensed physician.

In addition to health insurance, or as part of it, your employer may

COST OF LONG-TERM MENTAL ILLNESS*

	Covered by Generous Federal Plan	Owed by Patient	Covered by Typical Private Plan	Owed by Patient
Hospitalization				
Acute care	$135,000			
Less intense	6,000			
Outpatient visits	66,200			
Drugs	87,600			
TOTAL	$294,800	$75,000	$219,800	$50,000	$244,800

* Based on diagnosis of schizophrenia in 1988 at age 20, expected to live to age 60, with some hospitalization every three years.

provide disability insurance, which pays a fixed sum per day or per week while you cannot work and which can be used to pay for treatment and/or hospitalization.

Another form of private insurance is the prepaid health plan, or *health maintenance organization (HMO)*. All HMOs are by law required to provide mental health services, but the actual coverage and provision varies. The basic difference between HMOs and other health insurance is that here the insurer and provider are one and the same. HMOs are among the least expensive forms of private health insurance and their number has grown rapidly. Nevertheless, they are not available everywhere.

There are two other kinds of prepaid health plan, *preferred provider organizations (PPOs)* and *competitive health plans (CHPs)*. PPOs provide services on a contract basis at a predetermined price, for example, $64 for an office visit to a psychiatrist. Under this arrangement, subscribers find that the services purchased from PPOs are paid in full, whereas services from other health providers may be paid only in part. The business or the insurance carrier is free to negotiate rates with medical providers in advance. CHPs tend to significantly limit allowances for mental health care; often they conform only to the minimum coverage, if any, set by state law.

Still another employer-paid plan is the *employee assistance program (EAP)*, a system of on-site counseling and consultation by a company psychologist. Originally a method of rehabilitating alcoholic employees, the EAP has come to include such diverse elements as marital and family counseling, drug rehabilitation, psychological screening, and referral to private psychotherapists.

PUBLIC INSURANCE (MEDICARE AND MEDICAID)

There are two main forms of public (government) health insurance, Medicare and Medicaid, and two forms of disability insurance, Social Security and Supplemental Security Income. (In addition, armed services personnel and their dependents have special insurance, also described below.)

Medicare is a federal health insurance program run by the Social Security Administration for persons who are sixty-five or older and for some persons under sixty-five who are disabled. Medicare pays a portion of some medical expenses and has two parts: hospital insurance (Part A) and medical insurance (Part B). Hospital insurance is financed by contributions from employers, employees, and the self-employed, and is free to anyone eligible for Medicare. Medical insurance is financed through monthly premiums paid by those who wish to have it. People over sixty-five who have not worked long enough to be entitled to Medicare hospital insurance can buy this protection by paying a monthly premium, but they must then buy both hospital and medical insurance.

You may apply for Medicare three months before you turn sixty-five. If you don't apply within three months before or after that date you may not apply again until the next general enrollment period, January 1 through March 31 of each year. Also, you pay a penalty for not enrolling at sixty-five, not only in lost benefits but in the form of a higher premium.

As of January 1989, Medicare covered unlimited inpatient care in any participating hospital in each benefit period except for a single annual deductible estimated at $564 in that year. (While Medicare covered all of the approved charges in excess of $564 a year, it did not cover extra services or conveniences, such as a private room, but extra insurance called Medigap, offered by various companies to supplement Medicare, extends the coverage.) However, there still was a lifetime limit of 190 days of care on inpatient psychiatric hospital services. In addition, Medicare covered up to 150 days in a Medicare-certified skilled nursing home, and home health care six days a week for as long as it is prescribed by a physician. It also covered unlimited hospice care for terminal patients.

Medicare medical insurance, available for a modest premium, covered 80 percent of covered medical costs per year (after the first $75). Included were all physician services, outpatient hospital services for diagnosis, treatment in an emergency room or hospital outpatient clinic, home health visits, outpatient physical or speech therapy, and any other treatment prescribed by a physician. However, it allowed only a modest amount per year ($500 in 1989) for outpatient treatment of mental illness (after the $75 deductible). As of January 1991 Medicare also will help pay for most outpatient prescription drugs, although there will still be a $600 deductible annually and a 50 percent copayment (the subscriber will get back *half* of annual prescription costs after paying the first $600 worth).

Although Medicare sounds like fairly good coverage for mental health care for the elderly, there is another catch. Medicare will pay only "reasonable charges," and exactly what constitutes "reasonable" is decided by the carrier, that is, the organization selected by the Social Security Administration to handle claims. In more than half of the states it is Blue Cross/Blue Shield; in the rest it is other insurance companies. Charges in excess of this amount may have to be paid by the individual.

Medicaid is a medical assistance program for needy and low-income persons supported by federal, state, and county taxes. In most states the Medicaid program is administered by the state department of public welfare through local welfare offices. The program pays for doctors' fees, inpatient or outpatient hospital care, laboratory tests, x-rays, care in a skilled (and sometimes intermediate) nursing home, and prescription drugs. In most states, anyone receiving Supplemental Security Income (SSI; see below) can be covered by Medicaid. To find out if you are eligible for Medicaid, you must contact your local welfare office. Some individuals are eligible for both Medicare and Medicaid.

Medicaid coverage varies from state to state, including the number of days of psychiatric hospitalization covered. In some states it will pay for a stay in the psychiatric unit of a general hospital and not for one in a psychiatric hospital. It does not cover halfway houses at all. In some states it covers outpatient visits but the amount paid to psychiatrists varies widely from state to state.

How easy it is to obtain Medicaid also varies widely. In some county welfare offices it is readily available to many individuals; in others one must be virtually without funds and wholly unable to work. Even if you can get Medicaid there is a catch. It covers all charges from qualified providers but it must pay practitioners and facilities considerably less than their normal fees, so many will not accept Medicaid clients. (In contrast, most practitioners and facilities do accept Medicare.)

If you expect Medicare or Medicaid to pay for your hospital costs, you must tell the business office of the hospital immediately upon admission, as must also generally be done with other forms of insurance. Often the hospital must first consult with the state before filing a claim to be paid, which takes time. Therefore, you may have insurance and still not be reimbursed for your hospital bill simply because you did not inform the hospital of your coverage soon enough.

SOCIAL SECURITY AND SUPPLEMENTAL SECURITY INCOME (SSI)

If you are a severely disabled worker of any age, with a physical or mental condition that will prevent you from working for at least one year (or that is expected to result in death), you may be entitled to disability pay from the Social Security Administration, called *Social Security Disability Insurance (SSDI)*. The amount will meet most of the medical and some of the living expenses of those who qualify. In order to qualify you must have worked and had Social Security payments withheld from your paycheck for a certain period of time (usually five of the previous ten years, but the law may have changed by the time you read this). If you do not qualify under Social Security you may be able to obtain Supplemental Security Income (see below).

If you are disabled, certain members of your family also can receive benefits from Social Security: unmarried children under eighteen (under twenty-two if they are full-time students), disabled children eighteen or over if they were disabled before the age of twenty-two, or your spouse if she is sixty-two or older. A person disabled before he could work long enough to build up Social Security benefits may be eligible for benefits based on his parents' Social Security contributions, beginning either when they reach sixty-five or upon their death.

Such benefits may be applied for at any age, and they continue for the duration of the disability; they do not stop with the parent's death, and they are available for adopted children as well.

If you are divorced, you may be eligible for benefits as a dependent of your ex-spouse if you were married for ten years or longer. A divorced and disabled wife who survives a worker to whom she was married for ten years or more becomes eligible for benefits at the age of fifty.

For all these forms of disability and survivors Social Security, apply at your nearest Social Security office (see your phone book) as soon as disability or death has occurred. Go either in person or telephone and ask to have an application mailed to you. For disability benefits you need a letter from your physician, and you also must give the Social Security office your physician's name, address, phone number, and a list of the dates when you saw the physician. Disability pensions may be discontinued if you return to work, even on a part-time basis, but sometimes allowances are made.

Supplemental Security Income (SSI) is a federal program that pays a monthly check to individuals in financial need who either are sixty-five or older or are, at any age, blind, mentally incapacitated, or disabled. Most states add to the amount that the federal government provides. You can get SSI even if you have never worked, or if you have some assets in the form of savings accounts, stocks or bonds, or jewelry or other valuables, provided that the value of those assets does not exceed a certain amount (in January 1989 that amount was $2,000 for a single person and $3,000 for a married couple). A house, personal effects, or household goods usually do not count as assets, and insurance policies or a car may not either, depending on their value. You may earn some income and still get SSI. You also may have unearned income (Social Security, interest on savings accounts, dividends, veterans' compensation, workers' compensation, pensions, annuities, gifts), provided it does not exceed a given amount (the figures change from year to year). However, living in the home of a relative may reduce the amount of SSI awarded.

SSI in most states makes one eligible for Medicaid medical insurance (see above) but does not provide survivors' benefits, that is, the children, widow, or other dependents of a person receiving SSI do not continue to receive money after that person's death. Also, SSI payments stop if one is hospitalized for more than thirty days. In order to apply for SSI, call your local Social Security Administration office.

It is important to try to get SSI even if the amount will be small (if one has other income), because it establishes eligibility for other programs: Medicaid, vocational rehabilitation, food stamps, and housing and rent assistance from the Department of Housing and Urban Development. In some states this eligibility occurs automatically; in others separate applications must be completed.

The application for SSI is reviewed by a disability examiner and a physician. If it is denied, the denial may be appealed within sixty days. If the local Social Security office denies the first appeal, a reappeal may be made before an administrative law judge of the U.S. Department of Health and Human Services. Such continued pressure often is successful.

You need both persistence and patience in dealing with Social Security offices. If you telephone, you may have to try many times to get a free line. The best times to get through are early in the morning or early in the afternoon, and late in the month. If you decide to go in person, be prepared to wait, possibly for several hours. Bring something to read and a snack. Be sure to bring all relevant papers and documents: any correspondence you may have had with the Social Security Administration, information about your doctor (name, address, phone number, dates when you saw the doctor), and a letter from the doctor confirming your disability.

Whether you telephone or go in person, be sure to make a note of the name of the person you speak with; it may be relevant if there are misunderstandings. Do not ignore any correspondence from Social Security. If you're not sure what a letter means, telephone the person who wrote it. If you don't answer a letter, your claim may be denied on grounds of "lack of cooperation."

When people are considered disabled because of mental illness, a question sometimes arises concerning their ability to handle their own finances. If the Social Security Administration determines that they are incapable of handling their own funds (a determination usually made by a psychiatrist), someone else—usually a relative or a friend but sometimes the director of an inpatient facility, such as a hospital or halfway house—becomes the "representative payee" and the checks are made out to that person. If the ill person is hospitalized, the representative payee usually turns the check over to the hospital; if it is a state or county hospital, in some places the check may be turned over to the state office of mental health or to whatever department in that state administers hospital bills.

Bear in mind that laws and regulations governing Social Security and SSI change, and interpretations of them differ. The best source of information is the frequently updated *Social Security Manual*, which is available at some large Social Security offices or can be obtained from the Superintendent of Documents, U.S. Government Printing Office, Washington, DC 20402.

Members of the armed forces are treated free of charge while they are in the service for any physical or mental illness, and after discharge for any service-connected conditions (see under Veterans Administration clinics, Chapter 13). While they are in the service their families are covered by CHAMPUS (Civilian Health and Medical Program of the Uniformed Services). It allows sixty days of hospital care for mental illness per year, and shares the cost of two outpatient visits per week, with periodic reports from the provider and periodic peer review required (to justify continued treatment). After discharge or retirement, CHAMPUS benefits end. However, a retired member of the armed forces who is entitled to retirement pay may apply for the Survivor Benefit Plan, in order to plan for caring for a disabled child, spouse, or other family member after his own death.

THIRD-PARTY PAYMENTS AND CONFIDENTIALITY

According to statements made by psychiatrists and psychologists connected with such organizations as the National Institute of Mental Health and the American Psychiatric Association's Committee on Confidentiality, thousands of men and women pay for mental health care out of their own pockets instead of applying for the mental health insurance coverage provided by their employers because they fear the consequences of admitting they have an emotional problem at their place of employment. One estimate stated that 15 percent of all adults who have such insurance and are currently in therapy waive reimbursement for this reason. And, of course, countless others forego treatment entirely rather than let their employers or colleagues know they are using their mental health benefits. They feel disclosure is too high a price. The same is true in the military, especially for career officers, who fear they will not be promoted if their superiors learn they have emotional problems.

Another source of concern is the security of information that is provided to the insurance companies in the course of making claims. This information is necessarily used by the insurers and, sometimes, by outsiders for purposes of claims review or legitimate research. Yet unrestricted access to diagnoses—and one must, after all, state what a claim is for—can cause serious problems for patients if the information is widely circulated.

Some psychiatrists try to protect their patients by deliberately falsifying diagnoses on claims forms. One study compared several thousand actual insurance claims for psychiatric care against diagnoses recorded in psychiatrists' private files in the same geographic area during the same period of time. The results revealed that when patients' names were reported (as they were in the claims), about 84 percent were diagnosed as neurotic, whereas when the patients' identities were concealed (in the information taken from the files) only about 28 percent were so diagnosed and the rest were diagnosed as having much more serious illnesses, such as schizophrenia.

One aid to greater confidentiality is for businesses offering health insurance to have claims sent directly to the insurer rather than being channeled through company personnel offices. Another, of course, is to educate the public so as to eliminate what has been called "mentalism," that is, the unreasonable fear of and prejudice against mental patients.

FINANCIAL HELP FROM OTHER AGENCIES

A variety of state and local agencies may directly and indirectly help pay some of the costs of mental health care. The trouble is that they are often hard to track down, and the services may be fragmented among several agencies. Free transportation to and from treatment and health-care centers may be available, for example, as may special education courses of various kinds. The best source of such information is a knowledgeable local social worker. You may find such a social worker on the hospital staff or through the community mental health center or a social agency such as a family service agency.

Another source of valuable information and help is your state or federal *vocational rehabilitation office*. The state offices usually operate a unit in every state mental hospital; the federal unit nearest you can be found through the phone book (look in the United States government section). These offices provide a wide range of services, including a physical examination to determine fitness for employment, counseling and testing to determine vocational aptitudes, job training (a huge area, including personal adjustment training, prevocational and vocational training for special fields, sheltered workshops, and on-the-job training), transportation to and from these services, and job placement. The evaluation, counseling, and placement are all free of charge, but there may be fees for job training and/or medical services, depending on economic need (fees are based on what clients can afford).

TYPICAL CHARGES FOR MENTAL HEALTH CARE

The fees charged for outpatient psychotherapy vary widely. In general, psychiatrists charge more than psychologists, who usually charge more than social workers and psychiatric nurses. However, this differential may be offset (or canceled out) by the fact that insurance coverage may be limited to psychiatrists, or to psychiatrists and psychologists, and not pay a penny toward therapy by an unlicensed social worker or nurse.

Therapists in private practice may adjust their fees to the client's ability to pay—some do and some don't—but the reduction may not be very great, usually no more than 15 or 20 percent. If you like the therapist but can't afford the fee, ask if it is negotiable. The worst you can get is a negative reply.

In general, clinics tend to charge less than private practitioners. Training institutes or the outpatient clinics of teaching hospitals, where therapists may be students (trainees or residents), may be cheaper yet. However, the name "clinic" does not guarantee a lower fee; some private clinics are very expensive. The lowest fees are those charged by community mental health centers, which are supported by local, state, and federal government funds, as well as by third-party (insurance) payments and grants and fees. They must by law consider the client's ability to pay, and they cannot refuse treatment on that ground alone. Their "sliding scale" of fees may go down to zero.

Hospitalization in the psychiatric unit of a general hospital costs, on the average, twice as much as in a private mental hospital, but again, the difference may be offset or canceled by the fact that insur-

COMPARATIVE FEES OF THERAPISTS
Individual Fees*

Profession	Median	Most Popular Fee
Psychologists	$75	$75
Social workers	$65	$60
Couples and family counselors	$70	$70
Other (non-M.D.)	$65	$60

Group Fees*

All professions	Median: $35	Most Popular: $35

Individual by Region*

Region	Median	Most Popular Fee
East	$70	$75
South	$75	$75
Midwest	$70	$75
West	$75	$70

Individual by Practice Setting*

Large Cities and Suburbs	$75
Small Towns	$70
Rural Areas	$65

Individual by Education*

Psychiatrist or psychoanalyst with M.D.	$75–$125
Clinical psychologist with Ph.D.	$50–$80
Psychiatric social worker with MSW	$40–$60

* Based on 1988 survey published in *Psychotherapy Finances*, volume 15, no. 3. Used by permission. Note that more than half of the 1,312 practitioners reporting offer a sliding fee scale, according to client's finances, and an additional one-third report that at least some of their clients pay less than their regular fee.

ance may cover much or all of the former and little or nothing of the latter. Most private mental hospitals do not accept Medicaid inpatients.

State and county mental hospitals must accept Medicaid patients but are *not*, contrary to popular opinion, totally free of charge. They collect as much as they can from their patients, and also from private insurance companies and Medicaid. For patients who have no insurance but do have financial assets of one kind or another, the hospital may charge a fee based on its judgment of what the patient can afford. Moreover, in most states certain relatives of patients are legally liable for paying the costs of hospitalization, or at least for as much as they can afford. In some states, for example, husbands or wives are legally liable for the hospital costs of their spouse, but parents and children are not. In other states, parents and adult children, as well as the spouse, are liable and in some states the law is altogether unclear. When relatives are so liable, they must pay as long as they (or the guardians of their estate) can do so, even out of a pension or Social Security payment. In order to find out the law in your state, investigate at your county courthouse and also discuss your finances with the hospital business office.

The costs of partial hospitalization—day care, night care, halfway houses, and so on—are a gray area. Some private plans treat it the same as full-time hospitalization. Most do not. In general, if it is under the auspices of a community mental health center it will be covered as outpatient care; if it is administered by a county or state hospital it is likely to be covered as inpatient care. A private facility, on the other hand, may receive little or no coverage.

Nursing homes or extended-care facilities nearly always accept Medicare patients but may or may not accept Medicaid. Medicare will pay for a skilled nursing facility provided the patient meets a series of other qualifications. The charges of nursing homes vary widely, from very expensive to quite cheap, and so does the quality of care (see Chapter 20). Some private insurance policies do cover extended-care facilities.

TIPS FOR CUTTING MENTAL HEALTH COSTS

- For psychotherapy, consider using a teaching hospital clinic or a community mental health center.
- If psychoactive drugs are prescribed, keep a list of medications that have been effective for you in the past; make sure your prescription is labeled and write on the label the reason for taking this drug (you may be able to use it again); shop around for prescriptions (prices vary considerably among different pharmacies); ask your doctor to prescribe by generic name instead of brand name if possible; don't buy from a hospital pharmacy unless it's an HMO pharmacy (hos-

pital drugstore prices tend to be higher); use the largest-size tablet available that is consistent with the prescribed dose (two 10-mg tablets can cost twice as much as one 20-mg tablet); buy in bulk— the largest supply you are likely to need—if your physician approves.

- If you are hospitalized, check your charges in advance so you know how much to expect; check your bill carefully to make sure your length of stay was the same as you are charged for, and to make sure you actually received the services you are being charged for.
- If you decide to leave the hospital against medical advice, check with your insurance company to make sure it will still cover your bill. (You probably should get a second opinion before checking out.)
- Deduct the cost of treatment from your federal income tax (and possibly also your state income tax) if it exceeds the percentage of your income specified by law. It counts as a medical expense, that is, money paid for preventing, treating, and alleviating diseases or disabilities of a taxpayer and his dependents. You may deduct the costs of psychotherapy by a psychiatrist or psychologist (or others if supervised by one of these professionals); special schooling for an emotionally disturbed or otherwise handicapped child; transportation to and from such a school; sheltered workshops, a group home, partial hospitalization, or other housing if a physician orders it as a transition to normal life; diagnostic tests and evaluations; prescribed medication (in excess of 1 percent of income), including drugs and vitamins; special instruction and training; half your premium for medical insurance; a certain amount of "child care" for a disabled relative (child or adult) in your home who needs supervision while you are at work.

Tax laws change frequently, and specific allowances are periodically adjusted for inflation, so be sure to check with your local Internal Revenue Service office for details. Do not fail to itemize and record all such expenses, and keep with them dated and signed notes from physicians and other professionals recommending the services whose costs you may wish to deduct.

Chapter

25

PREVENTING MENTAL ILLNESS

ONCE THE cause of a specific illness is known, there is a fairly good chance that researchers will discover not only a cure for it but a means of preventing it entirely. This, at least, has been the case with numerous infectious diseases—whooping cough, measles, diphtheria—that have been virtually wiped out by means of widespread immunization, and it may soon be the case for cancer. It may also one day be true for mental illnesses, but that time has not yet arrived. The causes of only a few disorders—mainly those involving organic brain disease—are known, and we cannot always prevent their occurrence. We do know, however, that there is increased risk of developing a mental illness for certain individuals or under certain conditions.

As with physical illness, the greatest risk is for those who are weakest: the very young, the very old, the convalescent (recovering from mental illness), and those who are undergoing a major life stress or who live in an unhealthy and stressful environment (the poor). Also like physical illness, the best chance of preventing serious mental illness is early detection, early intervention, and early treatment.

CHILDREN AT RISK

Schizophrenia, major depression, and manic-depressive psychosis all are believed to involve genetic factors, which also are suspected in antisocial personality disorders, alcoholism, and panic disorder (acute anxiety). A child with one schizophrenic parent has a 10 percent risk of developing schizophrenia (as opposed to 1 percent for the general population); when both parents have (or had) it, there is a 46 percent risk that their child will, too. That risk can rise with stress from disease, trauma, difficulties in the family, or other factors.

Such youngsters often show early signs of poor function, in the form of deficits in fine motor development, visual and motor coordination, and other neurological development. For families known to be at risk for transmitting such a susceptibility, genetic counseling, a careful examination of each child at the time of birth, and frequent pediatric evaluation of the children allow the possibility of early intervention, such as therapeutic nursery care and special language programs (for children showing delayed language development).

INHERITED DISORDERS

When one or both parents are found to carry a predisposition to a mental disorder or an actual defective trait, *genetic counseling* can be used to determine the probability of transmitting the disorder to a child and to consider the various options available. For example, if the husband carries the defect, the wife may be inseminated artificially, using a donor's sperm. For certain disorders, blood and urine tests can determine if either parent is a carrier, and sophisticated genetic tests are becoming available for such disorders as Huntington's chorea, for which no cure is yet known. For others, there may be no such evidence, but the strong possibility of transmitting a very serious disorder may be a deterrent to childbearing.

Some disorders or defects can be detected during pregnancy by testing the amniotic fluid surrounding the fetus. In these cases a decision can be postponed until that procedure, called *amniocentesis*, reveals whether or not a defect actually has been transmitted. Amniocentesis can be used to detect chromosomal defects associated with mental retardation, such as Down's syndrome and fragile X chro mosome, and certain inborn metabolic disorders, some of which can actually be treated *before* birth.

PRENATAL PREVENTIVE CARE

Some forms of mental disorder result from inadequate protection of the brain and nervous system during its early development in the womb. There is a clear relationship between lack of medical attention to a pregnant woman and her risk of bearing a child with a mental disorder such as retardation. Comprehensive prenatal care, with especially close attention to high-risk pregnancies (teenagers, women aged thirty-five or older, women with certain chronic diseases such as diabetes, and Rh blood incompatibility), can help lower the risk significantly.

The pregnant woman's diet can affect her baby. Inadequate amounts of vitamins and minerals or lack of protein can cause abnormalities in the baby's development. Her alcohol intake must be limited (some authorities say eliminated entirely). Too much can cause the baby to develop fetal alcohol syndrome, which can result in various growth deficiencies and retardation. There is definite risk to a baby whose mother has six drinks (9 ounces) of alcohol a day, and recent research indicates that even more than two drinks (3 ounces) is inadvisable. The use of addictive drugs can cause babies to be born addicted.

During pregnancy certain infectious diseases can harm the baby. The best known is rubella (German measles), for which immunization (by vaccine) has been available since 1969. Any woman considering pregnancy who has not already had rubella should be immunized against it and should put off conception for at least four months after vaccination (to make sure that the virus present in the vaccine is out of her system). Rubella can cause irreversible brain damage in the baby, as well as other serious abnormalities.

Toxoplasmosis, a flu-like illness caused by a parasite transmitted through rare or raw meat and also through the feces of domestic cats, can cause severe retardation in babies whose mothers are infected during pregnancy. A blood test before pregnancy can determine if a woman is immune; if she is not, she should avoid eating rare or raw meat and handling cat litter boxes during pregnancy.

Preventing Mental Retardation

Family Planning & Counseling

Identification of High-Risk Pregnancy

Prenatal Education

Diagnosis and Treatment Services
1. Genetic Screening and Counseling
2. Social Services
3. Nutrition Services
4. Nursing Services

Normal Pregnancy:
1. Nutrition Education
2. Nursing Services: Preparation for Labor & Delivery
3. Parental Education

Maternal/Fetal Transportation for Problem Delivery

Normal Labor and Delivery

High-Risk Obstetrical Unit

Identification of High-Risk Infant

Identification of Normal Infant

Intensive Care of Newborn:
1. Physician Services
2. Nursing Services
3. Nutrition Services
4. Social Services

Specialized Pediatric Care:
1. Diagnosis and Treatment for Genetic Defects and Inborn Errors of Metabolism
2. Social Services
3. Nutrition Services
4. Parenting Classes

Normal Pediatric Care:
1. Immunizations
2. Parenting Classes
3. Preventive Services

Measurement of Program Effectiveness:
1. Decrease in incidence of Down's Syndrome, especially in mothers over thirty-five years of age.
2. Decrease in perinatal mortality.
3. Decrease in low-birth-weight infants in primary hospitals.
4. Decrease in maternal chronic conditions.
5. Decrease in mental retardation from inborn errors of metabolism.
6. Other measures.

Courtesy of Roberta R. Coffin, M.D., Director, Medical Services Division, Vermont Department of Public Health, Burlington, VT.

Active genital herpes infection, a viral disease that can be sexually transmitted, may be deadly to the fetus and newborn. Some 75 percent of the babies that do survive suffer neurological damage and, often, retardation. No cure is known, but if active disease is detected in the mother before birth, a cesarean delivery is advisable so that the baby cannot be infected during its passage through the birth canal. If the mother has AIDS or has been exposed to the HIV virus, the baby has at least a 50 percent chance of being infected with this fatal disease.

PREVENTIVE CARE FOR THE VERY YOUNG

Even with careful prenatal care, some babies are at risk for conditions that can be detected only after birth. Screening at birth for one metabolic defect, phenylketonuria (PKU), now mandated by law in many localities, makes it possible to treat a baby by means of diet from infancy on, preventing brain damage. A simple blood test performed at birth for hypothyroidism (thyroid hormone deficiency) enables immediate treatment of the baby with thyroxin and thus helps prevent cretinism, a form of retardation caused by this deficiency.

Early detection and intervention are particularly useful for babies born of diabetic mothers, who are at risk for hydrocephalus and other abnormalities that benefit from prompt treatment, as well as for babies of alcoholics and drug abusers, who may be born addicted and suffer from withdrawal symptoms.

Proper nutrition for the mother who is breast-feeding and for the baby throughout infancy and early childhood may prevent developmental abnormalities in the brain and nervous system that contribute to mental defects. The removal or avoidance of environmental hazards like lead (in lead-based paint) is also important; the consumption of lead by small children can cause brain damage. A simple blood test, the FEP (free erythrocyte protoporphyrin) test, can be used to screen large numbers of children for lead poisoning and ensure early treatment of all who are ill.

Among the measures for preventive mental health care for youngsters that are badly needed are more and better day care for children of working parents, with greater emphasis on children's mental and emotional development; and periodic, comprehensive assessments of developmental status for every child (subject to parental consent), so that problems that might lead to emotional maladjustment or learning difficulties can be detected and treated early. Along these lines, one community mental health center instituted an Early Intervention Program to serve children under the age of thirty-six months who are lagging behind in walking, talking, or other areas; who are overly active or passive; who are born with cerebral palsy, Down's syndrome, or other developmental handicaps; who have problems with sleeping, eating, or toilet training; or who need help in learning to play with other children. After evaluation, the center offers a variety of services for the children and their parents. They include home visits by a specially trained teacher who brings selected materials to help a child with motor, language, and intellectual development; small groups for infants in a class setting with parent participation for learning of stimulation techniques; education and support groups for parents; small classes for toddlers to develop both individual and social skills; and help in locating and obtaining other community resources and services for special-needs children under the age of three.

INFANT PSYCHOTHERAPY

One of the newest fields in mental health care is infant psychotherapy, practiced by an estimated ten thousand professionals, including psychiatrists, psychologists, pediatricians, social workers, and nurses. It is believed that therapy for minor problems in infancy can prevent major problems in later life. In extreme cases, when the parent is much impaired or absent, therapy involves a team of caretakers who substitute for the parents. For most children, however, therapy focuses on evaluation of what is wrong between parent and child, and then teaching the parent to respond better to the baby's needs.

Partly because more is now known about the emotional development of babies, and partly because there has been an alarming increase in the number of infants born to mothers who are drug abusers or who are in their early teens (and in effect are still children themselves), there has been growing interest in preventing emotional problems in infants who are likely to have them. Surveys indicate that perhaps as many as 10 to 15 percent of infants brought to pediatricians' offices have a severe problem, such as depression or inability to respond to people. Another 10 to 15 percent appear to have milder problems that might benefit from short-term treatment.

The most serious disturbances in infants usually are attributed to parental abuse or to neglect of basic needs such as warmth and regular feeding. It is believed that such neglect can slow intellectual growth. Among the symptoms often encountered are continuous crying, frantic shaking, a tendency to shrink from touch, extreme sadness and lethargy, and indiscriminate rage.

For parents, this new field represents a source of expert advice on the emotional ups and downs of babies, which can both lay to rest ungrounded fears that something is wrong and, if something actually is found to be amiss, can provide help for a solution.

PREVENTIVE CARE FOR THE ELDERLY

The mental disorders of old age are not well understood either, but definite correlations have been discovered between symptoms of senility and such factors as hormone deficiency, poor nutrition, depression, and social isolation. Further, minor illnesses, chronic illnesses, or even a drastic change in environment can in older persons give rise to symptoms of senile dementia. A recent study found that 35 percent of a group of patients originally believed to have irreversible senile dementia actually had a treatable and reversible medical or psychiatric disorder.

Many, if not most, older persons suffer from one or another chronic physical problem that requires medication. However, an older person's body metabolizes drugs quite differently from younger individuals. Tranquilizers, barbiturates and other sleep medications, mood-altering drugs, and diuretic-type drugs used to treat high blood pressure and heart disease are common causes of dementia symptoms that often can be eliminated simply by reducing the dosage or altering the medication.

Depression, especially in reacting to loss, is common in the elderly and sometimes takes the form of senility symptoms. Many elderly persons suffer two important kinds of loss: the death of friends and relatives, and impaired health. Often handicaps in sight or hearing and difficulty in walking prevent older people from going out much, as well as from engaging in their usual indoor activities (reading, sewing, listening to music, watching television). These constraints limit their lives. Too often such individuals end up in nursing homes or long-term care institutions where their mental health degenerates even more.

ELDERLY HOME CARE

Comprehensive health care, including nutritional and other services, often can prevent such degeneration by enabling the elderly to remain in their own homes. Traditionally such services were provided by family members, but today, with families often scattered across the country, and with more and more old people outliving many of their relatives, it is no longer feasible.

In some areas community mental health centers are able to provide needed services, and in others the slack has been taken up by a relatively recent innovation, the home-care corporation, usually administered under a system established by the state department of elder affairs (known by a variety of names in different states). For example, Massachusetts instituted a system of twenty-nine nonprofit home corporations, each serving its own region. Some services are provided directly by the corporation staff, and others are purchased from providers in the various communities. One home care corporation provides the following services:

- Information and referral, providing answers to most questions of concern to persons sixty years of age or older. This service includes a brief interview to determine a person's needs for services, referral to the appropriate resource, and follow-up to make sure the service was rendered.
- Home care, coordinated by a case manager, an individual assigned to each client to obtain services designed to enable the elderly person to continue living at home, and to periodically reevaluate the services as circumstances change. Among them are homemaker service (for food shopping, personal errands, light housekeeping, laundry, and meal preparation); chore service (heavy cleaning and minor household repairs); home-delivered meals ("meals on wheels") for homebound elders unable to prepare their own meals; and companionship (regular visits by volunteers to isolated elders).
- Nutrition, providing a hot noon meal and a full schedule of activities to anyone over sixty at various central locations in the area.

- Transportation services, including rides for out-of-town medical and social service appointments (when no other means of transport are available) and to and from nutrition (noon meal) sites.
- Protective services, working with other agencies to provide immediate help for elders in crisis or those being abused or neglected, with a social worker coordinating help from medical, legal, and mental health agencies.
- Legal aid, providing counsel to elders through referral to the Senior Citizens Law Project.
- Planning, including identifying the most pressing needs of older residents in the area and creating a plan to coordinate community resources to meet those needs.

Under this excellent system, a case worker is sent to see any person over sixty who phones for help or for whom assistance is requested by the family, a hospital, or some other social agency. Most of the clients have a serious physical handicap, such as severe arthritis, but often they exhibit emotional distress as well, caused by anxiety over economic problems (rising fuel bills, for instance) and increasingly limited physical ability.

A major service provided is a day health center that can be used by *any* adult (sixteen years of age or older) whose medical or psychological condition indicates a need for nursing care, supervision, or therapeutic services as an *alternative* to institutional placement. The day center accepts both Medicaid and private-paying participants, and requires only that a person be willing to attend a minimum of two six-hour days a week. The program, open from 9 A.M. to 3 P.M. every weekday, provides health-care monitoring and supervision by a registered nurse (in collaboration with the client's own physician); personal care services; physical, occupational, and speech therapy; a hot lunch and two snacks; social, recreational, and educational activities; transport to and from the program; and referrals to and coordination of community health and social services with counseling for participants and their families.

Day-care centers specifically for Alzheimer's patients, with special support and education programs for their families, are being organized in various places. With a rapidly rising elderly population and the realization that institutional placement is regarded by most elderly persons and their families as a desperate last resort, home-care and day-care programs represent a less expensive and far more desirable alternative.

PREVENTIVE CARE FOR FORMER PATIENTS

Effective aftercare for persons who were hospitalized for mental illness is a significant factor in preventing relapse and readmission to the hospital. With the emphasis today on brief hospitalization and a rapid return to the community, there has been an enormous increase in the "revolving door" syndrome, that is, patients are discharged from the hospital only to require readmittance within a few months. Estimates vary, but most studies indicate that 50 to 60 percent of patients are rehospitalized within nine months of discharge.

A coordinated transition from hospital to community is extremely important to adjustment, yet it is often the weakest link in the aftercare chain. Without vigorous efforts to familiarize patients with community treatment facilities, they often get no aftercare whatever. Personal contact appears to be vital. Aggressive planning before hospital discharge, in which the patient can see the aftercare facility (day hospital, community mental health center, etc.) and meet the new therapist in charge, as well as careful follow-up to make sure the patient actually carries out the agreed-on plan, are essential. (The various forms of partial hospitalization that can be used in this transition are described in Chapter 21.) In addition, most studies indicate that keeping up sufficient medication and maintaining psychotherapy of some kind after discharge significantly reduces the rate of relapse. Self-help groups such as Recovery, Inc. (see Chapter 14) also are useful, particularly when used in conjunction with other forms of aftercare.

HOME MENTAL HEALTH-CARE SERVICES

Jennifer R., 54, divorced, with a twenty-five-year history of manic-depressive psychosis, is hospitalized after becoming increasingly paranoid, delusional, and suffering from insomnia. Her five grown children cannot or do not wish to have her live with them. The hospital will discharge her as soon as her symptoms are controlled somewhat, but she is not ready to manage alone in the apartment she shares with her elderly mother.* The solution: mental health home-care services.

In 1987 two Massachusetts nurses founded Mental Health Care at Home, a private service in which licensed clinicians provide needed mental health care in a client's home. This care includes individual, couple, or family therapy, administration of medication and mon-itoring of side effects, crisis intervention, blood tests to make sure medication levels are maintained, and referral and link-up with com-munity resources.

In Jennifer's case, the hospital social worker contacted Mental Health Care at Home to arrange a planning meeting in the hospital, attended by Jennifer, her family, her doctor, and her social worker. This meeting served to establish rapport with Jennifer and her family and to identify potential problems that might arise at home. Since her symptoms were not entirely controlled at discharge, home care visits began immediately. Her medication was closely supervised, and Jen-nifer was taught to prepare and take the drugs prescribed. At various times she developed severe side effects to some of the drugs, but early identification of these problems and prompt communication with her doctor, who then changed her prescriptions, helped stabilize Jen-nifer's symptoms. Her lithium blood level was regularly checked, and the family was taught about her problems and the various solutions.

Jennifer's case is serious enough so that a few weeks of home care to ease the transition between hospital and home are not enough. Conse-quently she has been put on a home-care maintenance program, with still regular but fewer visits. As a result she continues to take her medications regularly and her symptoms are well controlled. Most important, home care not only enabled her earlier discharge from the hospital but has prevented rehospitalization.

Among other clients who have benefited from mental health home care are Carol, an obese, passive seventeen-year-old who became suicidally depressed when her mother and her mother's live-in boy-friend moved with her to a new neighborhood (four weeks of intensive home visits, in addition to continued therapy at the local community mental health center, and she returned to school); Nellie, a ninety-year-old widow with a long-standing personality disorder (two weeks of intensive home care enabled her to return to the adult day center

* Adapted from case by Elizabeth Killian, co-founder, Mental Health Care at Home, Inc., Dedham, MA.

from which she had been suspended for her negative, aggressive behavior); Anna, 44, who has averaged two to three hospitalizations a year for manic-depressive psychosis and alcohol abuse (long-term home care has kept her stable and compliant with medication, as well as able to work full-time and live independently).

The cost savings of home services are considerable. A year's maintenance home care for Anna currently costs about $5,800, as opposed to several hospitalizations a year costing $20,000. Admission to a nursing home would cost Nellie $100 to $150 a day, whereas intensive home care for two weeks costs $1,000. A four-week stay in a hospital accepting adolescents would have cost Carol as much as $20,000, compared to $2,500 for four weeks of intensive home care.

OUTPATIENT COMMITMENT

Some mental disorders require long-term use of medication to prevent recurrence, yet refusing medication is a common problem. Sometimes the person refuses openly. More often noncompliance is secret, so that for weeks and months relatives and the therapist do not realize that the patient is not taking prescribed medication. The reasons for noncompliance vary: Manic-depressive patients may enjoy the "high" of their mania; schizophrenics may be distressed by side effects of antipsychotic drugs; or, often, a person simply denies being chronically ill and insists that medication is not needed.

Dealing with this problem is easier if the underlying reasons for refusal are known. If side effects are troublesome, which can be indicated by means of a daily diary kept by the patient, alternatives such as a lower dosage, a different type of drug, or intermittent medication may be considered. If none of these alternatives is feasible, outpatient commitment might be considered.

Outpatient commitment specifies that a patient must accept treatment in an outpatient program. It is not a conditional release from a hospital, since the client is committed as an outpatient without having first been committed as an inpatient. To ensure compliance, the medication can be given by injection, or in liquid form (so that a tablet can't be hidden in the mouth). With some medications, like lithium, blood levels can be periodically tested. Outpatient commitment is legally sanctioned in two-thirds of the states, but many mental health professionals are not familiar with the procedure, so at present fewer than 5 percent of all commitments are to outpatient status.

RETURNING TO WORK

Vocational rehabilitation is an important and often underrated element in aftercare. Obtaining employment after a mental illness, particularly after hospitalization, may be very difficult. As indicated earlier, mental illness is a stigma, and some employers are unwilling to hire former patients. The help of both a vocational counselor and a therapist can be useful in advising a person about the problems of a particular job and making recommendations to particular employers. The person's own expectations also play a role. An individual who is ashamed of her past illness or who expects employer discrimination may back away from a promising position and drift into marginal, ill-paid work that suits her low self-esteem more than her actual abilities and training.

Some mental patients have residual disabilities that prevent full-time employment. They may, however, function well in part-time jobs. Sometimes job sharing—with two persons sharing the work and responsibilities of one position—is a solution. Those with considerable handicaps may do well in sheltered workshops. (See also career rehabilitation in Chapter 21.)

FOR THOSE IN TROUBLE WITH THE LAW

With those forms of illness that lead to antisocial behavior of one kind or another, specifically criminal offenses and drug abuse, psychotherapy in a court clinic or correctional facility represents a kind of preventive mental health care. In some states court clinics provide evaluation and treatment for offenders, and they also may provide training in counseling for correction officers and prison guards (see also Chapter 26).

Nearly all of the states provide some form of psychiatric treatment in their prisons. However, the number of professional mental health workers in relation to the prison population is so small and their other administrative chores are so numerous that in practice very few prisoners have access to the services of a counselor.

The most promising group in terms of prevention would seem to be juvenile offenders. The findings of a recent report indicate that juvenile offenders—that is, anyone under the age of eighteen—may receive mental health services at one or more points, the most common of which are at intake, after the filing of a delinquency petition but before a court hearing (to determine the youngster's competency to proceed with the hearing); after the hearing (to help the court determine how to settle the case); after a judicial opinion or sentence has been pronounced (in place of disposition, usually taking the form of civil commitment to a mental health facility); and following the court's disposition (for example, as a condition of parole).

Although it sounds as though juvenile offenders receive considerable mental health services, in practice such services may consist of a single interview with a psychiatrist to determine competency. An extended period of individual or group therapy addressed to sorting out a youngster's emotional problems and preventing recurrence of antisocial behavior is rare.

For young drug abusers, experience with drop-in centers for young people on drugs indicates that such facilities may attract more youngsters than hospital-based or other "establishment" clinics, even when they are staffed by the same personnel (principally social workers and physicians). For both drug and alcohol dependency, which tend to have extremely high rates of relapse, self-help groups may help prevent backsliding for those individuals who are willing and able to use them.

COPING WITH LIFE CRISES

Certain stressful experiences are almost universal, and it has been found that programs can be designed to teach people to cope with them more effectively. The reduction of stress associated with these experiences lowers the likelihood of serious emotional problems. Included among such experiences are a child's admission to a hospital; separation of parent from child (even for a short period); death of a family member or a close friend; a serious illness or major surgery (especially open-heart surgery); the struggles of adolescence, marriage, pregnancy, child rearing, middle age, and old age; separation and divorce; loss of a job, prolonged unemployment and retirement. Careful preparation for effective handling of critical situations and prompt intervention when an emotional crisis does develop may prevent future problems.

CRISIS INTERVENTION

Telephone hot lines for individuals in various kinds of life crisis have sprung up all over the country in recent years. The most dramatic crisis they deal with is threatened suicide, but there also are hot lines for child abuse and other violence directed toward others. They can be located through the phone book. (See Chapter 2 for more specific information.)

Often a telephone hot line is a strictly local service, established and staffed by concerned professionals and/or volunteers in a particular city or town. One hot line, CONTACT, is a national network (in turn a member of Life Line International, consisting of similar "teleministries" in other countries). Each of several hundred CONTACT centers in the United States is an autonomous community service linked with the national network. It provides twenty-four-hour direct access by phone to trained lay volunteers who wait at a central location and respond to callers.

Each CONTACT volunteer is required to have fifty hours of training in counseling that is provided in weekly sessions over several months. Training sessions are devoted to such subjects as personality theory; emphatic listening; substance abuse; crisis theory; listening skills; loss, dying, and grief; human sexuality; and suicide prevention. Callers may remain anonymous if they wish. The service is used by more than 1.5 million persons a year, who call for a variety of reasons. At least 30 percent of the calls directly concern mental health or emotional problems.

Numerous communities and groups in the United States have set up suicide prevention centers. The essential elements for such a center are twenty-four-hour phone service and the availability of professional backup and consultation. The best centers form part of a community network and include emergency mental health services (including suicide prevention), partial hospitalization, full hospitalization, and outpatient counseling.

EMPLOYEE ASSISTANCE PROGRAMS (EAPS)

Originally a method of rehabilitating alcoholic employees, the Employee Assistance Program consists of one or more staff mental health professionals who counsel employees of their company and has come to encompass marital and family counseling, drug rehabilitation, psychological screening, and referral to private therapists. Many companies also use their program to ensure that the care provided to their employees is appropriate and cost-effective.

Screening and treating workers through the company EAP has become a preferable alternative to the expense of firing an employee who has problems. It is hoped that early screening and treatment will catch potential mental problems in their early stages and prevent some of the high costs of hospitalization, as well as improve productivity and employee relations.

REDUCING STRESS

A booklet published by the National Mental Health Association, *How to Deal with Your Tensions*, recommends a number of specific steps for anyone who is unusually tense and anxious. They include:

- Talk it out (with a relative, friend, doctor, minister, anyone).
- Escape for a while (with a book, movie, brief trip).
- Work off your anger and tension in vigorous physical activity.
- Give in occasionally; if you have frequent quarrels, make allowance for the fact that you *could* be wrong.
- Do something for others.
- Take one thing at a time.
- Don't expect too much of yourself.
- Go easy with criticism of others.
- Let up on your competitive urge.
- Make yourself available to others.
- Schedule your recreation.

Not everyone has a friend or relative or doctor to confide in. For many, however, a support group made up of other individuals with the same or a similar problem can be extremely helpful. Such support groups have been organized by family service agencies, mental health clinics, churches, and numerous other organizations. Sometimes they have been formed by putting up a notice on the bulletin board of a local library or grocery store, or putting an ad in the local paper.

In addition to groups for mental patients, alcoholics, and drug addicts, the self-help movement has given rise to numerous support groups for individuals coping with life stresses: Reach to Recovery (after a mastectomy), Parents Without Partners (with nearly a thousand active chapters in the United States and Canada), the La Leche League for breast-feeding women, Widows Helping Widows, groups for parents of children with physical and/or emotional handicaps, as well as groups for parents whose children have died (The Foundation for Sudden Infant Death and the Society of the Compassionate Friends). See Chapter 14 for how to find a self-help group.

DIVORCE MEDIATION

With nearly one-half of all American marriages now ending in divorce, the life crisis of separation and divorce has become commonplace, but how it is handled has a direct bearing on the mental health of the family members concerned.

Divorce mediation is a relatively new area of counseling that offers both crisis intervention and support. Mediation by an experienced and neutral person provides the opportunity for husband and wife to work out the terms of an agreement over such issues as custody, visitation, co-parenting, the present and future needs of children, financial arrangements, and division of property. In this process, the anger and conflict associated with separation and divorce may be significantly reduced, minimizing the disruption in the lives of all family members, particularly the children. For families with children, divorce mediators tend to see a divorce not as the end of a family but as a radical restructuring, which may, if either parent remarries, eventually involve new family members as well.

Divorce mediators are counselors, lawyers, and therapists especially trained in family mediation and divorce procedures. In addition to helping a couple reach an agreement, mediators may provide individual therapy and counseling, family and children's counseling, and a variety of support groups (for separating couples, children and/or adolescents of divorcing parents, stepparents, etc.). The accompanying illustrations show what issues a separation agreement should include, and a sample separation/divorce agreement negotiated by a divorce mediator.

SOCIAL AND ENVIRONMENTAL STRESS

While each of us has a degree of tolerance to stress, the presence of multiple sources of stress increases the likelihood of mental breakdown. For example, the combination of hunger, crowding, and racial

MATTERS TO BE INCLUDED IN A SEPARATION AGREEMENT*

The division of real and personal property, including its appraisal, terms of sale, and how proceeds are to be divided.

Financial obligations of one spouse to another, including support of spouse, support of children, financing of college education (sharing based on income, equally, or on savings or trusts), summer camp, medical and dental care (insurance), life insurance and retirement income, cost of living increases, reduction or other changes based on employment status.

Custody of minor children, including who has custody (one parent or shared), visitation arrangements (any time, specific times each week or month, school vacations, summer vacations, travel out of state or abroad).

Tax implications, including deductions for alimony and dependency exemptions.

Attorney's fees.

Relation of separation agreement to divorce judgment (separate from divorce terms or part of them).

Provisions for change (mediation clause, arbitration clause).

AGREEMENT OF JOHN AND MARY DOE
REGARDING THEIR SEPARATION AND DIVORCE*
FEBRUARY 25, 1991

John and Mary, who have been married twenty-five years, have lived separately for the last ten months. They have three children, Jane, age twenty-two, and Marjorie, age twenty, who both live in the city nearby, and John, Jr., age eighteen, who lives at home with Mary. They have acknowledged that an irretrievable breakdown of their marriage exists, and have drawn an agreement by which to legally separate and seek a divorce.

1. Property and possessions

John and Mary have agreed that she will continue to live in the marital home on Main Street, in Ourtown, until it is her decision to sell this house. The equity accrued (based on the value of the property at the time it is sold) will be shared equally by John and Mary.

John and Mary have agreed to divide their personal possessions to their mutual satisfaction by the time this agreement is presented in court.

2. Financial arrangements

In order to assume responsibility for liabilities to date, for maintenance costs, and for educational expenses, John and Mary have agreed to the following:

a. John will contribute $800 monthly to the support of Mary and son John; he will

_____
* Courtesy, Divorce Resource & Mediation Center, Inc., Cambridge, MA.

also continue to provide telephone service as possible through his employment, and to maintain Mary's car expenses.

b. Mary will find employment suitable to her skills and experience to provide income for expenses beyond those supported by John.

c. John will assume responsibility for the debts (known to both of them) incurred as of the date of the court appearance.

d. John will contribute to the college expenses of Marjorie and John, Jr., to the best of his ability, and as arranged between him and these children.

3. Insurances

John and Mary have agreed that health insurance for this family will be maintained by John's current policy as long as it is possible for Mary and the children to be covered under this plan.

They further agree to maintain their respective life insurance policies naming each other as primary beneficiaries.

4. Privacy

Pending a final divorce decree, John and Mary agree to respect each other's privacy and to allow one another to live their public and private lives as though they are unmarried individuals.

5. Mediation

In the event of any major change of circumstance, such as loss of employment, substantial increase or decrease in either of their incomes, illness or disability, John and Mary agree to discuss and negotiate any needed changes in the terms of this agreement. Should they fail to reach a suitable and workable modification of any issue, they agree to use mediation for resolution.

or ethnic discrimination in our city ghettoes can become intolerable and produce unhealthy behavior in some individuals. Whereas schizophrenia afflicts approximately 1 percent of the overall population, the incidence of this disorder may be as high as 6 percent in a city ghetto. In such areas, community services potentially can play a large role in preventive mental health care.

The poor carry the biggest risks of mental handicap. It is the poor who account for the most high-risk pregnancies and the least prenatal care. It is the poor who are likely to skip medical checkups for their children, where mental problems could be discovered and treated at early stages. It is the poor who are likely to be nourished inadequately and receive insufficient care for the many physical conditions associated with mental impairment. It is the poor who are more likely to become drug abusers, and to suffer serious head injuries.

Programs like Head Start, which enhance the physical, social, and educational capacities of preschool children in economically disadvantaged areas, are a form of preventive mental health care. So are programs teaching young mothers (often still adolescents themselves) how to care for their infants, programs to help teenagers avoid drug and alcohol dependency, and programs to help the elderly. Such programs are costly, but in the long run they may cost society less than the illness they help prevent or mitigate, in terms of both institutional care and lost productivity.

COMMUNITY MENTAL HEALTH CARE

The basic premise of community mental health care (or community psychiatry or social psychiatry) is that the community should be the focal point for treatment and prevention of mental illness. Beginning in the 1960s with the establishment of community health centers, this care was intended to include a complete range of mental health services in every neighborhood in the nation, along with the conquest of destructive social forces that contribute to mental illness: poor housing, unemployment, and prejudice. In the broadest sense, prevention includes prenatal care, nursery and school care, the development of creative skills, satisfactory job placement, and special help in emergency situations.

Community mental health care was not a new concept. Individual mental health facilities have from time to time extended their activities by going into the community to provide services. As early as 1909 Dr. Adolph Meyer conceived an integrated program of prevention, treatment, and aftercare in which hospital psychiatrists worked with teachers, general practitioners, welfare workers, and the police. In the 1920s the child guidance clinics, ancestors of today's mental health clinics, emphasized prevention of mental illness in adults through early detection and treatment in childhood.

What was new about community care as planned in the 1960s was that its aims were so broad, and that it recognized that community resources must be linked. Although it is the poor who need mental health care the most, outsiders cannot barge into a ghetto community and hand down help from on high. A system of community cooperation and participation is necessary for any such measures to be truly effective.

Changes in funding have placed considerable constraints on these programs. Moreover, some authorities believe that the community mental health clinics have failed particularly those with serious, chronic mental illness, who as a result of deinstitutionalization and the lack of community resources have swelled the ranks of the homeless. These critics believe that there is a basic confusion of mental health and mental illness, and that the myth persists that good mental health represents an antidote to mental illness. In serious mental illness, they say, the cause is organic, and no amount of good social services will help a person with schizophrenia or manic-depressive psychosis who is not properly treated to control his symptoms. People with these illnesses are different from those who are in "poor" mental health, people who have problems in interpersonal relations or in some other area of their lives but are not actually ill. Mental health care, say these critics, is a misnomer. In order to allocate funds and resources appropriately, there must be a separation between the mentally ill and what they call the "worried well."

THE MENTAL HEALTH ASSOCIATION

Although many communities may not have a single mental health center that serves multiple needs, there often are numerous resources available. However, they may be hard to find. A central role in linking community resources can be played by the local Mental Health Association (MHA), which serves as an *advocate* for mental health. It works to prevent mental illness and help the mentally ill. A major form of advocacy by the MHA chapters is to work for necessary changes in federal, state, and local laws. Another is to make sure that the mental health providers in the area are actually meeting the community's needs. The MHA monitors the quality of care regardless of the client's ability to pay, and helps people who are having trouble with providers. It also tries to get services started to fill existing needs. Some MHA chapters perform clinical services themselves, but most do not.

In addition to advocacy, the other main jobs of the MHA are information and referral. Its staff members go into the community to run special programs in schools and businesses. It provides general information and referral services in all areas of mental health, including substance abuse and chronic mental illness. It helps individuals, family members, and the community to find and take advantage of appropriate services and resources.

Formerly supported mainly by government funding, the MHAs now rely on grants from local community chests, foundations, membership dues, and corporations. One chapter, for example, has a library including films and videos available to individuals, students, schools, businesses, and community groups, on such topics as child abuse, domestic violence, substance abuse, chronic mental illness, stress, families, children, and therapy specialties. It also offers a support group for families of the mentally ill, and a social club for formerly hospitalized mentally ill persons and other lonely or isolated community members. It runs a widowed persons' service, a one-on-one outreach program for the newly bereaved by volunteers who have been widowed for eighteen months or more. It also helps run a twenty-four-hour crisis hot line.

Finally, it brings together individuals, groups, and agencies interested in specific mental health topics, and helps local agencies keep in touch with each other and with the community they serve. It conducts in-service training programs for personnel in schools and nursing homes, for the clergy and the police, probation officers, and other community members who are likely to come in contact with the mentally ill and to be in a position to provide preventive mental health care and referrals. It sends speakers to churches and schools, clubs, and other organizations to talk about rape, domestic violence, parenting, and child development. It runs a social club with weekly meetings for people who are lonely, isolated, and experiencing difficulty in everyday living situations. By educating the public about these issues, and by supporting individuals who are coping with critical life situations, the MHA performs a valuable service.

REGULAR CHECKUPS?

Preventive mental health care encompasses such a broad area of concerns that it might seem impossible to achieve, at least for a large number of people. However, one mental health professional interviewed suggested a remarkably simple remedy that she hopes will one day be universally applied: regular mental health checkups.

Clearly this measure would cover the entire developmental gamut—from genetic counseling and prenatal care through old age. To an extent, some primary-care physicians—family doctors, obstetricians, pediatricians, internists—already perform this function, but it could be greatly expanded and legitimized. There would be no more hesitation about going for an annual mental health checkup than there is about going for a physical checkup. Such examinations would be widely available, through school and industrial health programs and multiservice neighborhood clinics, as well as through private practitioners. This kind of program would greatly increase the chances for early detection and early treatment, if only through increasing public acceptance of mental disorders as illnesses for which effective treatment is both possible and available.

Chapter

26

MENTAL ILLNESS AND THE LAW

MENTAL ILLNESS can affect one's judgment or behavior so as to endanger oneself or others. When it does, the law may intervene to protect the individual and the community. It may judge a person incompetent and assign someone else to conduct his affairs. It may require her to enter a protective environment, that is, a mental hospital. Should a mentally ill person commit a crime, the law may shield him from ordinary punishment, either by finding him incompetent to stand trial, or, after a trial, by finding him "not guilty by reason of mental disease or defect (insanity)," or "guilty but mentally ill." In either case, the law usually will require the person so judged to seek treatment for the illness, most often in a hospital, which may be either an open or a "secure" (locked) facility, depending on the nature of the crime. Thus, unlike any physically ill individual, a person who has been judged to be mentally ill may be forced to be hospitalized and be deprived of control over her own life, at least for a time.

In practice, few mentally ill persons commit crimes against others or become involved in criminal proceedings. However, other questions involving the law may arise. Can a mentally ill person enter into a contract and be bound by it? Can he make a will, declaring, "I, Robert Roe, being of sound mind and body . . . ?" Can a mentally ill person sign out of the hospital? To what extent are a person's conversations with a psychotherapist confidential?

This chapter gives an overview of the principal legal issues involved in mental illness and its treatment, including such matters as responsibility for a crime, court-ordered psychiatric treatment, involuntary hospitalization (commitment), mental patients' civil rights, questions of competency (to stand trial or to conduct one's own affairs), guardianship for those who are minors or are incompetent, and a brief discussion of certain kinds of crime that are, by and large, considered mental health problems, specifically child abuse and other domestic violence, and juvenile delinquency.

A TYPICAL CASE

John B., 25, lost his job last week after getting in a fist fight with a fellow worker. It is the fourth time in less than a year that his violent behavior has gotten him in trouble. This time the other man, whose jaw he broke, is planning to sue him.

John's offense, in legal terms, is a tort, a civil wrong done to another person. Injury has occurred, but it is up to the injured person to decide whether or not he wants compensation. In this case he does. Is John liable?

John's family knows that he is unstable. How could they not, since this violent outburst is his fourth in less than a year? They tell his lawyer that he has always behaved in this way, that he can't seem to help himself when his temper "takes over." His behavior has kept him from getting decent jobs that pay well enough for him to save some money, and he doesn't have enough money now to pay damages.

Unfortunately for John, he is indeed liable. In tort cases a person may be judged to have a mental disease or defect, but that is not considered an excuse. Therefore, John will have to pay as much of the damages awarded to his co-worker as he can. Luckily for his family, they are not liable for the injury he does to others (although if John were a minor, in some states they would be). Unless John can be

successfully treated for what is almost certainly a mental illness and
can learn to control his violent impulses, about the only thing that
might help in the future is to make sure he has good personal liability
insurance, in order to protect both him and others. With his past
history, however, it may be difficult for him to get such an insurance
policy.

Can John be forced to seek treatment? Not as a result of this civil
case. If he had been charged with a crime, and if his lawyer had
decided to plead "not guilty by reason of mental defect," and if court-
appointed psychiatrists had agreed that John was indeed ill and could
not be held responsible for his actions, then the court might have
ordered him to be placed in an institution, most likely a secure one,
such as a hospital for the criminally insane. But to have treatment
imposed, a guardianship hearing would be required and John would
have to be declared incompetent (guardianship and competency are
discussed later in this chapter).

COURT CLINICS

Treatment ordered by a court of law does not necessarily involve
hospitalization.

*Jimmy R., 12, small for his age, got in a street fight with a playmate
and knocked the other child unconscious with a lead pipe. It was the
first time he had ever appeared in court.*

Jimmy lived in Massachusetts. Because it was his first court appearance, the judge handling the case requested a psychiatric evaluation, a
very common practice in that state since the passage of the Briggs Act
in 1921. The court-appointed psychiatrist talked with Jimmy and
with his mother, a single parent of four children, and he also tested the
youngster. A psychological profile emerged of a timid, nervous, frightened child, seemingly incapable of aggression.

The court granted a continuance, carrying the case for a year with
no finding. Jimmy was put on probation, and part of his sentence was
that he had to attend the court clinic for a year, in order to receive
psychotherapy.

Massachusetts has a staff of 130 professionals serving 62 (of that
state's 64) district courts and 13 (of 14) superior courts. These court
clinics treat several thousand persons a year. Most clinic clients do not

come of their own accord but on a mandatory, court-ordered basis. They are sent for evaluation, to discover whether or not they are competent to be tried (see below for more about competency), and for treatment. The clients who come for treatment are usually young (most are between the ages of fifteen and twenty-five, and few are older than thirty-five), because most crimes are committed by young people. Their crimes range from arson and robbery to drug abuse, wife-beating, and child abuse. Many of them have acted out their personal problems by injuring the persons and property of others.

Most of the court clinics are located in district courts, which dispose of 90 percent of all criminal cases. The goal is, through proper sentencing, to make the first offense the last. It is estimated that about 70 percent of first offenders do not come before the courts again.

Massachusetts is not the only state that has court clinics but its system is considered the most sophisticated of its kind. However, even its clinics are not sufficient: There is a pressing need for more such services.

Jimmy's crime, like most, was an impulsive one. Law enforcement professionals maintain that the majority of offenses are not premeditated but arise out of unpredictable, volatile situations. Teaching clients the need to control their impulses is a major goal of therapy in any court clinic.

"NOT GUILTY BY REASON OF . . . "

On April 6, 1988, Lonnie L. Gilchrist, Jr., a black stockbroker at Merrill Lynch's Boston office, was fired for poor sales performance by his boss, George W. Cook, who was white. Around noon on the following day he stormed into Cook's office and repeatedly shot, pistol-whipped, and kicked Cook, who died. Gilchrist, who had no history of violent crime, was charged with first-degree murder and pleaded not guilty by reason of insanity.

The case came to trial almost exactly a year later. Nearly two-thirds of the nine days of trial testimony came from mental health authorities who examined Gilchrist following the shooting. His lawyers did not attempt to refute the eyewitness testimony concerning the crime. Instead, they maintained that he was temporarily insane at the time and thus was not criminally responsible for his actions. Two psychiatrists and one psychologist testified for the defense that Gilchrist suffered from a long-standing personality disorder that led him to harbor irrational beliefs that he was being persecuted because he was black. The stress of being fired, combined with his irrational beliefs, triggered a temporary psychosis that made Gilchrist unable to control his actions.

The prosecution, on the other hand, held that Gilchrist had cold-bloodedly calculated the murder. A former colleague testified that on the day he was fired, Gilchrist had declared he had two options: one a legal one and the other that he would show Cook not to "mess with a real man." Further, during the hours immediately before the shooting, Gilchrist apparently was not behaving in any unusual way. He completed a $125,000 bond transaction and he canceled a dentist appointment. A psychiatrist for the prosecution testified that Gilchrist's supposedly paranoid beliefs did not constitute a mental illness but merely were intended to justify the shooting in his own mind. Furthermore, the psychiatrist believed Gilchrist was in fact able to distinguish right from wrong and could have chosen to control his actions. In order to judge Gilchrist legally insane, the jury would have to find Gilchrist substantially lacking in either the ability to judge right from wrong, or the ability to control his actions.

After more than four days of deliberations, the jury declared they could not reach a verdict. However, the judge urged them to resume deliberations, telling them there were no other twelve persons who could better decide the charges and no clearer evidence that could have been presented. Less than four hours later the jury reached their verdict—guilty as charged of first-degree murder, which in Massachusetts carries a mandatory sentence of life imprisonment.

Gilchrist's lawyer declared he would appeal the verdict to a superior court on issues raised by the judge's instructions to the jury (who had twice asked, during their deliberations, for a repetition of the legal definition of insanity).

COMPETENCY TO STAND TRIAL

Had the question of Gilchrist's sanity been raised sooner, the court would have ordered a psychiatric evaluation to determine if he was competent to stand trial at all. A defendant is found incompetent for trial if he is considered unable to understand the charge against him or unable to participate in his own defense. Such an evaluation is usually performed in a hospital, where the individual can be subjected to a variety of tests and can be observed by professionals for a few days.

Even then, the standard of competency is very loosely applied. Many psychiatrists believe that it is better to stand trial than to wait for a prolonged period. Moreover, in the past, those found incompetent almost invariably were committed to a state mental institution for a long period of time—here, as in other specifics, the law varies from state to state—and were released only when one or more psychiatrists determined that they were no longer dangerous. (In theory, a person could be incompetent but not dangerous to others; in practice, this issue seldom arises because the question usually comes up only in cases involving a serious crime, such as murder. In Utah, in 1979, however, a court ruled that one must be *both* dangerous and incompetent in order to be committed.) Since then courts have tended either to bring the accused person to trial or to drop the charges.

The defense used for Gilchrist, "Not guilty by reason of insanity" at the time the crime was committed, is not invoked very often—indeed, only in an estimated 2 percent of cases, and usually only as a last resort. Most lawyers believe a jury won't be convinced by it, so they tend to use it only in cases of homicide where there is strong proof that the defendant actually did the killing. When it is invoked, each side usually gets a psychiatrist (or several psychiatrists) to testify in its behalf, and very frequently the two sets of psychiatrists present conflicting opinions, as they did in Gilchrist's case.

Until Gilchrist killed his boss he had no criminal record. Had the jury in this case chosen to believe his psychiatrist, they might have acquitted Gilchrist as "not guilty by reason of insanity." In the case of Jack Ruby, who killed President John F. Kennedy's assassin, Lee Harvey Oswald, the jury did not believe the defense experts who maintained that Ruby had shot Oswald during a psychomotor epileptic seizure. In the case of John Hinckley, who tried to shoot President Ronald Reagan in 1981, they voted for acquittal, a decision that was widely criticized. However, at this writing Hinckley is still (after nine years) confined in a mental ward.

SANITY IS A LEGAL TERM

Sanity is a purely legal concept. It refers to an individual's capacity for assessing reality, making choices, and taking responsibility for her actions.

The rules for "not guilty by reason of insanity" vary among different jurisdictions. One of the oldest, long in use in American state and federal courts, is the M'Naghten Rule. In 1843 Daniel M'Naghten shot to death British Prime Minister Robert Peel's secretary, whom he mistook for the prime minister. He believed that Peel had been pursuing him because he had voted against him, and that Peel had devised the Corn Laws to ruin him. M'Naghten was found not guilty of the crime by reason of insanity, which, it was determined, meant that he did not know that his action was wrong. The problem with this rule lies in the words *know* and *wrong*: How does one not know? How does one not understand the consequences? Is the action wrong in the sense of the law or according to prevailing moral standards? In a number of states and in the federal courts, therefore, the very restrictive M'Naghten Rule was broadened by a rule called "irresistible impulse" stating that even though a person might know that an action is wrong, he is not responsible if unable to resist the impulse to commit it anyhow.

In 1954 Judge David L. Bazelon of the United States Court of Appeals for the District of Columbia handed down still another standard, called the Durham Rule. It said "an accused person is not criminally responsible if his unlawful act was the product of mental disease or defect." At first it was hailed as a huge improvement, since "mental disease" could now be interpreted according to the most recent medical knowledge. Later many lawyers and judges (including Bazelon himself) decided the rule was too ambiguous, since it now could be argued that merely committing a crime was evidence of mental illness, and in practice psychiatrists who testified in court generally could not explain their reasoning to juries in a satisfactory way.

In 1972 the American Law Institute proposed still another definition, the Model Penal Code, whereby a person should not be held responsible for a criminal act if, as a result of mental disease or defect, he lacks the substantial capacity either to appreciate the wrongfulness of his conduct or to conform his conduct to the law.

All these rules represent attempts to answer once and for all the question of responsibility for crime. None is totally satisfactory, and indeed, some authorities believe that this question can have no single answer but must be resolved in every specific instance. Further, because the insanity defense is imprecisely defined, it is open to abuse.

In April 1982 Idaho enacted a law eliminating the plea of mental illness as a defense in criminal cases, although such illness would be considered by the judge in sentencing. Soon afterward Montana and Utah followed suit, and most other states have since passed laws restricting the use of the insanity defense, among them a modification that allows defendants to be found guilty but mentally ill. The Federal Insanity Reform Act of 1984 made still more changes, including making the "not guilty by reason of insanity" defense an affirmative defense that the defendant must prove by clear and convincing evidence. It also created a special *verdict* of not guilty by reason of insanity and instituted a comprehensive, complicated commitment procedure. And indeed, acquittal of a crime on grounds of mental illness generally does lead to a kind of imprisonment: confinement in a mental institution. As pointed out, John Hinckley was and remains so confined.

Understandably, the public does not want a person who was acquitted of a crime on the grounds of insanity to be released immediately, or after a short period of treatment, and then commit new offenses. Many states try to minimize this possibility by making it easier to commit insanity acquittees and making them subject to more restrictive release laws than those applicable to mentally ill persons who have been civilly (noncriminally) committed. For those who are judged guilty but mentally ill, a few states require that treatment be provided but most at present do not.

VOLUNTARY AND INVOLUNTARY CIVIL ADMISSION

There are several forms of voluntary and involuntary civil (noncriminal) admission to a mental hospital. Bear in mind, however, that each state has its own laws governing this matter. In order to learn about the law in your state (or your relative's state), you may have to consult a local lawyer, or the legal department of your state department of mental health. You can read the relevant statutes in your state at the library in your county courthouse. Another useful source of information is the *Mental Disabilities Law Reporter*, a bimonthly publication of the American Bar Association.

If you or your relative want a lawyer to represent you, you may need one who is expert in mental health law; you can find one either through your state bar association or by contacting the American Civil Liberties Union. Also, your state judicial department may have an agency that can help, such as the Mental Health Advisors Committee, which trains attorneys in mental health law and provides information and referrals.

The least restrictive form of voluntary admission in practice is *informal admission,* but few mental hospitals allow it, although it may be used for admission to some general hospitals with a psychiatric unit. Informal admission consists simply of signing into the hospital, exactly as though for medical or surgical treatment. The patient then can request a discharge or leave at will, without giving advance notice. However, she will usually be required to sign a form releasing the hospital and its staff from all responsibility if the discharge is against "medical advice."

For *voluntary admission* a person comes to a mental hospital and signs a paper indicating that she seeks admission and treatment of her own free will. Such a patient may leave the hospital at any time, although in some states she may have to give a few days' notice. The precise period varies from three to ten days. It allows the hospital to petition a court for commitment of any patient it believes should not be released because she represents a danger to self or others. (This practice is uncommon, but instances of it have occurred.) However, a discharge order can be written at any time by the patient's attending doctor, and then no waiting period (or advance notice) is required.

As indicated above, each state has its own laws. In Massachusetts it is not up to a patient to prove that she should not be hospitalized. Rather, it is up to the party seeking to prolong hospitalization and treatment (the hospital or, more often, family members) to prove in a court of law that the patient should be retained against her own will. Further, in such cases, actual behavior that demonstrates the patient's dangerousness or incompetence must be established. Once it has been established, however, a patient's voluntary admission can, in effect, be converted into an involuntary admission. Hospitalization by court order is likely to be for a much longer period than most voluntary admissions—in Massachusetts for a period up to six months for a first court order and for a period up to twelve months for second and subsequent court orders.

Another form of commitment allowed in numerous states is outpatient commitment, basically an agreement whereby a patient is committed to outpatient treatment. (It is described in the previous chapter under preventive care for former patients.)

Involuntary admission, also called *commitment* or *certification,* was at one time fairly easy to obtain. Often a family simply got two physicians to certify that one of its members was mentally ill and in need of treatment, and then that person could be hospitalized for an indefinite period. As a result, thousands of individuals were unreasonably and unjustly confined in mental hospitals and deprived of their liberty and basic civil rights, often under conditions far worse than those found in penal institutions.

THE MENTAL PATIENTS LIBERATION MOVEMENT

In the 1960s the civil rights movement that swept the country was extended to mental patients as well, assisted by a small but vocal group of mental health professionals who insist there is no such thing as mental illness. Among them was Thomas Szasz, a well-known American psychiatrist who maintained that it is only our intolerance to those who are different from ourselves that leads us to label them as "mentally ill." Mental illness, according to Szasz and others, is a social definition imposed on individuals who either represent a threat to the community (the criminal and the deviant), or who disturb or frighten those around them (such as a person who hears "voices" or claims to be Jesus Christ), or who represent a burden (old people). Consequently, they oppose involuntary psychiatric treatment of any kind, including involuntary hospitalization. Hospitals for the criminally insane, civil liberties lawyer Bruce Ennis pointed out in his *Prisoners of Psychiatry* (1972), contain only a very few patients who actually have been convicted of a crime; most of the inmates have merely been accused of a crime and then judged mentally incompetent to stand trial. Moreover, said Ennis, for those confined because they represent a danger to others, the judgment often is interpreted as "potentially dangerous"; no one can predict accurately which person will actually harm others.

In response to these ideas, in the early 1970s mental patients began to organize liberation groups that stressed political action rather than treatment. One of the first groups formed was the Mental Patients Liberation Project in New York (a similar group was formed about the same time in Vancouver, Canada). Among other things, it formulated a mental patients' bill of rights, consisting of basic rights that its members believed were frequently denied to mental patients. These early groups (another was called Network against Psychiatric Assault) basically agreed with Szasz's concept that mental illness does not exist (it is society that is sick), and therefore no one should be treated or hospitalized involuntarily.

In the 1980s, as it became increasingly clear that the chronic serious mental illnesses not only exist but are organic in nature, a number of newer patient self-help groups were organized, and in 1985 they banded together to form the National Mental Health Consumers Association, which works more in a public relations than a legal capacity.

NEW LAWS CONCERNING INVOLUNTARY HOSPITALIZATION

In response to pressure both from civil liberties advocates and from the deinstitutionalization movement, new laws and court decisions have radically changed concepts and practices concerning the rights of mental patients. Today there are two kinds of involuntary hospitalization: emergency and long-term. Emergency commitment in most states is for seventy-two hours, not including weekends and holidays. Both kinds of commitment involve numerous guarantees of the individual's rights. The basic purpose of commitment laws is to enable mentally ill individuals to be put forcibly into a hospital so that they will not harm themselves or others and so that they can be treated.

In 1972 a federal district court in Wisconsin ruled that involuntary commitment must involve the following:

- Timely notice of the charges justifying confinement
- Notice of the right to a jury trial
- An initial hearing on probable cause for detention beyond a period of forty-eight hours
- A full hearing on the necessity of detention beyond a period of two weeks
- Legal counsel to represent the detained person at the hearing
- No admission of hearsay evidence at the hearing
- Protection of the detained person against self-incrimination under the Fifth Amendment
- Proof of mental illness and dangerousness to self or others "beyond a reasonable doubt"
- Inquiry into less restrictive alternatives than involuntary hospitalization

• No treatment until the detained person has had a probable cause hearing

This ruling was hailed by civil rights advocates as the "Ten Commandments" for the mentally ill. Virtually all the procedural questions (concerning the right to a hearing) have been further litigated, and many of the court's decisions have been incorporated into state law (all of them in Wisconsin and various ones in other states). The substantive proof of mental illness "beyond a reasonable doubt," however, has been interpreted in a variety of ways, and in 1979 the Supreme Court ruled that only "clear and convincing proof" was needed. Further, numerous states now mandate periodic review of patients who have been committed to see if they really must remain hospitalized.

In the early 1980s the trend to making commitment more difficult began to be turned around, partly in response to the thousands of mentally ill homeless individuals who wandered the streets. In 1983 the American Psychiatric Association proposed a model commitment law based on "significant deterioration" as opposed to "potential dangerousness." Although it was strongly criticized by legal experts who believed it infringed on mental patients' civil rights, a number of states subsequently passed laws enabling the commitment of individuals who would suffer severe and abnormal mental, emotional, or physical distress if they were not hospitalized. The new laws allow hospitalization to prevent the worsening of an already existing mental illness or to prevent the physical harm such deterioration might cause. Again, they are supported by psychiatrists and by the families of chronic patients who want to be able to hospitalize a patient with dispatch during a crisis, and they are opposed by those who feel mental patients do not have enough legal protection as it is.

Despite the changes in law, however, in practice the decision to hospitalize a person against his will tends to remain in the hands of the court-appointed review officer, and in the end a decision to commit is usually made by a judge, attorney, or physician.

The bulk of involuntary commitments are made on a temporary, emergency basis. For this, too, each state has its own laws. In Massachusetts, a physician or police officer may apply for involuntary hospitalization at a mental hospital for a period of up to ten days. If the person is unwilling to go to the hospital, he may be transported by medical or police personnel, who may use restraints if necessary.

However, no person may be admitted involuntarily unless he (or his parent or guardian) has been given the right to apply for a voluntary admission.

Once the person arrives at the hospital, a psychiatric examination must be conducted within two hours to determine if failure to hospitalize this person would create a likelihood of serious harm by reason of mental illness. Finally, the ten-day period of involuntary hospitalization can be extended only by court order.

RIGHTS IN THE HOSPITAL

Even when a person is hospitalized involuntarily, her civil rights cannot be curtailed. In many states a bill of rights for mental patients must be posted in the patient area of all hospitals. Among the rights protected are the right to send and receive mail, to keep and use personal possessions, to communicate with an attorney, to vote, and to hold a driver's license. Further, in all states civilly committed hospitalized mental patients have two other basic rights: *the right to refuse treatment*—in practice this usually refers to drug treatment, electroconvulsive (shock) treatment, or surgery—except in emergency situations when there is immediate risk of physical injury, and *the right to treatment* for their illness. In other words, no one can be forced to take drugs or undergo shock treatment,* nor can one be held in a mental hospital where no treatment is offered. By extension, therefore, any involuntarily confined patient who is not dangerous must be offered treatment or be released.

Before the development of psychoactive drugs, violent mental patients frequently had to be restrained for long periods, or confined in padded cells, or both. Today, however, *restraint* and *seclusion* may be used only under highly controlled conditions, if at all, and informed consent must be secured for various forms of specific treatment. The issue of informed consent is also controversial. Can a severely ill mental patient understand the side effects or benefits of medication, or the risk of an experimental drug? One study of schizophrenic patients showed that only 27 percent realized they needed medication.

---

* Except in emergency situations where there is substantial likelihood of extreme violence, personal injury, or suicide, or the patient is found incompetent by a judge following a formal hearing. Also, in some cases a guardian can authorize treatment (see guardianship below).

Concerning restraints and seclusion, each state has its own statutes and regulations establishing procedures and limitations on their use. In New York, for example, a patient may be put in a seclusion room for two hours only; if further seclusion is believed necessary, a physician must renew the order for it, again for only two hours. Also, most states require hospitals to keep detailed records of their use of seclusion that they must submit to the state department of mental health. (See also Iowa's Bill of Rights for Persons with Mental Retardation, Developmental Disabilities, and Chronic Mental Illness, in Appendix B.)

How to Get Out

Psychiatric patients increasingly have the means to end a commitment and leave the hospital. In more and more states they now have the right to counsel, a jury trial, and to appeal a decision. In some states they can demand a "probable cause" hearing before a judge to assess if they should be held longer than the initial seventy-two hours. They or relatives or friends on their behalf may petition for a writ of habeas corpus to question the legality of their detention and ask the court for release.

Many areas of the United States now have legal organizations specifically charged to defend the rights of mental patients. Some are funded by local or federal government, and others by small groups of independent lawyers. To locate resources in your area, call your local bar association or the National Legal Aid and Defender Association (see Appendix A).

PRACTICAL PROBLEMS RAISED BY
CIVIL RIGHTS SAFEGUARDS

Although the new laws and regulations do protect patients from abuse of their rights as citizens, they sometimes impose constraints that raise both clinical and ethical questions.

The legal process for obtaining involuntary hospitalization is cumbersome, and although it protects against unnecessary confinement, it does not always serve the severely psychotic patient who is not dangerous but badly in need of treatment. For example, when does the homeless "bag lady" who wanders the city streets in icy weather and sleeps in doorways under cardboard coverings represent a "danger" to self?

Then, hospitals sometimes find themselves in a double bind: They must by law provide treatment, but patients may by law refuse any or all treatment. The right to refuse treatment and the application of the rule of informed consent for accepting treatment may be fine for those patients rational enough to make a considered judgment. That may not be the case for some acute schizophrenics, for example, who are not lucid enough to realize they need antipsychotic medication and whose behavior without such treatment has a detrimental effect on fellow patients.

This issue has become the focus of a number of legal battles. Prolonged use of antipsychotic drugs, as indicated in Chapter 18, sometimes leads to serious and irreversible side effects. In one court case a former aircraft pilot who had been hospitalized for seven years in a New Jersey state hospital insisted that involuntary hospitalized patients who have not been legally declared incompetent have a constitutional right to refuse antipsychotic drugs regardless of doctor's orders (under New Jersey law at that time only voluntarily committed patients could refuse medication). Hospital psychiatrists countered that lawyers and judges should not interfere with their professional decisions about what is best for a hospitalized mental patient.

Nevertheless, the federal district court judge who heard this case in 1978 ordered the state of New Jersey to provide "informed consent" forms, listing all the adverse effects of any drug, which had to be signed by all patients in state mental hospitals (or by their guardians if they had been declared incompetent) before medication could be administered. He also directed the state to establish a system of autonomous patient advocates to serve as informal counsel to patients who wished to refuse medication, and to provide a panel of independent psychiatrists to review all decisions to medicate a patient against his will.

The state appealed to a higher court to overturn this ruling, calling the restrictions it imposed complex, highly intrusive, unprecedented, and unsound. The state's director of mental health and hospitals testified that the order had caused an increase in patient violence because medication had not been taken or had to be delayed, and the order had led to morale problems among the staff and deterioration in the condition of some patients who had refused their medication. The federal district court in this case upheld the patient's right to refuse drugs except in instances of presenting a danger to self or others, or if found incompetent.

A similar question arises with respect to suicidal patients. Should one honor such a patient's right to forego treatment or to be discharged? Should a man who says he wants to die be permitted to end his life? Or should his expressed desire be considered a symptom of illness that will presumably disappear when the illness has been effectively treated? In California, a person who is suicidal may be committed for fourteen days to a mental hospital for intensive treatment, and, if still suicidal after that period may be required to remain another fourteen days. At the end of that period, however, even if the patient is still suicidal but is not shown to be dangerous to others, he must be released.

Even the right to treatment, which has given rise to court actions setting standards for staff-patient ratios and treatment programs, among other things, has created problems in some hospitals. For example, as a result of such action, treatment teams in one large mental hospital were required to review and revise each patient's treatment plan once a month. One large ward in this hospital housed both acutely ill young adults and a group of older, chronically ill patients. The treatment team for this ward, which formerly met for two hours a week, now needed an extra ten hours a week in order to interview each patient once a month to review his treatment plan, even for those chronic patients whose mental status had not changed in years. As a result, the time available for treating the acutely ill younger patients, who were far more likely to benefit from intensive treatment, was sharply curtailed.

Finally, the principle of placing a person in the least restrictive environment consistent with proper care often means discharge from the hospital because such care costs money that the states do not have. For those who lack family and community supports, such discharge poses grave problems. It is estimated that one-third of the nation's growing homeless population suffer from a major mental illness.

THE RIGHT TO CONFIDENTIALITY

State laws differ concerning protection of the privacy of psychiatric patients. As indicated in Chapter 24, the very fact of making an insurance claim can jeopardize confidentiality, depending on who has access to this information. When seeing a private practitioner there usually is no danger that a client's revelations will be disclosed. This privacy is necessarily less exclusive in a clinic, however, where details of treatment are discussed at staff meetings. Most clinics keep records for all their clients, and they vary in the extent to which they limit access to their records. In some the records may be used for research, training, or demonstration purposes.

Should clients and patients be allowed to examine their own records? Laws and opinions concerning this issue differ considerably. The federal government and consumer rights advocates hold that people should be able to find out what is written about them; many of the states as well as many hospitals and individual practitioners disagree. In Massachusetts the current law states that psychiatric records are to be private and not open to public inspection except upon a judicial order, whether or not there are pending judicial proceedings, or upon the written request of a patient's attorney when accompanied by an authorization from the patient, or when determined by a hospital's medical director to be in the patient's best interest. A patient may demand to see her own records, however.

The confidentiality of conversations with a therapist is not protected by law in the same way that conversations with either a priest or a lawyer are. Most states consider it "privileged" communication, which protects patients from disclosure unless they waive that privilege, but there are still exceptions. A therapist who is subpoenaed by a court may be required to reveal confidential information about a client, especially in a criminal case but sometimes also in civil matters, such as child custody.

Suppose a person tells a therapist of a wish or plan to harm someone else. In 1976 the California courts ruled that mental health professionals in such a situation have a duty to warn the potential victim. This ruling, called the Tarasoff decision, has been extended to numerous other states. Further, the immediate family of a hospitalized, seriously ill person also is entitled to some information about the patient's illness and progress. Although state laws differ, families should be receiving as much information as they would for a patient with Alzheimer's or multiple sclerosis.

New problems of confidentiality for health professionals—not just mental health—have arisen with the rising number of patients with AIDS or AIDS-related complex. Mentally ill individuals who are intravenous drug abusers are at particularly high risk for this fatal infection. And, of course, they can infect sexual partners or anyone with whom they share a needle. Under what obligation is the therapist who learns of a client's infection to tell his family or other intimates? There are conflicting issues here, and the law has not yet developed clear guidelines.

INCOMPETENCY AND GUARDIANSHIP

For a person who is judged incompetent (some states call it "gravely disabled"), a court may appoint another individual who then exercises that person's rights and handles their personal and/or financial affairs.

Note that competency here is used in a different sense from competency to stand trial, described earlier. Legally it means the capacity to make one's own decisions.* A person who has jurisdiction only over someone's property is generally called a *conservator;* when it also extends to personal decisions, he is called a *guardian.*

When the person who is judged incompetent, called the *ward,* is hospitalized—and many if not most individuals who are judged incompetent need the extensive supervision or care available only in an institution of some kind—the guardian acts on the patient's behalf, deciding to accept or refuse medication, apply for hospital discharge,

---

* For a long time the standard of competency was the ability to manage property. However, in recent decades advocates for the mentally retarded have pointed out that individuals unable to handle finances might still be capable of choosing whom to marry, for example, and urged standards appropriate to the activity under consideration. These principles extend to the mentally ill as well. Consequently the law in various jurisdictions has become more specific, requiring court decisions on individual, relevant issues. For example, in Massachusetts an incompetent person is one "incapable of taking care of himself by reason of mental illness." How this capability is defined depends on the methods used to assess competence: interviews, observation, etc., by a qualified clinician.

and so on. A guardianship may be temporary, commonly lasting for ninety days or less, or it may be permanent.

A guardianship may serve as a mechanism whereby parents ensure care for a chronically ill child after their death, in which case the guardian may be a relative, family friend, or person appointed by the judge. The guardian may make personal decisions regarding where the ward is to live, the right to travel, and the right to medical and/or psychiatric treatment. Property decisions, made by a conservator, include the right to sign checks or withdraw funds from a bank account.

The person who is judged incompetent usually loses a number of rights, among them the right to vote, to enter into a valid contract, to practice a profession, to hold a driver's license, to adopt children or to prevent the adoption of her own children, or to sell (or give away) property. Incompetency also is considered evidence of inability to execute a valid will, although in practice this question usually does not arise until after a person has died (when a dissatisfied family member sues to have a will set aside on the ground that the testator was incompetent). Although marriage is also a contract, a person who is judged incompetent and then marries usually is considered to be legally married unless such a marriage is set aside (by annulment). As far as divorce is concerned, a person judged incompetent may have trouble initiating divorce proceedings, and, similarly, his spouse may have trouble suing for divorce.

Persons who have been judged incompetent remain so until a court certifies them to be competent. Only then can they regain control over their affairs and property. One can contest being placed under guardianship. In an emergency a temporary guardianship sometimes is ordered without giving the person prior notice. However, in this instance notice usually must be given within a specified time, such as three days. At the time the notice is received, a person may request a court hearing to object either to the guardianship itself or to the specific individual nominated as guardian. Again, state laws vary. In Massachusetts when a person seeking guardianship applies for authority to admit his ward to a mental health facility, a hearing must be held with the ward in attendance (or, if impossible, in the presence of the ward's attorney).

For minors, the parents are usually considered the guardians, but according to a recent Supreme Court ruling, their request to hospitalize their child against his will need only be reviewed by a neutral and independent physician.

DOMESTIC VIOLENCE

Certain mental health problems frequently entangle a person with the law. Antisocial personality disorder, the name given to the illness of John B. (see above) and others whose violent behavior gets them in trouble, is one example. Domestic violence—child neglect and abuse, spouse abuse, abuse of elderly parents—is another example, as is juvenile delinquency.

Child neglect and abuse is a growing problem in America, found among all social classes. Legally a child is any person under the age of sixteen. A neglected child is one deprived of adequate food, clothing, shelter, education, or medical care by parents who either can afford to provide them or who have been offered help to do so. An abused child is one whose parents or guardians have inflicted physical injury or sexual abuse on him or her, or have allowed such injury to be inflicted by others.

Most states have laws requiring teachers, physicians, nurses, and social workers to report child abuse and neglect, but once a situation has been reported the solution is not easy. Mental health professionals believe that it requires the cooperation of a mental health professional, pediatrician, social worker, and the court if violence is not to recur, and that both parents—not just the abusing one—should receive counseling. Because many parents who maltreat their children were themselves maltreated by their own parents, it is believed they need extensive support and therapy to improve their poor self-image and to learn to control their violent impulses, as well as education in the proper care of children and in child development. A national self-help organization, Parents Anonymous, has an extensive network of local chapters where parents can turn for help, remaining anonymous if they wish (see Appendix A).

The abuse of wives by their husbands (and, less common but occasionally found, of husbands by wives) also is an increasing problem, as is abuse of the elderly by their children or other family members. In 1981 New York became one of the first states to establish a twenty-four-hour toll-free hot line for victims of domestic violence, who could call for crisis counseling and referrals to shelters and service programs in their localities. Subsequently, hot lines and shelters have sprung up all over the country. Although the courts may stop individual instances of wife-beating, for example, by temporarily restraining a husband from access to his wife and children, legal action alone is rarely enough to resolve such cases. Extensive counseling for all the members of the family—abuser, victim, and children—is needed if the family is to remain together (or separate) without a repetition of violence, with potentially tragic results.

JUVENILE DELINQUENCY

Juvenile delinquency is essentially a legal term. A juvenile delinquent or juvenile offender is a child who comes to the attention of a juvenile court for having committed acts that would be considered crimes if they were committed by an adult, or for certain statutory offenses that pertain only to children, such as truancy, running away from home, and, in some jurisdictions, disobedience to parents and teachers.

The term *juvenile delinquent* thus covers a broad range, lumping together youngsters who have committed armed robbery with those who have merely played hookey from school. Richard Bush, a child psychologist, suggests that it should be applied only to adolescents who exhibit a recurring pattern of antisocial behavior, who show little or no regard for the rights or feelings of others, who have little concern for their own safety or for the consequences of their acts, and who tend to associate in groups or gangs with other young people who share similar values and behavior patterns. Before adolescence these youngsters are called *predelinquent*.

Traditional insight psychotherapy is generally not very successful with such youngsters. Behavioral therapy tends to work better (see Chapter 16). For the younger ones whom family courts are likely to leave in the charge of their parents, a coordinated effort among teachers, parents, social worker, and mental health specialist to provide a firm, structured environment with close supervision may help. For older teenagers, an out-of-home placement of some kind often is indicated.

Some juvenile delinquents have other, identifiable mental disorders, such as brain damage or retardation. Indeed, some authorities believe there is a definite link between learning disabilities and juvenile delinquency. Certain kinds of learning disability, they feel, are associated with behavior patterns that tend toward delinquency, specifically impulsiveness, limited ability to learn from experience, and limited ability to decipher social cues (understand what is considered acceptable behavior). The child with learning problems develops little self-esteem and may feel the need to compensate for school failure through absenteeism, suspension (for disciplinary reasons), or dropping out altogether. Although these theories may seem speculative, and many others believe that the underlying causes of juvenile delinquency are more readily found in poverty, broken homes, cultural alienation, and social disadvantages—in other words, an environment such as an urban ghetto—studies of high delinquency areas indicate some differences between those youths who get in trouble with the law and those who do not.

One major problem for juvenile delinquents is the lack of facilities where adequate treatment is provided. The families of these youngsters often cannot afford private treatment, and state hospitals, as indicated above, have little room for children or adolescents. Some communities have established halfway houses for adolescents, but to date the need for such facilities far exceeds the supply. As a result, juvenile offenders may end up in a highly inappropriate setting, such as a state hospital for the criminally insane, that is, a maximum security facility for the mentally ill who represent a grave danger to the community. One man in his mid-twenties, for example, who had been in trouble since his teens, in and out of state hospitals and police lockups, spent six months in a hospital for the criminally insane after he was arrested for trespassing on his parents' property. Though originally scheduled for only twenty days of pretrial observation, a legal mixup kept him living among murderers, rapists, and assaulters—those considered the most deranged and violent criminals—for half a year. His case is unfortunate but not unusual.

To improve the delivery of mental health services to juvenile offenders, the following improvements have been recommended:

- The juvenile court system should have available to it preadjudication and predisposition mental health services for diagnosis, evaluation, and consultation.
- Ambulatory (outpatient) mental health services should be provided in youth development centers, youth forestry camps, and state-supervised juvenile facilities.

- A certain number of decentralized maximum-security beds should be provided in the youth services system for violent juvenile offenders, with specialized mental health treatment and research services available.

In addition, there is a need for secure beds in mental hospitals for mentally ill juvenile offenders, aftercare services, liaison between mental health and social service offices, and review of the laws relating to the mentally ill juvenile offender.

Few if any states today offer this range of facilities and services—indeed, only a minority have developed any juvenile programs—yet without adequate intervention juvenile offenders almost invariably become adult offenders.

Chapter

27

THE FUTURE—
AVENUES OF RESEARCH

THE FIELD of mental health and our understanding of mental illness have grown immensely in recent decades. There is overwhelming evidence that some illnesses are disorders of the brain and central nervous system. To date only the most severe disorders are so implicated, but it is possible that one day we will find that all mental disorders ultimately have organic causes. Research in this area has mushroomed with the development of more sophisticated technological equipment, including computers.

The growth of genetic research—the mapping of the body's thousands of genes, the basic units of heredity—is uncovering more about who is at risk for developing an illness. At the same time, although our understanding of causes is far from perfect, we are continuing to develop newer and better kinds of treatment.

THE BRAIN

The brain is often described as a complex message center, receiving signals from outside the body and from different organs within the body, and sending messages to other organs. The brain itself consists of nerve cells, or neurons. Within the brain messages are transmitted from neuron to neuron, a process that occurs in fractions of a second. The brain contains perhaps 50 billion neurons. Each message must pass over minuscule gaps between the neurons, called *synapses*. There are far more synapses than neurons: Each neuron has one thousand to ten thousand synapses over which it may transmit messages, and it may receive messages from some one thousand other neurons, making for a total of perhaps 20 trillion synapses.

NEUROTRANSMITTERS

The message transmitted by a neuron is actually an electrical signal. In order to cross a synapse, the electric signal must be momentarily turned into a chemical one. To accomplish this, a special chemical substance called a *neurotransmitter* is released at the synapse by the transmitting cell. The neurotransmitter comes in contact with the receiver cell across the synapse and either activates or inhibits the receiver cell. Then the neurotransmitter either is broken down by the chemical action of an enzyme (a special protein) or it is reabsorbed into the fiber from which it came.

About 70 neurotransmitters have been identified so far. They are vital in the transmission of messages. Each carries either a stimulating or inhibiting message across the synapse from the first, or presynaptic, neuron to the second, or postsynaptic, neuron. In order to receive this message, the postsynaptic neuron must have an appropriate receptor, which is a certain kind of protein molecule. Just as many different brain chemicals serve as neurotransmitters, many others serve as receptors. In addition, still other chemicals called *neuromodulators* influence the neurotransmitters.

The neurotransmitters are vital in the transmission of all messages, and at least some of them are believed to be central to regulating mood, perception, thought, and behavior. The effect on behavior of many drugs, ranging from the caffeine in coffee and hallucinogens like mescaline and LSD to the medications used to control mania and depression, arises from their ability to disrupt or change the chemical transmission of messages between neurons.

Among the neurotransmitters believed to be involved in certain mental illnesses are norepinephrine, serotonin, dopamine, acetylcholine, and gamma-aminobutyric acid (GABA). Dopamine and norepinephrine are chemical compounds called catecholamines. They are produced in the body from two amino acids, phenylalanine and tyrosine, through changes mediated by enzymes (protein molecules made by the body). Serotonin is synthesized from another amino acid, tryptophan, also through enzyme action. Ultimately, the amino acids come from protein in the food we eat (see below, under the blood-brain barrier).

Dopamine is related to arousal, alertness, and euphoria. Serotonin is related to states of drowsiness. Mood disorders—major depression and manic-depressive psychosis—are related to these neurotransmitters. Depression is linked with an underactivity of the neurons that respond to the catelochamines (norepinephrine and dopamine), in effect a functional deficiency of these brain chemicals. But some depressions appear to be related to an abnormality of serotonin, and perhaps other neurotransmitters also are involved. The tricyclic antidepressants (see Chapter 18) work by making more norepinephrine available (blocking its reabsorption); the monoamine oxidase inhibitors (MAOIs) work by blocking the breakdown of neurotransmitters by the enzyme monoamine oxidase and therefore increase their concentration. The mania of manic-depressive disorder is thought to be due to overactivity of the catecholamines. Lithium, used to control mania, inhibits the release and reuptake of norepinephrine and may increase the turnover rate of serotonin; it may also somehow suppress acetylcholine.

The neurotransmitter dopamine is believed to be connected also with the development of schizophrenia. The phenothiazines, the most effective of the antipsychotic drugs developed so far, act by blocking the effects of what seems to be an excess of dopamine. Amphetamine, on the other hand, which is a powerful stimulant, triggers the release of dopamine; a large dose of amphetamine can disrupt a person's thought processes and give rise to hallucinations and delusions of persecution like those found in acute schizophrenics. One of the products produced from the breakdown of dopamine is homovanillic acid (HVA). HVA concentrations have been found to be significantly higher in the blood plasma of psychotic persons—individuals with schizophrenia who are experiencing delusions and/or hallucinations—and decrease with the use of antipsychotic drugs.

The symptoms of parkinsonism, a disease of the central nervous system of unknown cause, are related to a deficiency of dopamine, and since the late 1960s this formerly untreatable disease has been treated with L-dopa, a chemical precursor of dopamine. (An overdose of L-dopa also leads to schizophrenia-like symptoms.) Because L-dopa is not effective for all parkinsonism patients, neurosurgeons have been pursuing a new approach: the implantation directly into the brain of tissue from the adrenal glands, which produce dopamine as a chemical step in synthesizing certain hormones. This procedure has been used in some human patients, but it is still considered highly experimental.

Another class of brain chemical are the *peptides*, which sometimes act as neurotransmitters and at other times as pituitary, adrenal, and gastrointestinal hormones. Research in peptides in the 1970s revealed that two kinds, the *endorphins* and *enkephalins*, are involved in pain perception, the control of respiration, thirst, memory, and sexual behavior. Peptides are believed to be much more specific in their effects than neurotransmitters, possibly being capable of conveying specific ideas, moods, memories, emotional states, and behaviors. With advanced laboratory techniques scientists have created a number of peptides synthetically, including synthetic endorphins. One peptide, vasopressin, closely related to the endorphins, appears to enhance the brain's ability to learn and to store information.

TECHNOLOGICAL ADVANCES

The fact that the nerves in the brain emit electrical signals was discovered only in 1924. When large numbers of brain cells are engaged in coordinated activity, they cause measurable currents to flow through the brain, the membranes surrounding it, the bony skull that encases it, and the scalp (skin) that covers it. These currents can be detected by means of electrodes placed on the skin, along with suitable amplifiers. A record of the currents is called an electroencephalogram (EEG).

The crude picture of brain function yielded by an EEG is useful for some diagnostic purposes—for diagnosing epilepsy, for example—but it is not refined enough to diagnose learning disability or mental retardation with any certainty. One line of research now being pursued is a battery of tests that measure the EEG from a score of electrodes under a large variety of test conditions. The huge amount of data generated is then analyzed with a computer. During the early decades of EEG technology, most neuroscientists assumed that the squiggly wave patterns were simply a random summation of the electrical impulses of the individual neurons. Computerized research, however, suggests that the EEG does not result from individual nerve impulses but from slow, graded electrical potentials produced by the bodies of the nerve cells. As these potentials sweep across vast numbers of neurons they become synchronized. Thus it is large groups of neurons working together that form the patterns seen.

Some scientists have found direct correlations between certain patterns and specific cognitive processes. One brain research center is focusing on amassing and analyzing large numbers of EEG patterns in the hope of developing precise profiles of a variety of brain states. With this technique, called *neurometrics*, it is hoped that instead of making vague diagnoses of mental problems such as learning disability or hyperactivity it will be possible to compare an impaired person's EEG with those of normal subjects in the same age group and discover the exact location and kind of abnormality, allowing for more specific treatment.

Another promising approach involves the measurement and analysis of infinitesimally small pulses of electricity in the brain that are called *evoked potentials* (EPs) because they are generated (evoked) by stimulation of different sensory nerves. This new tool reveals a good deal about the brain's workings in brain-injured patients, even when they are in a coma, and may help to predict how much brain damage has occurred and how much dysfunction can be expected. The technique already is used to assess the brain status of stroke victims and multiple sclerosis patients, as well as patients before, during, and after brain surgery.

Another form of EEG is *brain electrical activity mapping* (BEAM), whereby a computer analyzes the activity by means of electrodes placed on different parts of the skull and presents the results on a screen. This method can show brain-wave responses to various stimuli. Some BEAM experiments have shown that a particular positive electrical wave, called P-300, which in normal patients arises very fast after it receives an unusual stimulus requiring a revision of plans, is both delayed and smaller in schizophrenic patients. This situation occurs particularly in the left temporal lobe and associate limbic system—areas of the brain where memories are stored and matched to sensory stimuli. In another study, BEAM was used to find abnormal electrical brain waves in depressed patients who failed to respond to conventional treatment. In some of them BEAM produced patterns that were suggestive of seizure disorder (epilepsy), and some of these patients subsequently improved when treated with antiseizure medications.

BRAIN IMAGING

The computer also has been useful in producing very sophisticated x-rays of the brain. The *CAT* or *CT* (*computerized axial tomography*) scanner, introduced in the early 1970s, gives cross-sectional views of soft-tissue structures of the body. It has shown, for example, that the fluid-filled brain cavities known as ventricles are much larger than average in 15 to 20 percent of schizophrenic patients. Moreover, those patients with the largest ventricles have the most severe symptoms and are less likely to respond to antipsychotic medication.

A cousin of the CT scanner is the *PET* (*positive emission tomography*) scanner, which gives a metabolic portrait of the brain, revealing the rate at which sick and healthy tissues consume various chemicals. The patient is given a substance containing short-lived radioactive (positron-emitting) atoms that can be traced as they disintegrate. A computer turns these traces into images. The substance most commonly used in PET scans is glucose, the body's main source of energy. Glucose measurements indicate where metabolic activity is most intense. In another use of the PET scan, drugs are radioactively tagged to measure abnormalities in neurotransmitter pathways where the drugs act. Some studies using PET scanning with radioactive glucose suggest that schizophrenic patients have low metabolic activity in the front lobes of the brain, especially in the prefrontal area of the cerebral cortex (which governs planning and abstract thinking, and modulates social judgment and the expression of feelings).

PET scan studies also have shown that parts of the brains of patients with obsessive-compulsive disorder metabolize glucose at a substantially faster rate than the same brain regions in subjects with different mental illnesses or no illness. Patients who responded well to drug treatment for this disorder show PET scan results different from those not benefiting from treatment. The areas in question, the frontal lobes and the basal ganglia, are believed to play a role in the control of movements and also in some aspects of learned behavior.

The PET scanner also has been used to assess the brain of a person who is comatose owing to heart attack, stroke, Alzheimer's, drug overdose, or head injury. The patient is alive but unresponsive, often appearing awake but giving little or no evidence of awareness of the environment or ability to express thoughts. The PET scan can measure the biochemical activity of the brain and to some extent help assess the likelihood of recovery.

Still more sophisticated is *nuclear magnetic resonance imaging* (*MRI*), in which a patient is placed in a strong magnetic field that alters the alignment of hydrogen atoms in the body. With the help of a radio signal and computer, this magnetic effect is converted into a picture of a cross-section of the brain. MRI provides clearer and more complete pictures than CT, and furthermore, three-dimensional ones. MRI studies suggest that schizophrenic patients have smaller than average frontal lobes, as well as the possibility of atrophy in the temporal lobes.

Both faster and potentially more accurate than the PET scan is *MEG* (*magnetoencephalography*). Unlike PET or MRI, MEG does not use radioactive tracers or x-rays. Rather, it measures the miniscule magnetic fields in the brain that accompany the electrical activity generated when cells orchestrate the movement of a finger, the recognition of a face, or the solution of a math problem. Whereas EEG signals provide a view of diffuse brain activity, MEG measures cell function at exact locations in the brain, showing, for example, the different parts of the brain that become active during a specific motor activity.

Still another newer technique is *regional cerebral blood flow* (*RCBF*) measurement. The patient inhales a radioactive form of xenon gas, and as the gas disintegrates and emits radiation, its path in the brain is tracked by detectors placed around the head. This test reveals the flow of blood and, by implication, the intensity of activity in various brain regions. RCBF studies have shown, for example, that schizophrenics find it hard to activate the prefrontal cortex when they need it. Two tasks that produce high blood flow there in normal subjects—tests that require sustained attention, pattern recognition, and the ability to change in response to new stimuli—produce relatively little change in blood flow in schizophrenic patients.

THE BLOOD-BRAIN BARRIER

Where do the neurotransmitters come from? Their precursors (chemical forerunners) are nutrient substances that modify their release. Unlike other organs, which can use a variety of food substances (sugars, fats, amino acids), the brain can use only blood glucose. Moreover, much of the brain is believed to be protected by a selective filter system called the blood-brain barrier, which isolates it from the rest of the body's circulatory system. Through this barrier only small molecules, such as those of oxygen, can pass very readily. Fat-soluble molecules also can pass through, as do antibiotics, antihistamines, tranquilizers, and hormones. Most water-soluble molecules and the larger ones required by brain cells, like those of glucose, must be actively taken up by special transporting mechanisms. This phenomenon has particular significance for medications intended to affect the neurotransmitters or to treat cancer: In order to be effective they must penetrate the blood-brain barrier.

Since the neurotransmitters are in effect converted food substances, it seems reasonable to presume they can be affected by food intake. In fact it has been found that the consumption of carbohydrate foods, for example, triggers the release of serotonin, which increases sleepiness, decreases sensitivity to pain, and also decreases the craving for carbohydrates. The rate at which serotonin forms depends on how much of its chemical precursor, the amino acid tryptophan, gets into the brain. When one eats meat or another protein-containing food, the protein is broken down by digestion into its constituent amino acids, which then enter the bloodstream. Six of the amino acids, including tryptophan, are carried into the brain.

Although tryptophan is found in many foods, it is outnumbered by the five other amino acids that compete with it for entry into the brain. Therefore, eating lots of protein does not increase tryptophan (or serotonin) levels in the brain. However, consuming carbohydrates triggers the pancreas to produce insulin to process these foods. Insulin lowers the blood levels of the five amino acids that compete with tryptophan and therefore allows more tryptophan to reach the brain, so that more serotonin can be formed. Tyrosine, also an amino acid, is the precursor of norepinephrine, but eating more protein does not increase that neurotransmitter's levels and thereby help combat depression.

Other neurotransmitters are influenced by diet. For example, choline, which is consumed in foods like soybeans and egg yolks, is a precursor to acetylcholine, and increases the level of that neurotransmitter in the brain. Since acetylcholine plays a role in memory, researchers are now trying to determine if treatments that increase choline levels in the brain can counter memory loss in patients with Alzheimer's disease.

WEATHER, SUGAR, AND MOOD

Wind and light appear to affect people's moods. Certain weather conditions, notably such warm dry winds as the foehn in alpine Europe, the sharav in Israel, the sirocco in Italy, and the Santa Ana in southern California, have long been suspected of affecting mood to the point where they trigger accidents, crimes, and suicides. A recent experiment on human volunteers showed that weather changes caused by such winds (and also by other factors, such as pollutants, radioactivity, and high-voltage electric lines) generate a large number of positive ions in the atmosphere, which appear to increase tension and irritability in susceptible individuals as well as a slowdown in reaction times. These results are supported by experiments with mice, in whom exposure to high levels of positive ions raises the blood levels of serotonin and depletes brain levels of this neurotransmitter.

Sunlight also appears to affect both fertility and mood. In Finland, for example, the conception rate peaks in June and July, when Finns are exposed to about twenty hours of sunlight a day, and dips in the dark winter months. In the temperate and polar zones, there are seasonal patterns in depression, mania, and suicide attempts. Indeed, this condition has been recognized as a legitimate syndrome and is now called *seasonal affective disorder (SAD)*.

Our bodies have daily and annual rhythms as well as seasonal ones. A number of events take place in the course of every twenty-four-hour day: biological events that are endogenous (arise within the body). The sleep–waking cycle is the most familiar, but there are others, some of which can be determined or measured only by means of special techniques. For example, body temperature regularly rises every day, from its lowest point at dawn to its highest point in the evening. At night the pineal gland secretes the hormone melatonin, which reaches its peak levels in the body sometime between 11 P.M. and 7 A.M. The secretion of melatonin appears to be directly related to a person's exposure to light.

Although these body rhythms are largely self-sustained, they can be influenced by the environment. Sunlight, drugs, and hormones—

particularly the sex hormones estrogen and testosterone—can change the timing. These variations, may, some researchers suspect, help account for the high incidence of affective disorders (depression and mania) at certain times of life—during puberty, pregnancy, at certain times in the menstrual cycle, and menopause. The female body experiences these endocrine variations more than the male, and women suffer far more frequently from affective disorders than men do.

A classic symptom of major depression, as was noted in Chapter 6, is early-morning wakening; depression is at its worst at this time, and a gradual improvement of mood occurs during the course of the day. It is suspected that this situation may be due to some upset in the body's regular circadian (daily) rhythms. (Similarly, in temperate climates depression has a seasonal peak, in April, and a secondary peak, in fall.) Some researchers believe that depression involves what they call a *phase advance* of circadian rhythm, that is, everything occurs a little sooner than it should, and hence the whole twenty-four-hour cycle is shortened; thus, instead of waking up at the normal time, one wakes up several hours earlier. The cause of this advance is not known. It may be that some individuals have intrinsically shorter cycles owing to genetic factors, hormonal factors, or exceptional light sensitivity. Indeed, exposure to high-intensity light—simply sitting under fluorescent lights for several hours a day for a week or less—has proved to be an effective treatment for numerous SAD sufferers.

About the same time that such *phototherapy* began to be used for SAD, in the mid-1980s, research with obese patients who overeat only carbohydrates and with women who suffer from premenstrual syndrome (PMS) showed a similar cyclical pattern. Both carbohydrate-craving obesity and PMS have common symptoms: depression, lethargy, inability to concentrate, and episodic bouts of overeating carbohydrate foods and excessive weight gain. Moreover, they are cyclic, occurring in the afternoon and evening for overeaters and just prior to menstruation for PMS. The symptoms, it was observed, are similar to those of SAD, which of course is also cyclic (fall and winter).

The connection between SAD and melatonin has been definitely established, although it is not, at this writing, wholly understood. Why individuals with SAD, PMS, and carbohydrate-craving obesity all tend to crave sweets is not yet known. It would appear to be related to the neurotransmitter serotonin, that is, eating carbohydrates triggers insulin production, which in turn allows for more serotonin formation (see above). Normally the level of serotonin influences the amount of carbohydrates a person chooses to eat. When the body has enough serotonin, the desire for carbohydrates subsides. Researchers believe that when this feedback mechanism is upset, the brain fails to respond when carbohydrates are consumed, and so the desire for them persists longer than it should. The disturbance apparently occurs cyclically in all three disorders—SAD, PMS, and obesity. Oddly enough, carbohydrate cravers sometimes respond to treatment with light, just as SAD patients do.

GENETIC RESEARCH

Long-term studies of mental illness among natural and adoptive families of schizophrenic patients, as well as studies of identical twins, point to the strong probability of a hereditary component in this illness. Similar findings exist for alcoholism, manic-depressive disease, and major depression. To date the evidence suggests that it is a genetic *tendency* to develop these disorders that is passed on, and that only those who are exposed to certain environmental factors—brain injury during delivery, stressful life or work situation, physical trauma, abrupt changes in diet, infection with a virus—are the ones who become ill.

When one identical twin suffers from depression, there is a 57 percent likelihood that the other twin will also be affected, and only a 14 percent chance if the twins are fraternal. (Identical twins have the same genes; fraternal twins are no more alike than ordinary siblings.) For schizophrenia the chances are about 63 percent for identical twins and only 21 percent for fraternal twins; for alcoholism the chances are about 50 percent for identical twins and 30 percent for fraternal twins. If one identical twin has manic-depressive psychosis, the other has an 80 percent chance of having it, too.

In recent years researchers have actually begun to find specific genetic markers—one or more genes on one of the forty-six chromosomes that contain the body's complete blueprint of heredity—associated with a specific mental illness. Several such markers have been found for manic-depressive psychosis, and others for schizophrenia. The National Institute of Mental Health has sponsored a major molecular genetics research project in which they hope to locate the genes involved in inheriting vulnerability to both these conditions. If and when preliminary evidence is confirmed, it may enable very early detection of persons at risk, possibly even before birth (by analyzing the fetal chromosomes). It also may eventually enable molecular biologists to identify the substance(s) produced by the genes that is responsible for susceptibility.

The implications of an inherited vulnerability to mental illness have numerous potential clinical applications. A chronic inborn susceptibility suggests that there may be need for long-term treatment even in the absence of symptoms. Genetic counseling may be required, since family members are vulnerable to the same disorder as they enter the age of highest risk, for example, late adolescence and early adulthood for the depressive disorders and schizophrenia. And new medication could be developed to counteract the action of the genes responsible.

STRESS AND RISK

In the late 1970s formal studies confirmed what had long been suspected—that people in particular life situations are more likely to develop mental illnesses. Among the groups so identified were individuals who had recently been divorced, individuals who were physically disabled, and elderly persons who live alone. By pinpointing such groups it is possible to take preventive measures as well as to plan early intervention. For example, the establishment of community youth centers (some of them consisting of mobile vans) in poverty areas has made available such vital services as drug and alcohol programs conducted by former addicts, discussion groups for personal problems, job counseling, and the like to teenagers who otherwise would be unwilling or unable to seek out such services.

For individuals who have undergone some terrible experience, such as being taken hostage or abducted by terrorists, research indicates that various kinds of short-term crisis-oriented therapy begun as soon as possible after their ordeal can prevent the development of serious long-term emotional difficulties.

DEVELOPMENTS IN TREATMENT

During the past decade there has been increasing emphasis on briefer forms of treatment that address themselves more to specific problems than to changing a client's overall personality. Rather than taking a single doctrinaire approach to one form of therapy, clinicians have been increasingly inclined to borrow from various disciplines and adapt the treatment to the client. In some cases this process has been informal (see the description of eclectic therapy at the end of Chapter 17), but in others there have been formal amalgamations of separate schools, as, for example, with cognitive behavior therapy. No doubt this process is in part a reflection of the current consensus regarding the causes of mental illness, that is, it results from a multitude of factors, including hereditary predisposition, childhood experience, social environment, and stress, rather than *only* from learned maladaptive behavior or *only* from unresolved inner conflict.

One promising development in psychotherapy involves the use of *biofeedback* to control symptoms, an area greatly aided by the development of more sophisticated technical equipment to monitor blood pressure and other physical phenomena affected by one's emotional state. Biofeedback has been useful in controlling migraine headache and high blood pressure, two physical conditions affected very much by mental states, as well as physical symptoms of acute anxiety.

Biofeedback principles have been used by experimenters with electronic machinery to alter brain patterns and activity. One such machine, the CAP (computerized automated psychophysiological) scan, projects an EEG picture in the form of a multicolor map onto a television screen while the subject is undergoing the procedure. By changing thoughts and feelings, the subject actually can see changes in his brain-wave activity.

Researchers in this field (beginning with the German physician, Hans Berger, 1873–1941) distinguish different kinds of electrical activity in the brain: *alpha* waves, fairly slow and of high amplitude, associated with concentration on inner experiences, such as deep relaxation, meditation, and contemplation; *beta* waves, of lower amplitude and more rapid frequency, associated with outer-directed mental activity, such as verbal, linear, logical thinking; and *theta* waves, also slow but of lower amplitude than alpha, associated with calm, relaxation, and the emergence of long-forgotten memories. It is believed that one can learn to control such wave activity and thus alter mood and behavior. However, more research is necessary to determine the exact nature of these mind–body manipulations, before they can be considered a reliable form of therapy.

Another promising area of investigation is the influence of the mind on the body's immune system. Recent studies show that altering a patient's mental state can actually boost the immune system. This new field, called *psychoimmunology*, is based on the idea that there is definite interaction between the brain and central nervous system, and the body's immune system. Cells in the immune system have been shown to have receptors for brain chemicals, and there also are direct physiological links between the nervous system and the lymph nodes and spleen, where some immune cells are manufactured or stored.

For example, in order to prevent the recurrence of some cancers that are in remission, patients were given an eight-week course in relaxation and in cognitive therapy (focusing on changing self-defeating beliefs and attitudes). Following the course, blood tests revealed a rise in their active natural killer cells, which protect against tumor growth, unlike a second group of patients who received only standard medical treatment. Similar results have been reported for AIDS and other diseases.

Human behavior, the human brain, the human body, the human being in relation to the environment—all these are topics of vast complexity that may never be understood well enough to enable precise and accurate prediction of how people will feel and act. Nevertheless, we are making increasing progress in improving our understanding of mental illness and how to treat it successfully.

Appendix A

USEFUL ADDRESSES AND PHONE NUMBERS

(Note: Addresses and phone numbers listed are the latest available but could have changed by the time you read this. If so, check the local yellow pages, or call or write to ODPHP National Health Information Center, P.O. Box 1133, Washington, DC 20013-1133, (800) 336-4797; (301) 565-4167 in MD and metropolitan DC, and ask this government office to check their data base of information resources.)

American Academy of Child and Adolescent Psychiatry
3615 Wisconsin Ave., NW
Washington, DC 20016
(202) 966-3700

American Association of Acupuncturists and Oriental Medicine
5473 66th St., N.
St. Petersburg, FL 33709
(813) 541-2666

American Association for Marriage and Family Therapy
1717 K St., NW
Washington, DC 20006
(202) 429-1825

American Association of Orthomolecular Medicine
900 N. Federal Highway
Boca Raton, FL 33432
(305) 393-6167

American Association for Partial Hospitalization
1411 K St., NW
Washington, DC 20005
(202) 347-1649

American Association of Professional Hypnotherapists
P.O. Box 731
McLean, VA 22101
(703) 448-9623

American Association of Sex Educators, Counselors, and Therapists
11 Dupont Circle, NW
Washington, DC 20036
(202) 462-1171

American Board of Examiners in Professional Psychology
2100 E. Broadway
Columbia, MO 65201
(314) 875-1267

American Family Therapy Association
1255 23rd St., NW
Washington, DC 20037
(202) 659-7666

American Group Psychotherapy Association
25 E. 21st St.
New York, NY 10010
(212) 477-2677

American Mental Health Counselors Association
5999 Stevenson Ave.
Alexandria, VA 22304
(703) 823-9800 (Ext. 383)
(800) 354-2008

American Psychiatric Association
1400 K St., NW
Washington, DC 20005
(202) 682-2000

American Psychological Association
1200 17th St., NW
Washington, DC 20036
(202) 955-7600

Association for Advancement of Behavior Therapy
15 W. 36th St.
New York, NY 10018
(212) 279-7970

Association for the Advancement of Psychoanalysis (of the Karen Horney Institute)
329 E. 62nd St.
New York, NY 10021
(212) 751-2724

Canadian Mental Health Association
52 St. Clair Ave., E.
Toronto, Ontario, Canada
(416) 789-7957

Canadian Psychiatric Association
Suite 103, 225 Lisgar St.
Ottawa, Ontario K2P OC6, Canada
(613) 234-2815

Canadian Psychological Association
Suite 46, 1390 Sherbrook St., W.
Montreal, 109, Quebec, Canada

Family Service of America
11700 W. Lake Park Drive
Milwaukee, WI 53224
(414) 359-2111

Institute for Rational-Emotive Therapy
45 E. 65th St.
New York, NY 10021
(212) 535-0822

Institute for Reality Therapy
7301 Medical Center Dr.
Canoga Park, CA 91307
(818) 888-0688

International Institute for Bioenergetic Analysis
144 E. 36th St.
New York, NY 10016
(212) 532-7742

International Transactional Analysis Association
1772 Vallejo St.
San Francisco, CA 94123
(415) 885-5992

National Academy of Counselors and Family Therapists
225 Jericho Tpke.
Floral Park, NY 11001
(516) 352-1188

National Alliance for the Mentally Ill
2101 Wilson Blvd.
Arlington, VA 22201
(703) 524-7600

National Association for the Advancement of Psychoanalysis
80 Eighth Ave.
New York, NY 10011
(212) 741-0515

National Association of Private Psychiatric Hospitals
1319 F St., NW
Washington, DC 20004
(202) 393-6700

National Association of Social Workers
7981 Eastern Ave.
Silver Spring, MD 20910
(301) 565-0333

National Center for (Divorce) Mediation Education
2083 West St.
Annapolis, MD 21401
(301) 261-8445

National Clearinghouse for Mental Health Information
(301) 443-4514

National Council of Community Mental Health Centers
12300 Twinbrook Parkway
Rockville, MD 20852
(301) 984-6200

National Mental Health Association
1021 Prince St.
Alexandria, VA 22314
(703) 684-7722

Public Citizens Health Research Group
2000 P St., NW
Washington, DC 20005
(202) 872-0320

Radix Institute
Route 2, Box 89-A
Granbury, TX 76048
(817) 326-5670

Rolf Institute
P.O. Box 1868
Boulder, CO 80306
(303) 449-5903

Veterans Administration Information Service
(202) 389-2443

FOR SPECIFIC PROBLEMS

ADDICTION

Al-Anon Family Groups
1372 Broadway
New York, NY 10018
(212) 302-7240

Alcohol and Drug Problems Association of North America
444 N. Capitol St., NW
Washington, DC 20001
(202) 737-4340
(provides list of major state and provincial agencies for alcoholism)

Alcoholics Anonymous
P.O. Box 459
Grand Central Station
New York, NY 10163
(212) 686-1100

Narcotics Anonymous
P.O. Box 9999
Van Nuys, CA 91409
(818) 780-3951

National Council of Alcoholism
12 W. 21st St.
New York, NY 10010
(212) 206-6770
(lists nonprofit agencies in many cities making referrals to private physicians
and public and private agencies that provide treatment)

ALZHEIMER'S

Alzheimer's and Related Disorders Association
70 E. Lake St.
Chicago, IL 60610-5997
(800) 621-0379; in IL (800) 572-6037

AUTISM

Autism Society of America
1234 Massachusetts Ave., NW
Washington, DC 20005
(202) 783-0125

DEPRESSION AND MANIC-DEPRESSIVE DISEASE

Depressives Anonymous
329 E. 62nd St.
New York, NY 10021
(212) 689-2600

Foundation for Depression and Manic-Depression
7 E. 67th St.
New York, NY 10021
(212) 772-3400

National Depressive and Manic Depressive Association
Merchandise Mart
P.O. Box 3395
Chicago, IL 60654
(312) 993-0066

National Foundation for Depressive Illness
20 Charles St.
New York, NY 10014
(800) 248-4344

EATING DISORDERS

National Association of Anorexia Nervosa and Related Disorders
Box 7
Highland Park, IL 60035
(312) 831-3138

LEARNING DISABILITIES

**Accreditation Council on Services for People with Developmental
    Disabilities**
120 Boylston St.
Boston, MA 02116
(617) 426-7909

Association for Children and Adults with Learning Disabilities
4156 Library Rd.
Pittsburgh, PA 15234
(412) 341-1515

Council for Exceptional Children
1920 Association Dr.
Reston, VA 22091
(703) 620-3660

SCHIZOPHRENIA

Schizophrenics Anonymous
1209 California Rd.
Eastchester, NY 10709
(914) 337-2252

TOURETTE'S DISORDER

Tourette Syndrome Association
42-20 Bell Blvd.
Bayside, NY 11361
(718) 224-2999

Health and Welfare Canada
Social Service Programs Branch
Ottawa, Ontario K1A 1B5
(613) 957-2913

National Mental Health Consumers' Association
311 S. Juniper St.
Philadelphia, PA 19107
(215) 735-2465

National Self-Help Clearinghouse
Graduate Center of City University of New York
33 W. 42nd St.
New York, NY 10036
(212) 840-1259

Recovery, Inc.
802 N. Dearborn St.
Chicago, IL 60610
(312) 337-5661

Self-Help Center
1600 Dodge Ave.
Evanston, IL 60201
(312) 328-0470

Self-Help Clearinghouse
St. Claires-Riverside Medical Center
Denville, NJ 07834
(201) 625-7101

HOSPITALS FOR CHILDREN

American Association of Children's Residential Centers
440 First St., NW
Washington, DC 20001
(202) 638-1604

Association of Child and Adolescent Psychiatric Hospitals
Pine Rest Christian Hospital
300 68th St., SE
Grand Rapids, MI 49508

NURSING HOMES

American Association of Homes for the Aging
1129 20th St., NW
Washington, DC 20036
(202) 296-5960
(nonprofit homes)

American Health Care Association
1200 15th St., NW
Washington, DC 20005
(202) 833-2050
(proprietary homes)

LEGAL QUESTIONS

American Bar Association Commission on the Mentally Disabled
Washington, DC
(202) 331-2240

Mental Health Law Project
2021 L St., NW
Washington, DC 20036
(202) 467-5730

National Legal Aid and Defense Association
1625 K St., NW
Washington, DC 20006
(202) 452-0620

CHILD ABUSE

Parents Anonymous
6733 S. Sepulveda
Los Angeles, CA 90045
(213) 410-9732

National Council on Child Abuse and Family Violence
1155 Connecticut Ave., NW
Washington, DC 20036
(202) 429-6695

Appendix B

STATE OF IOWA
BILL OF RIGHTS FOR PERSONS WITH MENTAL RETARDATION, DEVELOPMENTAL DISABILITIES, AND CHRONIC MENTAL ILLNESS*

225C.25 Short title.

Sections 225C.25 through 225C.28 shall be known as "the bill of rights of persons with mental retardation, developmental disabilities, or chronic mental illness."

85 Acts, ch 249, §2

225C.26 Scope.

These rights apply to any person with mental retardation, a developmental disability, or chronic mental illness who receives services which are funded in whole or in part by public funds or services which are permitted under Iowa law.

85 Acts, ch 249, §3

225C.27 Purpose.

Sections 225C.25 through 225C.28 shall be liberally construed and applied to promote their purposes and the stated rights. The division, in coordination with appropriate agencies, shall adopt rules to implement the

* Effective July 1, 1987, dependent on enactment of funding formula.

purposes of sections 225C.25 through 225C.28 which include, but are not limited to the following:

1. Promotion of the human dignity and protection of the constitutional and statutory rights of persons with mental retardation, developmental disabilities, or chronic mental illness in the state.

2. Encouraging the development of the ability and potential of each person with mental retardation, developmental disabilities, or chronic mental illness in the state to the fullest extent possible.

3. Ensuring that the recipients of services shall not be deprived of any rights, benefits, or privileges guaranteed by law, the Constitution of the State of Iowa, or the Constitution of the United States solely on account of the receipt of the services.

85 Acts, ch 249, §4

225C.28 Rights.

The rights of persons described in section 225C.26 include, but are not limited to:

1. Comprehensive evaluation and diagnosis. A person suspected of being mentally retarded, developmentally disabled, or chronically mentally ill or applying for developmental disabilities services, has the right to receive a comprehensive diagnosis and evaluation adapted to the cultural background, primary language, and ethnic origin of the person.

2. Individual treatment, habilitation, and program plan. Persons with mental retardation, a developmental disability, or chronic mental illness who require services have the right to an individual treatment, habilitation, and program plan.

3. Individualized treatment, habilitation, and program services. A person with a known or suspected mental retardation, developmentally disabled, or chronic mental illness condition shall not be denied treatment, habilitation, and program services because of age, sex, ethnic origin, marital status, ability to pay, criminal record, degree of disability or illness, or mental retardation condition.

4. Periodic review of treatment, habilitation, and program. A mentally retarded, developmentally disabled, or chronically mentally ill person receiving services has the right to a periodic, but at least annual, reevaluation and review of the individual treatment, habilitation, and program plan to measure progress, to modify objectives if necessary, and to provide guidance and remediation techniques.

5. Participation in the formulation of the plan. A person with mental retardation, a developmental disability, or chronic mental illness or the person's representative has the right to participate in planning the person's own treatment, habilitation, and program plan and to be informed, in writing, of progress at reasonable time intervals. Each person shall be given the oppor-

tunity to make decisions and exercise options regarding the plan, consistent with the person's capabilities.

6. Least restrictive environment and age-appropriate services. A person with mental retardation, a developmental disability, or chronic mental illness has the right to live and receive age-appropriate services in the least restrictive setting consistent with the person's individual treatment and habilitation needs, potential, and abilities.

7. Vocational training and employment options. A person with mental retardation, a developmental disability, or chronic mental illness has the right to vocational training which contributes to the person's independence and employment potential.

8. Wage protection. A person with mental retardation, a developmental disability, or chronic mental illness engaged in work programs shall be paid wages commensurate with the going rate for comparable work and productivity.

9. Insurance protection. Pursuant to section 507B.4, subsection 7, a person or designated group of persons shall not be denied insurance coverage by reason of mental retardation, a developmental disability, or chronic mental illness.

10. Due process. A person with mental retardation, a developmental disability, or chronic mental illness retains the right to citizenship in accordance with the laws of the state.

85 Acts, ch 249, §5

INDEX

= 389 =

ABOUT THE AUTHORS

Christine Ammer has written reference books for many years. A former publisher of *Hospital Purchasing Management,* she also has led workshops on women's health issues. Her *A to Z of Women's Health: A Concise Encyclopedia* was selected as an outstanding reference source by the American Library Association and has recently been published in a new expanded edition by Facts on File. A graduate of Swarthmore College, she lives in Lexington, Massachusetts.

Nathan T. Sidley, M.D., is a fellow of the American Board of Psychiatry and Neurology, and associate professor of psychiatry at Boston University Medical School. He serves as director of medical and forensic services for the Department of Correction of the State of New Hampshire and as a psychiatrist at Edith Nourse Rogers Memorial Veterans Hospital in Bedford, Massachusetts. He is a graduate of the University of Minnesota Medical School.